Transition Economies after 2008

The economic crisis of 2008, starting from the US banking crisis, affected economic and political development in varied ways around the world. This edited volume examines the impact of the crisis on Eastern Europe and Russia, and the resulting policy responses. Taken as a whole, the economies of the former state socialist countries—frequently still referred to as transition economies—were hit hard by the crisis, suffering falls in GDP in 2009 that were deeper than the average around the world. However, there was considerable variety in the effects on individual countries, whilst some continued to grow, others suffered quite exceptional falls in output. Policy responses were also quite diverse and do not obviously fit with the nature and severity of economic factors. The more general impacts on political life were also varied. In many cases very much the same governments continued in power, while in others there were significant changes and signs of a growing instability in party and political structures. The chapters in this book explore these differences between countries and set them in a wider international context.

This book was originally published as a special issue of *Europe-Asia Studies*.

Martin Myant is Head of Unit European Economic, Employment and Social Policy at the European Trade Union Institute (ETUI) in Brussels, Belgium.

Jan Drahokoupil is a Project Director at the Mannheim Centre for European Social Research (MZES), University of Mannheim, Germany, and Senior Researcher at the ETUI in Brussels, Belgium.

Routledge Europe-Asia Studies Series

A series edited by Terry Cox
University of Glasgow

The **Routledge Europe-Asia Studies Series** focuses on the history and current political, social and economic affairs of the countries of the former 'communist bloc' of the Soviet Union, Eastern Europe and Asia. As well as providing contemporary analyses it explores the economic, political and social transformation of these countries and the changing character of their relationships with the rest of Europe and Asia.

Challenging Communism in Eastern Europe
1956 and its Legacy
Edited by Terry Cox

Globalisation, Freedom and the Media after Communism
The Past as Future
Edited by Birgit Beumers,
Stephen Hutchings and
Natalia Rulyova

Power and Policy in Putin's Russia
Edited by Richard Sakwa

1948 and 1968 – Dramatic Milestones in Czech and Slovak History
Edited by Laura Cashman

Perceptions of the European Union in New Member States
A Comparative Perspective
Edited by Gabriella Ilonszki

Symbolism and Power in Central Asia
Politics of the Spectacular
Edited by Sally N. Cummings

The European Union, Russia and the Shared Neighbourhood
Edited by Jackie Gower and
Graham Timmins

Russian Regional Politics under Putin and Medvedev
Edited by Cameron Ross

Russia's Authoritarian Elections
Edited by Stephen White

Elites and Identities in Post-Soviet Space
Edited by David Lane

EU Conditionality in the Western Balkans
Edited by Florian Bieber

Reflections on 1989 in Eastern Europe
Edited by Terry Cox

Russia and the World
The Internal-External Nexus
Edited by Natasha Kuhrt

Civil Society and Social Capital in Post-Communist Eastern Europe
Edited by Terry Cox

New Media in New Europe-Asia
*Edited by Vlad Strukov, Jeremy Morris
and Natalya Rulyova*

Many Faces of the Caucasus
*Edited by Nino Nino Kemoklidze,
Cerwyn Moore, Jeremy Smith and
Galina Yemelianova*

**Explaining Policy Change in the
European Union's Eastern
Neighbourhood**
*Edited by Julia Langbein and
Tanja A. Börzel*

Transition Economies after 2008
Responses to the Crisis in Russia and
Eastern Europe
*Edited by Martin Myant and
Jan Drahokoupil*

Transition Economies after 2008
Responses to the crisis in Russia and Eastern Europe

Edited by
Martin Myant and Jan Drahokoupil

First published 2014
by Routledge
2 Park Square, Milton Park, Abingdon, Oxon, OX14 4RN, UK

and by Routledge
711 Third Avenue, New York, NY 10017, USA

Routledge is an imprint of the Taylor & Francis Group, an informa business

© 2014 University of Glasgow

All rights reserved. No part of this book may be reprinted or reproduced or utilised in any form or by any electronic, mechanical, or other means, now known or hereafter invented, including photocopying and recording, or in any information storage or retrieval system, without permission in writing from the publishers.

Trademark notice: Product or corporate names may be trademarks or registered trademarks, and are used only for identification and explanation without intent to infringe.

British Library Cataloguing in Publication Data
A catalogue record for this book is available from the British Library

ISBN 13: 978-0-415-74544-4

Typeset in Times New Roman
by Taylor & Francis Books

Publisher's Note
The publisher accepts responsibility for any inconsistencies that may have arisen during the conversion of this book from journal articles to book chapters, namely the possible inclusion of journal terminology.

Disclaimer
Every effort has been made to contact copyright holders for their permission to reprint material in this book. The publishers would be grateful to hear from any copyright holder who is not here acknowledged and will undertake to rectify any errors or omissions in future editions of this book.

Contents

Citation Information	ix
Notes on Contributors	xi

1. Transition Economies after the Crisis of 2008: Actors and Policies
   Martin Myant & Jan Drahokoupil   1

Policy Paradigms and Forms of Development in and after the Crisis   11

2. The Political Economy of Crisis Management in East–Central European
   Countries
   Martin Myant, Jan Drahokoupil & Ivan Lesay   13

3. Avoiding the Economic Crisis: Pragmatic Liberalism and Divisions over
   Economic Policy in Poland
   Gavin Rae   41

4. The Baltic Republics and the Crisis of 2008–2011
   Rainer Kattel & Ringa Raudla   56

5. Russia's Response to Crisis: The Paradox of Success
   Neil Robinson   80

6. Belarus' Anti-Crisis Management: Success Story of Delayed Recession?
   Dzmitry Kruk   103

Continuity and Change in the Enterprise Sector   119

7. Crisis and Upgrading: The Case of the Hungarian Automotive and
   Electronics Sectors
   Magdolna Sass & Andrea Szalavetz   121

8. Actions and Reactions of Russian Manufacturing Companies to the Crisis
   Shocks from 2008–2009: Evidence from the Empirical Survey
   Ksenia Gonchar   140

CONTENTS

Banks—the Role of Ownership and Regulation 161

9. Central and East European Bank Responses to the Financial 'Crisis':
   Do Domestic Banks Perform Better in a Crisis than their Foreign-Owned
   Counterparts?
   Rachel A. Epstein 163

10. The Return of Political Risk: Foreign-Owned Banks in Emerging Europe
    Zdenek Kudrna & Daniela Gabor 183

    Index 203

Citation Information

The chapters in this book were originally published in *Europe-Asia Studies*, volume 65, issue 3 (May 2013). When citing this material, please use the original page numbering for each article, as follows:

Chapter 1
Transition Economies after the Crisis of 2008: Actors and Policies
Martin Myant & Jan Drahokoupil
Europe-Asia Studies, volume 65, issue 3 (May 2013) pp. 373–382

Chapter 2
The Political Economy of Crisis Management in East–Central European Countries
Martin Myant, Jan Drahokoupil & Ivan Lesay
Europe-Asia Studies, volume 65, issue 3 (May 2013) pp. 383–410

Chapter 3
Avoiding the Economic Crisis: Pragmatic Liberalism and Divisions over Economic Policy in Poland
Gavin Rae
Europe-Asia Studies, volume 65, issue 3 (May 2013) pp. 411–425

Chapter 4
The Baltic Republics and the Crisis of 2008–2011
Rainer Kattel & Ringa Raudla
Europe-Asia Studies, volume 65, issue 3 (May 2013) pp. 426–449

Chapter 5
Russia's Response to Crisis: The Paradox of Success
Neil Robinson
Europe-Asia Studies, volume 65, issue 3 (May 2013) pp. 450–472

Chapter 6
Belarus' Anti-Crisis Management: Success Story of Delayed Recession?
Dzmitry Kruk
Europe-Asia Studies, volume 65, issue 3 (May 2013) pp. 473–488

CITATION INFORMATION

Chapter 7
Crisis and Upgrading: The Case of the Hungarian Automotive and Electronics Sectors
Magdolna Sass & Andrea Szalavetz
Europe-Asia Studies, volume 65, issue 3 (May 2013) pp. 489–507

Chapter 8
Actions and Reactions of Russian Manufacturing Companies to the Crisis Shocks from 2008–2009: Evidence from the Empirical Survey
Ksenia Gonchar
Europe-Asia Studies, volume 65, issue 3 (May 2013) pp. 508–527

Chapter 9
Central and East European Bank Responses to the Financial 'Crisis': Do Domestic Banks Perform Better in a Crisis than their Foreign-Owned Counterparts?
Rachel A. Epstein
Europe-Asia Studies, volume 65, issue 3 (May 2013) pp. 528–547

Chapter 10
The Return of Political Risk: Foreign-Owned Banks in Emerging Europe
Zdenek Kudrna & Daniela Gabor
Europe-Asia Studies, volume 65, issue 3 (May 2013) pp. 548–566

Please direct any queries you may have about the citations to clsuk.permissions@cengage.com

Notes on Contributors

Jan Drahokoupil is a Project Director at the Mannheim Centre for European Social Research (MZES), University of Mannheim, Germany, and Senior Researcher at the ETUI in Brussels, Belgium. His book publications include *Transition Economies: Political Economy in Russia, Eastern Europe, and Central Asia* (with Martin Myant, 2011), *Globalization and the State in Central and Eastern Europe: The Politics of Foreign Direct Investment* (Routledge, 2008) and a number of journal articles on political economy and development. He co-edited *Contradictions and Limits of Neoliberal European Governance* (2008). He is an Associate Editor at *Competition and Change: The Journal of Global Business and Political Economy*.

Rachel A. Epstein is an Associate Professor of International Relations and European Politics at the Josef Korbel School of International Studies at the University of Denver, USA. She holds a PhD from the Department of Government at Cornell University, USA. Her 2008 book, *In Pursuit of Liberalism,* examined the denationalising and depoliticising effects of international organisations on post-communist financial sectors and military-security apparatuses. Her work has also appeared in the *Journal of Common Market Studies, Comparative Political Studies, Journal of European Public Policy* and *Security Studies.*

Daniela Gabor is a Senior Lecturer at Bristol Business School, UK. Her research focuses on three areas broadly related to financialisation. First, she is interested in shadow banking activities, in particular collateral intermediation, and the implications for central banking, sovereign bond markets and regulatory activity. Second, her research develops the theme of transnational banks' involvement in policy deliberations around capital controls and crisis management in both global settings and in emerging markets. Finally, she researches the IMF's conditionality and advice on capital controls. Publications include *Central Banking and Financialization: A Romanian Account of How Eastern Europe Became Subprime* (2011), 'Capital account management in emerging countries: lessons from the global financial crisis' in *Journal of Development Studies* (2012) and 'Learning from Japan: (European) central banking in crisis' in *Review of Political Economy* (2013).

Ksenia Gonchar is a leading Researcher at the Institute for Industrial and Market Studies and Associate Professor in Economics of Industrial Innovations at the Economic Faculty of the National Research University Higher School of Economics, Moscow, Russia. She holds a PhD from the Institute of World Economy and International Relations of the Russian Academy of Sciences. Her research focuses on

NOTES ON CONTRIBUTORS

empirical studies of firm productivity, innovations and location in the country, regional and global context. Apart from publications in Russian academic journals she has published papers in *Post-Communist Economies, Post-Soviet Affairs, International Regional Science Review* and *Defence and Peace Economics.*

Rainer Kattel is Professor of Innovation Policy and Technology Governance, and Head of Ragnar Nurkse School of Innovation and Governance, Tallinn University of Technology, Estonia. His main research area is industrial and innovation policies in catching-up economies, especially Central and Eastern Europe and Latin America. He has published extensively on innovation policy and development economics. His recent books include *Ragnar Nurkse: Trade and Development* (co-edited with Jan A. Kregel and Erik S. Reinert, 2009), *Knowledge Governance: Reasserting the Public Interest* (co-edited with Leonardo Burlamaqui and Ana Celia Castro, 2012) and *Public Procurement for Innovation Policy: International Perspectives* (co-edited with Tarmo Kalvet and Veiko Lember, 2013).

Dzmitry Kruk is a Researcher at the Belarusian Economic Research and Outreach Center. He is also a Lecturer at the Belarusian State University, Minsk, Belarus. His research interests are finance and growth, monetary economics and transition agenda. He holds an MA in Economics from the Belarusian State University, and currently is a PhD candidate in the same University. His PhD thesis deals with the specifics of financial intermediation in the transition economies and its impact on economic growth.

Zdenek Kudrna is an Assistant Professor at the Institute for European Integration Research, University of Vienna, Austria. He has been an advisor to the IMF and World Bank, UNDP and the Czech Minister of Finance. His work recently appeared in *Journal of Common Market Studies, Post-Communist Economies* and in a volume *The EU's Decision Traps: Comparing Policies* (2011).

Ivan Lesay is a Senior Researcher at the Institute of Economic Research, Slovak Academy of Sciences, Bratislava, Slovakia, and Advisor to the Slovak Finance Minister. He holds Masters Degrees in Political Science and Political Economy from the Trnava University and Central European University, Budapest, Hungary, and a PhD in Economic Theory from the University of Economics, Bratislava, Slovakia. His research interests include international financial institutions, welfare state, and post-communist transition in Central and Eastern Europe.

Martin Myant is a Senior Researcher and Head of the Research Unit on European Economic, Employment and Social Policy at the European Trade Union Institute (ETUI) in Brussels, Belgium. He has been researching the economic and political development and recent history of East-Central Europe for many years with a primary focus on the Czech Republic. His publications include *The Czechoslovak Economy 1948–1988: The Battle for Economic Reform* (1989, paperback, 2010), *Transforming Socialist Economies: The Case of Poland and Czechoslovakia* (1993), *The Rise and Fall of Czech Capitalism: Economic Development in the Czech Republic Since 1989* (2003) and *Transition Economies: Political Economy in Russia, Eastern Europe, and Central Asia* (with Jan Drahokoupil, 2011).

Gavin Rae is an Associate Professor at Kozminski University in Warsaw, Poland. He has researched and published on issues connected to the transition from

NOTES ON CONTRIBUTORS

communism, particularly in Poland, the enlargement of the EU, the economic crisis in Eastern Europe and austerity and the welfare state. He is author of *Poland's Return to Capitalism: From the Socialist Bloc to the European Union* (2008) and a member of the editorial board of *Debatte: Journal of Contemporary Eastern Europe*.

Ringa Raudla is a Senior Research Fellow in the Ragnar Nurkse School of Innovation and Governance at Tallinn University of Technology, Estonia. She holds a doctoral degree in economics from the Faculty of Law, Economics, and Social Sciences, University of Erfurt, Germany. Her main research interests are political economy, public finance and postcommunist transition. She has published numerous articles and book chapters in areas such as constitutional political economy, social insurance reform, public procurement, fiscal governance, and fiscal sociology. Her recent publications include articles in *Governance, Constitutional Political Economy, European Journal of Law and Economics, Public Administration, Journal of Public Policy* and *Policy Studies*.

Neil Robinson is a Professor in the Department of Politics and Public Administration and Director of the Institute for the Study of Knowledge in Society, University of Limerick, Ireland. His research interests are Russian political economy and state and regime development in post-communist countries. He is the author or editor of several books on Russian and comparative politics, most recently *The Sage Handbook of Comparative Politics* (2009) and *The Political Economy of Russia* (2012), as well as articles in journals such as *Communist and Post-Communist Studies, Review of International Political Economy* and *East European Politics*.

Magdolna Sass has been a Senior Research Fellow at the Research Centre for Economic and Regional Studies, Institute of Economics of the Hungarian Academy of Sciences since 1996. Her main research topics are inward and outward foreign direct investments and foreign trade and related policies in the East-Central European countries, with special attention to developments in Hungary. She participated in and led numerous international and Hungarian research projects in these fields. Her latest publications include articles in *European Urban and Regional Studies, European Planning Studies, Post-Communist Economies* and *Eastern European Economics*.

Andrea Szalavetz is a Senior Research Fellow at the Research Centre for Economic and Regional Studies of the Hungarian Academy of Sciences. She holds a PhD from the Marx Károly University of Economics, Budapest, Hungary (currently: Corvinus University). Her research interest is the economics of innovation and global value chain research. Her latest publications include 'Micro-level aspects of knowledge-based development: Measuring quality-based upgrading in MNCs Hungarian subsidiaries' in *International Journal of Knowledge-Based Development* and 'The Hungarian Automotive Sector: A Comparative CEE Perspective with Special Emphasis on Structural Change' in *Clusters in Automotive and Information and Communication Technology* (2012).

Transition Economies after the Crisis of 2008: Actors and Policies

MARTIN MYANT & JAN DRAHOKOUPIL

THE ECONOMIC CRISIS OF 2008, STARTING FROM THE CRISIS in banking in the USA, affected economic and political development in varied ways around the world. This collection covers the impact and policy responses in the former state socialist countries of Central and Eastern Europe and the Commonwealth of Independent States (CIS). Taken as a whole, the economies of the former state socialist countries—frequently still referred to for convenience as transition economies—were hit hard by the crisis, suffering falls in GDP in 2009 that were deeper than the average around the world. However, there was considerable variety in the effects on individual countries, with a few continuing to grow while some others suffered quite exceptional falls in output. Policy responses were also quite diverse and do not obviously fit with the nature and severity of economic factors. The more general impacts on political life were also varied. In many cases very much the same governments continued in power, while in others there were significant changes and signs of a growing instability in party and political structures.

The essays in this collection aim to explore these differences between countries and to set them in a wider international context. Table 1 shows the course of GDP changes over the period of the crisis as the most basic indicator of economic performance. Data are provided for 11 countries referred to in some significant detail in the essays in this collection,[1] as well as for Bulgaria and Ukraine and, to provide a wider context, five other countries, three EU members with rather different experiences and two countries from other parts of the world that illustrate the diversity of experiences. Despite the obvious heterogeneity, there are some approximate groupings of countries in terms of how they were hit by the crisis and also in how they reacted. These can be set against the experience of the five chosen comparators.

The Central and East European countries and South-East European countries, with the exception of Poland, experienced a fall in GDP in 2009 followed by gradual recovery. The experiences of Germany, and to some extent those of the UK and USA, appear very similar. The Baltic republics experienced substantially deeper falls in GDP, but also more rapid

---

The preparation of this collection was generously supported by the COST Action ISO 902 'Systemic Risk and Financial Crisis'.

[1] The Czech Republic, Hungary, Poland and Slovakia are grouped together as Central and East European countries (CEECs) while Estonia, Latvia and Lithuania are referred to as the Baltic republics. Bulgaria and Romania are referred to as SEECs (South-Eastern European countries).

TABLE 1
Percentage Change in GDP, Constant Prices for Selected Transition Economies and Five Comparator Countries, 2007–2011

	2007	2008	2009	2010	2011
Czech Republic	5.7	3.1	−4.7	2.7	1.7
Hungary	0.1	0.9	−6.8	1.3	1.7
Poland	6.8	5.1	1.6	3.9	4.4
Slovak Republic	10.5	5.8	−4.9	4.2	3.3
Slovenia	6.9	3.6	−8.0	1.4	−0.2
Estonia	7.5	−3.7	−14.3	2.3	7.6
Latvia	9.6	−3.3	−17.7	−0.3	5.5
Lithuania	9.8	2.9	−14.8	1.4	5.9
Bulgaria	6.4	6.2	−5.5	0.4	1.7
Romania	6.3	7.3	−6.6	−1.6	2.5*
Belarus	8.6	10.2	0.2	7.7	5.3*
Russia	8.5	5.2	−7.8	4.3	4.3
Ukraine	7.9	2.3	−14.8	4.1	5.2*
Germany	3.4	0.8	−5.1	3.6	3.1
Greece	3.0	−0.1	−3.3	−3.5	−6.9*
United Kingdom	3.5	−1.1	−4.4	2.1	0.7
United States	1.9	−0.3	−3.5	3.0	1.7
China	14.2	9.6	9.2	10.4	9.2

Note: *, estimate.

Source: IMF, available at: http://www.imf.org/external/pubs/ft/weo/2012/01/weodata/weoselgr.aspx, accessed 15 August 2012.

recoveries. The three CIS countries covered here were very diverse. The fall in Russian GDP in 2009 was quite high, but recovery was reasonably rapid. Ukraine suffered an even steeper decline while Belarus joined Poland as a country that continued to grow. The international comparisons show that no country considered here followed the road of seemingly uninterrupted rapid growth exemplified by China or the road of steadily deepening recession exemplified by Greece.

Differences in experiences of the crisis followed from somewhat different economic structures, developed over the preceding two decades, and also somewhat different political structures that led to different policy choices.

Central and East European countries, and to a lesser extent South-East European countries, are characterised by both political and economic integration into the EU. They have export-oriented economies, heavily dependent on incoming multinational companies, and political systems that comply fully with requirements for democratic life, albeit with evidence of less stable party structures and less developed interest representation than in Western Europe. The Baltic republics differ from this both in economic structures, with weaker export potential that left them with persistent current account deficits, and in political structures which gave less influence for interest representation.

Russia differs from these patterns by having a less open economy—producers for the domestic market are better protected against external competition—and a much higher reliance on exports of raw materials, notably oil and gas. Its political life is also substantially different, with political power much more closely linked into business interests than in Central, let alone Western, Europe. Ukraine differs from this largely in economic structure, depending more on exports of semi-manufactures which have provided a less reliable and substantial source of income. Finally, Belarus appears as a unique case with less of the trappings of democracy, but its economic structure is not that unique. The big differences appear in the choices of policies made by its autocratic government.

The impact of the crisis on economic life is covered elsewhere (Myant & Drahokoupil 2012). It depended on the modes of integration into the international economy. Many, but by no means all, of the countries considered here had covered their current account deficits by financial inflows, exploiting the easy credit conditions in the world up to 2008. This included the Baltic republics, South-East European countries and Ukraine and Hungary, with Belarus joining that club in the last years up to 2008. As previous growth had been heavily dependent on the availability of this source of credits, the end of easy lending was an important factor pushing countries into depression.

This is shown in Table 2 for the countries for which the International Monetary Fund (IMF) has provided comparable data of bank loans to domestic economies. How loans were used within economies varied considerably: some countries emphasised credits to households and much of this was long-term credit for housing, and credits to households were most prominent in Hungary, Poland and Estonia; others, notably Russia, emphasised credits to businesses. The financial inflows fuelled rising credit levels to households in Hungary, Slovenia, Estonia and Lithuania. As indicated in Table 2, these countries experienced a reduction in the volume of credits at some point. This was a significant factor reducing levels of GDP. In other countries too, banks had become more cautious in lending.

The restrictions on credits were typically visible in falling construction output, that being a sector particularly dependent on credits to both producers and final consumers. Where construction continued to grow, it was typically helped by government spending replacing the private credits that had been important in the past. It is noteworthy here that a few countries experienced an increase in credits to businesses, although much less to households. This was the case for Belarus and, to a lesser extent, for Russia. In the former case government encouragement of credit expansion was an important part of policies that countered other factors that would lead to declining GDP.

TABLE 2

BANK LOANS TO HOUSEHOLDS AND BUSINESSES AS A PERCENTAGE OF GDP, SELECTED TRANSITION ECONOMIES AND INTERNATIONAL COMPARATORS, 2007–2010

	2007	2008	2009	2010
Czech Republic	72.5	77.6	81.5	83.8
Hungary	47.2	54.1	52.1	51.6
Poland	37	47.2	47.4	49.1
Slovenia	97.2	106.1	120.8	116.3
Estonia	89.8	94.8	106.6	96
Lithuania	56.1	58.7	65.4	58.6
Bulgaria	61.3	70.2	73.8	73
Belarus	29.8	34.5	46.6	54.5
Russia	42.8	48	50.7	49.3
Germany	24.1	24.5	24.7	23.5
United States	48.3	49.9	47.1	46.1

Source: IMF, available at: http://elibrary-data.imf.org/DataReport.aspx?c = 2529610&d = 33120&e = 170185, accessed 15 August 2012.

Countries dependent on the export of manufactured goods were hit by falling demand, but often only for a relatively short period. As indicated in Table 3, recovery came quite quickly as demand in Western Europe for their exports recovered. This applied to all the countries covered here outside the CIS. It applied to countries that continued growing—China, Belarus and Poland—and to those that experienced falling GDP. The fall in exports can be shown to be a major factor in falling GDP: the relatively small drop in exports in Poland is a partial explanation for that country's relatively good GDP performance. However, the data also imply that other factors compensated for falling exports in a number of countries, notably China. The key factor here was state spending.

The negative effects of falling exports deepened the depression in countries that had previously been dependent on financial inflows. Thus Baltic republics experienced a permanent loss in economic activity from the fall in financial inflows, but export activity recovered very quickly, leading to high rates of growth from the deepest point of the crisis.

Russia faced a fall in oil and gas prices, and the resulting loss in revenue contributed to the sharp drop in GDP in 2009. Later price increases for exports helped economic recovery and the crisis could soon appear as a thing largely of the past. Ukraine was less fortunate, suffering both from the halt to financial inflows, depressing all activities previously dependent on credit, and from falling demand for its exports which was only partly compensated for by renewed growth after 2009. Belarus was a somewhat different case, previously dependent on its relationship with Russia, including the ability to export manufactured goods to that country. The course of its development can only be explained after a closer look at economic policy frameworks.

TABLE 3

PERCENTAGE CHANGE IN EXPORTS OF GOODS AND SERVICES, CONSTANT PRICES FOR SELECTED TRANSITION ECONOMIES AND FIVE COMPARATOR COUNTRIES, 2007–2011

	2007	2008	2009	2010	2011
Czech Republic	11.2	4.0	−10.0	16.4	11.0
Hungary	15.0	5.7	−10.2	14.3	8.5*
Poland	9.1	7.1	−6.8	12.1	7.3
Slovak Republic	14.3	3.1	−15.9	16.5	10.8
Slovenia	13.7	2.9	−17.2	9.5	6.8
Estonia	13.0	7.7	−23.1	17.4	31.5
Latvia	10.0	2.0	−14.1	11.5	12.6
Lithuania	3.1	11.4	−12.5	17.4	13.7
Bulgaria	11.9	9.9	−8.3	−0.7	11.0
Romania	7.8	8.3	−6.4	14.1	9.9
Belarus	7.4	2.9	−10.7	6.2	28.2
Russia	7.2	−5.6	−8.8	7.1	4.9
Ukraine	3.2	2.3	−24.2	9.3	7.1*
Germany	8.0	2.7	−13.6	13.7	8.3
Greece	6.9	3.0	−19.5	4.2	−0.2
United Kingdom	−1.3	1.3	−9.5	7.4	4.6
United States	9.7	6.3	−12.0	14.4	7.4
China	19.8	8.4	−10.3	28.4	8.2

Note: *, estimate.

Source: IMF, available at: http://www.imf.org/external/pubs/ft/weo/2012/01/weodata/weoselgr.aspx, accessed 15 August 2012.

In most cases the fact of economic depression led to a worsening of public finances. Budget deficits rose as tax revenue declined and, in some cases, public spending increased either to cover the higher social costs or as part of a deliberate attempt to lessen the effects of the crisis or, in some cases, reflecting continuity with previously decided policies. These differing effects are shown in Tables 4 and 5. Table 4 shows changing state spending in real terms. Divergences among countries are quite substantial. The only case of consistent and continuing decline over the whole period reviewed here was Hungary. In 2009 it was joined by a number of other countries. As argued in some of the following contributions, some were forced by external difficulties to seek help from the IMF—this applied to Hungary, Latvia and Ukraine—and the conditions attached pushed them into austerity measures. However, in a number of countries, either by continuity with past policies or by deliberate changes in policy, spending increased such as to compensate for the reductions in credits and/or exports. China appears as a clear example of this, followed by Russia and Slovakia and, to a lesser extent, Poland and the Czech Republic. In this they appeared to follow the example of the UK, USA and Germany. The trends in following years show continuing variety, but signs of a tendency towards austerity.

Table 5 shows the trends in government budget deficits and Table 6 shows the resulting effects on levels of gross government debt. The wider international comparisons suggest a very comfortable position for transition economies. None experienced the levels of deficits and escalating international debt demonstrated by Greece and, to a lesser extent, by the UK and USA. Hungary was the closest in terms of debt levels, albeit without a similar continuing growth. It should be added however, that the absolute level of debt is not the only factor to be considered in assessing a country's vulnerability. Repayment structures,

TABLE 4

PERCENTAGE CHANGE IN GOVERNMENT SPENDING, CONSTANT PRICES FOR SELECTED TRANSITION ECONOMIES AND FIVE COMPARATOR COUNTRIES, 2007–2011

	2007	2008	2009	2010	2011
Czech Republic	3.4	3.4	4.0	0.9	2.7*
Hungary	−2.8	−2.0	−2.7	−2.5	−0.4*
Poland	2.7	7.6	4.7	5.9	2.3
Slovak Republic	3.5	8.3	13.1	2.7	−3.5
Slovenia	1.1	6.6	2.9	3.1	1.1
Estonia	8.4	13.4	−0.4	−4.0	3.8
Latvia	6.6	16.9	−16.0	−1.9	−4.4
Lithuania	13.4	10.2	0.4	−2.9	−1.0
Bulgaria	10.5	6.9	−2.8	1.7	−4.1
Romania	11.7	12.3	−2.9	−1.0	−6.0*
Belarus	8.2	10.4	−2.3	1.5	−6.6
Russia	15.3	9.1	11.2	−1.6	−1.6
Ukraine	6.0	10.7	−12.8	3.9	−1.9*
Germany	−1.3	2.1	3.7	3.1	−1.8
Greece	7.7	6.3	3.2	−9.7	−6.7*
United Kingdom	2.7	5.6	5.0	0.1	−0.6*
United States	4.2	6.5	8.3	−1.3	−0.1*
China	14.1	16.3	25.9	7.4	14.6

Note: *, estimate.

Source: IMF, available at: http://www.imf.org/external/pubs/ft/weo/2012/01/weodata/weoselgr.aspx, accessed 15 August 2012.

TABLE 5
GOVERNMENT REVENUES MINUS GOVERNMENT SPENDING AS A PERCENTAGE OF GDP FOR SELECTED TRANSITION ECONOMIES AND FIVE COMPARATOR COUNTRIES, 2007–2011

	2007	2008	2009	2010	2011
Czech Republic	−0.7	−2.2	−5.8	−4.8	−3.8
Hungary	−5.1	−3.7	−4.5	−4.3	−3.0
Poland	−1.9	−3.7	−7.3	−7.8	−5.2
Slovak Republic	−1.8	−2.1	−8.0	−7.9	−5.5
Slovenia	0.3	−0.3	−5.6	−5.4	−5.7
Estonia	2.8	−2.3	−2.1	0.4	1.0
Latvia	0.6	−7.5	−7.8	−7.2	−3.4
Lithuania	−1.0	−3.3	−9.2	−7.1	−5.2
Bulgaria	3.3	2.9	−0.9	−3.9	−2.1
Romania	−3.1	−4.8	−7.3	−6.4	−4.1
Belarus	2.3	3.4	−0.4	−1.8	3.3
Russia	6.8	4.9	−6.3	−3.5	1.6
Ukraine	−2.0	−3.2	−6.3	−5.7	−2.7
Germany	0.2	−0.1	−3.2	−4.3	−1.0
Greece	−6.7	−9.7	−15.6	−10.6	−9.2
United Kingdom	−2.7	−4.9	−10.4	−9.9	−8.7
United States	−2.7	−6.7	−13.0	−10.5	−9.6
China	0.9	−0.4	−3.1	−2.3	−1.2

Source: IMF, available at: http://www.imf.org/external/pubs/ft/weo/2012/01/weodata/weoselgr.aspx, accessed 15 August 2012.

TABLE 6
GOVERNMENT GROSS DEBT AS A PERCENTAGE OF GDP FOR SELECTED TRANSITION ECONOMIES AND FIVE COMPARATOR COUNTRIES, 2007–2011

	2007	2008	2009	2010	2011
Czech Republic	28	28.7	34.3	37.6	41.5
Hungary	67	72.9	79.7	81.3	80.4
Poland	45	47.1	50.9	54.9	55.4
Slovak Republic	29.6	27.9	35.6	41.1	44.6
Slovenia	23.1	21.9	35.3	38.8	47.3
Estonia	3.7	4.5	7.2	6.7	6
Latvia	7.8	17.2	32.9	39.9	37.8
Lithuania	16.8	15.5	29.4	38	39
Bulgaria	18.6	15.5	15.6	16.7	17
Romania	12.7	13.6	23.8	31.2	33
Belarus	18.3	21.7	34.9	41.0	50.2
Russia	8.5	7.9	11	11.7	9.6
Ukraine	12.3	20.5	35.4	40.1	36.5
Germany	65.2	66.7	74.4	83.2	81.5
Greece	105.4	110.7	127.1	142.8	160.8
United Kingdom	43.9	52.5	68.4	75.1	82.5
United States	67.2	76.1	89.9	98.5	102.9
China	19.6	17	17.7	33.5	25.8

Source: IMF, available at: http://www.imf.org/external/pubs/ft/weo/2012/01/weodata/weoselgr.aspx, accessed 15 August 2012.

meaning the need to repay a large volume of debt in a short period, may lead to serious difficulties even for a country with a low level of debt relative to GDP. Also, owing to lower credit ratings, transition economies in general needed to pay higher interest charges on debt than the richer and more trusted countries in Western Europe and North America.

Nevertheless, the data do not point to particularly serious and general problems of growing government debt levels, at least for the foreseeable future. Indeed, in some countries they were extremely low, notably in Estonia and Russia, and to some extent also Bulgaria. Russia was also well protected by reserves built up in the preceding years that made increased government spending appear a low-risk option. However, concerns over growing debt levels were a factor in a number of countries' policy making, reflecting perceptions of both political elites and populations as they watched unfamiliar economic events in Greece and other countries.

A key question for the essays that follow is whether policy responses, and responses of economic actors more generally, should be seen as the logical, or even the only possible, response to economic conditions. The essays look at the reactions of political actors and governments—the most complex of all actors on the economic stage because they have to respond to a wide variety of different pressures and interests—and of industrial enterprises and banks, which in turn contribute to setting the framework within which politicians make their decisions.

Studies of individual countries or comparisons within groups of similar countries cover Central and East European countries, the Baltic republics and Russia. They had contrasting experiences in terms of the economic impact of the crisis, but that alone does not explain the differences in responses. Policy choices depended on the strength of particular political and social forces, on opportunities for interest representation, on public and elite perceptions of the nature and causes of crisis, probably shaped by past histories and experiences, and on the strength of, and receptiveness to, possible external pressures. That alternative views on the most appropriate policies existed is beyond serious dispute. Different policies were proposed by different political and social forces and changes of government were frequently associated with changes in policy.

For Central and East European countries, as compared in the essay by Martin Myant, Jan Drahokoupil and Ivan Lesay, a division between 'social-democratic' and 'neo-liberal' policy directions has broad plausibility, although it is not an exact fit. These countries are, in political and economic structures, the closest to Western Europe and, also as EU members, many of the same policy themes emerged. The social-democratic label applies to a mix of policies including elements of Keynesian-inspired expansionary policies, employment protection and/or creation and likely emphases on support for public sector activities and on protecting lower-income sections of society. Governments are likely to listen to social interests, seeking agreement through tripartite structures. In this view the crisis was caused by a failure of a free-market economy and it was therefore appropriate for the state to take steps to correct for the failures of the market.

The neo-liberal label applies to a mix of policies that aim for a smaller role for the state and typically for achieving this by cutting spending. There is a consistent opposition to the state playing a role in redistribution of income and cuts in state benefits may even be balanced by cuts in taxes on business and high personal incomes. Such governments are unlikely to listen to organised interests, although their policies clearly are favourable to particular groups in society.

TRANSITION ECONOMIES AFTER 2008

In the countries considered here, the case of neo-liberal policy making was more complex than a simple reaction to the crisis. On the one hand, it was clear from politicians' rhetoric that they were using the fact of the crisis as an opportunity to push through policies, for a small state and for a state that played as small a role as possible in redistribution from higher to lower income groups, on the pretext of balancing the state budget and preventing an escalation of state debt. On the other hand, ideology was often tempered by economic and political realities and, above all, by the prospect of electoral defeat. Gavin Rae pursues this theme in the context of the development of Polish neo-liberal thinking, showing how the perceived need for caution contributed to the continuation of economic growth in that country.

The contribution by Martin Myant, Jan Drahokoupil and Ivan Lesay develops a comparison across four countries to show how policy responses varied with governments. Both voter perceptions—swayed either more by fears generating over rising state debt levels or more by concern at cuts in the public sector—and pressure from social interests were important in dictating the shifts. The authors hypothesise, albeit cautiously, that the effects of the crisis will lead to a higher salience of issues relating to income distribution and the return to a main political division between left and right.

The Baltic republics' experience, discussed by Rainer Kattel and Ringa Raudla, represents a purer form of neo-liberal policy making with less sign of voter rebellion or public discontent. The solution of 'internal devaluation', meaning very sharp cuts in public spending and reductions in wage levels rather than currency devaluation, was not followed by other countries: they typically combined currency devaluation with a more tempered degree of public austerity. There were specific economic conditions, but the acceptance of the policy approach is related by the authors to 'simple polities', with limited input from social partnerships, constitutional veto players and corporatist structures. The dominant form of nationalism in these countries was fully compatible with a 'hard' course in economic policy, incidentally doing whatever was required to satisfy conditions set from the EU for admission to the Euro, that being presented as the means to ensure the survival of the nation. In Hungary, the Central and East European country most affected by external debt problems, there was a different form of nationalism which did not lead to such willing acceptance of external conditions. The rhetoric behind policy was therefore not that of a clearly neo-liberal agenda and there was more verbal resistance towards outside advice and pressures. In practice, government's policies in all the countries under consideration included elements of compromise and pragmatism that make it difficult to characterise them clearly along a spectrum from social-democrat to neo-liberal. Moreover, terms with broad applicability in Western Europe appear more distant for the CIS countries. Apart from differences in economic conditions, these countries' policy responses reflected the differing natures of politics and, in particular, the close links between business 'oligarchs' and political power. It was also important that help to individual businesses by a government is practically impossible inside the EU as this conflicts with strict rules against anti-competitive policies.

In Russia, as discussed by Neil Robinson, support for individual businesses was a central part of anti-crisis policy thinking. That also helped others in society, in so far as employment was protected, but there was no other social interest comparable to the informal power of large business groups. Some elements of Russian policy appeared distinctly Keynesian, as is consistent with the rising government spending shown in Table 5, and support for businesses was not linked to any ideological inspiration from neo-liberal thinking. Politicians' rhetoric revolved more around means to restore Russia's economic standing and there was plenty of scope for state action in view of the financial reserves built up over previous years.

Belarus, covered by Dzmitry Kruk, appears as a unique case among the countries considered here. The key government policy tool was the use of directed credits. These were not formally ruled out by the IMF terms, but they were clearly against the spirit of the policy package that was intended to restrict government intervention in the economy. Policy making did not involve direct input from social interests—although the desire not to generate major opposition could still influence government choices—or much of an input from economic theory. Policy remained the preserve of an authoritarian government that had presided over a specific kind of semi-directed economy over the preceding years. Higher domestic demand, generated by government or from government directives, compensated for falling exports and ensured continued growth while other countries were experiencing depression. There are questions over the sustainability of the approach. Growth was associated with external and internal imbalances which threatened to push the country into depression just as others were recovering.

Industrial enterprises are considered directly in two contributions. In Central and East European countries the most important enterprises for setting the direction of recent economic development have been incoming multinational companies. The essay by Magdolna Sass and Andrea Szalavetz reports results from an investigation of the reactions of firms in the Hungarian automotive sector. Their operations had undergone continual change, but with a general trend towards the upgrading of activities in subsidiaries. Albeit with variations between firms, this appeared to accelerate during the crisis. It remains to be seen whether this is a temporary phenomenon or representative of a more fundamental change.

Ksenia Gonchar uses very detailed survey evidence from Russia to show the complexity and variety of enterprise reactions. There was no single transmission mechanism for the effects of the crisis. Some were hit by falling export demand, some by credit restrictions and some by higher import prices after devaluation. Moreover, reactions varied partly because of other factors, such as financial reserves, that affected enterprises' resilience. This complexity helps explain the sharp fall in Russian output despite the apparently low level of Russia's integration into the international economy.

Banks are considered directly in two studies. Rachel Epstein compares banks in four countries—Latvia, Poland, Hungary and Slovenia—to investigate the importance of foreign compared to domestic ownership. The straightforward expectation was that a high level of foreign ownership would lead to vulnerability. Individual case studies demonstrate a more complex picture in which ownership was only one factor. Domestic ownership, in some cases, carried additional risks and increased state-budget difficulties as governments felt obliged to help out their banking systems. In other cases, depending on the past histories and policies pursued by domestically-owned banks, domestic ownership provided greater stability.

Political risk in banking has typically been studied as an asymmetric problem, meaning that banks investing abroad fear adverse reactions from that country's government. Zdenek Kudrna and Daniela Gabor follow the reactions of banking authorities in Hungary, Austria, Romania and Latvia, demonstrating that political risk is a symmetrical phenomenon. Risks arise from unilateral reactions from governments on either side. These have been tempered, but only by *ad hoc* interventions from international agencies. Dangers of uncertainty and instability therefore still remain.

The variety of responses from industrial enterprises, from banks, and even more clearly among the countries followed, weighs against any notion of a post-communist model for effects of, and political reactions to, economic crisis. Nevertheless, there are signs of some common features. This is less clear in economic conditions, although there evidently was a tendency for several of the countries to become dependent on financial inflows that led to high levels of debt. That was particularly likely in those that were the most enthusiastic in adopting policies of free markets and loose financial regulation. That was precisely the policy mix that could give a country a good reputation in international financial communities, encouraging inflows of finance, but it then led to the greatest immediate vulnerability to the effects of the crisis.

There was also a tendency among transition economies in Central and Eastern Europe towards export structures closely linked into Western Europe. The result was a high susceptibility to economic developments in the EU, and especially Germany. In the same vein, CIS countries frequently suffered from narrow export bases, largely inherited from the Soviet past, that left them vulnerable to fluctuations in demand for those particular products.

Political reactions to the crisis also show variation but some signs of a common 'post-communist' heritage. This is reflected in a sense of political insecurity making the countries more willing to accept externally-inspired neo-liberal models and tough austerity measures, in the cases of the Baltic republics and Central and South-Eastern Europe, or rule by more authoritarian regimes that had little time for consultation with representatives of social interests, as in CIS countries.

These are matters of degree. There were limits that populations would accept, and the position of those limits marks an important difference between the Baltic republics and Central and East European countries. However, it is a reasonable generalisation that both of these groups of countries differed from Western European countries in their lower levels of popular opposition to austerity measures, in the lower willingness of governments to respond to social interests, in the weaker acceptance of the need for a government role in overcoming the effects of the crisis, and in greater public concerns over levels of government debt. These were not primarily issues of political structures,[2] but rather of views and attitudes within society that shaped perceptions of the crisis and appropriate responses. How far that represents a clear difference from Western Europe, supporting the trend towards 'simple polities', is a theme beyond the scope of this volume.

European Trade Union Institute, Brussels
Universität Mannheim & European Trade Union Institute, Brussels

Reference

Myant, M. & Drahokoupil, J. (2012) 'International Integration, Varieties of Capitalism, and Resilience to Crisis in Transition Economies', *Europe-Asia Studies*, 64, 1, pp. 1–33.

---

[2]For example, tripartite structures provided formal channels for social consultation, but their use was very varied.

Policy Paradigms and Forms of Development in and after the Crisis

The Political Economy of Crisis Management in East–Central European Countries

MARTIN MYANT, JAN DRAHOKOUPIL & IVAN LESAY

Abstract

The financial and economic crisis in the Central and East European countries raised the profile of economic policy themes that relate to the role of taxation and state spending. The key policy differences related to public budgets and support for a demand stimulus. Responses fall broadly into two categories that we link to a social-democratic and a neo-liberal response. The distinction indicates that the policy responses were linked to the party affiliation of the government on the left–right spectrum. There were some remarkable common trends that cannot be explained by the logical requirements of the economic situation alone. There are differences in timing and in severity, but every country has at some point moved towards a policy of balancing the budget by making cuts. In all cases there were cuts in benefits for marginal groups in society and a switch towards indirect rather than direct taxes. These carry clear distributional implications.

THIS ESSAY ANALYSES POLICY RESPONSES TO THE FINANCIAL and economic crisis in the Central and East European countries (the Czech Republic, Hungary, Poland and Slovakia), a group of countries with broadly similar economic and political backgrounds that were affected by the crisis slightly differently. Thus Hungary was hit much harder by the financial side of the crisis while the Polish economy was overall less vulnerable to external shocks. However, there was a wide variety of, often contradictory, policy reactions, with important differences both between countries and between periods in individual countries. The aim of this essay is to explain the differences in policy reactions as linked to the differences in interpretations of the causes and nature of the crisis by key actors.

We start by looking at the economic impacts of the crisis in terms of GDP, finance, export performance, state spending and state debt. This follows the framework set out in an earlier article (Myant & Drahokoupil 2012) which was designed for analysing the impact of the crisis on economic performance in 2009. An analysis of political responses needs a different, and more flexible, framework because of the complex and varied interactions between economic and political phenomena. Indeed, some of the indicators referred to

Ivan Lesay thanks Tatiana Bujňáková for her help and acknowledges support from the VEGA grant (#2/0104/12).

above relate to the direct impact of external shocks—governments had very little short-term control over exports—but some are also partly indicators of policy responses. Only two types of economic problems, as argued in the second section, constituted hard constraints that limited the room for governments to manoeuvre: problems in the financial sectors invariably led to implementation of support measures for domestic banks; problems with financing government debt then made countries dependent on the IMF and other institutional lenders, preventing the governments from pursuing anti-cyclical policies.

The key policy differences relate to state budgets and, amid the huge number of individual measures that were adopted, responses fall broadly into two categories that we link to a social-democratic and a neo-liberal response. The terms are imprecise. Government policies were not guided by strict adherence to theories, either political or economic. However, as we argue in the third section, the division proves applicable and helpful for all of these four countries. The distinction indicates that the policy responses were linked to the party affiliation of the government on the left–right spectrum. Political contexts—type of ruling parties and their electoral strategies—shaped the interpretation of the crisis and the nature of policy reactions. The remaining sections thus analyse the politics of crisis management in individual countries in detail.

The varied responses demonstrate the extent to which conflicts depended on conditions and past histories specific to individual countries. Debates took different forms in each one, but the following three points summarise the general features of Central and East European countries when compared with other groups of countries.

First, governments did need to take account of public opinion and that set limits to any neo-liberal strategy. The Baltic recipe would lead to electoral defeat. However, quite substantial cuts in public-sector pay and state benefits could be implemented and this marks Central and East European countries out from Western European countries where the level of social acceptability seemed to be reached more quickly.

Second, fears over the level of state debt were easy to arouse and that set limits to any social-democratic strategy. That is not obviously justified by figures on government debt as a percentage of GDP, but reflects the reality of international constraints imposed on Hungary and fears in other countries that they could easily lose the confidence of financial institutions, and also perhaps that their electorates are easier to frighten than those of Western Europe.

Third, there was little concern over long-term economic weaknesses that might be revealed by the crisis. Indeed, issues such as the desirability of greater emphasis on research and high technology played only peripheral roles in government rhetoric. Essentially, the assumption was that the crisis would be weathered without any new economic thinking.

The conclusion is that the crisis did not lead to a uniform pattern of policy responses, but similar policy issues were brought to the fore. However, there were both similarities and differences in policy responses that cannot be explained by the logical requirements of the economic situation alone. The crisis, partly through its real and partly through its imagined effects, raised the profile of debates over levels of taxation and state spending, over levels of provision for pensions, health and education services and, above all, over measures affecting the distribution of income. It did not determine which side would triumph, or in what particular form, but political divisions, even when masked by other rhetoric, resembled much more the classic division between left and right than had been common in the region. There was very little change in thinking on longer-term economic policy making so this political change may prove to be the most important outcome in policy terms of the financial and economic crisis of 2008.

The economic impacts of the crisis

An analysis of all transition economies shows that the variations in GDP decline from 2008 to 2009 can largely be explained by falling financial inflows, falling exports and reductions in state spending.[1] First came a sharp halt to credits which affected most severely those countries that had been dependent on financialised growth, but also led to increased caution from banks in all countries. Next came a fall in demand for exports from those countries exporting products that were sold with the help of credits, meaning motor vehicles and other high-value consumer goods. The reductions in incomes through lower profits and wage payments led to a further reduction in domestic demand and to lower tax revenues and this, plus any additional spending undertaken in the context of the crisis, led to deepening state-budget deficits.

Differences between Central and East European countries followed from differing levels of past dependence on financial inflows, that being an important factor only in the case of Hungary, differing levels of dependence on exports, that being lowest in the case of Poland, and differing levels of willingness to incur state-budget deficits. That was the most constraining in Hungary owing to pressure to comply with terms from the IMF, given the country's dependence on IMF financing from November 2008. The responses of economic actors—enterprises, banks and households—were broadly consistent and predictable but, particularly after 2009, governments' reactions were more complex and varied. The course of economic development therefore reflected partly the continuing influence of external economic events and partly the choices made by governments which can therefore be seen both as a response to economic developments and as a factor shaping the course of those developments.

Table 1 shows changes in key economic indicators that were the least subject to government influence and could therefore be considered as creating the conditions from which policy choices had to be made. GDP declined in 2009 in all cases apart from Poland, where the previous rate of growth declined markedly, and then recovered across all countries in 2010. The major stimulus was the renewed growth in exports. There was also some recovery in the volume of credits, following restriction in all countries in 2009, but there was no return to the very rapid expansions of the pre-2008 period. Hungary was hardest hit here, because of the country's previous dependence on financial inflows, but recovery was also hampered in other countries because banks, following concerns with the world financial situation, became more cautious. In no case was there a recovery to the levels of lending of the mid-2000s.

These indicators point to areas of possible policy response. Declining exports led immediately to falling industrial output and hence a threat of rising unemployment. Governments could react passively or could respond with measures to maintain employment, to create new employment opportunities or to raise demand levels to compensate for the fall in export demand. Lower levels of credit caused particular problems

---

[1]The impacts of the crisis on individual countries up to the end of 2009 are discussed elsewhere (Myant & Drahokoupil 2011, 2012).

TABLE 1

ANNUAL PERCENTAGE GROWTH IN GDP, EXPORTS AND VOLUME OF CREDITS, 2008–2011.

	GDP				Exports				Credit to enterprises and households			
	2008	2009	2010	2011	2008	2009	2010	2011	2008	2009	2010	2011
Czech Republic	3.1	−4.7	2.7	1.7	6	−10.2	17.6	11	16	1.5	4.1	5.9
Hungary	0.9	−6.8	1.3	1.7	4.2	−12.7	16.9	10.2	10.5	−4.6	−1.4	1.3
Poland	5.1	1.6	3.9	4.4	7.1	−6.7	10.1	7.5	36.7	7.2	8.8	14
Slovakia	5.8	−4.9	4.2	3.3	3.2	−14.8	10.6	16.9	18.2	3.1	6	8.6

Notes: The figures are December values.
Sources: For GDP and exports, IMF database, available at: http://www.imf.org/external/pubs/ft/weo/2012/01/weodata/weoselgr.aspx, accessed 16 August 2012. For Credits, December to December annual growth, from central banks, available at: http://www.cnb.cz/cnb/STAT.ARADY_PKG.PARAMETRY_SESTAVY?p_sestuid=1148&p_strid=AACA&p_lang=CS; http://www.nbp.pl/home.aspx?f=/statystyka/pieniezna_i_bankowa/nal_zobow.html; http://www.nbs.sk/sk/statisticke-udaje/menova-a-bankova-statistika/zdrojove-statisticke-udaje-penaznych-financnych-institucii/uvery, all accessed 16 August 2012.

for the construction sector and governments could, again, respond passively or by substituting state spending for previously credit-financed activities. These differences are pursued in discussion of individual countries.

Table 2 gives a broad indication of the nature of government responses. Government spending increased in 2009 in all cases covered here apart from Hungary. Growth was particularly marked in Slovakia. There was then rapid retrenchment in 2010, albeit with Poland continuing the upward trend. Figures for 2011 suggest a continuing, albeit not universal or consistent, trend for government spending to switch from countering depression into a factor holding back the pace of economic recovery. Differences between countries are also clear from the fiscal deficits, which grew somewhat more rapidly in Poland. The constraint on budget deficits was fear over growing state debt. The figures in Table 2 suggest that the high level of public debt in Hungary was an exception, while in general the region was characterised by low debt levels in international terms.

As already argued, changes in the economy were partly a consequence of government policies. However, the changes outlined above also set an agenda for governments and for political parties and representatives of particular interests. There were likely to be pressures from particular groups: those suffering declining living standards, those hit by the reduction in credits, those seeking to combine security in employment with flexibility in the face of economic fluctuations and those threatened by cuts in public spending.

Governments in all countries interpreted the nature of the crisis and adopted policies in response. However, it is not sufficient to take at face value government presentations of their anti-crisis policies. They often presented packages of measures which included steps, some of which had been decided beforehand and some of which were never implemented. Governments came under pressure to appear to be doing something and responded, at least in part, by dissembling.

Moreover, measures adopted under an 'anti-crisis' heading were arguably often irrelevant to the crisis. It is therefore very difficult to separate out clear cut, anti-crisis policy measures from continuity with past policies or from new policies that were adopted at the time of the crisis, often using economic difficulties as a pretext. The two sections that follow set out the basis for a framework that makes sense of policies adopted, starting with a consideration of external and internal constraints. The key point is the linking of economic theories and political ideologies to actual policy responses and this points towards a re-emphasis of an underlying, but often blurred, left–right distinction.

External and internal constraints

There were hard constraints, both economic and political, that limited the room for manoeuvre for governments regardless of their ideological affiliation. The centrality of the financial sector for the rest of the economy meant that all governments were under pressure to ensure stability of banking systems, but that was generally done by government guarantees without any direct expenditure. Banks were largely under foreign ownership and enjoyed a degree of security thanks to international agreements, as discussed by Kudrna and Gabor (this issue), so that stability of the financial system, a major issue for the crisis at the global level, was an issue that in Central and East European countries required an active response only in Hungary where the financial sector was in a more difficult situation.

TABLE 2

ANNUAL PERCENTAGE GROWTH IN GOVERNMENT SPENDING, FISCAL BALANCE AS PERCENT OF GDP AND GOVERNMENT DEBT AS PERCENT OF GDP, 2008–2011.

	Government spending growth				Fiscal balance				Government debt			
	2008	2009	2010	2011	2008	2009	2010	2011	2008	2009	2010	2011
Czech Republic	3.4	4.0	0.9	0.9	−2.2	−5.8	−4.8	−3.1	28.7	34.4	38.1	41.2
Hungary	−2.0	−2.7	−2.5	0.6	−3.7	−4.5	−4.2	4.3	74.0	79.8	80.2	80.6
Poland	7.6	4.7	5.9	1.6	−3.7	−7.4	−7.8	−5.1	47.1	50.9	54.85	56.3
Slovakia	8.3	13.1	2.7	−1.3	−2.1	−8	−7.7	−4.8	27.9	35.6	41.1	43.3

Source: Eurostat, available at: http://epp.eurostat.ec.europa.eu/portal/page/portal/statistics/search_database/, accessed 16 August 2012.

TRANSITION ECONOMIES AFTER 2008

Financing external debt could become a major constraint on policy, but this was an issue only in Hungary which, unable to finance its government debt in October 2008, was forced into seeking external financing from the IMF and EU under terms that implied budgetary restriction. That was not an absolute determinant of policies as governments could interpret external conditions with some flexibility. Nevertheless, it rather sets Hungary apart from the other Central and East European countries.

The EU had some influence over all Central and East European countries' fiscal policies. Having joined the EU in 2004, they were committed to joining the euro at some time in the future. Slovakia joined in 2009 and was thereby formally tied to the Maastricht criteria, meaning that the budget deficit should not exceed 3% of GDP and public debt should not exceed 60% of GDP. In practice, these were not hard constraints in the first years after 2008 when many EU members failed to meet the targets. The other countries were expected to abide by timetables, negotiated and embodied in Convergence Programmes, which set target dates for fulfilling the criteria. For Hungary this was overshadowed by conditions set out in agreements with the IMF. For Poland it was significant as a factor reinforcing internal pressures for austerity which led to the dramatic fall in the budget deficit in 2011. In Slovakia, the pressure from the European Commission was a factor that contributed to the commitment to bring down the deficit. For the Czech Republic its significance varied as governments changed with the oddity that the main political force advocating austerity was the least eager for early accession to the euro and the least interested in following EU directives and guidelines.

Apart from this, the EU did impose an important constraint through its competition rules which effectively ruled out help to individual enterprises or sectors. Any government assistance could not discriminate between EU member countries and that marked a striking difference from Russia and Ukraine, where much of the anti-crisis policy took the form of help to particular firms (as well as from the USA). Policy making in Central and East European countries therefore took the form of more general measures which appeared less susceptible to individual lobbying.

Finally, the most important internal constraint on a government was the possibility of defeat in an election. However, that was not a universal determinant of particular policies. It is clear that no government can ignore all opinions and pressures and pursue a course based on pure ideology. All make some compromises so as to win elections that give them the power to pursue their priority objectives. All listen to some extent to social interests even if, as indicated for individual countries, the influence of formal tripartite structures varied greatly, depending in fact on the willingness of particular governments to listen which, in turn, varied with the ideological complexion of governments.

Economic theories and political ideologies

The crisis of 2008 brought back memories of the depression of the 1930s and with that, thoughts of a solution true to Keynesian theory. If the problem originated in the failure of the banking system to provide credits, then that implied a case for states to substitute for private-sector failure and to stimulate demand. This implied running a budget deficit, and trying to prevent that by cutting spending was, in the Keynesian view, a mistaken approach. Cutting spending would further depress demand and hence national income and tax revenues, leading to long-term depression if not a downward spiral of decline. The aim of a

19

countercyclical policy was to prevent not only an immediate economic decline but also a permanent loss of potential output that the latter was likely to cause. It thus made more sense to endure a period of rising government debt which could be reduced when economic growth was restored.

The alternative perspective of fiscal prudence put all the emphasis on preventing an escalation in the level of government debt. In this view the crisis was a crisis of the state budget and the solution was to restore balance. Within such a perspective the fear was not of lasting depression but of state bankruptcy. That was a live issue in Hungary, leading to the need to seek IMF help, and the fear could be evoked across Central and East European countries as a number of other EU member countries experienced extreme difficulties with continued borrowing.

However, the key division in policy choices is closest to an ideological divide between what can loosely be termed social-democratic and neo-liberal responses. That differs from dividing policy responses by the attitude towards the state budget alone for four reasons. The first is that the budget can be balanced by a number of different methods. Both raising taxes and cutting spending are options and the ways in which they are done can have very different distributional impacts. The second is that spending and tax policies can have quite specific effects, such as maintaining employment in a particular sector or demand for a particular product, that are not captured by a distinction between stimulus and depression. The third is that governments used further measures that related only indirectly to the state budget, such as labour-market policies. The fourth is that crisis management was often used as an opportunity to implement policies that the parties in power wanted to implement regardless of the crisis.

The interpretation of the nature of the crisis and the respective policy response pursued was conditional upon the party-ideological affiliation on the left–right dimension. There had been an inexact fit between political parties and easily definable economic thinking (Tavits & Letki 2009), such that the division between left and right in Central and East European countries, with the exception of the Czech Republic, was blurred by the nationalist–populist (right) compared to the modernising (left) dimension (Kitschelt 1995; Kitschelt *et al.* 1999). The crisis raised the profile of economic policy in general and the role of the state in providing social security and services and in affecting the distribution of income in particular. The left–right dimension thus started to play a more prominent structuring role. At the same time, in the context of unstable party systems where social constituencies are not clearly defined, it is difficult to assign policy positions to political parties *a priori*. Specific crisis narratives used by party leaders in voter mobilisation played a key role in shaping the party agenda (Hanley *et al.* 2008). The policy of individual governments thus has to be linked to the specific electoral strategies of the parties that compose the governments.

In general, the left subscribed to the social-democratic response, including acceptance of Keynesian thinking alongside responsiveness to pressure from employee representatives and support for progressive taxation. There was no presumption in favour of a reduction in the weight of the public sector in the economy. The neo-liberal response of the right was likely to ignore Keynesian thinking and to centre on the dangers of a budget deficit. This was to be solved by cutting public spending, especially benefits for the unemployed and those on lower incomes, and any increases in taxes should not be progressive. The neo-liberal approach cannot be defined simply as giving priority to budget balance. Indeed, evidence is clear from many countries, including Central and East European countries, that over preceding years governments with a social-democratic complexion had been the more determined and successful at reducing budget deficits (Tavits & Letki 2009). Thus the neo-liberal approach should be seen as primarily concerned with cutting back on state activity in total, and particularly on any role it plays in reducing the extent of inequality created by a free-market system.

This highlights one of the difficulties in interpreting responses to the economic crisis. It has been claimed that every successful politician is aware of the possibility of using a crisis to implement otherwise unpopular policies. All political trends could theoretically act in such a way, including those advocating Keynesian or nationalist approaches. However, in the context of the post-2008 situation, advocates of the neo-liberal approach appeared the most adept in this. The slogan of reducing the budget deficit, so as to avoid state bankruptcy was used to justify moves towards lower levels of state benefits and also of taxes and towards overall less progressive tax systems, steps which have the primary effect of shifting the pattern of income distribution.

Table 3 indicates the broad differences in starting points and in the policy reactions to the crisis that relate to public spending. In the Czech Republic, the first reaction of a

TABLE 3
GOVERNMENT SPENDING, % OF GDP.

Czech Republic	2007	2008	2009	2010	2011
Total government expenditure	41	41.1	44.9	44.1	43.4
Gross capital formation	4.1	4.6	5.1	4.3	3.7
Compensation of employees	7.3	7.3	7.8	7.6	7.3
Social benefits	17.6	17.6	19.5	19.7	20

Poland	2007	2008	2009	2010	2011
Total government expenditure	42.2	43.2	44.5	45.4	43.6
Gross capital formation	4.3	4.6	5.3	5.7	5.9
Compensation of employees	9.6	10	10.3	10.2	9.8
Social benefits	19.3	19.2	20.6	20.7	20.1

Hungary	2007	2008	2009	2010	2011
Total government expenditure	50.7	49.2	51.4	49.5	48.7
Gross capital formation	3.7	2.9	3.1	3.4	2.9
Compensation of employees	11.7	11.6	11.5	10.9	10.1
Social benefits	18.4	18.6	19.4	18.5	17.9

Slovakia	2007	2008	2009	2010	2011
Total government expenditure	34.2	34.9	41.5	40	37.4
Gross capital formation	2	2	2.3	2.6	2.3
Compensation of employees	6.6	6.8	7.7	7.7	7.1
Social benefits	16.1	16.1	19	19.5	18.5

Note: Government spending on social benefits differs from total expenditure on social protection.
Sources: Eurostat, Government Finance Statistics, available at: http://epp.eurostat.ec.europa.eu/portal/page/portal/government_finance_statistics/introduction, accessed 16 August 2012.

right-wing government was limited: continuation of past policies led to continued growth in the weight of public spending in GDP, affecting all its main elements. A caretaker government that ruled from May 2009 led to reductions in some areas alongside increases in others as it listened to diverse inputs from political parties and society. Elections in May 2010 gave a strong mandate to a right-wing government that then pursued a neo-liberal approach, reflected in the declining share of state spending.

In Poland, the policy of the right-wing government that pursued a careful strategy of re-election—which was ultimately proven successful in March 2011—can be seen as partially Keynesian oriented, with continued growth in public-sector pay and capital spending. It changed in 2011 with more evidence of retrenchment.

Hungary, in contrast, started from the position of the highest level of state spending, but dependence on financing from the IMF led to the imposition of pro-cyclical policies on the then left-wing government. The arrival of the conservative-right government in March 2010 changed the situation. It was able to gain more independence through unorthodox one-off revenue-raising measures, but a radical neo-liberal agenda, albeit with a specific nationalist–populist colouring, led to the reductions in capital formation, public-sector pay and social benefits shown in Table 3.

In Slovakia, state involvement in the economy and in social protection was lowest in the Central and East European countries. The social-democratic government implemented an anti-crisis policy, but the data in this table show powerful effects from elements that were not explicitly part of the anti-cyclical package. Increases in spending in 2009, including social benefits, public-sector pay and capital spending—an element made up largely of infrastructure expenditure—were part of the government's broader policy of increasing public spending after the period of cuts by the right-wing government before 2006. The approach was reversed by the neo-liberal approach of the new right-wing government from June 2010.

Table 4 sets out matching data on government revenues as a percent of GDP. It is noteworthy that only Hungary consolidated its budget through revenue increases in 2011. In the rest of the Central and East European countries, the apparent urgency of balancing budgets did not lead to a significant increase in tax and insurance contributions as a percent of GDP after 2007. A further striking feature is the common switch from direct towards indirect taxes, although the former had already been relatively low by international standards. The latter tend to be less progressive, falling on the whole population, while direct taxes are more likely to fall more heavily on higher earners,[2] and on businesses. Social contributions are less clear cut, with part nominally paid by employers and part nominally paid by employees. Reductions in this period frequently followed from reductions in business contributions. The data in Table 4 are therefore consistent with the crisis leading to a strengthening of the neo-liberal relative to the social-democratic approach.

The aggregate data are indicative of important differences, but the complexity of the politics and policy of crisis management requires a detailed analysis of developments in individual countries. That is provided in the sections that follow.

---

[2]This is true even where so-called flat tax systems have been introduced as they contain significant allowances before tax is levied.

TABLE 4
GOVERNMENT REVENUE, % OF GDP.

Czech Republic	2007	2008	2009	2010	2011
Total revenue	40.3	38.9	39.1	39.3	40.3
Indirect taxes	10.8	10.6	11.1	11.2	11.5
Direct taxes	9	8	7.3	7	7.5
Social contributions	15.7	15.6	15	15.3	15.5

Hungary	2007	2008	2009	2010	2011
Total revenue	45.6	45.5	46.9	45.2	52.9
Indirect taxes	15.9	15.6	16.6	16.9	16.6
Direct taxes	10.3	10.6	9.9	8	6.4
Social contributions	13.9	13.8	13.3	12.1	13

Poland	2007	2008	2009	2010	2011
Total revenue	40.3	39.5	37.2	37.5	38.5
Indirect taxes	14.1	14.2	12.9	13.6	13.7
Direct taxes	8.6	8.6	7.4	6.9	7
Social contributions	12	11.3	11.3	11.1	11.4

Slovakia	2007	2008	2009	2010	2011
Total revenue	32.4	32.8	33.5	32.3	32.6
Indirect taxes	11.1	10.4	10.3	10.1	10.4
Direct taxes	6.2	6.5	5.5	5.4	5.6
Social contributions	11.9	12.2	12.9	12.6	12.5

Source: Eurostat, Government Finance Statistics, available at: http://epp.eurostat.ec.europa.eu/portal/page/portal/government_finance_statistics/introduction, accessed 16 August 2012.

The Czech Republic

Czech politics were characterised by a reasonably clear division between left and right. Governments broadly of the right dominated up to 1998 and were in power again from 2006. Social Democrats were dominant in the intervening period. Thus the right was in power in 2008 and had been able to implement neo-liberal policies of a flat tax, some reductions in welfare benefits and initial charges for health treatment. Its parliamentary majority was very tight, but it showed no desire to compromise with the opposition or to listen to representatives of social interests. The first reactions to reports from outside of a developing economic crisis were dismissive: this would not affect the Czech economy in view of its stable financial system and policies of low taxes, low state spending and low budget deficits. The state budget for 2009 was therefore approved with the assumption of real GDP growth of 4.8%.

Changes came in early 2009, following pressure from inside the country. Both employers and trade unions pointed to the collapse in manufacturing output and, following thinking in other EU member countries and advice from the EU as a whole, formulated their anti-crisis measures. The EU was of special significance as the Czech Republic held the presidency of the union for the first half of the year and it was not desirable to ignore calls for anti-crisis strategies embodying a fiscal stimulus. However, the dominant party in the Czech government, the *Občanská demokratická strana* (ODS, Civic Democratic Party), had a record of Euroscepticism that, combined with ideological aversion to any economic policies associated with Keynesian theories, ruled out full compliance with EU thinking.

Thus the first Czech reaction was essentially to give some appearance of complying with pressures from the EU for an anti-crisis policy, but to complement this with a defiant pronouncement that no significant rethinking was required, irrespective of the external or internal pressures. The crisis was seen as a minor, short-term phenomenon which should not be allowed to disrupt the neo-liberal direction of its policies.

In February 2009 the government published its National Anti-Crisis Plan *(Národní protikrizový plán vlády)*. Prime Minister Topolánek introduced the programme with the words: 'It is a plan which, unlike those of many other countries, is free from the populism and bribery which we could smuggle in under the cloak of a crisis situation'.[3] It was a plan 'of which we would not need to be ashamed even in a time of growth' (Vláda ČR 2009, p. 5). There were some nods of recognition towards EU pressure for a stimulus package, but dangers were not seen as very great and the main one was not seen as coming from the crisis at all. A key statement in the programme was that 'taking note of the fact that the cyclical slow-down of the economy is a lesser threat than long-term indebtedness', the package of measures was aimed at 'maintaining employment and the stability of the public finances' (Vláda ČR 2009, p. 32). The aim was not to create a demand stimulus, in line with Keynesian thinking, but to 'make labour cheaper' (Vláda ČR 2009, p. 3), keeping people in employment, preventing unemployment from rising at all, and enabling firms to invest and grow (Vláda ČR 2009, p. 32).

The plan was presented as stimulating the economy to the extent of 2.9% of GDP, adding a cost equivalent to 1.9% of GDP to the state budget. In fact, almost half of the package was from measures already decided and approved (such as the annual pay increase for state-sector employees which had been agreed following strong pressure from trade unions and opposition parties) so that the new fiscal stimulus, introduced after acknowledging the crisis, amounted to only 1.1% of the GDP that was actually achieved in 2009. Fully 74% of the stimulus was to come from reductions in taxes and social insurance obligations on businesses, thereby continuing with the previous neo-liberal policy direction. There was no commitment to major infrastructure investment, no serious thought of a demand stimulus either by raising the lowest incomes or by supporting particular sectors and a reversal rather than expansion of measures for direct employment creation, which had been financed out of the company social insurance contributions that were being cut as a measure apparently to help overcome the crisis.

The only new form of policy discussion was cosmetic. The government established the National Economic Council of the Government *(Národní ekonomická rada vlády, NERV)*, on 8 January 2009 as an advisory body. It had a strong representation from business and only two of its nine members were academics, in the limited sense of being employed by academic institutions. Although not all clear and active supporters of the government, none were known as its opponents. It produced three reports, with a final one in September 2009, and broadly supported the government's approach, concluding that 'the main priority should not be growth in GDP but rather reducing indebtedness' (NERV 2009, p. 66).

[3] Addressing parliament on 18 February 2009 (PSP 2009).

The outcome in practice is clear from the 267-page report on the results of the 2009 state budget (MFČR 2010). There were only seven references to anti-crisis measures, one very general, four relating to easier tax conditions for businesses and two relating to export guarantees which were a relatively small item. Indeed, the only noteworthy consequence of the anti-crisis plan was the introduction of additional tax relief on small businesses, which were the only social interest that visibly affected government decisions.

Changes on the expenditure side largely reflected previously planned cuts in some state benefits, reduced spending on anti-unemployment measures, presented, as indicated above, as part of an anti-unemployment measure, and higher unemployment benefit payments, reflecting higher levels of unemployment, up from an average of 5.4% in 2008 to 8.0% in 2009 and 9.0% in 2010. The increase was small in relation to the state budget as a whole, amounting to only 1.3% of total expenditure, against 0.66% in 2008.

A change in approach in the Czech Republic was brought about by the defeat of the Topolánek government in a vote of no-confidence in March 2009—over issues not related to the anti-crisis policy—and its replacement by a caretaker government, given support by the main parties of the right and left. It was intended that the new government would not take any major political decisions and just tide things over until new parliamentary elections. Those were delayed until 28–29 May 2010. This interlude therefore gave some voice to the Social Democratic Party, which supported following the advice coming at the time from the EU and IMF for a fiscal stimulus. It succeeded in winning approval for reversal of some previous state benefit reductions. The new government was also more willing to consult through tripartite structures, even agreeing with unions and employers on 2 February 2010 to a 38-point plan (RHSD 2010).

This was a government that acknowledged the presence of a crisis and the need to take measures. A number were even approved, such as a car-scrap scheme, lobbied for by the motor industry and supported by the Social Democrats, which was approved by parliament in September 2009. However, very little was actually done. The 38-point plan remained at the level of points for consideration, despite pressure from both employers and unions for decisive action. Indeed, both employers and trade unions were openly frustrated by the government's approach, preferring a shorter list of measures that would be treated as priorities. A prime example was support for implementation of the German *Kurzarbeit* system, whereby an employee could work shorter hours while partially supported from state benefits. That was not possible under existing Czech law, so the call was for some simple amendments. The government's response was to discuss and consider rather than to implement.

Reluctance over spending measures reflected one clear decision that the government did take: the budget deficit for 2009 was not to exceed 5% of GDP and the same was to apply for 2010. The background to this was the desire of the government—more sympathetic to the EU than its predecessor—to engage fully with the process of joining the eurozone. This required compliance with the Convergence Programme, negotiated with the European Commission, which set the timetable for reaching the Maastricht criteria. Terms were renegotiated in early 2010, with the prediction that the budget deficit target of 3% of GDP could be met in 2013. Despite a lack of enthusiasm for early entry to the Euro, the ODS were quick to approve. The Social Democrats were more sceptical.

The clear deficit target, alongside opposition to significant tax increases, inevitably pointed to spending cuts. With Social Democrat support for public services, the immediate blow fell on new infrastructure projects and on areas such as the government's commitment to R&D spending. Thus stimulus and retrenchment met in one contradictory programme and the stimulus measures were the ones to face delay.

This, then, was neither an explicitly neo-liberal nor an explicitly social-democratic response. There was a willingness to listen to the views and interests that pointed in the social-democratic direction, but little action was taken. It rather marked a period of indecision and waiting in which the course of economic development was left unaffected by government policies, despite the crisis being a major theme in economic policy discussions. It differed from the approach of the Topolánek government in that social-democratic measures were held in check by inaction rather than outright rejection.

The Czech political situation was transformed by parliamentary elections in May 2010 which led to a right-wing government with a clear majority, effectively the first time since 1996 that a government had not had to struggle to maintain a parliamentary majority. A major factor in the electoral outcome was undoubtedly the situation in the eurozone at the time. Parties of the right used this in the last weeks of campaigning and the outcome of the elections deviated markedly from previous opinion polls which had pointed to a decisive victory for the left. Evidently, with continued public-sector pay rises and with recovery in export-oriented industries meaning that real wages for those still in work were rising, the threat of falling living standards and rising unemployment appeared less serious to much of the population than the fear of possible state bankruptcy following rising debt levels. Thus, at this point the most important political effect of the economic crisis appeared to be a decisive move to the right, opening the way for a clearly neo-liberal policy direction.

The new government came with a reinterpretation of the crisis. The only issue of concern, to judge from its rhetoric, was the budget deficit and state debt, mixed with a more general neo-liberal agenda. They were going beyond just exploiting a crisis as an opportunity to implement unpopular policies. The outcome can be seen from the results of the 2010 state budget (MFČR 2011). The 'crisis' was presented as an external constraint, not as a reason for adopting any particular policies. Anti-crisis measures were mentioned only in relation to some reductions in business tax obligations. The important changes from the previous year included reduced unemployment benefit payments, following stricter rules that reduced the numbers eligible, and a 2.5% reduction in spending on pay throughout state administration. Research institutes and universities also experienced significant cuts.

Spending in 2011 (MFČR 2012) was further reduced by cuts in state benefits and public-sector pay but, as confirmed by the data in Table 3, the impact on public spending was relatively small. Thus a 22.5% cut in spending on unemployment benefits and an 11.7% cut in social benefits in 2011 were equivalent to only 0.2% of GDP, as these items were already quite small. All of these savings were outweighed by a 6.3% increase in pension payments, due to an increasing number of retired people and to the government's compliance with the existing law on indexation of pensions, equivalent to 0.6% of GDP.

In fact, the government appeared to be motivated as much by a clear neo-liberal agenda as by restoring budget balance and when the two came into conflict it faced a difficult dilemma. In contrast to the initial reaction in 2008 of denying that there was a crisis, the new approach seemed to be to magnify its scale so as to provide a pretext for a broader policy agenda. The government's programme included greater private roles in the pension system and the employment service, a two-tier health system allowing additional payments for better services and fees for students in higher education. The state budget deficit was set to

TRANSITION ECONOMIES AFTER 2008

increase with the transition to a partly private pension system and this was to be held in check by increases in VAT while taxation on business and personal incomes were to remain unchanged.[4] Results for 2011 showed revenue from indirect taxes increasing by 3.9% while revenue from direct taxes fell very slightly, up 3.6% from personal incomes and down 4.6% from companies.

Not surprisingly, government policies met with opposition in the form of large and persistent public protests and demonstrations, particularly from trade unions and universities, and other informal groups also took some forms of action. This of itself need not influence government decisions, but the overall political effect of the economic crisis appeared to be a reassertion of a classic left−right division, with high-profile disputes over policies that directly affect the distribution of income. Parliamentary elections, due in 2014, could be expected to reveal which side in that divide could command more public support.

Poland

The left−right division was less prominent in Poland than in the Czech Republic or Slovakia. The left had suffered a resounding defeat in 2005 and the main political division was between the *Platforma Obywatelska* (PO, Civic Platform) and *Prawo i Sprawedliwość* (PiS, Law and Justice). The former brought together politicians from neo-liberal backgrounds, but they had repeatedly failed with some of their favoured policies, notably the flat tax, advocacy of which contributed to electoral defeat in 2005. PiS was more nationalist than neo-liberal and had a continuing association with the Solidarity trade union. PO won the 2007 election, albeit on a more cautiously neo-liberal policy than in the past and set about governing, in coalition with the party representing farmers, with an approach aimed at winning a second term in power. That had not been achieved by any Polish government since 1989.

When contrasted with the experience of other Central and East European countries, Poland differed in three respects. The first was that one government remained in power for some years after the start of the crisis and that was associated with more stability in policy making. The second, marking it out from other governments of the right, was that it was a pragmatic right-wing government, listening to social interests and influenced by fears over the social costs of its policies. The third was that it was concerned over budget deficits and rising debt, ultimately placing these considerations ahead of a narrower neo-liberal agenda that would place all the emphasis on a small state and privatisation.

The Polish government responded to the crisis slightly more quickly than its Czech counterpart, following reports of reduced exports from foreign- and domestically-owned firms and as banks cut lending in the autumn of 2008. The response was to reduce the growth forecast for 2009 from 4.8% to 3.7% and to set out the Stability and Development Plan (*Plan stabilności i rozwoju*) on 30 November 2008. The underlying assumption was that Poland

---

[4]The actual costs of the reform were uncertain as the entry into the private pillar was made voluntary. There was thus uncertainty about the number of people who would divert part of their insurance contributions to the private pillar and thus reduce revenues of the budget. Costs for a compulsory private pillar were expected to peak at 1.1% of GDP by 2040. The reform thus involved substantially lower costs than was common in the earlier reforms in other Central and East European countries (see Drahokoupil & Domonkos 2012).

was unlikely to be severely affected by the crisis owing to the relative stability of its banking system. The plan was billed as costing zł 91.3 billion (0.7% of GDP), but most of this was in guarantees to keep the finance system functioning. It was intended to balance reduced revenue from the lower level of GDP by reduced spending. The effect of the plan was to allow the budget deficit to rise when growth was even lower than expected.

However, in early 2009 the Polish government came under pressure to take more positive action from opposition parties and the Solidarity union which argued that the country was ideally placed to implement a Keynesian policy of fiscal stimulus. This position was neither explicitly accepted nor explicitly rejected. Instead, negotiations through the tripartite commission led to a 13-point anti-crisis package which came into force on 22 August 2009 with the intention that it should operate for two years with the possibility of further extension (MPiPS 2009).

The measures included a number of proposals for changes in employment legislation to make it easier for enterprises to maintain employment by temporary layoffs and short-term working and proposals to ease financial difficulties for businesses suffering from the immediate effects of the crisis, largely by reducing tax burdens. Much of the necessary legislation was passed fairly quickly. Some longer-term measures, such as an agreement to raise the minimum wage to the level of half the average wage, were set aside for further discussion. This, then, was largely a programme for immediate relief rather than a significant economic stimulus. The main help to investment was to be from helping co-financing for EU-funded projects.

Overall the impact of newly adopted government policies on economic development was very small. However, the continuation of government spending decided in the past, including increases in public-sector pay and pensions significantly above the increases in private-sector pay, helped to maintain consumption-led growth through 2009 and 2010 (MFRP 2011, p. 7). Government spending also continued on road building and the output of the construction sector continued to rise every year while it moved into decline in all other Central and East European countries as they cut public capital spending.

Polish government policy underwent a shift in 2011 towards much greater concern over the budget deficit. The stimulus was partly external, as the European Commission called on the government to take steps to get back in line with its programme for joining the eurozone. The stimulus was also internal, partly in the sense that complying with eurozone rules did matter to this government but primarily because a previous right-wing Polish government had set strict rules on the level of state debt. Should this reach 55% of GDP, the government was required to cut spending and freeze the indexation of pensions. The constitution set 60% as an absolute maximum and that was also the level set by the Maastricht criteria. As indicated in Table 2, these levels were looming large and the government was embarrassed by criticisms from outside its ranks that it was on course for a debt crisis. The response was a programme of changes on the expenditure and revenue sides.

The main spending-side measures were a freeze on public-sector pay (saving 0.46% of GDP in 2011), pension reductions achieved by limiting early retirement (saving 0.30% of GDP in 2011) and cuts in employment creation measures (saving 0.28% of GDP in 2011). On the revenue side the biggest changes were an increase in VAT (0.41% of GDP) and a change in the system of financing pensions which increased state revenue by the equivalent of 0.64% of GDP. The effect on the state budget was quite significant as the deficit fell in 2011 to little over half its 2010 level (based on nine months of 2011 (MFRP 2012)). This

TRANSITION ECONOMIES AFTER 2008

also brought a shift in the driving forces for Poland's economic growth. In 2011, pensions and pay in both public and private sectors stagnated in nominal terms and fell in real terms. Public investment projects continued but, as in other Central and East European countries, the main stimulus to growth had become rising exports.

There were still important differences from the Czech experience both in the rhetoric surrounding, and in the content of, policies. In terms of rhetoric, the fiscal deficit was only 'one of the serious threats to Poland's development' (MFRP 2011, p. 11), rather than the biggest and most pressing. In content too the reform of the pension system indicated a significant difference. Under the system established in 1998, a proportion of pension contributions went into private funds while a proportion went into a smaller state pension system. Changes from May 2011 reduced the share going to private funds to less than a third of its previous level, increasing revenue that flowed through the state budget. This was therefore a significant reversal of a key neo-liberal reform measure, arousing some wrath from free-market purists. It reflected both the desire to reduce state debt and a more realistic assessment of the costs and performance of the private pension system (Drahokoupil & Domonkos 2012). However, the pragmatic approach appeared to work in that the PO government triumphed in parliamentary elections in October 2011, returning for a second spell in power.

Slovakia

The Slovak government in 2008 was dominated by the *Smer—sociálna demokracia* party (Direction—Social Democracy) under Prime Minister Robert Fico. It had come to power after elections in 2006 following a period of right-wing dominance during which standard neo-liberal policies, including a flat tax and partial privatisation of the pension system, had been introduced with vigour and considerable consistency. The share of public spending in GDP was the lowest among all Central and East European countries and among the lowest in the EU. The *Smer* government had been committed to reintroducing more progressive elements in the personal income tax system but, at a time of rapid economic growth and rising living standards, did little to reverse those previous neo-liberal policies.

However, the Slovak government reacted to the economic crisis in a clearly Keynesian, and also social democratic, manner. As indicated in Table 3, it produced the largest rise in state spending in 2009 of any Central and East European country. This primarily reflected continuation of expenditure planned before under a budget based on the assumption of 4.6% growth in GDP. This included increases in public-sector pay, higher social spending and increased capital spending, all contrasting with the previous government's approach of reducing the role of the state and all to be financed out of continuing rapid economic growth. This outweighed the impact of a formal anti-crisis package which was nevertheless of some significance when set against those of neighbouring countries. Between November 2008 and February 2009 the government adopted 62 explicit anti-crisis measures, plus a series of further steps targeted at a number of levels and sectors, covering macroeconomic policy, the financial sector, the business environment and the labour market.

Slovakia went further than other countries in systematic formal consultation with representatives of particular interests, building from the established tripartite structure. An Economic Crisis Committee was established in January 2009 as an advisory body with responsibility for approving all anti-crisis measures. It brought together representatives of trade unions, employers' organisations, regions and municipalities, the central bank, the banking sector and ministers. The enormous number of measures approved reflected the number of interests represented and some measures were adopted explicitly after consultations with interest groups, such as the Motor Industry Association or the Slovak Banking Association.

There was an element of confusion as discussion of policies was rather informal and episodic. The prime minister, ministers or their advisors were pressing for speed, leading to a substantial amount of stress, confusion, political direction and improvisation. Indeed, as has been pointed out (Filadelfiová 2010, p. 52), anti-crisis measures were often copied from the concepts of other countries or the EU rather than being based on an analysis of local contexts. The government's approach to consultation meant that the 'economy' was understood rather narrowly. The perspectives of economic actors took centre stage and economic tools and employment measures were prioritised. The public sector and social services were not considered under the anti-crisis heading (Kusá & Gerbery 2009, p. 17).

In the field of macroeconomic policy, the stated rationale, in line with accepted Keynesian thinking and with the first pressures from the EU, was to raise aggregate demand, and thus consumption and production. Besides the passive anti-crisis policy of continuing with past plans for higher spending, the government also actively decided to provide liquidity to citizens and firms by various tax measures, including a higher basic tax allowance on personal income tax and higher employee tax credit, in effect a negative income tax. These changes were therefore very unusual for the time in that they increased the progressiveness of the tax system. This tax cut stimulus amounted to €455 million (approximately 0.7% of GDP).

There were also a number of measures benefiting particular sectors. A refundable aid package of €236 million (0.36% GDP) was provided to the railway companies and later reclassified as a non-refundable capital transfer. The registered capital of the Slovak Guarantee and Development Bank (SZRB) was increased by €32.4 million (0.05% GDP), and that of Eximbanka (Export–Import Bank) by €11.4 million (0.018% GDP). These additional sources were aimed at the development of small and medium-sized enterprises and at promoting their exports. Car producers enjoyed the €55 million (0.085% GDP) subsidy supporting the purchase of new cars conditioned by liquidation of old cars (the car-scrap scheme). Interest-free subsidies for house insulation, amounting to €71 million (0.11% GDP), were beneficial for the construction sector.

Given the relatively good shape of the financial sector, the Fico government did not need to intervene and spend any money on saving banks. However, the Bank Stabilisation Assistance Act adopted in June 2009 provided a legal basis for state aid to banks, should they be hit by the global crisis. Another preventive measure was adopted in November 2008, a Bank Deposit Protection Act. Another set of anti-crisis measures related to the business environment. They were intended to boost the competitiveness of companies, to support applied research and innovation, explicitly at the cost of basic research, and to target energy-related sectors. However, these measures were not allocated significant budgetary resources and had minimal impact.

Labour-market measures included a contribution to support the maintenance of employment, along the lines of the German *Kurzarbeit* scheme that could make little progress in the Czech Republic. This policy required a public subsidy for short-time working schemes. Employers who wanted to prevent or minimise layoffs, and were willing temporarily to limit companies' operating activities by reducing their employees' weekly working time by at least 4%, were eligible for this subsidy. Government documents were also presented supporting the creation and maintenance of social enterprises and raising the work commuting allowance as anti-crisis measures, although they were launched or planned before the crisis. Taken together, all the labour-market anti-crisis measures had approximately 126,000 beneficiaries, but accounted for only €52 million (or 0.08% of GDP) from the state budget and EU funds.

The difference in approach from that of Czech governments is clear. It was recognised from early on that there was a crisis and the government took steps to counter its effects. Other steps, such as short-time working and the car-scrap scheme, indicate the influence of business and employee interests. However, the actual impact of all these measures over the period 2009–2010 was rather small. Changes in GDP depended much more on continuity in past spending plans and on export performance, including the decline in 2009 and renewed growth in 2010. Indeed, not only were planned measures set to have a relatively small effect, but only about half of the promised resources were actually disbursed. Whereas the expenditures were planned on the level of €2.02 billion (3.14% of GDP), the real sum represented only €1.03 billion (1.6% of GDP).

A detailed breakdown also shows wide variations between measures (Lesay & Bujňáková 2011, p. 216). Implementation was effectively full for tax reductions, but much less reliable where non-state actors were expected to apply for support. Thus, implementation of planned expenditure was minimal in support for social enterprises, subsidies for employment and programmes aimed at improving energy efficiency. The car-scrap scheme was fully subscribed, but measures to help research, using subsidies and tax allowances, were grossly undersubscribed.

Parliamentary elections in June 2010 led to a right-wing coalition government. That did not imply electoral punishment for the social-democratic *Smer* party. The party won more votes than in the previous elections in 2006, but failure by its previous coalition allies meant that the right succeeded thanks to its ability to lead a viable coalition.

The newly formed government of Prime Minister Iveta Radičová openly resigned from anti-crisis policies. In a government report dated October 2010, it was claimed that anti-crisis measures 'had mostly a formal character and the impact of their implementation to mitigate the negative crisis impacts on the Slovak economy is questionable'. The text further reads that 'at the moment it is not necessary to prepare further measures to mitigate the impacts of the global economic crisis' (MHaV 2010, pp. 3, 5).

In many ways, the Radičová government acted in the opposite way to the government of Prime Minister Fico. The new administration was active in trying to balance the budget deficit and consolidate public finances, and was reluctant to promote deliberate stimulus policies. It has to be stated though that after the initial fiscal stimulus for the period 2009–2010, Social Democrats planned to launch fiscal consolidation in 2010, too. Pressure from the European Commission on this eurozone member arguably contributed to the commitment to fiscal consolidation. The budget deficit was clearly going well over the 3% limit already in 2009. This was judged to be acceptable by the European Commission in view of the economic crisis and of the fact that Slovakia had followed advice in adopting a stimulus package, but the recommendation was to eliminate the excessive deficit (i.e. above

3%) by 2013.[5] The Social Democrats responded by adopting a budget for 2010 aimed at eliminating the excessive deficit by 2012 (MFSR 2009). It is difficult to estimate to what extent things would have been different had *Smer* formed the government again.

Unlike its predecessor, the right-wing government did not enact any sector-specific anti-crisis measures. It was also relatively inactive towards the financial sector, partly because the banks did not need state aid, and partly because the deposit guarantee scheme enacted by the previous government was still effective. Somewhat surprisingly, however, the Radičová administration did introduce a bank levy, amounting to 0.4% of selected banks' liabilities, with an expected yearly contribution of €80 million, to go into a special reserve fund for handling a potential future banking crisis. Such a proposal was not raised during the Fico government, but when back in opposition *Smer* proposed a higher rate of 0.7%. The initial opposition of the Slovak right-wing Minister of Finance Ivan Mikloš to a bank levy probably changed due to pressing budgetary problems and to the influence of the EU.

However, much more than in introducing progressive measures, the Radičová government was active in further implementation of neo-liberal reforms. On the revenue side, the VAT rate increased from 19% to 20% and excise duties were also increased. On the expenditure side, two focal areas for cuts were core expenditures of the state and public-sector wages, leading to a contraction by almost 16% in 2011–2012 in real terms. A constitutional debt threshold for public finances at 60% of GDP, to be lowered gradually to 50% after 2017, was also enacted in 2011. It has to be stated that all the parliamentary parties, including Social Democrats, supported this proposal. The overall trend by the right-wing government was to cut expenditures to match the level of revenues, although the latter, measured as a share of GDP, were among the lowest in Europe. The anti-crisis measures introduced by Social Democrats in the labour market were set to be temporary, running only to the end of 2010. The right-wing government did not prolong their operation. It is obviously an open question whether the Social Democrats would have acted differently.

The Radičová government's policies inevitably generated opposition and hostility from part of the population. This came to the fore when, albeit for reasons not directly related to the economic crisis, her government fell and was forced into early elections in March 2012. This time *Smer* won a clear overall majority in parliament and Fico returned as prime minister. In view of past promises, his government could be expected to move back to social-democratic policies. In view of the tight budget situation, higher spending could not be achieved without some tax increases and that implies a re-emphasis on progressive taxation of personal incomes.

Hungary

Hungarian politics have not fitted easily into a left–right divide. The main parties from both of these sides competed in the past through promises of spending increases before elections and both shared responsibility for the continuing budget and current account deficits of the years up to 2008 (Ohnsorge-Szabó & Romhányi 2007). A number of policies which had the effect of stimulating domestic demand, including a mortgage subsidy for households, were introduced by the right-wing government in 2000. The Socialist Party (*Magyar Szocialista*

---

[5]An IMF mission reported on 19 July 2010 indicating that significant cuts would be needed to reduce the deficit to below 3% by 2013 (IMF 2010).

Párt) came to power after the 2002 election and accentuated the trend of unfunded spending increases, introducing a 13th-month pension[6] and continuing with public-sector wage increases (amounting to 37% in real terms in 2002 and 2003). This is the background to Hungary's high level of public spending relative to GDP and to its persistent current account deficits that made it more vulnerable than any other Central and East European country to the effects of the financial crisis.

The Socialists, re-elected in 2006, were obliged to pursue a policy of fiscal consolidation given the aim of joining the eurozone and the problems in financing debt. Approximately half of this was to be achieved by revenue increases, higher VAT in particular. Expenditure reductions were to include lower investment spending and reduced public-sector employment. There were no plans for cutting public-sector pay or pensions, although the extensive early retirement system was to be tightened. Thus, in contrast to other Central and East European countries, Hungary entered the crisis in a period of fiscal stabilisation and low growth while both the public and private sectors were heavily indebted and reliant on financing from abroad.

The Hungarian situation was specific also as far as the vulnerability of the financial sector was concerned. Banks had relied heavily on external financing. The drop in cross-border loans was unlikely to lead to liquidity problems for foreign-owned banks, but it put pressure on domestic banks that experienced difficulties in accessing funding and they had to rely on government support. Moreover, a large part of loans in Hungary were in foreign currencies. Devaluation made repayment more difficult for borrowers. The risk of a growing share of non-performing loans was an issue for all banks and all governments involved in crisis management, both left and right, were prepared to work with the banks on resolving this issue (OECD 2012, pp. 64–65).

The crisis hit the country directly in the early stages of the 'credit crunch'. The government bond market had already experienced problems in the first half of 2008, with several undersubscribed bond issuances. The collapse of Lehman Brothers led to a sell-off of government securities, a failed bond auction, and a sharp currency depreciation in early October 2008 leading the government to seek a stand-by arrangement with the IMF and the EU which was agreed on 28 October 2008 (IMF 2011). Conditions included limits on government deficits and the establishment of a Fiscal Council, an independent watchdog that was to ensure that the fiscal rules were followed and to evaluate the effects on the state budget of legislative changes.

Thus in this first period, and in contrast to other Central and East European countries, the Hungarian government was pursuing a pro-cyclical fiscal policy. The measures followed agreement with, and were formally approved by, the IMF, but the latter did not intervene in the policy process. This followed the resignation of Prime Minister Ferenc Gyurcsány, who lost credibility to pursue reforms in a series of political scandals that followed his confession to having lied in the run up to the 2006 elections.

The new, reconstructed government relied extensively on policy input from the Reform Alliance, an organisation consisting of representatives of all major Hungarian business associations, the president of the Hungarian Chamber of Commerce and Industry, and a number of economists. Its proposals were also supported by representatives from multinational companies. The new finance minister was an important Reform Alliance

---

[6]The pensioners thus received an additional monthly pension in a calendar year.

figure. Trade unions were formally consulted through a tripartite body where they expressed their disagreement with policies pursued, but they did not have a significant influence on policy.

In 2008, the reduction of expenditures had been achieved by not using reserves that had been built into the budget. The stand-by agreement with the IMF envisaged a general government deficit of 2.6% of GDP for 2009, implying a fiscal adjustment of about 2.5% of GDP, 2% more than envisaged earlier in 2008. The focus was on the expenditure side, including pay cuts for public-sector employees, equivalent to 1% of GDP, the elimination of the 13th monthly pension for early retirees and a cap on the 13th monthly pension for other pensioners, equivalent to 0.2% of GDP. The indexation of selected social benefits was to be postponed or eliminated (0.2% of GDP), and other spending was to suffer a general reduction (0.5% of GDP).

The budget for 2009 was consistent with the goals in the stand-by agreement, with the exception of a smaller cut in public-sector wages. With the 2009 recession larger than foreseen, the IMF was prepared to agree to a revised deficit target of 3.9% of GDP in May 2009, a figure that was, in practice, surpassed although, as indicated in Table 2, Hungary's deficit was by then relatively low by Central and East European standards. In 2009 and 2010 expenditures were reduced by the equivalent of 1.6% and 3.6% of GDP, respectively (NM 2011a). This included cuts in pensions, by various means, and cuts in various social benefits. Public-sector pay was frozen for 2010 and 2011 and cut through abolition of the 13th-month salary from 2009.

The reconstructed government also pursued a tax reform, presented as revenue neutral, that can be directly linked to Reform Alliance proposals, shifting taxation to consumption and cutting the burdens on business and high earners. In 2009, there was a minor reduction in the lowest bracket of personal income tax while VAT was increased from 20% to 25%, albeit with a preferential rate of 18% for food. In 2010, employers' insurance contributions were reduced by 5% and personal income tax was cut. A 3% increase in the corporation tax rate went in parallel with the cancellation of a 4% solidarity tax, a levy on most businesses and high-income individuals that had been introduced as a part of the 2006 package. Finally, a property tax was introduced.

There was also a package of anti-crisis measures to help the private sector suffering from funding problems, a fall in the value of the currency and the collapse in export demand. In contrast to the other Central and East European countries, measures relating to banking and finance were very prominent. Thus the government introduced a foreclosure moratorium for mortgage loans, about two-thirds of which were denominated in foreign currency, mostly Swiss francs. There was also a bank support package that had an important role in reducing funding pressures at three domestically-owned banks.

A number of measures were introduced to support non-financial enterprises, including credit guarantee programmes, direct lending through the development bank, interest subsidies and participation in venture companies to address the deteriorating credit market conditions. As in other countries, uptake was low (OECD 2010, p. 13). The employers, most notably the multinationals in the automobile industry as in other Central and East European countries, pressed for more employment flexibility to deal with the drop in demand. Negotiations involving trade unions led to a reduced-working-hours scheme allowing workers on a four-day schedule to receive 80% of pay for the fifth day, provided that they met a number of conditions, including the use of training. However, this, unlike the German-

TRANSITION ECONOMIES AFTER 2008

style *Kurzarbeit* scheme, did not involve a state wage subsidy. Take up was low and the law remained little more than a gesture towards protecting employment places as employers were in a powerful enough position to adjust labour inputs through wage cuts and layoffs.

The situation was transformed after elections in May 2010 when the right-wing *Fidesz* party came to power, gaining a constitutional majority, meaning that it had the power to do as it liked. It took a firm approach on the country's international standing and, in July 2010, negotiations with the IMF and EU about future funding collapsed. The IMF was most concerned with a lack of 'commitment on the 2011 budget to preserve the ... fiscal target of below 3 percent of GDP' and referred to a disagreement about taxation policies (IMF 2011, p. 23). The government cited disagreements about previous commitments based on a growth forecast that was 'too optimistic'.[7] It preferred to implement reforms without consulting the IMF or EU and to rely on market-based funding in the future.

Fidesz represented a conservative right that mobilised through a nationalistic and populist agenda. It had vehemently opposed spending cuts during its period in opposition and argued that a large reduction in the tax burden was needed to stimulate growth and employment. Its economic ideology incorporated some nationalist elements and there was rhetoric about overcoming the failure of standard, neo-classical economics, as apparently exposed by the world crisis. Nominally, then, this was a new approach to economic policy but, once the rhetoric is stripped away, much actually fitted with the neo-liberal thinking the government claimed not to accept. Indeed, elements that appeared novel were largely unsustainable or far less effective than the government claimed. The dominant features were therefore to remain a shift towards a less progressive tax system, cuts in redistributive state spending, most notably on the unemployed, and attacks on employee and union rights.

Tax reforms implemented from mid-2010 included a 'flat tax' on personal income,[8] and other tax reductions, most notably for SMEs, resulting in revenue loss estimated at around 1.8% of GDP (EC 2011). Revenue increases were achieved through a temporary bank levy and one-off 'crisis taxes' on energy, retail and telecommunications companies. That played on nationalist rhetoric as these were sectors controlled primarily by multinational corporations. These measures raised revenue of 0.7% and 1.3% of GDP, respectively (EC 2011; OECD 2012). Importantly, the private pension pillar was effectively nationalised, switching the budget balance into the sizeable surplus shown in Table 2, due to the one-off transfer amounting to 10% of GDP. *Fidesz* traditionally opposed pension privatisation, but the decision, similar to that made in Poland, reflected a realisation of its high costs and a negative evaluation of the performance of private funds that was widely shared across the spectrum (Drahokoupil & Domonkos 2012).

The new government showed no interest in wider social consultation. It reduced external control over its own activities and it severely constrained policies of future governments through constitutional changes. In 2010, it effectively abolished institutionalised social dialogue by replacing the tripartite National Interest Reconciliation Council (*Országos Érdekegyeztető Tanács*, OÉT) with the much more symbolic National Economic and Social

---

[7]Comments on the stand-by arrangement programme submitted to the IMF by the Hungarian Ministry for National Economy, the Central Bank and the Hungarian Financial Supervisory Authority (IMF 2011, pp. 37–38).

[8]A so-called 'flat tax' on the personal income implied a real rate of 20.3% for those on the average wage, a level comparable with that in Slovakia and the Czech Republic (Myant & Drahokoupil 2011, p. 180). It included a substantial allowance for families with children and the latter, together with the high-income earners, therefore benefited. In contrast, lower-income workers without children could lose almost 10% of their net income (Szabó 2013).

Council (*Nemzeti Gazdasági és Társadalmi Tanács*, NGTT). The latter was an advisory body with no government representatives and incorporating various civil society organisations, such as churches, universities and consumer protection groups (Szabó 2013). In late 2010, the government downgraded the Fiscal Council, removing its staff and replacing independent economists elected by parliament by the central bank governor, the head of the State Audit Office—both government appointees—and an economist to be appointed by the president. However, the new constitution, approved in 2011, gave the Council the power to veto fiscal laws, meaning that, at least nominally, it had the power to bring down the government. The new constitution, taking effect from 2012, also stipulated that public debt be capped at 50% of GDP, albeit at some unspecified point in the future. A debt rule, adopted in December 2011, taking effect from 2016, stipulated that until that level of debt-to-GDP ratio is reached, the public debt can increase only by expected inflation minus half of expected real GDP growth.

Fiscal consolidation was set out in a plan of structural reforms for 2011–2015 introduced in March 2011 and to come into effect from January 2012. It was given the nationally inspiring title of the Széll Kálmán Plan, after the fiscally prudent prime minister of 1899–1903. The programme aimed at keeping deficits below 3% of GDP, thereby reducing indebtedness from 80% to 65% of GDP by 2015. About three-quarters of this consolidation was to come from expenditure cuts, equivalent to 1.8% of GDP in 2012 and 2.8% in 2013. The major focus was savings in employment and labour-market policy, advertised as pushing people into the labour market (estimated at 0.7% GDP/year). The measures included reducing support in unemployment, disability pensions and sick pay. Disability pension eligibility cuts and early retirement revision were intended to save 0.4% of GDP per annum. The plan also included a reform of drug subsidies, stimulating price competition and favouring generics (0.4% of GDP), and savings in public administration (0.4% of GDP).

There were some implementation delays in 2011. More seriously, the spending side of the plan was not clearly specified, as exemplified by the vague estimates of savings and promises of efficiency savings in the public sector. Moreover, many of the measures, such as the freeze in public-sector wages and cuts in benefits, could not fail to arouse political opposition. June 2011 saw large demonstrations against the scrapping of early retirement benefits. In September 2011, the government confirmed its commitment to follow the deficit targets in the Kálmán Széll plan even after a downward revision of the growth outlook. The deteriorating growth prospects led to the adoption of additional fiscal measures on the revenue side: there was an increase in employer's social security contributions and various excise taxes. Moreover, VAT was increased to 27%, the highest level in the EU.[9] On the spending side, there was a 2.5% reduction in public-sector employment in 2011, excluding public employment schemes.

In the labour market, the new labour code undermined employee rights and allowed for flexibilisation of employment relations (Szabó 2013). The government also pursued reforms and policies ostensibly aimed at increasing labour-market participation. These included mainly punitive measures with little economic rationality, most notably the public employment schemes (OECD 2012, pp. 87–118).[10] They seemed driven by a populist

[9] By 2011, the government expected the contribution of expenditure-side adjustment to 2012 consolidation to drop below 60% (NM 2011b).

[10] Subsidised public-sector employment programmes are widely considered to be the least effective form of active labour-market policies (Card *et al.* 2010). Public-works scheme experiments in the past had failed to improve the employability of participants and to provide a foothold in the open labour market (Fleck & Messing 2010; Budapest Institute 2011).

agenda, rewarding those in low-paid jobs by increasing wages at the bottom of the labour market while punishing the unemployed. Public employment schemes had been launched in early 2009 to bring down long-term unemployment. The *Fidesz* government introduced a new public employment scheme, managed by the Ministry of the Interior. Aimed also at the long-term unemployed, the schemes provided higher income than social assistance but lower than the minimum wage. More than 100,000 were enrolled in 2009 and 2010 and 220,000 people—100,000 full-time equivalents—participated in 2011. At the same time, the duration of unemployment benefits was cut from 270 days to only 90 days and capped at the level of the minimum wage. Moreover, an additional job-search benefit, previously available for 90 days, was abolished in 2011, except for workers close to retirement. The government also attempted to raise the lowest wages—compensating low-income workers for the possible losses from the new tax regime—and increased the minimum wage in 2012 by 19%. Public institutions received subsidies to finance the increases. Firms that did not implement the low-wage increases were to be excluded from public procurement, but this sanction mechanism was not in use by 2012. Many employers, particularly in the private sector, thus did not implement any compensatory wage increases at all (Szabó 2013).

The austerity course, combined with large one-off revenue boosts, stabilised the budget in the mid-term, but a downgrading of the sovereign rating to non-investment grade—first by Moody's on 25 November 2011 followed by other major agencies in December 2011 and January 2012—precipitated the failure of several debt auctions. The government thus went back to the IMF and the EU to request financial assistance from the end of 2011.[11]

Conclusion

The initial impact of the crisis, measurable by the fall in GDP in 2009, can be broadly explained by factors external to the four countries considered here. However, the crisis did not end with the recovery in exports from their low point in early 2009. It continued to dominate economic performance in the following years and differences between countries became less explicable in terms of external economic shocks. Domestic policy making became a more important determinant and the policies chosen differed between countries and over time.

Thinking was not very imaginative. In no case was there an attempt to rethink the basis of past strategies, for example by trying to switch to a 'knowledge-based economy', relying more on innovation, research and higher education. Controversies and choices centred rather on a limited range of themes that fit quite well into a social-democrat as opposed to a neo-liberal framework. Increasingly, the state budget became the key arena and the key conflict was over the priority to be ascribed to, and the distributional consequences of, reducing deficits. The choices depended primarily on internal politics—the ideologies of ruling parties, the interests they listened to and their ability to weather public opposition and win elections—but external pressures also played a role. This was clearest in the case of Hungary, reflecting that country's sorry financial position, but even there a government could try to defy the demands of the IMF and EU. In other cases external pressures were less direct and played a role essentially by giving greater backing and political credibility to political forces favouring austerity.

[11]No agreement was concluded by November 2012, but further discussions were anticipated for early 2013.

One effect of economic crisis was to increase political volatility, with some dramatic changes in parties' electoral fortunes. However, that was not the case everywhere—Poland stands out as an exception—and, when detailed policies are examined, there are striking similarities in the ideas that came forward in all countries. In all cases there were cuts in benefits for marginal groups in society and a switch towards indirect rather than direct taxes: these carry clear distributional implications. The unemployed were penalised with varying degrees of determination and business was typically given help through reduced taxes. Again, the distributional implications would appear to be that support was given to those already on higher incomes. Differences include varying levels of support for a demand stimulus, maintained the longest in Poland through infrastructure spending, and for a private pension scheme. This is an important difference as it represented an additional cost to the state budget. It was pursued most enthusiastically in the Czech Republic, the one country yet to introduce such a scheme, even at the cost of increasing the budget deficit. The implication is that an ideologically driven quest for a small state and bigger role for private enterprise could take priority over the quest for a balanced budget.

Thus the link from economic difficulties to these economic policy changes is not direct. To some extent politicians were using the crisis as a pretext for pursuing polices they had always wanted to impose. Nevertheless, the fact of rising budget deficits at a time of low growth forced governments into choices with clear distributional implications and these led in some countries to powerful social protests. It can therefore be hypothesised that the crisis is reasserting the distinction between left and right as a central dividing line in Central and East European politics. We conclude with the question of which 'side' will prove the more influential in a constantly changing political scene. There are differences in timing and in severity, but every country has opted for balancing the budget by cuts at some point. The legacy of the crisis so far looks like being a move towards a smaller state and more unequal society.

European Trade Union Institute, Brussels
Universität Mannheim & European Trade Union Institute, Brussels
Institute of Economic Research, Slovak Academy of Sciences, Bratislava

References

Budapest Institute (2011) *The Efficiency of Municipal Public Works Programmes* (Budapest, Budapest Institute for Policy Analysis).

Card, D., Kluve, J. & Weber, A. (2010) 'Active Labour Market Policy Evaluations: A Meta-Analysis', *The Economic Journal*, 120, 548, pp. F452–77.

Drahokoupil, J. & Domonkos, S. (2012) 'Averting the Funding-Gap Crisis: East European Pension Reforms after 2008', *Global Social Policy*, 12, 3, pp. 283–99.

EC (2011) *Assessment of the 2011 National Reform Programme and Convergence Programme for Hungary*, European Commission Staff Working Paper, SEC(2011), 725 final, available at: http://ec.europa.eu/europe2020/pdf/recommendations_2011/swp_hungary_en.pdf, accessed 16 August 2012

Filadelfiová, J. (2010) 'Rodové dimenzie krízy: Situácia na trhu práce a vládne protikrízové opatrenia', in Cviková, J. (ed.) *Rodové dôsledky krízy: Aspekty vybraných prípadov* (Bratislava, Aspekt), pp. 11–68.

Fleck, G. & Messing, V. (2010) 'Transformations of Roma Employment Policies', in Fazekas, K., Lovász, A. & Telegdy, A. (eds) *The Hungarian Labour Market: Review and Analysis 2010* (Budapest, Institute of Economics, Hungarian Academy of Sciences and National Employment Foundation).

Hanley, S., Szczerbiak, A., Haughton, T. & Fowler, B. (2008) 'Sticking Together: Explaining Comparative Centre–Right Party Success in Post-Communist Central and Eastern Europe', *Party Politics*, 14, 4, pp. 407–34.

TRANSITION ECONOMIES AFTER 2008

IMF (2010) *Slovakia: 2010 Article IV Consultation Concluding Statement of the Mission* (Washington, DC, International Monetary Fund), available at: http://www.imf.org/external/np/ms/2010/071910.htm, accessed 16 August 2012.

IMF (2011) 'Hungary: Ex Post Evaluation of Exceptional Access Under the 2008 Stand-By Arrangement', *IMF Country Report*, 11/145, available at: http://www.imf.org/external/pubs/ft/scr/2011/cr11145.pdf, accessed 16 August 2012

Kitschelt, H. (1995) 'Formation of Party Cleavages in Post-Communist Democracies', *Party Politics*, 1, 4, pp. 447–72.

Kitschelt, H., Mansfeldová, Z., Markowski, R. & Tóka, G. (1999) *Post-Communist Party Systems: Competition, Representation, and Inter-Party Cooperation* (Cambridge, Cambridge University Press).

Kusá, Z. & Gerbery, D. (2009) *Slovak Republic: Impact of the Economic and Financial Crisis on Poverty and Social Exclusion* (Brussels, European Commission).

Lesay, I. & Bujňáková, T. (2011) 'Financná a ekonomická kríza a protikrízová politika na Slovensku', in Tiruneh, M. W. (ed.) *Determinanty ekonomického rastu a konkurencieschopnosti: Výzvy a príležitosti* (Bratislava, Ekonomický ústav SAV), pp. 187–222.

MFČR (2010) *Návrh státního závěrečného účtu České republiky za rok 2009* (Prague, Ministry of Finance of the Czech Republic), available at: www.mfcr.cz/cps/rde/xbcr/mfcr/SZU2009_C_pdf.pdf, accessed 16 August 2012.

MFČR (2011) *Návrh státního závěrečného účtu České republiky za rok 2010* (Prague, Ministry of Finance of the Czech Republic), available at: www.mfcr.cz/cps/rde/xbcr/mfcr/SZU2010_C_pdf.pdf, accessed 16 August 2012.

MFČR (2012) *Návrh státního závěrečného účtu České republiky za rok 2011* (Prague, Ministry of Finance of the Czech Republic), available at: http://www.komora.cz/download.aspx?dontparse=true& FileID=8210, accessed 16 August 2012.

MFRP (2011) *Program konwergencji: Aktualizacja 2011* (Warsaw, Ministerstwo Finansów Rzeczypospolitej Polskiej), available at: http://www.mf.gov.pl/index.php?const=1&dzial=90&wysw=4, accessed 16 August 2012.

MFRP (2012) *Informacja kwartalna o sytuacji makroekonomicznej i stanie finansów publicznych styczeń 2012* (Warsaw, Ministerstwo Finansów Rzeczypospolitej Polskiej), available at: http://www.mf.gov.pl/ dokument.php?const=5&dzial=3502&id=283502, accessed 16 August 2012.

MFSR (2009) *Zaradenie Slovenska do procedúry nadmerného deficitu* (Bratislava, Ministerstvo financií Slovenskej republiky), available at: http://www.finance.gov.sk/Default.aspx?CatID=84&NewsId=344, accessed 16 August 2012.

MHaV (2010) *Analytická správa o dopadoch finančnej a hospodárskej krízy* (Bratislava, Ministerstvo hospodárstva a výstavby Slovenskej republiky).

MPiPS (2009) *Pakiet antykryzysowy* (Warsaw, Ministerstwo Pracy i Polityki Społecznej), available at: http:// www.mpips.gov.pl/praca/pakiet-antykryzysowy/, accessed 16 August 2012.

Myant, M. & Drahokoupil, J. (2011) *Transition Economies: Political Economy in Russia, Eastern Europe, and Central Asia* (Hoboken, NJ, Wiley-Blackwell).

Myant, M. & Drahokoupil, J. (2012) 'International Integration, Varieties of Capitalism, and Resilience to Crisis in Transition Economies', *Europe-Asia Studies*, 64, 1, pp. 1–33.

NERV (2009) *Závěrečná zpráva* (Prague, Národní ekonomická rada vlády), available at: http://www.vlada. cz/assets/media-centrum/dulezite-dokumenty/zaverecna-zprava-NERV.pdf, accessed 16 August 2012.

NM (2011a) *Hungary's Structural Reform Programme 2011–2014: Based on the Political Thesis of the Széll Kálmán Plan* (Budapest, Nemzetgazdasági Minisztérium), available at: http://www.kormany.hu/ download/b/23/20000/Hungary%27s%20Structural%20Reform.pdf, accessed 22 January 2013.

NM (2011b) *Measures to Attain the Sustainable Reduction of Public Debt* (Budapest, Nemzetgazdasági Minisztérium).

OECD (2010) *OECD Economic Surveys: Hungary* (Paris, Organisation for Economic Co-operation and Development).

OECD (2012) *OECD Economic Surveys: Hungary* (Paris, Organisation for Economic Co-operation and Development).

Ohnsorge-Szabó, L. & Romhányi, B. (2007) 'How Did We Get Here: Hungarian Budget 2000–2006', *Journal of Public Finance*, 52, 2, pp. 243–91.

PSP (2009) 'Transcript of the 48th Session of the Chamber of Deputies, Czech Parliament', *Library of Czech and Slovak Parliaments, 2006–2010*, available at: http://www.psp.cz/eknih/2006ps/stenprot/048schuz/ s048304.htm#r1, accessed 16 August 2012.

RHSD (2010) *Návrh krátkodobých opatření pro východiska z krize a řešení jejích důsledků* (Prague, Rada hospodářské a sociální dohody), available at: http://www.vlada.cz/assets/media-centrum/tiskove-zpravy/38-navrhu-opatreni.pdf, accessed 16 August 2012.

Szabó, I. (2013) 'Between Polarization and State Activism: The Effect of the Crisis on Collective Bargaining Processes and Outcomes in Hungary', *Transfer: European Review of Labour and Research*, 19, 2.

Tavits, M. & Letki, N. (2009) 'When Left is Right: Party Ideology and Policy in Post-Communist Europe', *American Political Science Review*, 103, 4, pp. 555–69.

Vláda, ČR (2009) *Národní protikrizový plán vlády* (Prague, Vláda České Republiky), available at: www.vlada.cz/assets/media-centrum/predstavujeme/narodni-protikrizovy-plan.pdf, accessed 16 August 2012.

Avoiding the Economic Crisis: Pragmatic Liberalism and Divisions over Economic Policy in Poland

GAVIN RAE

Abstract

Although liberalism has been the dominant economic ideology in post-communist Poland, liberal parties have tended to struggle to win political majorities. After winning the 2011 parliamentary elections, Citizens' Platform (*Platforma Obywatelska*) became the first party in Poland's democratic history to win two consecutive elections. Despite its liberal ideological background, *Platforma Obywatelska* took a more pragmatic and cautious approach to economic policy, avoiding the introduction of strong austerity economic policies. This paper considers the debate within the liberal camp about *Platforma Obywatelska*'s economic policies, with particular reference to the reform of pensions. It also looks at the plans of the government for more strident liberal economic reforms in its second term, at what impact these will have on the popularity of *Platforma Obywatelska* and at how this reflects a tension between the party's pragmatic concerns of government and commitment to liberal ideology.

ALTHOUGH THE ECONOMIC CRISIS DISPROPORTIONATELY affected the countries of Central and Eastern Europe, it did not hit the region evenly. As highlighted in the Introduction to this volume, the Polish economy continued to grow throughout the crisis, with its slowest growth being 1.9% in 2009. Poland enjoyed the status of having been the most successful economy after the outbreak of the financial crisis, not only in Central and Eastern Europe but in the whole of the EU, and was the only EU member state not to experience recession, at least up to 2012.

This does not mean that the economic crisis had no negative effect on the Polish economy. Unemployment once again rose into double figures, after significantly falling following EU entry, and public debt continued to rise towards its constitutional limit. The country suffered from a series of severe social and structural problems and living standards remained below the levels of most of its neighbours. It had the highest number of people of any EU country working on temporary, insecure contracts, known as 'junk contracts'.[1] The

---

[1] 'Junk contracts' refer to various forms of temporary employment contracts that can offer very little protection against arbitrary management, or even contracts based on civil and not employment law, which enable employers to avoid all legal obligations towards employees. Whilst the average percentage of workers employed on a contract of a limited duration stands at less than 15% in the EU, in Poland it reaches 27%.

country continued to retain some of the largest economic inequalities in the region, with many of the poorest regions in the EU situated in the country. Poland faced a potential demographic crisis, caused by the emigration of huge numbers of young people abroad and a low birth rate. For historical reasons it had some of the least developed infrastructure, such as transport, in the region and many of its public services were severely underfunded and in a state of decline.

Yet, despite these difficulties, Poland was protected from the worst effects of the economic crisis. Although living standards fell, they fell by less than in other Central and Eastern European countries and were more in line with the Western European average (EBRD 2011). The point at which Poland entered the crisis—both economically and politically—greatly impacted upon the policy choices that were made in the following period. This essay considers the policies of the government at the time within the framework of a discussion about liberalism in Poland. The governing party—Citizens' Platform (*Platforma Obywatelska*, PO)—came from a strong liberal tradition, but took a more pragmatic approach to economic policy once in government. This policy was heavily criticised by many within the liberal camp and the government was put under pressure to change its cautious approach to economic reform due to domestic and international pressures to implement a programme of austerity-style spending cuts.

Liberal consensus

As the communist system began to disintegrate in the late 1980s, so liberalism moved into the political mainstream. Its leading intellectual and political representatives had shifted their attention to the economy, believing that individual freedom would best be guaranteed within the realm of a 'non-ideological' market system. This emphasis on the economy was often explained as being a continuation of the tactic of 'anti-politics'. Throughout the 1980s the opposition movement had interpreted this as involving a change in consciousness, through living 'outside the system' (Michnik 1985; Ost 1990). Thereafter, it was primarily employed as justification for rapidly removing the state from economic life.

Despite the ideological dominance of liberalism in Poland, it failed to consolidate itself as a political force capable of governing independently. The various liberal parties that emerged in the early 1990s tended to either splinter or disappear. After the political backlash, caused by the implementation of the shock-therapy reforms, governments ostensibly from the 'post-communist' left or 'post-solidarity' right assumed responsibility for implementing economic reform. Liberalism therefore existed not as a viable political option for government, but rather as a hegemonic structure that set the limits of public debate and policy making.[2]

Furthermore, this has increased by more than five times since the beginning of the century, with just over 5% of workers employed on such contracts in 2000 (Eurostat, 'Employees with a Contract of Limited Duration (annual average) % of Total Number of Employees', available at: http://tinyurl.com/7c56bab, accessed 9 August 2012). A report by the government, *Raport Młodzi 2011* (Szafraniec 2011), revealed that over 60% of workers aged under 25 are employed on 'junk contracts'. This is further compounded by the large number of self-employed workers in Poland. A total of 19% of all those working are self-employed, which is the fifth highest number in the EU after Greece, Italy, Portugal and Romania (Szafraniec 2011).

[2]This neo-liberal hegemony has an international dimension. For example, neo-Gramscian theorists have analysed the post-communist transition and integration of new members into the EU as an extension of the

TRANSITION ECONOMIES AFTER 2008

Within this overarching liberal consensus, any discussions on such things as different economic systems or forms of economic transformation were essentially excluded or marginalised. Although the conservative criticism of liberalism has often centred on its relativism and moral neutrality, Polish liberalism has actually been characterised by its economic fundamentalism, which reduced the scope for social and political liberalism to develop.

PO and economic liberalism

PO and its leader, Prime Minister Donald Tusk, had strong ideological roots originating in the small neo-liberal faction of the opposition movement existent in Gdańsk during communism. This current criticised the leadership of the Solidarity movement for concentrating on issues such as democracy and equality and for not supporting a rapid transformation of the socialist economy (Ost 1991). It looked to promote individual freedom through economic activity and advanced a programme of mass privatisation. Tusk developed a dogmatic support for the free market, to the extent that he even claimed at the end of the 1980s that he would prefer a free-market economy without democracy to socialism with free elections.

Although no one from the Gdańsk Liberals took part in the Round Table talks that negotiated the transition from communism, they took centre stage after one of their main figures, Jan Bielecki, was appointed prime minister by President Lech Wałęsa in 1991. Representatives of this current were central in creating the Liberal Democratic Congress party (*Kongres Liberalno-Demokratyczny*, KLD) and then the Freedom Union (*Unia Wolności*, UW) in the 1990s. Leading figures such as Donald Tusk and Janusz Lewandowski were members of the Solidarity Electoral Alliance–Freedom Union (*Akcja Wyborcza Solidarność*, AWS) government from 1997 to 2001, which included Leszek Balcerowicz as Finance Minister. They then went on to help form PO, which became the leading liberal economic party in Poland.

Once Poland had entered the EU in 2004, so the liberal consensus began to disintegrate. For the first time politics became dominated by two parties of the right—the Law and Justice Party (*Prawo i Sprawiedliwość*, PiS) and the Citizens' Platform (PO)—which, to different degrees, argued that the socioeconomic problems in Poland were due to the existence of a political and economic network that had its roots in the previous communist system and those from the Solidarity movement who had 'collaborated' with it.[3]

PiS won the 2005 presidential and parliamentary elections, after opposing PO's neo-liberal economic programme, particularly its proposal for a flat tax, meaning a single rate of personal income tax. PO's vote was restricted primarily to a wealthy, urban electorate, while PiS had managed to win the votes of a broader section of society, including a strong vote in the countryside. The coalition government formed by PiS, with populist and nationalist

hegemony of international capital and the expansion of neo-liberal hegemony (Bieler 2002; Bohle 2006; Bohle & Greskovits 2007).

[3]This included the idea of building a new Fourth Republic in Poland. Although this idea became associated with PiS it was actually first prominently aired by the historian and PO MP Pawel Spiewak (2003). By the mid-1990s Tusk had advanced a general critique of the Polish transition. He claimed that a political 'vain class', numbering around 100,000 people, had usurped power and created a corrupt political system. He promoted the politics of anti-elitism, opposing the liberal establishment and drawing upon the historical tradition of Józef Piłsudski and his campaign to cleanse the state known as *Sanacja* (Rae 2007).

43

parties, only lasted until 2007. The weakness of the left meant that PO attracted the votes of those parts of the electorate that were concerned with the creeping authoritarianism of the PiS government. PO also restrained its neo-liberal agenda, promising to raise public sector wages and improve the lives of pensioners, thus widening its base of political support (Rae 2008).

The election of PO in 2007 was met with great enthusiasm and self-congratulation by sections of the liberal intelligentsia. For example, former Solidarity leader and editor of the liberal daily newspaper *Gazeta Wyborcza*, Adam Michnik, praised the Polish intelligentsia for having uncritically supported liberal economic reform, claiming that the previous two decades had been the best in Poland for over 300 years. He derided both the left and right critics of the transition and economic liberalism as being populist (Michnik 2008).

In response to this enthusiasm of the liberal intelligentsia, one of the leading authorities on Polish liberalism—Andrzej Walicki—argued that the Polish intelligentsia had lost its concern for the lives of the poor and had instead concentrated purely on the needs of capital and the market (Walicki 2008). Such a fear had been expressed by Jerzy Szacki in the early 1990s, who had predicted that liberalism in post-communist societies would become a caricature of itself through turning into an inversion of Marxism and associating itself purely with financial power rather than liberty and human rights (Szacki 1994). Liberals in Poland have therefore tended to align themselves with thinkers such as Hayek and von Misses, who seek to remove the restrictions placed by the state upon the individual believing that the free market is the best guarantor of individual liberty, rather than with liberals such as John Gray or Isiah Berlin.[4]

Return of the state

Despite the hopes of its liberal supporters, PO had been partly successful during the 2007 parliamentary elections by restraining some of its liberal economic policies. Moreover, PO had not won an overall majority and needed to form a coalition government with the Polish Peasants' Party (*Polskie Stronnictwo Ludowe*, PSL), which provided a potential brake on PO's reform agenda. The further political obstacle facing Tusk's new administration came from the veto power of Lech Kaczyński from PiS who was president until his death in a plane crash in Smolensk in April 2010.

Despite its liberal background, the PO leadership was developing a different approach to government. As discussed above, the idea of 'anti-politics' had been deployed by neo-liberals in Poland, as a means to promote the primacy of the 'neutral' market economy. In the late twentieth century leaders from the left, such as Tony Blair, had used the idea of anti-politics and ideology to justify the promotion of free-market economics, arguing that previous doctrinal disputes over the state and market had been overcome. However,

---

[4]Berlin for example put forward two concepts of liberalism: positive liberty and negative liberty. Negative liberty concerns the removal of constraints that the state places upon an individual. In contrast positive liberty refers to the resources and power available to fulfil one's own potential. The idea of positive freedoms had previously been postulated by T. H. Green in the nineteenth century, who regarded them as freedoms that allow an individual to pursue something that is truly good and therefore implies doing good for others. He challenged the traditional idea that freedom concerns being free from state intervention and argued that freedom should not be seen as a person's power to do as he or she likes, but rather as the power to do something valuable for other people. Green strongly supported the new legislation being introduced in Britain from 1868 that regulated spheres such as employment and education (Dimova-Cookson 2003).

conversely, a result of this has now been that some previously committed ideological liberals have begun to countenance the prospect of the return of a more interventionist state. After all, if economic policy is to be formed in a non-ideological manner, then the option of increasing state intervention is available (Judt 2008). This can be observed in the policy approach taken by Tusk's administration.

The pragmatic turn by the political leadership of PO was partly influenced by its understanding of the stage of development of Polish capitalism. Previously, liberal reformers in Poland had considered the transition to a market capitalist system to involve following the 'well-trodden path' of development previously taken by the developed capitalist countries in the West (Balcerowicz & Gelb 1995). This therefore involved foreign capital playing an important and essential role in the building of Polish capitalism, with little attention paid to its own capital base.

The change in emphasis was articulated by one of Tusk's major political mentors, the former prime minister and head of the government's Economic Council, Jan Bielecki. He argued that the government should attempt to build firms into large, effective state companies that could be 'national champions'. He claimed that, rather than rapidly privatising some of Poland's largest state companies, such as the insurance company PZU, bank PKO BP and petrol concern PKN Orlen, they should be reformed and run more efficiently. He also stated that it was better that the largest banks in Poland should be situated in the country, in order to avoid an outflow of money, particularly in a period of economic crisis. Bielecki stated that he was not critical of the process of privatisation that occurred in the 1990s, but that an altered economic strategy was needed as the country was now at a different stage of development.[5]

This strategic change within Polish liberalism was most comprehensively laid out in a government document *Polska 2030*, prepared by the Board of Strategic Advisors to the government, led by Michał Boni (BoSA 2009). This document represents a significant change in emphasis for Polish liberalism, suggesting that the government should prioritise investment in social capital, in order to help make Polish society more open and trustful. It stated that social polarisation and a lack of equal opportunities hinder the development of social capital and that the state needed to become more efficient and caring. This included facilitating social integration, enhancing social mobility and investing in education. The document also recognised that many of the country's social and economic problems were connected to a low level of participation in the labour force.

Despite these important changes, the document still remained within the constraints of liberalism, albeit one that was more suited to the conditions in which PO was governing. The report recognised economic growth as the key to raising employment levels and social integration in Poland. The blame for the low level of employment was placed on insufficient human capital, the system of retirement and benefits and low culture of work. This paved the way for recommendations such as reforming the labour code and raising the age of retirement. Importantly, it also included a suggestion that the welfare state should be replaced with a so-called workfare society. This reflects a trend within European social policy of moving away from the concept of universal de-commodified welfare systems towards the commercialisation of welfare services and providing social benefits that are selected only for the poorest in society and aimed at overcoming social exclusion (Holden

---

[5]'Pierwszy po premierze', *Gazeta Wyborcza*, 31 January 2012.

2003). The document also identified controlling the budget deficit and public debt as being an essential element of an economic growth strategy. It proposed achieving this primarily by reducing public spending and offered no reform of the largely regressive tax system, apart from harmonising VAT rates.

A Thatcherite strategy?

The strategy of the PO-led government from 2007 was laid out retrospectively by the Finance Minister Jacek Rostowski. He stated that PO aimed to break the previous cycle of reform governments which had been unable to govern for more than one term due to the social unpopularity of their policies. This was the case at the beginning of the transition, when a succession of governments fell, following the implementation of shock-therapy reforms. It was also the case for the centre–right coalition government in the late 1990s. After introducing a series of reforms in sectors such as pensions, education and health, both participating parties, the AWS and UW, lost all of their seats in parliament. Accordingly, the main aim of Tusk and PO was to ensure that they could govern for two terms in order to carry through their programme of reform. Moreover, Rostowski claimed that they were attempting to emulate the example of Margaret Thatcher in Britain, who managed to implement her far-reaching reforms because she was able to govern for over a decade. In Rostowski's words:

> PO's project, defined by Donald Tusk, has always been conceived as being for at least two terms in office. We wanted to break from the 'yo-yo reform effect', which has damaged Poland's economic policy for the past twenty years. Instead, what Poland really needs is calm and step-by-step reform, although with the determined effort *à la* Margaret Thatcher, lasting even for a whole decade. Some politicians and commentators regard economic policy in an opposite way: liberals and reformers should act through implementing 'shock' policies in the first—and last—year of their term in office. (Rostowski 2012)

Rostowski argued that if they had immediately introduced policies such as reforming the early pension system for uniformed workers or abolished the existing health insurance scheme, then they would have played into the hands of their 'populist' opponents and lost power at the following elections. The government therefore rejected the so-called 'shock-therapy approach' in order to avoid the political risks associated with introducing a quick and radical set of liberal economic reforms.

Crisis and government intervention

PO's strategy for its first term in office was partially interrupted by the outbreak of the global financial crisis. Although the government was willing to use the state in some areas of economic policy, it was still aiming to repeat the 'Irish economic miracle' through enticing foreign investment into the country. The outbreak of the global economic crisis ruled out such a strategy. Rather than pushing PO back towards a more liberal economic strategy, to some degree it deepened its cautious approach to socioeconomic policy. Poland was able to avoid entering a recession and keep a positive course of economic growth for a number of reasons.

First, the country suffered no significant collapse in its banking and financial sectors. Personal debt in Poland was relatively low, mainly due to the fact that base interest rates had remained in double figures up until 2003 and therefore the credit bubble had only been inflated for a short period of time. Also the banking sector in Poland was relatively well regulated (Leven 2011).

Second, Poland was not as dependent on the inflow of private credit and capital as the small financialised economies, such as the Baltic republics. As the largest country in the region, the economy was more diversified and reliant upon internal demand and therefore did not suffer so much as international capital stopped flowing into other countries in the region.

Third, Poland was also not so heavily reliant upon exports and in particular not dependent upon one export industry, as is the case in the small export-led countries, such as Slovenia and Slovakia, which have well-developed car industries.

Fourth, Poland had not joined or tied its currency to the euro and therefore could retain some competitiveness through a devaluation of its currency.

Fifth, the Polish government increased its spending throughout the crisis, particularly by raising public investment, partly funded through an inflow of EU structural and cohesion funds.

This last point is of particular importance. Government expenditures continued to increase in Poland throughout the crisis, rising from €15.1 billion in 2008 to €16.5 billion in the first quarter of 2012. The level of government expenditure in Poland was slightly above the EU average, standing at around 49% of GDP.[6] One of the most important actions of the government was to increase public investment, through utilising available EU funds. Poland was the single largest recipient of EU funds from the 2007–2013 budget, set to receive up to €67 billion in structural and cohesion funds. This sum increases to €82 billion (€2,500 *per capita*) once the designated national government funds have been added. This helped the government initiate large investment projects in the country's infrastructure, particularly in preparation for the Euro 2012 football championship, making it the only country in Central and Eastern Europe to have increased its level of investment, as a share of GDP, between 2005 and 2010.

As shown in Table 1, the general level of investment in Central and Eastern European EU members fell by the equivalent of 5% of GDP between 2005 and 2010. This was taken up almost entirely by a sharp decline in business investment, decreasing on average from 22.9% to 16.4% of GDP. Every country in the region underwent falling business investment, although the depth of this decline was uneven. The largest collapses in private investment occurred in the Baltic republics, most dramatically in Estonia and Latvia where it fell by over 13%. In Poland, business investment only shrank slightly, by less than 1% of total GDP.

The level of public investment in the region actually slightly increased throughout the period of the economic crisis and was higher as a share of GDP than in the Eurozone countries in 2011. Public investment rose the most in Poland, by 2.2% of GDP, giving it the highest level of public investment as a share of GDP in Central and Eastern Europe, and one which was more than twice that in the Eurozone.

[6]Eurostat, 'Total Government Expenditures', available at: http://tinyurl.com/6of4mvce3lo2z, accessed 9 August 2012.

TABLE 1
PRIVATE AND PUBLIC INVESTMENT IN CENTRAL AND EASTERN EUROPEAN COUNTRIES, % OF GDP

	Private		Public		Total	
	2005	2010	2005	2010	2005	2010
Bulgaria	22.3	18.9	3.4	4.6	25.7	23.5
Czech Rep	24.9	21.3	4.9	4.6	20.0	16.4
Estonia	28.1	15.0	4.0	3.6	32.1	18.6
Hungary	19.1	16.1	4.0	3.2	23.1	19.3
Latvia	27.5	14.4	3.1	3.6	30.6	18.0
Lithuania	19.3	11.5	3.4	4.6	22.8	16.1
Poland	14.8	13.9	3.4	5.6	18.2	19.7
Romania	19.7	17.2	3.8	5.5	23.7	22.7
Slovakia	24.9	17.7	2.1	2.6	26.5	20.3
Slovenia	22.3	18.3	3.2	4.3	25.4	21.6
EU10	22.9	16.4	3.5	4.2	24.8	19.6
Eurozone	18.3	16.7	2.5	2.5	20.6	19.1

Source: Eurostat, available at: http://tinyurl.com/ccs3f6t, accessed 9 August 2012.

We can therefore see that the countries that suffered the largest falls in GDP were those in which investment as a share of GDP declined the most. This is most obviously the case in the 'financialised' economies of the Baltic countries, where the fall in investment was driven by a collapse in business investment and a small fall or insufficient rise in public investment. In many other countries, the maintenance or even small rise in public investment was not at a level sufficient to offset the far greater decrease in private investment levels. However, in Poland a combination of a small decline in private investment and a significant increase in public investment allowed the overall level of investment in the economy to increase.[7]

Debts and deficits

To some extent the PO government benefited from a fortunate mix of circumstances that has allowed the Polish economy to continue expanding throughout the period of the economic crisis. However, the government's more pragmatic economic policy also helped the country remain on this growth path, as it was prepared to allow its public debt and deficit to rise in order to finance public investment and spending. The government also did not embark on any extensive austerity reforms and in some cases it actually did the opposite, such as increasing the salaries of teachers.

Figure 1 shows both public debt and the budget deficit beginning to grow from 2007, which was partly the result of the previous PiS government's policies. While social spending marginally increased during this government's period in office, the income tax system moved in a more regressive direction. The previous three income tax bands of 19%, 30% and 40% were changed to two bands of 18% and 32%, thus implementing almost a *de facto* flat-tax system as 98.5% of tax payers paid the 18% rate.[8] Public debt continued to increase as the economy slowed from 2008. Although a budget deficit of under 8%, and particularly a public debt level of less than 55% of GDP, were relatively low in Europe at the time, a

---

[7]It should also be borne in mind that there is a relationship between public and business investment, as increases in public investment can help to maintain investments by private companies.

[8]This came after the Democratic Left Alliance (*Sojusz Lewicy Demokraticznej*, SLD) government had cut the business tax rate from 27% to 19% in 2004 (Szumlewicz 2011).

number of external and internal pressures led the government to seek to reduce the level. First, Poland agreed with the European Commission to reduce its budget deficit over the next few years (see below). Second, the Polish constitution, adopted in 1997, limits public debt at 60% of GDP, meaning that the government cannot take on any financial obligations if it exceeds this level. In order to ensure that this is not breached, Poland has a self-imposed threshold of 55% of GDP and if this is crossed then the government has to take action to balance the budget.

Public debt rose in Poland by more than zł300 billion between 2008 and 2011, equivalent to 11.7% of GDP. However, the growth of public debt in the EU during this time was 23.5% and 20 EU states had higher levels than Poland. Nevertheless, primarily due to its own internal limits, the Polish government concentrated during its first term on ensuring that its public debt did not cross 55% of GDP. Thus, despite its politically pragmatic approach, the government moved to freeze the pay of public sector workers—apart from teachers—reduce funeral subsidies, cut money allocated to the labour fund and increase the effective retirement age for those who had access to early retirement by five years. The government also raised VAT and ruled out any return to a more progressive tax system. It attempted to introduce a series of reforms, such as 'commercialising' the health service, that were vetoed by the late President Lech Kaczyński. Also, despite its previously stated commitment to building up state industries, the government significantly increased the pace of privatisation.

The aim of the Ministry of the Treasury was to reduce the share of state ownership in the economy from over 20% to 10%.[9] It recognised privatisation as a means to bring down its deficit and as an alternative to raising taxes. Between 2008 and 2011 the government completed the sale of 562 companies, which brought an income of around €10.3 billion. It planned the sale of a further 300 companies in 2012–2013, which it hoped would bring in

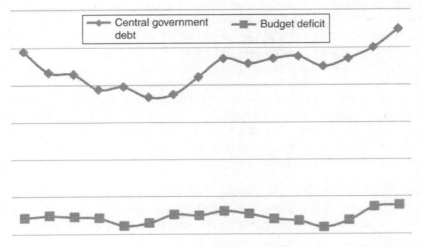

FIGURE 1. GOVERNMENT DEBT AND THE STATE BUDGET DEFICIT, % OF GDP, 1995–2009
Source: Eurostat, available at: http://tinyurl.com/6mxfmvu; http://tinyurl.com/yd5mf54, accessed 9 August 2012.

---

[9]In Poland the Ministry of the Treasury is separate from the Ministry of Finance and is responsible mainly for the management of nationally-owned assets.

revenue of €3.5 billion.[10] However, one of its most significant policy decisions, designed to reduce the level of public debt, was its partial reform of the private pension system. This is an example of where the government took a more pragmatic approach to economic policy and broke from those ideologically committed to liberalism. For this reason we shall consider this issue and its surrounding debate in some detail.

Reversing the pension reform

The question of whether governments can afford to provide universal pensions has been raised in the context of ageing societies and economic pressures to cut government spending and deficits. One proposed solution to this dilemma was the introduction of compulsory private pension schemes, as were implemented in a number of Latin American and Eastern European countries throughout the 1980s and 1990s. The perceived advantages of such a system are that the burden of providing pensions is passed from the government to the individual, thus easing fiscal pressures on state budgets and encouraging people to work longer, whilst pensions valorise through investments in the stock-market.

In the context of austerity programmes introduced globally following the financial crisis, many governments sought to reduce their spending on pensions, as it accounted for more than 16% of total public spending and over 6% of GDP in the OECD countries.[11] It could have been legitimately hypothesised that the crisis would have been used as an opportunity to widen and deepen private pension reform around the world, particularly in those countries most in need of external financial help. However, in contrast to previous economic crises, many governments actually either completely scrapped, or partially rolled back, these private pension systems. Thus while the programmes of austerity reduced the role of the state in providing public services, the opposite was true for the private pension schemes. This was primarily due to the fiscal pressures on governments to reduce budget deficits.

One of the major incentives for governments to introduce compulsory private pension systems was their wish to lessen the long-term burden upon the state to provide for people in their retirement.[12] However, in doing so, the system created short-term and medium-term pressures on the governments' budgets that were exposed by the financial crisis. This is because, while a part of people's salaries was transferred to the private pension funds, the government still had to keep paying for current pensions. This double burden on public finances lasts for a number of decades, until all those insured under the pay-as-you-go system are no longer alive. In essence, the compulsory private pension system entails the present generation defaulting on paying for current pensions in order to save privately for its own.

These combined pressures instigated partial or complete reforms of these systems in a number of Latin American countries (Chile, Argentina and Bolivia) and Central and Eastern European countries (Bulgaria, Estonia, Hungary, Lithuania and Poland). These governments

---

[10]'Rzęd: przychody z prywatyzacji w latach 2012–13—ok. 15 mld zł', *onet.biznes*, 27 March 2012, available at: http://biznes.onet.pl/rzad-przychody-z-prywatyzacji-w-latach-2012-13-ok-,18543,5072475, news-detal, accessed 7 August 2012.

[11]OECD Social Expenditures Data Base, 2011, available at: http://www.oecd.org/document/9/0,3746,en_2825_501397_38141385_1_1_1_1,00.html, accessed 7 August 2012.

[12]This reform introduced a three-pillar system that maintained a state fund but introduced a compulsory second private pension pillar and a third optional private pillar.

TRANSITION ECONOMIES AFTER 2008

had begun to question the wisdom of transferring money to the private pension funds, while also paying for existing state pensions. When the Polish pension system was reformed during the AWS–UW government in 1999, it was established that those aged 50 and over at the time would remain within the old pay-as-you-go system. This meant that the Polish National Insurance Company (ZUS) was required to continue paying these pensions, while 7.3% of total gross salaries was transferred to the private pension funds. It was estimated that this added up to a total of zł162 billion from the beginning of the reform, equivalent to 11.4% of Poland's GDP in 2010 (OECD 2011).

The initial proposal from within the government, for a reform of the system, was made by the Minister for Work and Social Policy, Jolanta Fedak, a member of the Polish Peasants' Party (PSL). She was soon supported by Rostowski, who saw a reform of the private pension system as a means to reduce social expenditures. Rostowski described the private pension scheme as being 'a cancer, which attacks reform and has risen to a gigantic size, damaging the whole pension system and now public finances'.[13] Bielecki also argued that the private pension system was too costly for the government's budget and that 'contrary to expectations the private pension funds had not become machines to increase the money of future pensioners'.[14] However, many within the government and PO were hostile towards any move away from the compulsory private pension scheme. For example, Boni argued that the suggestions for reform coming out of the government would equate to the dismantling of the system, which he argued was an essential element of Poland's general transition from communism.

After a period of negotiation it was agreed that the share of people's salaries being passed to the private pensions would be reduced from 7.3% to 2.3%, with the proviso that this would rise to 3.5% by 2017. The PO government thereby moved a significant sum of money away from the private pension funds and into the state budget, thus helping to control its public finances.

Liberal opponents

The decision of the PO government to avoid a radical programme of spending cuts during its first term in office opened up the most serious dispute between the supporters of liberal economics since the onset of the transition. The opposition to the government was led by supporters of Leszek Balcerowicz, grouped within the influential think-tank the Civil Development Forum (*Forum Obywatelskiego Rozwoju*, FOR).[15] They saw the most serious threat to the Polish economy as rising public debt and that in order to address this issue the government had to act quickly and decisively.

The fiercest dispute between these two groups occurred around the issue of reforming the compulsory private pension system. This included an open conflict between two former close political allies—Balcerowicz and Rostowski—who even held a live televised debate over the issue.[16] Despite their wish to bring down public debt, FOR opposed any reform of the private pension system and believed that the changes being proposed by the government

---

[13]'Co Dalej z Emeryturami? Dzisiaj Decyzja Rzędu', *Gazeta Wyborcza*, 8 March 2011.

[14]'Co Dalej z Emeryturami? Dzisiaj Decyzja Rzędu', *Gazeta Wyborcza*, 8 March 2011.

[15]See the website of the institute, available at: http://www.for.org.pl/pl, accessed 9 August 2012.

[16]Rostowski had been Balcerowicz's adviser from 1989 to 1991 and then led the Macroeconomic Policy Council in the Ministry of Finance from 1997 to 2001. The fact that many members of the PO government,

were tantamount to a betrayal of the ideals and practices of the transition. They saw the private pension system as being an essential component of the transition and that the attempts to reform it were interfering with individual rights and freedoms.

The importance of the private pension system was summed up by Ryszard Petru, a former adviser to Balcerowicz who had helped to draw up the pension reforms introduced in 1999. He explained that the private pension system was brought in with two main purposes in mind: first, to link an individual's pension to their own payments and therefore encourage people to work longer; and second, to break the monopoly of the state in organising pensions and create new financial bodies with a steady source of funding that could act as long-term investors in the Polish stock-market and be participants in future privatisations. The proposals of the PO–PSL government were seen as dismantling these essential reforms and reversing the course of the transition taken over the previous two decades.

Those grouped around Balcerowicz and FOR proposed a series of alternative public spending cuts, in place of reforming the pensions' system, that included: speeding up privatisation; halting salary rises for teachers; abolishing subsidies for mines; cancelling subsidies for newborn children; reducing unemployment benefit; raising the age of retirement and making it equal for men and women; withdrawing pension privileges for farmers, miners and uniformed workers; not increasing maternity leave; and reducing subsidies for funerals.[17] Such an alternative programme amounted to the type of full-scale austerity programme that Tusk's government was actively attempting to avoid during its first term in power.

A radical second term?

PO's first term in office was marked by a pragmatism, shaped in its partial move away from the ideology of liberalism and by the realities of governing during a period of economic crisis. However, it also had the declared strategy of seeking a second term in office in order to speed up its programme of liberal economic reform. PO won the parliamentary elections in October 2011 and formed its second coalition government with the PSL. This was the first time in Poland's history that a party had won two democratically contested elections in a row. A number of other factors made it more likely that PO would push ahead with a clearer liberal agenda.

First, the government had more political leeway during its second term. In July 2010 PO's candidate Bronisław Komorowski was elected president, after winning the elections that followed the death of Lech Kaczyński in the Smolensk tragedy. Komorowski was likely to support and even encourage PO to push ahead with its economic reforms.

Second, the continuing crisis in the Eurozone made an economic slowdown in Poland more likely. The European Commission predicted that the Polish economy would grow by 2.5% in 2012, down from more than 4% in 2011. Although this still makes the Polish economy one of the fastest growing inside the EU, its slowdown could lead to a further increase in public debt.

including Tusk himself, had been members of the government that introduced the initial private reform of the pension system added to the political tension between these two groups.

[17]'Rzęd Miksuje Emerytury', *Gazeta Wyborcza*, 1 December 2010.

TRANSITION ECONOMIES AFTER 2008

Third, connected to this was the increasing pressure coming from the EU for member states to reduce their deficits and debt. Poland signed a bilateral agreement with the European Commission, committing itself to bringing down its budget deficit to below 3% of GDP by the end of 2012.

Fourth, there was a possibility that the programme of public investment, that spurred Poland's economic growth, would come to an end during the PO government's term in office. The impetus for the surge in public investment programmes was reduced once the Euro 2012 football championships were completed. Also, the government's drive to bring down its deficit and debt left it with fewer resources for its own investment programmes. This was particularly the case as the central government was pressuring local governments, often the main initiators of investment projects and the largest beneficiaries of EU funds, to reduce their deficits.[18] Finally, in 2012 the negotiations over the next EU budget, to run from 2014 to 2020, were to be completed. Due to the economic and political climate in Europe it was possible that Poland would receive less than in the previous budget.

Prime Minister Donald Tusk presented his economic programme during his opening speech in parliament, in the midst of the Eurozone crisis, with ratings agencies threatening to reduce Poland's standing if it did not show a willingness to bring down its debt levels. In this context Tusk stated that he did 'not hide the fact that the aim of this is to stabilise the financial situation of Poland' adding that this was 'positive for the reputation of Poland and connected to the security of our bonds'.[19] The government set a target of reducing its public debt to 42% of GDP by the end of 2015 and budget deficit to just 1% by the end of the government's term in office.

In order to achieve this aim, Tusk announced a series of planned spending cuts. Behind some of these lay the goal of moving social policy away from the principle of universalism. Therefore, child benefits and tax relief would no longer be made available for those earning more than zł85,000 a year. Another major announcement from Tusk was that from 2013 the retirement age would be progressively raised from 65 for men and 60 for women until it reached 67. Tusk also declared that the government would be seeking to move away from the annual percentage rise in pensions and that the early retirement privileges of certain social groups, such as uniformed workers and coal miners, would be abolished. The government sought further to increase its revenues by abolishing health insurance concessions for farmers, while employers would have to pay 2% more in their social insurance contributions. The only rise in spending announced by Tusk was a salary increase of zł300 for soldiers and the police.

Despite the change in socioeconomic policy, the proposals of the Polish government were still relatively modest in comparison with the austerity programmes introduced in some other EU countries. Furthermore, many liberal critics doubted whether the government possessed the political will to complete its proposed reform package. What was clear is that due to internal and external pressures it was unlikely that the government would be able to continue with its previous economic policy. Some of the main advocates of more radical economic reform inside the government praised the government's approach to economic

---

[18]'Rostowski znów dokręca śrubę samorządom', *Gazeta Wyborcza*, 10 December 2012.

[19]'Premier wygłosił expose. Będę cięcia w ulgach i zmiany w emeryturach', *Gazeta Prawna*, available at: http://tinyurl.com/cln9vre, accessed 9 August 2012.

policy in its second term and underlined its Thatcherite credentials. For example, the Minister of Justice, Jarosław Gowin, stated in an interview:

> Donald Tusk has followed in the footsteps of Margaret Thatcher, who in her first term in office concentrated on holding onto power and the reforms for which she became renowned for she introduced only in her second term .... I admit that at the end of our first term I had lost hope that after winning the election the reforms would be speeded up. That is why, this doubting Thomas, is standing next to the PM with greater determination.[20]

The main question hanging over the new PO government was whether it would push ahead with its plans to introduce more austerity-style policies, even in the face of large social and political opposition. For example, an opinion poll showed just 7% of society supporting the government's plans to raise the retirement age and only 3% supporting equalising it for men and women.[21] Would the government instead seek other revenue-raising policies as an alternative, such as fully nationalising the pension system or reversing the previous tax reforms?

Conclusions

Liberalism in Poland has been characterised by its emphasis on free-market economics. This restricted the support for liberal political parties in Poland, although liberalism remained the hegemonic ideology that structured economic debate and policy making. The PO government took a more cautious approach to economic reform, despite its ideological background, seeking to gain a second term in office. It was prepared to consider using the economic instruments of the state more and even to dismantle some previous reforms that had been considered essential by liberals in Poland.

This more pragmatic approach to economic policy was also shaped by the effects of the global economic crisis and the need to increase government spending and investment to counter declining economic growth. However, as the crisis in Europe deepened, so pressure was placed on the Polish government to come into line with other EU states and implement more spending cuts and reduce its debts and deficit. This resonated with PO's declared intention to implement more radical economic reforms in its second term in office, which could see it return to its liberal ideological roots. However, the Tusk government remained relatively popular and successful by following a pragmatic and cautious approach to economic policy making. Diverging from this could lead to a rapid loss of political support and it is this contradiction that can be expected to determine the course of the PO government and the outcome of subsequent elections.

Kozminski University, Warsaw

---

[20] 'Jestem prawicowym mastodontem', *Gazeta Wyborcza*, 14 March 2012.

[21] 'Badanie TNS OBOP: Polacy nie chcę dłużej pracować', *WP.pl*, available at: http://finanse.wp.pl/kat,9231,title,Badanie-TNS-OBOP-Polacy-nie-chca-dluzej-pracowac,wid,14348403,wiadomosc.html?ticaid = 1e5d, accessed 9 August 2012.

TRANSITION ECONOMIES AFTER 2008

References

Balcerowicz, L. & Gelb, A. (1995) 'Macro-policies in Transition to a Market Economy: A Three Year Perspective', *Proceedings of the World Bank Annual Conference on Development Economics, 1994* (Washington, DC, The World Bank), 4548.

Bieler, A. (2002) 'The Struggle over EU Enlargement: A Historical Materialist Analysis of European Integration', *Journal of European Public Policy*, 9, 4, pp. 575–97.

Bohle, D. (2006) 'Neoliberal Hegemony, Transnational Capital and the Terms of EU's Eastwards Expansion', *Capital and Class*, 30, 1, pp. 55–86.

Bohle, D. & Greskovits, B. (2007) 'Neoliberalism, Embedded Neoliberalism and Neocorporatism: Towards Transnational Capitalism in Central–Eastern Europe', *West European Politics*, 30, 3, pp. 433–66.

BoSA (2009) *Raport Polska 2030: Wyzwania rozwojowe* (Warsaw, Board of Strategic Advisors), available at: http://zds.kprm.gov.pl/en, accessed 9 August 2012.

Dimova-Cookson, M. (2003) 'A New Scheme of Positive and Negative Freedom Reconstructing T.H. Green on Freedom', *Political Theory*, 31, 4, pp. 508–32.

EBRD (2011) *The Transition Report 2011: Crisis in Transition, A People's Perspective* (London, European Bank for Reconstruction and Development), available at: http://www.ebrd.com/pages/research/publications/flagships/transition.shtm, accessed 9 August 2012.

Holden, G. (2003) 'Decommodification and the Workfare State', *Political Studies Review*, 1, pp. 303–16.

Judt, T. (2008) *Reappraisals: Reflections Upon a Lost Twentieth Century* (London, Penguin Press).

Leven, B. (2011) 'Avoiding Crisis Contagion: Poland's Case', *Communist and Post-Communist Studies*, 44, 3, pp. 183–7.

Michnik, A. (1985) *Letters from Prison and Other Essays* (London, University of California Press).

Michnik, A. (2008) 'Mowa pogrzebowa nad grobem IV Rzeczypospolitej', *Gazeta Wyborcza*, 1 January.

OECD (2011) *Pensions at a Glance 2011: Retirement-Income Systems in OECD and G20 Countries* (Paris, Organisation for Economic Co-operation and Development), available at: www.oecd.org/els/social/pensions/PAG, accessed 9 August 2012.

Ost, D. (1990) *Solidarity and the Politics of Anti-Politics: Opposition and Reform in Poland since 1968* (Philadelphia, PA, Temple University Press).

Ost, D. (1991) *Shaping a New Politics in Poland: Interests and Politics in Post-Communist East Europe* Working Paper Series #8 (Cambridge, MA, Program on Central and Eastern Europe, Harvard University).

Rae, G. (2007) 'Back to the Future: The Resurgence of Poland's Conservative Right', *Debatte: Journal of Contemporary Central and Eastern Europe*, 15, 2, pp. 221–32.

Rae, G. (2008) 'Two Rights Make a Wrong? The Remaking of Polish Politics after the 2007 Parliamentary Elections', *Debatte: Journal of Contemporary Central and Eastern Europe*, 16, 1, pp. 73–86.

Rostowski, J. (2012) 'Do przyjaciół ekonomistów', *Rzeczpospolita*, 2 February.

Spiewak, P. (2003) 'Dlaczego IV Rzeczpospolita?', *Res Publica*, April.

Szacki, J. (1994) *Liberalism After Communism* (Budapest, Central European Press).

Szafraniec, K. (2011) *Raport Młodzi 2011* (Warsaw, Kancelaria Prezesa Rady Ministrów), available at: http://www.premier.gov.pl/download/e4/55/baa84af2abb1adcac51a4b3e49676f04f945.pdf, accessed 9 August 2012.

Szumlewicz, P. (2011) 'Reformy podatków sprzyjaję najbogatszym', *Podatki. Przewodnik Krytyki Politycznej*.

Walicki, A. (2008) 'Odpowiedź Michnikowi', *Gazeta Wyborcza*, 13 January.

The Baltic Republics and the Crisis of 2008–2011

RAINER KATTEL & RINGA RAUDLA

Abstract

This essay explores how the Baltic republics responded to the crisis of 2008–2011. We argue that while there are significant differences in how the Baltic economies responded to the crisis, these responses not only remain within the neo-liberal policy paradigm characteristic of the region from the early 1990s, but that the crisis radicalised Baltic economies and particularly their fiscal stance. We show that there are a number of unique features in all three Baltic republics' political economies that made such a radicalisation possible. However, these unique features make it almost impossible for the Baltic experience to be replicable anywhere else in Europe.

EUROPE, AND THE REST OF THE DEVELOPED WORLD, SEEMS to be mired in a debate over whether austerity brings growth or not. While there seem to be fewer candidates for actual European cases where fiscal retrenchment resulted in economic recovery and growth, the Baltic republics persistently attempt to claim that austerity works. All three countries were affected painfully by the global financial crisis in 2008–2009 and experienced one of the highest levels of GDP contraction globally. All three responded to the crisis by adopting a series of austerity measures. In 2010, the Baltic republics started to recover and recorded GDP growth between 5.5% and 7.6% in 2011. In the light of such temporal sequences of events, there has been a temptation in policy circles, both inside the Baltic republics and internationally, to draw a causal conclusion and to claim that it was the austerity that led to growth. This has led to well-publicised arguments in the media with, for instance, Paul Krugman arousing the ire of the Estonian president by questioning the impressiveness of the Baltic recovery, noting that the data show a huge downturn followed by positive but modest growth.[1] This was preceded by a high-level conference in Riga, Latvia where the IMF's Christine Lagarde and others praised the austerity measures applied there and in the rest of the Baltic countries.[2] Most of these debates

Research for the essay is partially funded by the Estonian Science Foundation (grant no: 8418), Mobilitas Grant of the European Social Fund (no: MJD43) and the EU FP7 project COCOPS. We would like to thank Aleksandrs Cepilovs for his help with researching this essay, and Jan Kregel and Ken Shadlen for their comments on earlier versions of this essay.

[1] The debate between Krugman and President Ilves took place in blog posts and twitter tweets, mostly in June 2012. A brief summary is available at: http://www.washingtonpost.com/blogs/reliable-source/post/estonian-president-hammers-paul-krugman-on-twitter/2012/06/07/gJQApU0zLV_blog.html, accessed 6 August 2012. See also Grennes (2012).

[2] Dani Rodrik offers a measured discussion of the conference in his blog entry, available at: http://rodrik.typepad.com/dani_rodriks_weblog/2012/06/what-i-learned-in-latvia.html, accessed 6 August 2012.

were rhetorically charged leaving little room for reflection and details. However, the question of whether austerity is effective or not, and whether the Baltic republics managed to recover with the help of fiscal measures, remains highly relevant and deserves careful consideration, especially if their model of 'crisis resolution' by fiscal adjustment is to be held up as an example to be emulated in the ailing European periphery. In what follows, we attempt to dissect in some detail the story of Baltic crisis management and its impact on the economy. While our approach is clearly informed by economic heterodoxy, we follow a historical institutionalist perspective in which 'temporal sequences, durations, paths, and cycles are important explanatory factors' (Pollitt 2012, p. 39). We thereby concentrate our discussion on institutional and policy processes and on their description.

Specifically, this essay sets out to explore the following questions: first, how did the Baltic republics respond to the crisis? Second, to what extent did the responses across the three countries differ and to what extent were they similar? Third, how can these differences and similarities be explained? Fourth, did the austerity measures work and is the Baltic experience replicable in other countries of the European Union as well?

As we will show, policy responses in all three Baltic economies exhibit a similar pattern of hardening the neo-liberal paradigm. Indeed, while there are significant differences in how the Baltic economies responded to the crisis, we will argue below that these responses not only remain within the neo-liberal policy paradigm characteristic of the region since the early 1990s, but that the crisis in fact radicalised the Baltic economies and particularly the fiscal stance. Indeed, as Åslund argues, 'the East Europeans have emerged as the successful pioneers of a new, more liberal, and fiscally responsible all-European economic system' (Åslund 2010, p. 101).[3] We will argue that there were a number of unique features in all three Baltic republics' political economies that made such a radicalisation possible. However, these unique features make it almost impossible for the Baltic experience to be replicable anywhere else in Europe.

The essay is structured as follows. We first give a brief overview of the origins of the crisis and proceed to a discussion of policy responses. We then examine how the societies reacted to the governments' anti-crisis measures and inquire into factors that help to explain the policy responses by the Baltic governments. We conclude with a brief examination of the impacts of the internal devaluation strategy adopted by all three states and discuss whether the Baltic 'model' of crisis resolution could be replicable in other European countries.

Origins of the crisis

Since regaining independence, the Baltic republics have stood out among the European transition countries as radical pro-market reformers. In the early 1990s, all three countries adopted a mix of policies advocated by the Washington consensus, including currency boards with fixed pegs (acting as nominal anchors for securing stabilisation), fiscal discipline, liberalisation of prices and trade, and wide-ranging privatisation. The economic environments created as a result of such neo-liberal policy choices appeared to have put the Baltic republics on an impressive growth track, only interrupted by the Russian crisis at the end of the 1990s. After accession to the EU, all three economies witnessed an unprecedented boom. Between 2004 and 2007 the Baltic republics stood out among the EU

[3]See also Åslund (2009, 2012).

countries for their high growth rates: the average annual growth rates for this period were 10.3% in Latvia, 8.5% in Estonia and 8.2% in Lithuania. These remarkable figures were, however, accompanied by signs of overheating, including double-digit inflation, a housing boom,[4] appreciating real exchange rates, accelerating wage growth—that exceeded productivity growth, especially in Latvia and Estonia and, to a lesser extent, in Lithuania—a fast accumulation of net foreign liabilities and soaring current account deficits. To a significant extent, the growth was fuelled by cheap credits, available through foreign-owned banks, which drove up domestic demand and which were channelled into real estate, construction, financial services and private consumption. Figure 1 depicts financial account dynamics in the Baltic republics during the boom years of 2000–2007. All three economies were rapidly building up debt towards the rest of the world. Thus, during 2007, the last boom year, the current account deficit exceeded 20% of GDP in Latvia and 15% in Estonia and Lithuania; credit to non-financial corporations and households exceeded 75% of GDP in Lithuania and 100% in Latvia and Estonia (Deroose *et al.* 2010; EC 2010).[5]

This massive growth of imbalances coincided with rapid wage growth and slow gains in productivity. Figures 2 and 3 show the evolution of nominal wage costs and labour

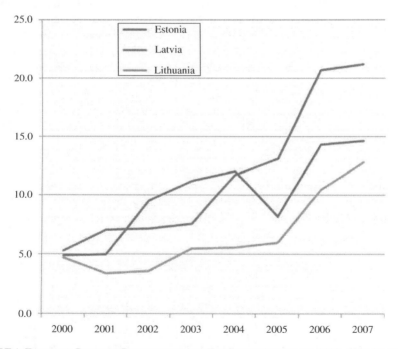

FIGURE 1. FINANCIAL DCCOUNT DEVELOPMENTS IN THE BALTIC REPUBLICS, 2000–2007 (% OF GDP).
Source: Eurostat, available at: http://epp.eurostat.ec.europa.eu/portal/page/portal/statistics/search_database, accessed 6 August 2012.

[4]Between 2003 and 2007 Latvia witnessed more than a tripling and Estonia and Lithuania more than a doubling of real-estate prices (EC 2010, p. 26).
[5]The European Commission (2010, p. 46) noted that the growth rates of mortgage loans were especially high in the Baltic republics, with growth rates 'among the highest recorded in emerging economies in recent times'. See Herzberg (2010) for a more detailed discussion on the private sector debt overhang.

productivity, measured against Germany's productivity, in Baltic economies in the 2000s. As we can see, all Baltic economies were rapidly losing competitiveness in addition to becoming massively indebted. Latvia, with the highest wage growth and the lowest productivity growth (Figures 2 and 3), became the most overheated of the three and Lithuania the least. Latvia also recorded the highest current account deficit, the highest GDP growth rate and the highest rate of inflation (see Table 1).

The high growth rates induced a lulling effect, leaving the political elites oblivious to the few warning signals that pointed to increasing external imbalances. Furthermore, the governments even added to the overheating of the economies by loose fiscal policies, including the spending of boom-generated windfall revenues from supplementary budgets adopted in the course of the fiscal year. This was more pronounced in Latvia and Lithuania than in Estonia, where the budget surpluses were accumulated into a rainy-day fund, referred to in the budget as the Stabilisation Fund (Purfield & Rosenberg 2010; Deroose *et al.* 2010).[6] Against the backdrop of such oblivious optimism, the magnitude of the economic downturn came as a surprise to the local policy makers. However, in academic circles critical analyses of the Baltic boom were also rare.

The crisis hit all Baltic republics quickly and painfully. The domestic bubbles burst in early 2008, when the credit supply decelerated and banks started tightening credit conditions. The downturn was further exacerbated by negative developments in the external economic environment after the Lehman Brothers' bankruptcy. As can be seen from Table 1, in 2009 GDP fell by 14.3% in Estonia, 14.8% in Lithuania and 17.7% in Latvia. The decline in industrial production in 2009 was the largest in Estonia at 25.9%, followed by 15.8% in Latvia and 14.6% in Lithuania. Purfield and Rosenberg (2010, p. 8) note that the decline in the real sector was driven by two factors: shrinking exports and the fall in domestic demand. The deterioration in private sector demand, resulting from the credit squeeze and plunging consumer confidence, was further exacerbated by reduced public sector spending.

Given such massive falls in both domestic demand and exports in 2008 and 2009, unemployment figures soared, rising most rapidly in Latvia—from the 2007 level of 6.0% to 18.7%, making it the largest increase in the EU—but closely followed by Estonia (from 4.7% to 16.9%) and Lithuania (from 4.3% to 17.8%) (see Table 1). In other words, in all three countries, unemployment rates at least trebled from 2007 to 2009 (Masso & Krillo 2011, p. 9).

Responses to the crisis: changes in policies and institutions

As the crisis deepened in 2008 most countries entertained, and many also implemented, some forms of Keynesian stimulus packages. The basic response in the Baltic republics amounted to fiscal retrenchment, combined with maintaining the fixed pegs and not engaging in expansionary monetary policies. The nature of the responses and their fiscal, economic and political success differed only in details within the same broader paradigm. In the following,

[6]With respect to financial markets, the Baltic governments did adopt some steps to cool the bubble, such as increasing reserve requirements and tightening the formula for calculating capital adequacy ratios, but these measures came either too late or were insufficient, given the largely foreign-owned banking sector which would have called for swifter and tighter cross-border cooperation between the authorities (Deroose *et al.* 2010, p. 5).

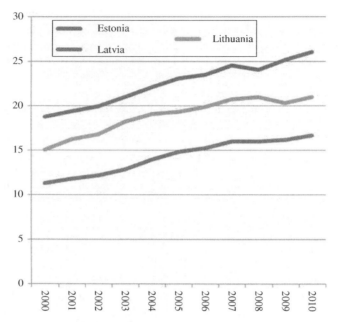

FIGURE 2. REAL LABOUR PRODUCTIVITY IN THE BALTIC REPUBLICS (% OF GERMAN LABOUR PRODUCTIVITY), 2000–2010 (EURO PER HOUR WORKED).
Source: Eurostat, available at: http://epp.eurostat.ec.europa.eu/portal/page/portal/statistics/search_database, accessed 6 August 2012. calculations by the authors.

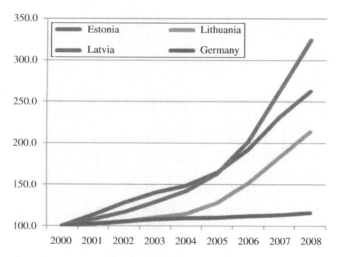

FIGURE 3. LABOUR COST INDEX IN THE BALTIC REPUBLICS AND GERMANY, 2000–2008 (2000 = 100).
Source: Eurostat, available at: http://epp.eurostat.ec.europa.eu/portal/page/portal/statistics/search_database, accessed 6 August 2012.

TRANSITION ECONOMIES AFTER 2008

TABLE 1
SELECTED ECONOMIC INDICATORS FOR THE BALTIC REPUBLICS, 2007–2010

	2007	2008	2009	2010	2011
Real GDP growth %					
Estonia	7.5	−3.7	−14.3	2.3	7.6
Latvia	9.6	−3.3	−17.7	−0.3	5.5
Lithuania	9.8	2.9	−14.8	1.4	5.9
Current account, % of GDP					
Estonia	−15.9	−9.7	3.7	3.6	3.2
Latvia	−22.4	−13.1	8.6	3.0	−1.2
Lithuania	−14.4	−12.9	4.4	1.5	−1.6
Annual inflation, %					
Estonia	6.7	10.6	0.2	2.7	5.1
Latvia	10.1	15.3	3.3	−1.2	4.2
Lithuania	5.8	11.1	4.2	1.2	4.1
*Unemployment rate (% of labour force) (European Union Labour Force Survey)**					
Estonia	4.7	5.5	13.8	16.9	12.5
Latvia	6.5	8.0	18.2	19.8	16.2
Lithuania	4.3	5.8	13.7	17.8	15.4
Gross pay (euro per inhabitant)					
Estonia	4200	4600	4000	3800	4100
Latvia	3700	4400	3300	3100	3400
Lithuania	2900	3300	2800	2700	3000
Real labour productivity growth per person employed (% change on previous period)					
Estonia	6.6	−3.8	−4.7	7.4	0.6
Latvia	5.8	−4.2	−5.3	4.7	14.8
Lithuania	6.8	3.6	−8.6	6.9	3.8
Real effective exchange rate (index 1999 = 100)					
Estonia	139.16	152.38	152.69	142.05	142.93
Latvia	142.97	165.30	150.30	132.59	134.41
Lithuania	128.09	134.79	132.51	121.20	120.99

Note: *European Union Labour Force Survey, available at: http://epp.eurostat.ec.europa.eu/portal/page/portal/microdata/lfs, accessed 5 February 2013.
Source: Eurostat, available at: http://epp.eurostat.ec.europa.eu/portal/page/portal/statistics/search_database, accessed 6 August 2012.

we will describe the policy responses and institutional changes undertaken by the Baltic governments in 2008–2011.

Fiscal consolidation

As can be seen from Table 2, all three Baltic republics implemented sizable fiscal consolidations in 2008–2010.[7] The fiscal adjustment was the largest in Latvia, adding up to around 14% of GDP between 2008 and 2011; the largest adjustment took place in 2009 when the consolidation measures constituted 9.5% of GDP. The 2009 consolidation figures for Estonia and Lithuania, quoted in those countries' convergence programmes, were around 8–9% of GDP.[8]

[7]By fiscal consolidation we mean the improvement of government's budget-deficit-to-GDP ratio via discretionary changes in fiscal policy (i.e. by expenditure cuts and/or revenue increases).

[8]Convergence programmes were required for new EU member states and contained commitments to policies and set timetables aimed at achieving compliance with the EU's Growth and Stability Pact which set the conditions for membership of the eurozone. All countries' convergence programmes are available at: http://ec.europa.eu/economy_finance/economic_governance/sgp/convergence/programmes/2012_en.htm, accessed 1 September 2012.

TABLE 2
Scope of Fiscal Consolidation (% of GDP) in the Baltic Republics, 2008–2010.

	Estonia	Latvia	Lithuania
2008 fiscal consolidation measures	2	0.5	0
2009 fiscal consolidation measures	8.9	9.5	8
2010 fiscal consolidation measures	2.9	4	3.7

Note: The size of fiscal consolidation for any given year is measured by adding up the changes in expenditures and revenues following the various deliberate consolidation measures undertaken by the government to improve the fiscal balance for that particular year.
Source: 'Restoring Public Finances', *OECD Journal on Budgeting*, 2011, no. 2, available at: http://ec.europa.eu/economy_finance/economic_governance/sgp/convergence/programmes/2012_en.htm, accessed 1 September 2012.

Why was fiscal consolidation chosen?

Broadly speaking, in order to deal with the crisis, the Baltic republics all opted for internal devaluation, instead of external devaluation, which implied the downward adjustment of nominal wages throughout the economy and fiscal contraction. Why did the Baltic governments prefer internal devaluation? As Kuokstis and Vilpisauskas (2010) argue, the choice of internal devaluation was 'anchored in the domestic consensus of policy makers and expert communities'. They point out that, although a number of foreign analysts, including Krugman, Rogoff and Roubini, advocated external devaluation as an adjustment strategy for the three Baltic republics, this option was, for the most part, not even given serious consideration.[9] The Baltic republics' governments strongly objected to external devaluation of the domestic currencies for a number of reasons, ranging from practical to symbolic.

Importantly, nominal exchange rate adjustment would have precluded joining the eurozone as an exit strategy from the crisis. Furthermore, given that a large proportion of loans in these countries had been denominated in euros,[10] external devaluation would have imposed large costs on significant parts of the population and reduced private sector net worth, potentially leading to a surge in loan defaults, with contagion effects for the rest of the economy.[11] Kuokstis and Vilpisauskas (2010) note that among local policy makers and experts, the prevalent belief was that devaluation of the currency would have been 'clearly wrong and potentially disastrous'.[12] It was felt that by devaluing the currencies, governments would lose an important focal point for action. In addition, none of the Baltic republics had had experience with alternative exchange rate regimes and hence no existing competencies to manage non-automatic systems (Raudla & Kattel 2011a).

Internal devaluation as an adjustment strategy was also supported by the European Union, which was afraid that devaluation of the Baltic currencies would cause havoc in the financial markets and, potentially, lead to spillovers to other Central and Eastern European countries, inducing capital flight from this region (Kuokstis & Vilpisauskas 2010; Åslund 2010).[13]

[9]See also Raudla and Kattel (2011a, 2011b).

[10]As of 2008, 88% of Latvia's private debt was in euros, followed by Estonia (with 85%) and Lithuania (with 64%).

[11]See also Purfield and Rosenberg (2010) and Raudla and Kattel (2011a).

[12]As Hansen (2010) put it, 'In all Baltic Republics devaluation, rightly or wrongly, is seen as Pandora's Box size XXXL and rapid euro introduction is seen, again rightly or wrongly, as an entry ticket to monetary Nirvana'.

[13]The IMF, in contrast, initially advocated external devaluation.

TRANSITION ECONOMIES AFTER 2008

In addition, when explaining the decision of all three Baltic governments to opt for internal devaluation, instead of external devaluation, the national-symbolic importance of the currencies and the corresponding exchange rates has to be kept in mind. As the creation of the new currencies and the corresponding exchange rate regimes in the early 1990s had coincided with the restoration of independence, democratisation and nation-building, the currencies acquired strong national-symbolic values and devaluing currencies came to be equated with devaluing the self-identity, sovereignty and statehood of these countries.

In addition to undertaking fiscal adjustment in order to maintain confidence in the peg and to aid internal devaluation, the Baltic governments also hoped that fiscal retrenchment would act as a signalling device, restoring the confidence of the markets and securing the return of foreign investment, which was seen as paramount for bringing the countries back to the growth path.[14]

The content of austerity measures

Fiscal consolidation in all three countries entailed both expenditure and revenue measures (see Table 3).[15] However, the relative importance of the measures shifted in time and followed somewhat different dynamics in the three countries. In Latvia, for example, the consolidation efforts were driven by spending cuts in 2009, but shifted more towards the revenue side in 2010. In Lithuania, the adjustment in 2009–2011 was driven by the expenditure side measures and the government was more willing to increase taxes at an earlier phase of adjustment than later on. In Estonia, the fiscal adjustment in 2008 and 2009 focused more on the expenditure side, whereas in 2010 the austerity measures were almost equally divided between the expenditure and revenue sides.

TABLE 3

CONSOLIDATION MEASURES TAKEN ON EXPENDITURE AND REVENUE SIDES OF THE BUDGET
(% OF GDP)

		Expenditure side	Revenue side
Estonia	2008	2	0
	2009	6.2	2.7
	2010	1.6	1.3
Latvia	2008	0.5	0
	2009	6.7	2.8
	2010	1.9	2.1
Lithuania	2009	5.8	1.6
	2010	3.7	?

Source: 'Restoring Public Finances', *OECD Journal on Budgeting*, 2011, no. 2, available at: http://ec.europa.eu/economy_finance/economic_governance/sgp/convergence/programmes/2012_en.htm, accessed 1 September 2012.

Cuts were applied to all expenditure categories, though operating expenses and transfers took a larger hit than investments. In all three countries, the governments curtailed those parts of capital budgets that were not financed from EU funds and accelerated spending on

[14]See, for example, Raudla and Kattel (2011a, 2011b) for a detailed analysis of the austerity discourse in Estonia.

[15]Detailed discussion of the austerity measures undertaken in all three Baltic republics is provided in Raudla and Kattel (2012).

EU-financed investments, facilitated by the new EU rules that allowed the governments to front-load the disbursements. The expenditure measures combined across-the-board cuts with targeted reductions. Among across-the-board measures, the cuts to operating expenses of the public sector—especially salary reductions—were the most prominent. Following a 'cheese-slicing' strategy, cuts in operating expenses took place in several rounds via negative supplementary budgets. In 2009, the largest wage cut took place in Latvia (by 18%), followed by Lithuania (10%) and Estonia (8%) (Masso & Krillo 2011).[16] Pay cuts continued in 2010 and 2011, especially in Latvia, although they were somewhat less dramatic than in 2009. Altogether, public sector employees faced the largest cut in Latvia: the salaries of central government officials, for example, were cut by 30% between 2009 and 2011 (IMF 2011). The wage bill expenditure decreased by 17% in Lithuania between 2008 and 2011 (Nakrošis *et al.* 2012). Pay cuts were less progressive in Estonia and Latvia than in Lithuania where cuts varied from 8% to 36%, depending on how high the previous level had been, with the highest earners taking the largest hits (Nakrošis *et al.* 2012).[17] In Estonia, teachers were subjected to a lower pay cut than the rest of the public sector (Jõgiste *et al.* 2012). In Latvia, in contrast, the education and health care sectors were particularly hard hit by cuts so that, for example, teachers' gross monthly pay was reduced from €494 to €358.

Among social benefits, pensions and sickness benefits took the first hit. Sickness benefits were curtailed in all three countries, either by cutting the benefits for the first days of sick leave, as in Estonia, or by reducing the payments that exceeded a certain threshold by 50%, as in Latvia. In Estonia, pensions were increased by 5% instead of following the indexing formula that would have led to a 14% increase. In Latvia and Lithuania, old-age pensions were cut, but in both countries the cuts were contested by judicial review and were found to be unconstitutional.[18] In Estonia a planned increase in unemployment benefits was postponed while those parts of the new employment law that made redundancies and layoffs easier were still enacted. In other words, from the so-called 'flexicurity' package, the flexibility aspects were introduced, while the security elements were postponed. In all three countries, significant savings were attained by diverting all or part of the contributions to the compulsory private funded pension pillar to the 'public pay as you go' pillar.[19]

Instead of increasing one particular tax significantly, the governments opted to spread increases across a large number of different taxes, both direct and indirect. Apart from increases in nominal tax rates, there was also extensive broadening of tax bases, especially in Latvia and to a lesser extent in Lithuania. Value added tax and excise duties on cigarettes,

[16]These numbers reflect annual wage changes in the entire public administration, including the local governments (Masso & Krillo 2010).

[17]In 2009 the pay of politicians, judges and civil servants was reduced by an average of 10%; the pay of employees in institutions and organisations supported by the state budget institutions was reduced by 8% on average and the pay of teachers and employees in the social sector and culture was cut by 5%. Although pay reductions were meant to be temporary in 2009, they were extended in 2010.

[18]Following a constitutional court ruling in Latvia, the government had to cancel the pension cut and compensate for the unpaid parts of the pensions. Nevertheless, the indexation of pensions was frozen from the end of 2013. In Lithuania, progressive cuts to pensions were implemented in 2010, with larger pensions facing larger cuts.

[19]In Estonia, the state-financed contributions to the second pillar were stopped from 1 July 2009 until 31 December 2010. In both Latvia and Lithuania, the part of the social insurance contributions transferred to the funded pillar was reduced (from 5.5% to 2% in Lithuania and from 6% to 2% in Latvia). The savings from this measure were considerable, ranging between 0.5% and 1% of GDP per year.

alcohol and fuel were increased in all three countries.[20] They all also broadened the base for personal income tax by reducing the number of allowances. Income tax rates also saw some changes. In Estonia, a planned reduction was postponed. In Latvia, the income tax rate was subject to fluctuations, first decreasing from 25% to 23% in 2009, then increasing again to 26% in 2010, followed by a reduction to 25% in 2011. In Lithuania, the 2009 increase in corporate income tax rate, from 15% to 20%, was reversed in 2010. In Estonia, unemployment insurance contributions were increased from 0.9% to 4.2% of gross wages. In Latvia, the employee's social insurance contribution rate was increased from 9% to 11% in 2011. Latvia also introduced a progressive real-estate tax, with higher rates applying to buildings with higher value, in 2009 and doubled the tax rates in 2011. Lithuania introduced a real-estate tax in 2011. No new taxes were introduced in Estonia during the crisis.

It is worth noting that, while in Estonia and Latvia the governments primarily imposed tax increases, in Lithuania the picture is more complex, with some reductions alongside increases, as exemplified by the reduction in personal income tax rates and the addition of exemptions to excise duties. In the autumn of 2009, in order to secure adherence to the Maastricht deficit criterion, the Estonian government also resorted to a number of one-off revenue-generation measures, such as taking dividends from state-owned enterprises and selling the shares of Estonian Telecom, with the condition that additional dividends would be paid out in 2009 and 2010 (Raudla 2011).[21]

Similar austerity measures, different fiscal outcomes?

In the light of their similar policy reactions—that of fiscal consolidation—in order to manage fiscal stress during dramatic economic decline, it may seem somewhat puzzling that fiscal performance, if measured in debt and deficit figures, was significantly better in Estonia than in Latvia and Lithuania (see Table 4).

Indeed, although all three Baltic republics implemented sizable fiscal adjustments in 2009–2011, there was, both within and outside the Baltic republics, a strong perception that Estonia was significantly more successful with fiscal consolidation than the others. Diverging fiscal performances were especially clear in 2009 (see Table 4), in the light of which Estonia came to be perceived as a shining poster-boy of crisis management, Latvia still looking troubled, while Lithuania lay somewhere in between. Estonia's apparent success can be attributed to a combination of political, institutional and economic factors.

First was timing. The Estonian government started consolidating the budget in 2008, whereas the other two governments still foresaw significant expenditure increases in planned budgets for 2009. Indeed, in terms of timing, the three Baltic economies had formed, since 1992, a peculiar kind of flying geese pattern of policy transfer and learning, and of growth, in the sense that in most policy reforms as well as growth dynamics, Estonia led the way, with Lithuania being in many cases the last to adopt certain reforms.[22] This is also true of growth

[20]In Latvia, the standard VAT rate was increased from 18% to 21% in 2009 and then to 22% in 2011. The VAT increases were from 18% to 21% in Lithuania and from 18% to 20% in Estonia. In addition, the lists of goods with favourable VAT rates were shortened and the favourable rates were increased.

[21]The revenue generated by additional dividends amounted to 0.78% of GDP in 2009 and 0.31% of GDP in 2010.

[22]For example, Lithuania explicitly waited in the early 1990s to see how the Currency Board would work in Estonia (Hanke 2009).

TRANSITION ECONOMIES AFTER 2008

TABLE 4
FISCAL INDICATORS FOR THE BALTIC REPUBLICS, 2007–2010.

	2007	2008	2009	2010	2011
General government deficit/surplus (% of GDP)					
Estonia	2.4	−2.9	−2.0	0.2	1.0
Latvia	−0.4	−4.2	−9.8	−8.2	−3.5
Lithuania	−1.0	−3.3	−9.4	−7.2	−5.5
General government gross debt (% of GDP)					
Estonia	3.7	4.5	7.2	6.7	6.0
Latvia	9.0	19.8	36.7	44.7	42.6
Lithuania	16.8	15.5	29.4	38.0	38.5
Total government expenditures (% of GDP)					
Estonia	34.0	39.5	45.2	40.6	38.2
Latvia	35.9	39.1	44.2	44.4	39.1
Lithuania	34.6	37.2	43.8	40.9	37.5
Total government revenues (% of GDP)					
Estonia	36.4	36.5	43.2	40.9	39.2
Latvia	35.6	34.9	34.6	36.1	35.6
Lithuania	33.6	33.9	34.3	33.8	32.0

Source: Eurostat, available at: http://epp.eurostat.ec.europa.eu/portal/page/portal/statistics/search_database, accessed 6 August 2012.

dynamics, notably of GDP and exports, where Estonia usually led and Lithuania was the last of the pack. True to the pattern, Estonia's economy was already showing clear signs of slowing down in early 2008 and this gave its policy makers something of an advantage. Latvia and Lithuania remained particularly optimistic and engaged in expansionary fiscal policies through 2008 (for example by increasing social expenditures), when Estonia was already reducing spending (Purfield & Rosenberg 2010, p. 16; Deroose *et al.* 2010, p. 6). The Estonian government adopted a negative supplementary budget as early as June 2008, when it became clear that the initial budget for 2008 had been adopted on the basis of unrealistic growth projections.[23]

Second was the availability or lack of reserves. While fiscal policies in all three countries had been pro-cyclical in the run-up to the crisis, leading to underlying fiscal imbalances in cyclically adjusted terms, they had been the least pro-cyclical in Estonia. There the government had accumulated significant reserves by channelling the windfall revenues into a rainy-day fund, which amounted to as much as 9% of GDP in the wake of the crisis (Klyviene & Rasmussen 2010; Brixiova *et al.* 2010). Thus, the resulting spending overhang was the largest in Latvia and the smallest in Estonia. In essence, with unchanged policies, the deficit for 2009 would have been around 10% of GDP for Estonia and 16–18% of GDP in Latvia and Lithuania (Purfield & Rosenberg 2010).

Third was the ownership structure of banks, as shown in Figure 4. As can be seen, the asset share of foreign-owned banks was almost 99% in Estonia, while amounting to just over 60% in Latvia. Given the need to bail out the Parex Bank in the absence of fiscal reserves, the

[23]Proceeding from the assumption that the GDP growth for 2008 would be 3.7% (instead of the projection of 7% growth that had been the basis for adopting the initial budget for 2008), the supplementary budget reduced projected revenues by €390 million (with the lower than originally projected GDP growth leading to lower tax revenues) and expenditures by €205 million (implying an expenditure cut of 3% compared to the originally planned budget and amounting to about 1% of GDP). Of those cutbacks, €44 million came from investments, €145 million from transfers and €11 million from operating costs.

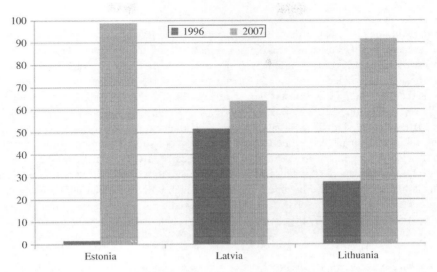

FIGURE 4. STRUCTURE OF FINANCIAL SECTOR BY OWNERSHIP IN THE BALTIC REPUBLICS: ASSET SHARE OF FOREIGN-OWNED BANKS (%).
Source: Kattel (2010, p. 46).

Latvian government had to ask for international support from the IMF, the EU and Nordic countries in November 2008.[24] The package that was approved in December/January helped to avoid the spillover of the liquidity crisis to the other Baltic economies as well (Purfield & Rosenberg 2010).[25] The lack of domestic banks gave Estonian and Lithuanian governments significantly more fiscal space as bailing out banks was essentially 'outsourced' to the Swedish central bank.

Fourth, the electoral cycle in Estonia favoured starting adjustment as early as 2008. At the height of the crisis in 2009, Estonia was in the middle of the electoral cycle, with the next general elections due in 2011. Both Latvia and Lithuania were in a somewhat different situation, with Latvia facing parliamentary elections in 2010, and Lithuania facing parliamentary elections in 2008 and presidential elections in 2009 (Kuokstis & Vilpisauskas 2010).[26] This meant that in both Latvia and Lithuania growth in public expenditure, and further promises of the same, was more recent and looming elections made the debates more difficult while Estonia had a relatively less fierce political climate. Finally, while in Latvia and Lithuania, the crisis brought about a dramatic fall in tax revenues, in Estonia the revenue shock was significantly smaller; this divergence has been attributed to better tax compliance and tax administration in Estonia (Purfield & Rosenberg 2010; Nakrošis *et al.* 2012).

[24]Parex held at the time about 20% of the domestic banking market (Purfield & Rosenberg 2010).

[25]In fact, Estonia was able to participate in this support action with €100 million. This lent considerable political support both domestically and internationally to the Estonian government. Furthermore, government reserves gave the Estonian government significantly more room in terms of building the case for fiscal retrenchment as international financial support with respective conditionalities was depicted as a loss of sovereignty: the politicians could argue that Estonia still needed to hold on to the accumulated reserves, in order to avoid a situation similar to Latvia's, which in turn necessitated fiscal retrenchment, rather than spending the entire rainy-day fund.

[26]Elections to the European Parliament were held in all three countries in 2009.

In sum, the coincidence of these five factors gave Estonia a considerable advantage in dealing with the crisis as it offered a great opportunity to unify all efforts behind one single goal: entrance into the eurozone. This option was not available to Latvia and Lithuania, mainly because these countries did not fulfil the inflation criteria on the eve of the crisis, while slowing growth was rapidly reducing inflation in Estonia. More importantly, in Estonia's case fulfilling deficit and debt criteria was realistic, while Latvia had lost out on the deficit criteria with one single act: bailing out the Parex Bank. It was feasible to fulfil all Maastricht criteria in 2009 and 2010 as the cuts started the earliest in Estonia and inflation was slowing because of the first signs of crisis. Lithuania had a much shorter window of opportunity for eurozone entry and it had a negative experience from 2005 when it missed by a 0.2% margin on the inflation criterion. As Estonia's next parliamentary elections were to be in 2011, the government had realistic hopes that it would be able to generate enough political capital domestically with eurozone entry to survive the crisis. Thus, the initial conditions made it possible for Estonia to have a straightforward realistic goal that the other two Baltic republics lacked.

Beyond fiscal consolidation: other policy measures adopted in response to the crisis

Besides fiscal consolidation, the second set of measures adopted during the crisis concerned the strengthening of (mostly already existing) policy measures for export-oriented activities, mostly via additional credit guarantees for exporters, but also shifting funding towards enterprise research and development and technology projects. In both sets of measures, the availability and use of EU Structural Funding played a crucial role. Figure 5 shows the level of EU Structural Funds in Baltic economies in comparison to Portugal, Ireland, Italy, Greece and Spain.

Finally, all Baltic republics undertook quite significant actions in the labour market, especially in the second part of 2009 and early 2010. Lithuania and Estonia introduced reforms to labour laws in 2009 in an attempt to make the labour markets more flexible.[27] Similar measures were enacted in Latvia in spring 2010. Latvia increased the duration of unemployment benefits to nine months, relaxed eligibility conditions and introduced a minimum floor (Purfield & Rosenberg 2010, p. 25). Latvia is also the only country to have raised the minimum wage during the crisis (Zazova 2011, p. 12). All three countries increased their spending on labour market policies, both in terms of absolute sums and as a fraction of GDP (Masso & Krillo 2011).[28] Again, all three countries made extensive use of EU funds for employment support measures. In the second half of 2009, the Estonian government introduced an action plan, foreseeing €45 million for creating 5,000 jobs and entailing a range of different measures, including business start-up support and broadening the conditions for wage subsidies (Masso & Krillo 2011, p. 44).[29] In 2010, a training voucher

[27]The new Employment Contracts Law in Estonia, enacted in July 2009, relaxed provisions pertaining to regular labour contracts, notice periods for redundancies were shortened, severance payments were curtailed and constraints on using fixed-term contracts were lifted. In Lithuania, the regulations concerning flexible work arrangements, such as temporary and part-time employment, were relaxed, but additional security for workers under fixed-term contracts was stipulated at the same time (Masso & Krillo 2011).

[28]Comparing 2008 and 2009, the expenditures on labour market policies increased from 0.2% to 1% of GDP in Estonia and from 0.4% to 0.9% of GDP in Lithuania (Masso & Krillo 2011, p. 43).

[29]For example, for start-up subsidies, the available sum was doubled, eligibility conditions relaxed and the self-financing rate decreased. The ceiling for subsidised loans available for start-ups was doubled (Masso & Krillo 2011).

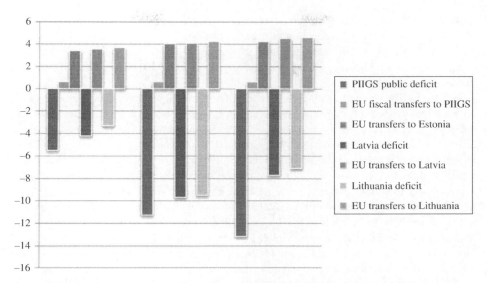

FIGURE 5. PUBLIC DEFICIT AND EU FISCAL TRANSFERS (COHESION FUNDS), AS % OF GPD, THE BALTIC REPUBLICS, 2008–2010.

Note: Fiscal transfers from the European Union are annual transfers through the Structural Funds. Here, the EU fiscal transfers include funds from three main sources: Cohesion, Rural Development, and Fisheries Fund. Data are available at: http://ec.europa.eu/budget/biblio/documents/fin_fwk0713/fin_fwk0713_en.cfm#alloc, accessed 6 August 2012.

Sources: Eurostat, available at: http://epp.eurostat.ec.europa.eu/portal/page/portal/eurostat/home/, accessed 5 February 2013; and European Commission, Cohesion Funds, available at: http://ec.europa.eu/regional_policy/thefunds/funding/index_en.cfm, accessed 5 February 2013; calculations by the authors.

scheme was introduced in Estonia, enabling small firms to purchase training from an established list of institutions. In Latvia, the government created a public works programme in 2011. Training programmes, including on starting a small business, were also offered. Other plans included training vouchers, wage subsidies and special support measures for young people. In Lithuania, a larger scale programme entailing a number of job support instruments was adopted in 2010 (Purfield & Rosenberg 2010).[30]

Institutional changes

On the level of institutions, Estonia changed the least during the crisis. Lithuania undertook some changes, mostly still in the implementation phase, but Latvia's response was rather dramatic. First, in Latvia the government became a significant actor in the banking sector. Second, more than half of government agencies were closed, as reported in the 2010 Convergence Programme.[31] Third, in particular in education and the health sector, there were significant changes and the Convergence Programme showed the numbers of schools and hospitals decreasing dramatically, including the closure of 24 out of 49 hospitals

---

[30] For a more detailed overview of the labour market measures adopted in the Baltic republics, see Masso and Krillo (2011, Appendix 1).

[31] See http://ec.europa.eu/economy_finance/economic_governance/sgp/convergence/programmes/2012_en.htm, accessed 2 September 2012.

TRANSITION ECONOMIES AFTER 2008

(Åslund 2010, p. 37). The number of general education institutions was reduced from 982 to 873, and vocational education institutions from 67 to 58.[32] Lithuania also initiated radical reforms in higher education and health care—under the general heading of 'optimisation'—which were still to be fully implemented in 2012 (Åslund 2010, p. 41; Jankauskiene 2010).

In terms of institutional capacities, crisis management brought two discernible changes in all three countries. First, the crisis led to politicisation of decision-making processes as decisions needed to be made in a relatively short time period, which meant that both analytical and consultative processes remained brief and highly centralised. This strengthened the position of executives relative to legislatures and, within the executive branch, ministries of finance, which were already important because of the role of EU Structural Funding management issues, became even more pivotal in policy making.[33] The planned changes to the budget process, for example in the form of the Fiscal Discipline Law in Latvia, are likely to further increase the power of the ministries of finance relative to that of line ministries. Second, the crisis further reinforced and strengthened the position of the EU as an institutional factor, which had already been substantial during the process of accession to the EU and later with the use of Structural Funds.[34] In the Latvian case, the EU and the IMF, as the largest donors in the €7.5 billion rescue package, were in direct dialogue with Latvian officials and in a position to raise demands directly. The IMF, at least initially, appeared open to more diverse solutions, including external devaluation, and the EU was more the hardliner in terms of fiscal policy (Lütz & Kranke 2010). In the Estonian and Lithuanian cases, the IMF's potential role, and even more its image from 1990s structural adjustment programmes, made the IMF a warning factor within domestic debates, which reinforced the EU's role as the key external advisor. The EU had two key advantages; first, as the source of Structural Funding, it had a lever to push for reallocation of resources within policy measures and to heighten the pace of funds' usage; and second, entry into the eurozone was an important source of policy discipline. Indeed, it can be argued that for all three Baltic policy makers, the EU became the key policy and epistemic peer community, the source of key policy ideas and of their positive feedback.[35]

Another key aspect on the institutional level was the reinforcement of path dependencies in policy capacities. Since regaining independence, fiscal retrenchment had worked in every major crisis the Baltic republics had faced: after 1992, after the Russian crisis in 1999, and particularly after Estonia's entrance into the eurozone (Raudla & Kattel 2011a, 2011b; Åslund 2010, p. 40).[36] While 2009 could in principle have offered a window of opportunity for a critical juncture in economic policy making—switching from a rather passive government role in the economy towards more active macro-management of the economy by the state—the policy choices made during the crisis imply the continuation of pre-existing policy and administrative capacities. Furthermore, both in Estonia and Latvia there

---

[32]See http://ec.europa.eu/economy_finance/economic_governance/sgp/convergence/programmes/2012_en.htm, accessed 2 September 2012.

[33]For a discussion on the evolution of budgetary institutions in Estonia, see Raudla (2010a, 2010b).

[34]See Suurna and Kattel (2010) for a case study.

[35]See also Ikstens (2010, p. 1056) for discussions on the role Commissioner Alumina played in the introduction of tax increases and the progressive real-estate tax in Latvia in 2009.

[36]In fact, Andrius Kubilius, Lithuanian Prime Minister from 2008, was also in office during the aftermath of the Russian crisis in Lithuania in 1999–2000, a fact that supported his credibility in the post-2008 crisis (see also Brozaitis 2005).

TRANSITION ECONOMIES AFTER 2008

were discussions on establishing the principles of fiscal discipline in their respective constitutions.[37]

Reactions to the austerity measures

In marked contrast to the public protests in Greece and other European countries, the population of Estonia broadly accepted the austerity measures quietly, or even supportively,[38] and there were no street riots.[39] There were some protests in Latvia and Lithuania, but brief one-day riots in January 2009 seem to have had political rather than economic causes, at least in the case of Latvia.[40] There were muted and sporadic protests by various trade unions and citizen interest groups throughout 2009 in all three countries,[41] but their impact remained limited.

Only in Lithuania was the voice of trade union protests heard. The government had totally avoided social dialogue when preparing austerity measures at the end of 2008, but it was forced to engage in consultations—at least to a certain extent—in the course of 2009[42] (Masso & Krillo 2011, p. 48). In the autumn of 2009, a social pact, or a national agreement, was concluded in Lithuania, endorsed by the trade union confederations, employers' unions and the government. The trade unions thereby promised to suspend protests in exchange for a government promise to protect living standards and to engage in social dialogue (Woolfson 2010, pp. 504–5).[43]

These mild reactions to the governments' measures can be explained in terms of immediate policy issues and of deeper political and historical factors. Importantly, the majority of the populations in these three countries were in favour of keeping the currency pegs, which made it easier for the government to sell the measures necessary for internal devaluation. In Estonia, the government was particularly successful in constructing a communicative crisis discourse that was simple, coherent and persuasive. It was built on three major elements: we cannot abandon the peg; we have to adopt the euro; we therefore have to adjust the budget.[44]

Although more protests could have been expected once the pain induced by the austerity measures was felt, a number of cultural and social factors prevented this. First, the Baltic

---

[37]In Estonia, the Union of *Pro Patria* and *Res Publica* (*Isamaa ja Res Publica Liit*), a conservative political party, campaigned for a balanced budget rule in the run-up to 2011 parliamentary elections. In Latvia, a set of fiscal rules on budget balance, debt level and countercyclical fiscal policy were being planned.

[38]As Kuokstis and Vilpisauskas (2010) point out, in Estonia public trust in the government actually increased at the height of the crisis in 2009: while in spring 2009, 38% of the population trusted the national government, the figure increased to 47% by the autumn of 2009, after three austerity packages had been adopted.

[39]In Estonia mass protests as a means of expressing discontent had been stigmatised in spring 2007, when Russian-speaking youths reacted with riots and looting to the relocating of the Bronze Soldier statue commemorating the Soviet victory over Nazi Germany from the city centre of Tallinn. Thus, as argued by Kattel (2010), the Estonian public feared that mass protests against the government's austerity measures would be likened to the rioters and looters during the Bronze Soldier events.

[40]See Ikstens (2010, p. 1055) on Latvia and Woolfson (2010, p. 496) on Lithuania.

[41]As Woolfson (2010, p. 502) notes, trade unions in Lithuania were reluctant to organise another major protest action as they did not want to be made responsible for provoking social unrest and violence.

[42]For example, in summer 2009 the Lithuanian trade union confederation protested against the government plan to cut basic monthly salaries in the public sector, which would have primarily affected the lowest paid employees, by organising a hunger strike in front of parliament. As a result of the protest, the government amended the plan and introduced more progressive pay cuts (Masso & Krillo 2011, Appendix 3).

[43]As Woolfson (2010, pp. 504–5) notes, the pact still entailed cuts to wages, pensions and parental benefits.

[44]For more detailed discussions, see Raudla and Kattel (2011a, 2011b).

republics were characterised by a patience culture, whereby society was willing to endure short-term pain for long-term gain in the form of independence, freedom and economic prosperity. This emerged in the late 1980s and early 1990s, but lingered on, even after the initial phase of transition was over (Greskovits 1998; Kuokstis & Vilpisauskas 2010). As Purfield and Rosenberg (2010, p. 4) rightly note, during the previous crises, in the early 1990s and then in 1998–1999, the populations of these countries had witnessed that the imposition of painful measures by the government, in the form of fiscal contractions, had paid off and led the countries back to a growth path.[45] Thus, the hope that the short-term pain would give rise to a long-term gain is likely to have made society more willing to accept the austerity measures in 2008–2010, although more so in Estonia than in Latvia and Lithuania, where a significant number of people chose to emigrate, rather than to stay and put up with the pain inflicted by contractionary policies.[46] Second, civil society in the Baltic republics was underdeveloped and therefore unable to mobilise significant protests. Third, the industrial relations in all three countries were 'highly individualised and dominated by employers' (Gonser 2011, p. 409) with trade union density the lowest in Europe,[47] meaning that trade unions could not stage significant protests.[48]

Discussion: from nationalist to pragmatic neo-liberalism

There are two constructs that help to understand the Baltic economies and their responses to the crisis: first, the idea of embedded neo-liberalism and its evolution in the region; and second, the concept of simple polity and its application to the Baltic republics.

Embedded neo-liberalism denotes a specific form of capitalism that developed in Eastern Europe after the demise of the Soviet Union.[49] This takes inspiration from Karl Polanyi's classic concept of embedded capitalism in which the state functions, by means of social protection mechanisms, as a curtailer of capitalist free market excesses (Polanyi 1957). In the Eastern European case, in a reversal of Polanyi's original idea which was epitomised in the European welfare state, self-regulating markets are seen as bringing social well-being.

One of the key features that enabled this construct to work in real polities is the instrumentalisation of the idea of nation and nationalism as a substitute for social well-being. That is, in the context especially of the Baltic republics, what capitalism can deliver is not so much a socially more balanced society, but rather the survival of the nation. While the notion of embedded neo-liberalism, where the embedding agent is nationalism, reflects developments in the entire Eastern European region and especially the Baltic republics, it is Estonia where it has evolved into perhaps its purest form.[50]

This nationalist neo-liberalism is reflected in a very open economy with governments looking for further avenues to liberalise and deregulate: low income tax for persons and

---

[45]See also Raudla and Kattel (2011a, 2011b).

[46]See also Kuokstis and Vilpisauskas (2010). In 2009, net migration from Estonia remained unchanged, but increased to 2% of the population from Latvia and to almost 5% from Lithuania (Eurostat, available at: http://epp.eurostat.ec.europa.eu/portal/page/portal/statistics/search_database, accessed 6 August 2012).

[47]In 2009, trade union density was 7.6% in Estonia and 10% in Latvia and Lithuania (Gonser 2011).

[48]As Gonser (2011, p. 412) points out, although on a number of occasions collective agreements were changed and pay cuts or freezes implemented without consultation with unions, employees accepted the changes without protests.

[49]See van Apeldoorn (2009); for a discussion of this concept in the context of the crisis, see Bideleux (2011).

[50]See also Thorhallsson and Kattel (2012).

TRANSITION ECONOMIES AFTER 2008

companies; relatively flexible labour markets (Zazova 2011; Masso & Krillo 2011); high levels of foreign direct investment; relatively stable governments;[51] increasing importance of the core executive (Drechsler *et al.* 2003) with weak to non-existent social partnerships; increasing importance of external ideas and policies in the sphere of economic policies (Karo & Kattel 2010); and language and cultural policies favouring the respective majority nations. This is significant for Estonia and Latvia which, unlike Lithuania, have sizable Russian-speaking minorities.[52] Ironically, in economic policies the Baltic republics exhibited practically no nationalist elements, for example eschewing domestic market protection. It is rather the functioning of the market that is seen as ensuring the survival of the nation.

The concept of simple polities denotes polities where social partnerships, constitutional veto players and corporatist structures—employers' unions, industry associations—play little role in actual policy making. The key policy-making capacity in simple polities is direct communication with the wider population. This can be contrasted with compound polities where social partnerships, veto players and/or corporatist structures play a pivotal role in decision making and where accordingly key capacities evolve around deliberation and consultation (Schmidt 2008, 2010; Raudla & Kattel 2011a, 2011b).

While constitutionally and historically, from the so-called first period of independence in the interwar period, the Baltic republics had a potential for both forms of polities, the nationalist neo-liberalism described above led to the emergence of decidedly simple polities in all Baltic republics.[53] This led to two phenomena. First, the evolution of specific institutional interactions and policy capacities; and second, implicit politicisation of the executive branch in terms of ideology and skills tacitly expected from new employees, meaning their adherence to the basic tenets of nationalist neo-liberalism.[54] This resulted in specific elite building with a discernible *esprit de corps*, visible in perhaps its purest form again in Estonia because of stable governments. In this setting, wide policy goals based on some form of implicit social consensus, such as entry into the EU and NATO, played a crucial role in mobilising the emerging elite and justifying the beliefs and value systems reflected in nationalist neo-liberalism. Reaching these goals became perhaps the key measure of efficiency and also opened channels of communication with the EU and its institutions. Indeed, for the emerging policy elites, these channels became key sources of ideas and positive feedback.

At the same time, domestically, the role of social partners in policy coordination remained undeveloped. The degree of insulation of the policy-making elites from social partners varies somewhat in the three countries, Estonia being the most detached and Lithuania the least. In Estonia, for example, although both the employers' union and trade unions made policy proposals about how to deal with the recession and reacted to the measures proposed by the government, they did not have sufficient power to force the government to amend its plans. Furthermore, as Gonser (2011, pp. 409, 412) argues, the crisis led to 'a deinstitutionalization of the collective bargaining system' and further weakened the trade unions, due to membership losses resulting from redundancies, implying further simplification of the polities in all three countries.

[51]Estonia's prime minister in 2012 had been in office since 2007; the leading coalition party, the Reform Party (*Reformierakond*), had been in the government since 1999.

[52]On Estonian minority politics, see Aidarov and Drechsler (2011).

[53]See also Woolfson (2010).

[54]See Peters and Pierre (2004) on forms of politicisation.

TRANSITION ECONOMIES AFTER 2008

Crisis management enforced the basic values of nationalist neo-liberalism, but it became more pragmatic during the course of the crisis.[55] Indeed, it is remarkable that both Estonia and Latvia returned to office in 2011 the governments responsible for heavy budget cuts under very high levels of unemployment. Lithuania elected a president who favoured the hard-line neo-liberal agenda of the government and brought with her also important changes in the government towards such pragmatic austerity (Krupavicius 2010, pp. 1062, 1066). Indeed, both Latvia and Lithuania had been crippled by the power of domestic oligarchs and the crisis intensified attempts to curb this (Woolfson 2010, p. 508).

This pragmatism is associated with one policy goal, entry into the eurozone. As argued above, this gave, particularly for Estonia, and after that country's success also to Latvia and Lithuania, a policy goal that unified the need to consolidate the budget, enforce more neo-liberal structural and administrative reforms, and implement economic reforms intended to support export-led growth.[56] Indeed, the Lithuanian government, the largest trade unions and several other social partners signed a national agreement in 2009 that expressed exactly this, subsuming policy goals, notably fiscal deficit reduction, under the aim of entry to the eurozone (Krupavicius 2010, p. 1071; Woolfson 2010, p. 505).

Eurozone entry as a general goal also engendered other specific goals that could be easily communicated to the public and that could be easily measured, following from the Maastricht criteria. As eurozone entry was realistic for Estonia, it also generated much stronger trust in the government and generally legitimised retrenchment. This enforced a much more pragmatic approach to policy as it subordinated the nationalistic goals to eurozone entry. Kuokstis and Vilpisauskas (2010) show how general levels of government trust remained significantly higher in Estonia than in Latvia and Lithuania, and this in turn translated into higher tax returns.[57]

Did the internal devaluation work?

After 2009 the worst seemed to be over for the Baltic republics. The economies returned to growth and in the second half of 2010 employment started picking up again. Exports followed a growth trend and current accounts turned into surplus. In the light of these developments, can we say that internal devaluation really worked?

The uniquely Baltic economic factors listed above indicate that the Baltic recovery did not result from internal devaluation but rather from other factors not under the control of the Baltic governments. While many analysts hasten to call the internal devaluation successful, the downward adjustment of prices and wages in the Baltics was relatively modest, especially in the light of how overheated the economies had become by the end of the boom. None of the three countries actually experienced any significant deflation. In fact, in 2010 and 2011, inflation in all three countries resumed an upward trajectory. The reduction of real wages from peak to trough was about 15–20% in all countries.[58] By the end of 2009, the real

[55]See also Åslund (2010, pp. 7, 32).

[56]See also Lütz and Kranke (2010) for interviews with the IMF staff.

[57]While in 2009 tax revenues fell by about 30% in Latvia and Lithuania, they declined by less than 5%, year on year, in Estonia (see also Staehr 2010).

[58]See Table 1; see also Krugman (2011) and Knibbe (2011). In 2009, the private sector outpaced the public sector in Lithuania in nominal pay adjustments. The pattern was similar in Estonia, while in Latvia the public sector led by a wide margin (see, for example, Table 4 in Purfield and Rosenberg (2010)).

74

TRANSITION ECONOMIES AFTER 2008

effective exchange rates had fallen by 10–20% from their boom-time peaks (Table 1). However, in the light of the preceding boom, the internal devaluation was rather modest and cannot fully explain the recovery in the Baltic republics from 2010.[59]

If not internal devaluations, then what was behind the Baltic recovery in 2011? There are three key factors: massive use of European funds; flexible labour markets; and integration of export sectors into key European production networks. Flexible labour markets have had two consequences. The first was persistently high unemployment, but this did not lead to higher social expenditure: automatic stabilisers were relatively unimportant, due to low levels of benefits and short periods of entitlement.[60] Moreover, active labour market measures were financed largely from EU Structural Funds. The second was accelerated emigration from all Baltic republics. The level had already been high in Lithuania before the crisis and Lithuania's and Latvia's censuses in 2011 showed dramatic falls in population numbers. Estonia's census in 2012 showed a more modest reduction in population (IMF 2011, p. 14). As the Baltic republics were simple polities, voice did not seem to be an option for many and exit became the preferred choice for increasing numbers of people (Kuokstis & Vilpisauskas 2010). However, both high unemployment and exit are forms of future costs in terms of future social issues and lack of a workforce. Thus, while during the crisis the costs of external devaluation were argued to be higher than internal devaluation—or adjustment, as it was mostly referred to in Baltic debates—it remains to be seen whether this is really so, given persistently high levels of unemployment and emigration.

Integration into European networks by a few dozen leading exporters is another key factor explaining the Baltic recovery. Figures 6 and 7 show the changes in exports and domestic demand. As is clearly visible from the figures, exports picked up in 2010, reaching record levels in 2011. In all three economies, however, domestic demand remained anaemic, hovering around the levels of 2004.

These developments had relatively little to do with domestic conditions or policy actions. Rather, they are an increasingly important symptom of the Baltic blend of capitalism, namely enclave industries. It has been recognised for some time that one of the key problems faced by Eastern European companies is the low embeddedness of foreign-owned exporting companies, reflected in the low level of linkages with domestic suppliers, partners, higher education and research institutions. For instance, one of the key electronics exporters from Estonia, Elcoteq, used up to 200 suppliers in 2012, none of which were domestic (Tiits & Kalvet 2012). While Baltic exports bounced back to their pre-crisis levels, the problem of linkages and feedbacks remained. In addition, the pre-crisis levels of exports were not enough to make up for the lack of foreign financing that fuelled Baltic growth in the mid-2000s. In sum, while the crisis hardened the Baltic neo-liberal resolve, the responses to the crisis did not bring substantial changes to Baltic economic structures and consequently their underlying fragility remained unresolved. However, as the Baltic economies are very open and small, their recovery and future growth depended heavily on European recovery. As the latter seemed likely to be slow and sluggish for some years, there is no reason to expect growth rates similar to those of the mid-2000s for some time to come.

The above factors made the Baltic cases unique. Their experience could not be reproduced in older EU members for three reasons (Grennes 2012). First, most EU countries, especially

---

[59]See also Grennes (2012).
[60]See also European Commission (2010, p. 64).

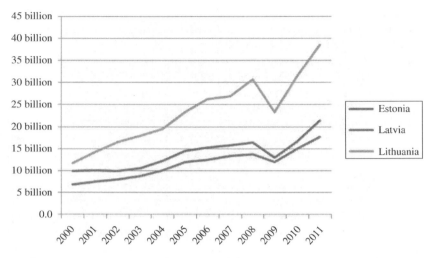

FIGURE 6. EXPORTS OF GOODS AND SERVICES FROM THE BALTIC REPUBLICS, MILLIONS OF PURCHASING POWER STANDARD, 2000–2011.
Source: Eurostat, available at: http://epp.eurostat.ec.europa.eu/portal/page/portal/statistics/search_database, accessed 6 August 2012.

in the troubled periphery, were already in the eurozone and therefore could not present short-term austerity measures and eurozone entry as a crisis exit strategy. Second, very few EU countries had civil societies as weak as those in the Baltic republics, and thus austerity bred visible unrest and instability. Third, few if any EU countries had such narrow and detached

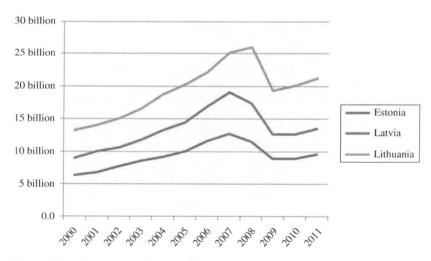

FIGURE 7. DOMESTIC DEMAND IN THE BALTIC REPUBLICS, MILLIONS OF EURO, CHAIN-LINKED VOLUMES, REFERENCE YEAR 2000, 2000 EXCHANGE RATES, 2000–2011.
Source: Eurostat, available at: http://epp.eurostat.ec.europa.eu/portal/page/portal/statistics/search_database, accessed 6 August 2012.

policy elites, accustomed to satisfying their European policy peers rather than their domestic partners.

Even if countries of the EU periphery could somehow replicate the aforementioned political conditions—by weakening civil society, retrenching the welfare state and relaxing labour regulations—they would still not face the same economic conditions. A number of economic and structural factors made the Baltic republics unique, including high levels of economic globalisation, both in terms of exports and in their financial sectors, and strong dependence on larger neighbouring economies, Scandinavia and Poland, for trade and, in the case of Scandinavia, technology transfer. Scandinavian economies recovered quickly, while Poland experienced no fall in GDP at all. Thus, while the EU was behaving more and more as if it were a small open economy where budget discipline was important for convincing investors and markets (Münchau 2011), the experience of the small open economies that dealt best with such fiscal policies is of very little use to other troubled EU members.

Tallinn University of Technology

References

Aidarov, A. & Drechsler, W. (2011) 'The Law and Economics of the Estonian Law on Cultural Autonomy for National Minorities and of Russian National Cultural Autonomy in Estonia', *Halduskultuur—Administrative Culture*, 12, 1, pp. 43–61.

Åslund, A. (2009) 'How Latvia Can Escape from the Financial Crisis', Presentation to the Annual Conference of the Bank of Latvia, Riga, 1 October, available at: http://www.iie.com/publications/papers/aslund1009.pdf, accessed 5 February 2013.

Åslund, A. (2010) *The Last Shall Be the First. The East European Financial Crisis* (Washington, DC, Peterson Institute for International Economics).

Åslund, A. (2012) *Southern Europe Ignores Lessons from Latvia at Its Peril*, Peterson Institute for International Economics, Policy Brief, 12–17, available at: http://boodstore.iie.com/publications/pb/pb12-17.pdf, accessed 6 August 2012.

Bideleux, R. (2011) 'Contrasting Responses to the International Economic Crisis of 2008–2010 in the 11 CIS Countries and in the 10 Post-Communist EU Member Countries', *Journal of Communist Studies and Transition Politics*, 27, 3–4, pp. 338–63.

Brixiova, Z., Vartia, L. & Wörgötter, A. (2010) 'Capital Flows and the Boom–Bust Cycle: The case of Estonia', *Economic Systems*, 34, 1, pp. 55–72.

Brozaitis, H. (2005) 'The Threat of State Default in Lithuania in 1999', in Buus, S., Newlove, L. M. & Stern, E. K. (eds) *Value Complexity in Crisis Management: The Lithuanian Transition* (Stockholm, Elanders Gotab), pp. 233–54.

Cassidy, J. (2011) 'The Demand Doctor. What Would John Maynard Keynes Tell Us to Do—and Should We Listen?', *New Yorker*, 10 October, available at: http://www.newyorker.com/reporting/2011/10/10/111010fa_fact_cassidy?currentPage=all, accessed 6 August 2012.

Daugeliene, R. (2011) 'Hypothetical Crisis Policy Framework for the Recovery of Lithuanian Economy: Searching for Impact of Globalisation', *European Integration Studies*, 2011, 5, pp. 116–24, available at: http://www.inzeko.ktu.lt/index.php/EIS/article/view/1086/1162, accessed 5 February 2013.

Deroose, S., Flores, E., Giudice, G. & Turini, A. (2010) *The Tale of the Baltics: Experiences, Challenges Ahead and Main Lessons*, ECFIN Economic Brief, 10, available at: http://ec.europa.eu/economy_finance/publications/economic_briefs/2010/pdf/eb10_en.pdf, accessed 5 February 2013.

Drechsler, W., Kattel, R., Kompus-van der Hoeven, M., Kallas, K. & Saarniit, L. (2003) *Managing Europe from Home. The Europeanisation of the Estonian Core Executive*, OEUE Occasional Paper, available at: http://www.oeue.net/papers/managing_europe_from_home_the_.pdf, accessed 6 August 2012.

European Commission (EC) (2010) 'Cross Country Study: Economic Policy Challenges in the Baltics', *Occasional Papers*, 58, available at: http://ec.europa.eu/economy_finance/publications/occasional_paper/2010/pdf/ocp58_en.pdf, accessed 5 February 2013.

Glassner, V. & Watt, A. (2010) 'Cutting Wages and Employment in the Public Sector: Smarter Fiscal Consolidation Strategies Needed', *Intereconomics*, 45, 4, pp. 212–19.

Gonser, M. (2011) 'More of the Same, but Faster?—The Financial Crisis and the Representation of Employee Interests in the Baltic Republics', *Transfer: European Review of Labour and Research*, 17, 3, pp. 409–14.

Grennes, T. (2012) 'Reduce Friction or it Might Break: Lessons for Euro Members from Latvia's Exchange Rate and Fiscal Policies', available at: http://www.voxeu.org/debates/commentaries/reduce-friction-or-it-might-break-lessons-euro-members-latvias-exchange-rate-and-fiscal-policies, accessed 6 August 2012.

Greskovits, B. (1998) *The Political Economy of Protest and Patience: East European and Latin American Transformations Compared* (Budapest, Central European University Press).

Hanke, S. H. (2009) 'Interview on the Lithuanian Currency Board System', CATO Institute, available at: http://www.cato.org/publications/commentary/interview-lithuania-currency-board-system, accessed 6 August 2012.

Hansen, M. (2010) 'Latvia: No Victory Yet, No Defeat Either', *A Fistful of Euros*, 4 March, available at: http://fistfulofeuros.net/afoe/latvia-no-victory-yet-no-defeat-either/, accessed 6 August 2012.

Herzberg, V. (2010) *Assessing the Risk of Private Sector Debt Overhang in the Baltic Republics*, IMF Working Paper, WP/10/250, available at: http://www.imf.org/external/pubs/ft/wp/2010/wp10250.pdf, accessed 6 August 2012.

Ikstens, J. (2010) 'Latvia', *European Journal of Political Research*, 49, 7–8, pp. 1049–57.

IMF (2011) *Staff Report, Republic of Latvia*, 10 May (Washington, DC, International Monetary Fund).

Jankauskiene, D. (2010) 'Management of Economic and Financial Crisis in Health Care Sector in Lithuania', *Management in Health*, 14, 4, pp. 3–10.

Jõgiste, K., Peda, P. & Grossi, G. (2012) 'Budgeting in a Time of Austerity: The Case of the Estonian Central Government', *Public Administration and Development*, 32, 2, pp. 181–95.

Karo, E. & Kattel, R. (2010) 'The Copying Paradox: Why Converging Policies but Diverging Capacities for Development in Eastern European Innovation Systems?', *The International Journal of Institutions and Economies*, 2, 2, pp. 167–96.

Kattel, R. (2009) 'The Rise and Fall of the Baltic Republics', *Development and Transition*, 13, July, pp. 11–13.

Kattel, R. (2010) 'Financial and Economic Crisis in Eastern Europe', *Journal of Post-Keynesian Economics*, 33, 1, pp. 41–60.

Klyviene, V. & Rasmussen, L. T. (2010) 'Causes of Financial Crisis: The Case of Latvia', *Ekonomika*, 89, 2, pp. 7–27.

Knibbe, M. (2011) 'Why Poland and Sweden Escaped the Crisis, to an Extent, and Some Other Baltic Republics Didn't', available at: http://rwer.wordpress.com/2011/10/25/why-poland-and-sweden-escaped-the-crisis-to-an-extent-and-some-other-baltic-states-didnt/, accessed 6 August 2012.

Krugman, P. (2011) *The Conscience of a Liberal, Krugman Blog*, entries for 21, 22, 24 October, available at: http://krugman.blogs.nytimes.com/, accessed 6 August 2012.

Krupavicius, A. (2010) 'Lithuania', *European Journal of Political Research*, 49, 7–8, pp. 1058–75.

Kuokstis, V. & Vilpisauskas, R. (2010) 'Economic Adjustment to the Crisis in the Baltic Republics in Comparative Perspective', Paper presented at the 7th Pan-European International Relations Conference, September, Stockholm, available at: http://stockholm.sgir.eu/uploads/Economic%20Adjustment%20to%20the%20Crisis%20in%20the%20Baltic%20States%20in%20Comparative%20Perspective.pdf, accessed 5 February 2013.

Lütz, S. & Kranke, M. (2010) *The European Rescue of the Washington Consensus? EU and IMF Lending to Central and Eastern European Countries*, LSE Europe in Question Discussion Paper Series, 22/2010, available at: http://www2.lse.ac.uk/europeanInstitute/LEQS/LEQSPaper22.pdf, accessed 5 February 2013.

Masso, J. & Krillo, K. (2011) *Labour Markets in the Baltic Republics During the Crisis of 2008–2009: The Effect on Different Labour Market Groups*, Working Paper (Tartu, University of Tartu, Faculty of Economics and Business Administration), available at: www.mtk.ut.ee/orb.aw/class=file/action=preview/.../Febawb79.pdf, accessed 6 August 2012.

Münchau, W. (2011) 'Why Europe's Officials Lose Sight of the Big Picture', *Financial Times*, 16 October.

Nakrošis, V., Vilpišauskas, R. & Kuokštis, V. (2012) 'Fiscal Consolidation during the Great Recession: The Case of Lithuania', paper presented at XVI IRSPM conference, Rome 11–13 April 2012.

Peters, B. G. & Pierre, J. (2004) 'Politicization of the Civil Service: Concepts, Causes, Consequences', in Peters, B. G. & Pierre, J. (eds) *Politicization of the Civil Service in Comparative Perspective. The Quest for Control* (London, Routledge), pp. 1–13.

Peters, B. G., Pierre, J. & Randma-Liiv, T. (2011) 'Global Financial Crisis, Public Administration and Governance: Do New Problems Require New Solutions?', *Public Organization Review*, 11, 1, pp. 13–27.

Polanyi, K. (1957) *The Great Transformation. The Political and Economic Origins of Our Time* (Boston, MA, Beacon Press).

Pollitt, C. (2012) *New Perspectives on Public Services: Place and Technology* (Oxford, Oxford University Press).

Purfield, C. & Rosenberg, C. B. (2010) *Adjustment Under a Currency Peg: Estonia, Latvia and Lithuania During the Global Financial Crisis 2008–2009*, IMF Working Paper, 10/213, available at: www.imf.org/external/pubs/ft/wp/2010/wp10213.pdf, accessed 6 August 2012.

Raudla, R. (2010a) 'The Evolution of Budgetary Institutions in Estonia: A Path Full of Puzzles?', *Governance: An International Journal of Policy, Administration, and Institutions*, 23, 3, pp. 463–84.

Raudla, R. (2010b) *Constitution, Public Finance, and Transition: Theoretical Developments in Constitutional Public Finance and the Case of Estonia* (Frankfurt am Main, Peter Lang, Europäischer Verlag der Wissenschaften).

Raudla, R. (2011) 'Fiscal Retrenchment in Estonia During the Financial Crisis: The Role of Institutional Factors', *Public Administration*, available at: http://onlinelibrary.wiley.com/doi/10.1111/j.1467-9299.2011.01963.x/full, accessed 5 February 2013.

Raudla, R. & Kattel, R. (2011a) 'Why did Estonia Choose Fiscal Retrenchment after the 2008 Crisis?', *Journal of Public Policy*, 31, 2, pp. 163–86.

Raudla, R. & Kattel, R. (2011b) 'The Development of Fiscal Policy in Estonia between 1991 and 2011: Insights from Discursive Institutionalism', Paper prepared for the 6th International Conference in Interpretive Policy Analysis: Discursive Spaces. Politics, Practices and Power, 23–25 June, Cardiff, available at: http://www.ipa-2011.cardiff.ac.uk/wp-content/uploads/file_uploads/24/24-Raudla.pdf, accessed 1 July 2012.

Raudla, R. & Kattel, R. (2012) 'Fiscal Stress Management in the Baltic Republics in 2008–2011', Paper prepared for IRSPM Conference (Panel on Fiscal Distress Management: Comparing Industrialized and Emerging Countries), 11–13 April, Rome

Schmidt, V. A. (2008) 'Discursive Institutionalism: The Explanatory Power of Ideas and Discourse', *Annual Review of Political Science*, 11, pp. 303–26.

Schmidt, V. A. (2010) 'Taking Ideas and Discourse Seriously: Explaining Change through Discursive Institutionalism as the Fourth "New Institutionalism"', *European Political Science Review*, 2, 1, pp. 1–25.

Staehr, K. (2010) 'The Global Financial Crisis and Public Finances in the New EU Countries in Central and Eastern Europe: Developments and Challenges', *Public Finance and Management*, 10, 4, pp. 671–712.

Suurna, M. & Kattel, R. (2010) 'Europeanization of Innovation Policy in Central and Eastern Europe', *Science and Public Policy*, 37, 9, pp. 646–64.

Thorhallsson, B. & Kattel, R. (2012) 'Neo-Liberal Small States and Economic Crisis: Lessons for Democratic Corporatism', *Journal of Baltic Studies*, 44, 1.

Tiits, M. & Kalvet, T. (2012) *Nordic Small Countries in the Global High-Tech Value Chains: The Case of Telecommunications Systems Production in Estonia*, The Other Canon and Tallinn University of Technology Working Papers in Technology Governance and Economic Dynamics, 38 (Tallinn, Tallinn University of Technology).

Van Apeldoorn, B. (2009) 'The Contradictions of "Embedded Neoliberalism" and Europe's Multilevel Legitimacy Crisis: The European Project and Its Limits', in van Apeldoorn, B., Drahokoupil, J. & Horn, L. (eds) *Contradictions and Limits of Neoliberal European Governance: From Lisbon to Lisbon* (London, Palgrave), pp. 21–43.

Weisbrot, M. & Ray, R. (2010) *Latvia's Recession: The Cost of Adjustment with an 'Internal Devaluation'*, CEPR Policy Paper, available at: http://www.cepr.net/index.php/publications/reports/latvias-recession-cost-of-adjustment-internal-devaluation, accessed 6 August 2012.

Woolfson, C. (2010) '"Hard Time" in Lithuania: Crisis and "Discourses of Content" in Post-Communist Society', *Ethnography*, 11, 4, pp. 487–514.

Zazova, A. (2011) 'Labour Market Institutions: An Obstacle or Support to Latvian Labour Market Recovery?', *Baltic Journal of Economics*, 11, 1, pp. 5–24.

Russia's Response to Crisis: The Paradox of Success

NEIL ROBINSON

Abstract

Russia's recovery from the deep economic crisis it experienced in 2008–2009 did not deliver clear political dividends for the Russian leadership. This is because of the context in which the crisis occurred and the way that the leadership, particularly President Medvedev, and many of its critics described the crisis. The oil-fuelled boom that preceded the crisis had the effect of deepening it. Economic recovery based on rising energy prices looks like a failure, rather than a success, and highlights the underlying structural problems of the Russian economy. Arguments about the need for modernisation from within government exacerbated this perception. This seems to have weakened the connection between approval for the leadership and economic growth, a staple of pre-crisis politics.

RUSSIA'S EXPERIENCE OF THE ONGOING INTERNATIONAL FINANCIAL crisis is unusual. The crisis hit Russia very hard in 2008, but its economy recovered quite quickly and it was soon beginning to post growth figures that would have gladdened the hearts of governments in many a eurozone country. The headline economic figures would seem to indicate that Russia dealt with the crisis relatively efficiently and effectively; the crisis had a severe impact on Russia but it did not plunge into depression for as long as some other former communist countries, or for as long as some established capitalist economies (Lane 2011; Myant & Drahokoupil 2012; Connolly 2012). Despite its relative success in dealing with the international financial crisis, the feeling lingers that Russia did not fully come out of crisis and that the way that it dealt with crisis was both sub-optimal and politically problematic. Any reader of the Russian press will have come across opinions from politicians and the commentariat that reflect this feeling. (We will return to some of them later in this essay.) However, dissatisfaction with the resolution of the crisis is widespread and goes beyond media moaning. In April 2012, 63% of respondents in a Levada Centre (2012) poll thought that the crisis was ongoing or had not yet even begun, against just 26% who thought that it had ended or at least had begun to end; a majority (57%), moreover, thought that a second wave of crisis would break out within the year.

This essay asks why there is this feeling and puts forward a tentative argument about the connection between it and the drop in support for Medvedev and Putin that developed into the protests around the 2011–2012 electoral cycle. According to the literature on the

TRANSITION ECONOMIES AFTER 2008

relationship between economic crisis and politics, the Russian government should have ridden out the crisis politically, so that the elections of 2011–2012 should have been largely the same as the previous two election cycles. Whilst there is some evidence that economic crisis can lead to regime change or to a change in government (Haggard & Kaufman 1995), it is generally accepted that only some types of crisis lead to regime or government change, and that there are constraints on crisis leading to regime change. A crisis caused by a trade shock, by major losses from trade caused by changes in global prices and in the volume of goods that traded internationally, is supposed to be less damaging politically than domestic financial crises. A trade shock is exogenous so incumbent governments can 'portray themselves as innocent victims' and duck blame at the ballot box (Peplinsky 2012, p. 136). Regime change is less likely in a democracy impacted by crisis and less likely in a resource rich country (Gasiorowski 1995; Smith 2004).

In the light of the literature Russia's leaders should have had a 'good' crisis, especially as recovery quickly followed. Russia's economic crisis was prompted by a trade shock so the government should have been able to pass blame off on economic misfortune. Russia's democratic credentials might be tarnished but the formal existence of democratic institutions might have had some mediating influence on the impact of crisis. This probably lessens over time in new democracies, especially after a repeated series of legislative elections (Bernhard *et al.* 2003). Some analysis of regime support as the crisis wave broke over Russia would support this having been the case in Russia. Russia has had a series of electoral cycles since 1993 that have not been contested significantly and domestically. This argues for a widespread acceptance of the regime and this, Rose *et al.* (2011, p. 155) have argued, blunted the impact of crisis politically. Familiarisation with the regime—'the passage of time' as they call it—meant that 'the world financial crisis ... lowered but did not reverse popular evaluations of the political regime', and this lowering of opinion was relatively small. Consequently, and overall, the Russian government 'appeared to have avoided any direct responsibility for what ... occurred in the economy' as McAllister and White (2011, p. 487) put it.

The limited impact of crisis on popular opinion recorded in 2008 and 2009, when the economic downturn was at its height, makes it difficult to link crisis to the events of 2011–2012. Even where findings about the impact of the crisis on political attitudes have been questioned, it is hard to connect the downturn to the slump in government popularity. Chaisty and Whitefield (2012), using another 2009 survey, have argued that there is evidence that Russians turned against the government when personally affected by the economic downturn. However, as they acknowledge, even if the 'events of December 2011 suggest ... that scholars may have underestimated the impact that the global financial crisis had in Russia' it will still be the case that 'establishing a causal link between the financial crisis and political developments in 2011 is problematic' (Chaisty & Whitefield 2012, pp. 192, 202). The time lag between crisis, the recording of opinions in 2009 and the electoral cycle was considerable and the Russian economy recovered in the meantime. Even if the reaction of public opinion to crisis is a delayed reaction—and such delays are not uncommon (Chaisty & Whitefield 2012, p. 202)—there is still much to explain to connect crisis and the weakening of regime support seen in the voting for United Russia, the protests and drop-off in Putin's personal vote.

This essay does not draw a definitive line between crisis and the political problems that were thrown up during the 2011–2012 electoral cycle. It reviews the economic experience of the crisis in Russia and some of the ideas that have been presented by Russian politicians, most notably President Medvedev, and analysts about the crisis. It shows that the crisis was, in part, severe because of Russia's dependence on energy sales and that recovery from crisis was helped by an upturn in such sales. This has meant that although the crisis was resolved relatively quickly it, and the government's response to it, have been portrayed as part of a longer crisis, as self-serving, and as reflecting political stagnation and paralysis. Parts of government have been keen to press this analysis of the crisis and the inadequacy of its resolution. This meant that the economic recovery that Russia experienced was probably not claimed as effective a success in a significant part of government rhetoric as it might have been. Medvedev's own analysis of the crisis and what needed to be done to resolve it set very high conditions for success and probably contributed to the notion that there was a substantive division between him and Putin over policy and reform. Cumulatively, and together with some of the social and economic problems of the Russian economy (some of which predate the crisis), these descriptions of the crisis and of the government's response to it seem to have contributed to the erosion of the popularity of the Putin–Medvedev 'Tandem', helped to create the tension apparent in the December 2011/March 2012 election cycle, and created the belief that crisis has not yet passed.

Russia before the crisis

Russia was in a good position to deal with crisis and at the same time vulnerable to it because of the economic boom of the 2000s. The boom saw steady and consistent economic growth and the improvement of state finances. Growth averaged just over 7% per year from 2000 to 2007. The boom was stimulated first by the aftershocks of the 1998 crisis as the falling value of the ruble stimulated demand for domestic goods and second, by the short-run expansion of production by private oil firms in the early 2000s as they sought to cash in on their assets in a time of uncertainty about property rights (Gaddy & Ickes 2005). Finally, the boom was sustained by the rise in energy prices from the mid-2000s onwards.[1] Figure 1 shows the close relationship between the price of oil and change in GDP between 2003 and January 2012. The high price of oil influenced the Russian economy across the board, boosting production in other sectors of the economy, stimulating stock-market growth and stabilising government finances.[2] Expanding energy exports and the rise in energy prices led to large current account surpluses, running at around 9–10% of GDP from 2000 to 2007. Taxes, transit charges and excise duties on oil rose across the 2000s, particularly quickly as the crisis approached and as the Russian government increased oil duties in response to high world prices and to fund plans for increased expenditure; export duties on a tonne of crude oil, for example, had averaged $177 between January 2005 and December 2007 while between January and August 2008 they rose to $495 per tonne (EEG 2012, p. 40). Before the crash 80–90% of all oil revenues went to the federal budget, accounting for about half of its revenue (Gurvich *et al.* 2009). Figure 2 shows the relationship between fiscal balances overall and the non-oil balance. In 2007, the last crisis-free year, the primary fiscal balance surplus was 5.9% of GDP, but the primary non-oil balance was negative (EEG 2008, pp. 31–32).

[1]For longer discussion of the boom and its bases see Ahrend (2006), Hanson (2007), Robinson (2007) and Rutland (2008). On oil and growth see also Gurvich *et al.* (2009) and IEPP (2010, pp. 170–74).

[2]For a fuller review see Gaddy and Ickes (2010).

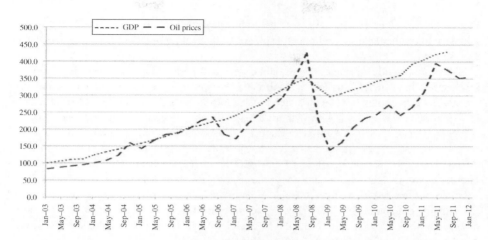

FIGURE 1. INDEXES OF GDP (2003 Q1 = 100, QUARTERLY, SEASONALLY ADJUSTED) AND CRUDE OIL PRICES (URALS, BASED ON MONTHLY $ PER BARREL, JANUARY 2003 = 100).
Sources: Calculated from data from OECD (2011a) and Urals oil price data collected from the monthly Expert Economic Group's *Obzor ekonomicheskikh pokazateleii*, 2003–2012, available online at: http://www.eeg.ru/pages/186, accessed 4 August 2012.

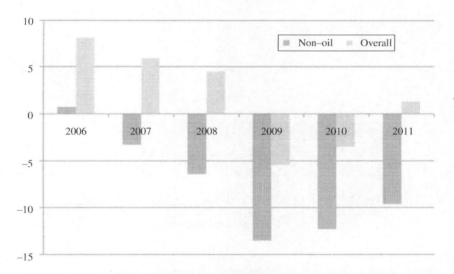

FIGURE 2. BUDGET BALANCES, 2006–2011 (% OF GDP).
Sources: Data collected from the Expert Economic Group monthly *Obzor ekonomicheskikh pokazateleii*, available at: http://www.eeg.ru/pages/186, accessed 4 August 2012.

Large fiscal surpluses meant that external debts were paid down and overall public debt was very low.[3] Foreign reserves grew to nearly $600 billion. Most of this was placed in two stabilisation funds, the Reserve Fund and the National Wealth Fund (for more details see

[3]External debt fell from the equivalent of 90% of GDP in 1999 to about 12% at the end of 2005. In June 2006, Russia announced that it would clear its remaining $22 billion debt to the Paris Club and pay an early repayment fee of $1 billion (Robinson 2009, p. 444).

Figure 7 below). These were built up to neutralise the inflationary potential of energy rents and were to be available to ameliorate the effects of fluctuating oil prices on the state budget and economy more generally.[4]

The positive budget balances, low public debt and large foreign reserves held in the stabilisation funds meant that Russia confronted crisis from a position of financial strength. However, the pattern of development across the 2000s meant that the crisis was to hit Russia in a particular way. Russia's growth in the 2000s was a 'commodity price-led boom' (Blanchard et al. 2010, p. 297). The effects of this became more apparent as the 2000s progressed; fiscal policy loosened and became more pro-cyclical and contributed to the heating up of the Russian economy (Vlasov 2011, p. 12).[5] Oil-led growth fuelled asset bubbles in non-tradable sectors like construction and services. The boom in construction, for example, is recorded in Figure 3. Outside of asset bubbles and non-tradable sectors foreign investment remained relatively low until late in the boom and Russia's overall competitiveness did not improve, either generally or in comparison to other emerging market economies (Cooper 2006a, 2006b; Garanina 2009).

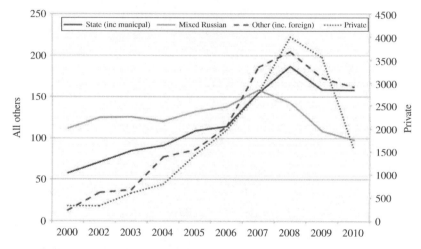

FIGURE 3. THE CONSTRUCTION BOOM AND SLUMP (BILLIONS OF RUBLES, BY SECTOR, CURRENT PRICES).
Sources: Based on data from Rosstat (2010, p. 270) and http://www.gks.ru/bgd/regl/b11_12/IssWWW.exe/stg/d01/17-02.htm, accessed 9 February 2012.

Growth was thus spectacular but its base, as the OECD (2009, p. 21) noted, rested more on 'temporary factors' than on deep-seated structural change and renewal. Central Bank of Russia (CBR) intervention in currency markets protected Russian industry from imports and maintained competitiveness on local markets. Revenues generated by record global energy prices and the easy availability of credit in the US and Europe meant that it was cheap for Russia's major businesses to borrow in foreign currency: on average the ruble cost of dollar

[4]On these funds see Kudrin (2006), Gurvich (2006) and Dmitrieva (2006).
[5]Gurvich et al.'s (2009) calculations point to pro-cyclical budgets even before the immediate run-up to the crisis because of the strength of the relationship between the budget deficit/surplus, GDP growth and oil revenues. The effect of Stabilization Fund savings and the efforts made at limiting the amount of oil revenues spent were therefore imperfect as means for controlling the commodity boom.

loans was 1% between 2003 and mid-2007 (OECD 2009, pp. 25–26). Russia's major firms borrowed to generate investment revenue for development in Russia in the absence of a developed domestic banking sector and to fund purchases outside of Russia as firms bought both up-stream and down-stream, and developed as global players in areas like metals and energy. The rise in private borrowing outstripped the decline in public debt by 2008. External borrowing reached $307 billion in June 2008, outside the financial sector, with that sector borrowing about $200 billion in June 2008, equivalent to about 40% of GDP.[6] These borrowing figures were low in comparison to other advanced economies, but low does not equal unproblematic: servicing borrowing depended on oil prices propping up the ruble's value.[7]

The impact of the crisis

Russia's vulnerability was exposed in the autumn of 2008 as the collapse of the oil price depressed the Russian economy sharply and deeply (IEPP 2010, pp. 10–19). The price of oil fell by $90 per barrel between July 2008 and the start of 2009. Government revenues were hit as tax and excise duties fell. The amount of excise duty levied on a tonne of oil, for example, fell from $495 to $100 from summer to year-end 2008 and remained low for a year. This and other revenue losses pushed the budget into deficit, as Figure 2 shows. Surpluses on the total primary budget and more or less balanced budgets on the non-oil component of the budget changed to a deficit in the last quarter of 2008. They both remained in deficit until 2011, when the total primary budget was again in surplus; the non-oil budget remained in deficit and at a level below where it had been when the crisis hit.

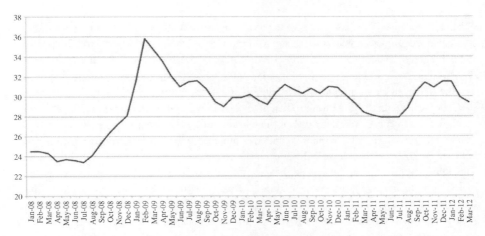

FIGURE 4. AVERAGE MONTHLY RUBLE–DOLLAR EXCHANGE RATES.
Source: Data collected from the Expert Economic Group monthly *Obzor ekonomicheskikh pokazateleii*, available at: http://www.eeg.ru/pages/186, accessed 12 August 2012.

[6]On this see Connolly (2009, p. 4); see also Kudrin (2009, p. 16).
[7]As Gaddy and Ickes (2010, p. 300) point out, the limited opportunity for foreigners to invest in energy sectors meant that the inflow of foreign capital could not help to revitalise the very sector that Russia derived rent from—an unintended irony of Putin's hydrocarbon economic nationalism.

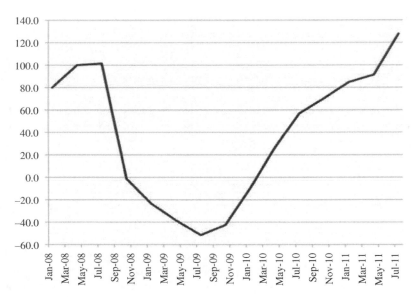

FIGURE 5. INDEX OF CHANGE IN VALUE OF STOCKS TRADED ON THE RUSSIAN STOCK EXCHANGE (2008 Q2 = 100, QUARTERLY, SEASONALLY ADJUSTED).
Source: Calculated from data in OECD (2011a).

The crisis caused by the changes in the terms of trade threatened a fiscal crisis—although this never developed thanks to the reserves held by the state—and also sparked a broader financial crisis. The value of the ruble fell on foreign exchanges and the value of stocks on the Russian stock exchange fell, as Figures 4 and 5 show. Both the fall in the ruble's value and the fall in stock values were inevitable given the predominance of energy stocks in the Russian market and the large foreign borrowings of many of the major Russian firms.[8] From its high point in July 2008, the value of the market plummeted, rapidly in the last quarter of 2008—when trading was frequently halted—and then more slowly through to the early autumn of 2009. It then took until June 2011 to return to its previous peak from 2008. The collapse of the stock market and the exposure of major firms to their foreign debts were matched by a sharp contraction in lending as Russian banks were exposed thanks to their foreign borrowings. The price of borrowing grew for banks, enterprises and households. Fears that banks would go under due to their foreign debts and their rising costs pushed the interbank rate from 4% in July 2008 to 16% in January 2009. As banks shifted their assets into dollars, to avoid being caught by further falls in the value of the ruble and to service debt, domestic interest rates rose; the average rate charged to firms rose from 11% in July 2008 to 17% in January 2009. Credit to households flat-lined across the end of 2008 and then began to fall through to December 2009, when there was a slight upturn (Blanchard *et al.* 2010, p. 300; EEG 2010, p. 33).

[8] Oil, electricity and metal producers accounted for 74% of market capitalisation, most of this concentrated in large firms, on both Russia's exchanges, MMVB and RTS. See Malle (2009, p. 31).

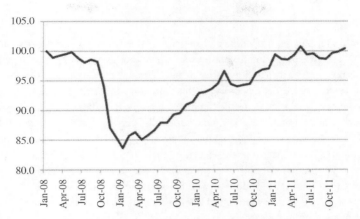

FIGURE 6. INDEX OF INDUSTRIAL PRODUCTION IN RUSSIA (JANUARY 2008 = 100, CURRENT PRICES).
Source: Calculated from data in OECD (2011).

The broadening financial crisis led to sharp contractions in construction, industrial production, wages and to an increase in unemployment. The headline figures, as the briefing papers for the 19 March 2009 government session on an anti-crisis package put it, were that in 'the fourth quarter of 2008, industrial production decreased by 6.1% compared to the same period of 2007. Manufacturing activities fell by 7.7%, the real after-tax incomes decreased by 5.8% and investment into fixed assets by 2.3%' (Russian Government 2009a). The contraction in construction can be seen in Figure 3; it was the major sector hit in 2009 (EEG 2010, p. 28). The reduction of lending by Russian banks led to a particularly sharp fall in the extent of construction being undertaken by the private sector; state and mixed state and private construction projects declined but more slowly. Figure 6 shows the contraction in industrial production as the crisis hits. The recovery is relatively quick in that the volume of production returns to its pre-crisis peak by late 2009/early 2010. The figures dip and rise thereafter but these changes are moderate and indicate neither a major downturn nor a major expansion of industrial production. Other sectors—apart from public administration, which grew—saw similar declines in activity: utility services contracted by 18.3%, hotels and restaurants were down 15.3%, trade 8.3%, financial services 5.7% and real estate operations 5.3%; transport and communications fell by 2.3%, with a particularly marked downturn in freight turnover of 10.2% (EEG 2010, p. 29). Unemployment rose from 6.1% to 8.4% of the working-age population between 2007 and 2009, before falling to 7.5% in 2010 (OECD 2011a).[9] This was a modest rise in comparison to unemployment rates in some eurozone economies, but the rise in unemployment was regionally differentiated, with sharper rises in Moscow city and the Central Federal District, the areas that had experienced larger growth in construction and service sectors during the boom and hence experienced a larger contraction in employment when it ended (Rosstat 2011b).

[9]Figures calculated from surveys according to International Labour Organization guidelines. Russian employment survey figures are a little different but show the same trends. Unemployment rose from 5.8% to 6.1% of the working-age population between 2007 and 2008, but then went up to 7.8% in 2009 before falling to 7% in 2010 (Rosstat 2011a).

The response to crisis

As the crisis was initially seen as a financial one, the CBR led the policy response (Gurvich *et al.* 2010, p. 10). This was not a totally unfair assessment, but as we will go on to argue, a fair assessment is not necessarily a politically astute one. Through the autumn of 2008 the CBR used its reserves to slow ruble depreciation and take pressure off firms that had to repay loans denominated in foreign currency. At the same time it propped up the stock market by allocating $5 billion from the National Reserve Fund initially—later increased to make a total of $20 billion by 2010—to buy shares and maintain their market value. This also eased pressure on firms with foreign borrowings since they had used their shares as collateral for loans. The CBR also provided $50 billion to the state foreign development bank, Vneshekonombank, to back up repayment of firm debts. Ruble liquidity in banks more generally was tackled as reserve requirements were raised; uncollateralised loans were provided to stabilise bank balance sheets and to prevent some from collapsing.

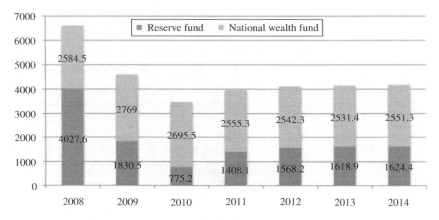

FIGURE 7. STABILISATION FUNDS, THE CRISIS AND PREDICTIONS FOR 2012–2014 (BILLIONS OF RUBLES).
Source: MinFin (2011, p. 5).

These actions did not prevent the crisis from impacting on wages, employment and the markets, although they may have eased that impact somewhat. The problem was twofold. First, the crisis was more than a financial crisis since it was centred on a trade shock and this, thanks to the commodity base of the boom that had preceded the crisis, spread out beyond the financial sector of the economy and quite rapidly. Second, support for the ruble was widely seen as unsustainable by Russian economic actors and the financial press. Russian reserves were quickly run down, although far from depleted. The funds accumulated in the Reserve Fund were particularly heavily hit, as can be seen in Figure 7: the amount held in the Reserve Fund halved between 2008 and 2009, and then halved again between 2009 and 2010. The rate of decrease of reserves was most marked in the last months of 2008, as reserves fell by $25 billion in September, $72 billion in October, $29 billion in November and $29 billion in December (Blanchard *et al.* 2010, p. 299). With capital flight the amount of foreign currency that was leaving Russia was even larger: Desai (2010, p. 143) estimates that $12–14 billion was leaving Russia each week at the end of 2008; households' exchange of rubles into other currencies did not peak until after January 2009 (EEG 2010, p. 82).

Tackling the crisis by defending the ruble so as to protect those firms and banks that had taken part in the huge expansion of borrowing in 2006–2008 was thus an expensive policy measure. The ruble could not be brought back to pre-crisis exchange rates, as can be seen in Figure 7. The ruble began to stabilise in January 2009 and this enabled firms and banks to cover a significant proportion of their foreign borrowings and more immediate debt obligations.

January 2009 and the slowing of the ruble's slide are generally seen as the moment when the focus of anti-crisis measures shifts (see for example the timetable on dealing with the crisis in Aganbegyan 2010). CBR exchange-rate policy changed in January and February 2009 to create a wide exchange-rate corridor and more flexibility in operational response to currency fluctuations (OECD 2011b, pp. 117–18). This change was perceived as moderating support for the ruble; foreign exchange support became less necessary after March 2009 since oil prices began to pick up and new export earnings, as opposed to earnings saved in the boom years, once more supported the ruble.

Following government discussions in December 2008, a process of developing more comprehensive anti-crisis measures through a revision of the 2009 budget began. The 2009 budget was clearly outdated given that it had assumed far higher oil prices. A revised budget was presented in March 2009 and the measures in it and the priorities identified eventually formed the basis of two anti-crisis policy documents for 2009 and 2010 (Russian Government 2009b, 2009c). The substance of the new measures was to shift use of financial resources from currency protection to direct economic stimulus by the state; from the second quarter of 2009 fiscal policy became countercyclical (OECD 2011b, p. 95). Money was also shifted from existing projects—cut in other words—to crisis management programmes. The volume of resources deployed in the stimulus package was substantial, equivalent to roughly 12–13% of GDP in both 2009 and 2010. The stimulus package has been estimated as being the third largest in the globe during 2009–2010 (Vavilov 2010, p. 229).

The stimulus package's priorities reflected longstanding governmental ambitions. The first substantive anti-crisis programme had seven main priorities, most of which— 'developing technological capabilities for future growth', for example, or stimulating 'innovation and restructuring the economy'—had been themes in both Putin and Medvedev's pre-crisis speeches. Anti-crisis policy incorporated a range of measures, particularly with regard to pensions and social policy, which had been announced pre-crisis. Spending on social policy rose from 8.6% to 13% of GDP between 2007 and 2010. Most of this increase was for pensions, where spending increased from 5.9% to 9.9% of GDP (OECD 2011b, p. 97). Much of the rest of the stimulus went on subsidies, particularly to the automobile industry and construction. State purchases were increased and preferential prices paid to Russian suppliers; there was direct support for industries affected by the downturn of the oil economy, such as transport firms, and support for regional budgets. A particular post-Soviet twist was the assistance for *monoprofil'nie gorody*, the 'monotowns' dominated by a single large economic enterprise as a legacy of Soviet planning. Fear of social collapse prompted political and economic intervention in these towns; the economic failure of their dominant enterprises would have not only caused mass localised unemployment but would have also led to the collapse of their social welfare infrastructures directly—many firms were still major welfare providers—and indirectly through the collapse of local tax bases. Togliatti and its dominant automobile plant AvtoVaz received a R25 billion loan in the first anti-crisis programme (Russian Government 2009a); the 2010 federal budget allocated R27 billion to a list of 27 monotowns (World Bank 2010, p. 23).

The stimulus measures combined with the steady revival of oil prices from mid-2009 to steady the Russian economy and to restart economic growth at the end of 2009. This growth has, with some stops and starts, been consistent since the end of 2009. GDP grew by 4% in 2010 and in 2011 (EEG 2012). The stimulus policies carried over into 2010 and, insofar as the increases in social expenditure had always been part of budgetary plans long-term, into 2011.

The reception of Russian crisis management: failing to deal with enduring crisis

We expect intuitively that economic crisis will impact governmental approval as economic downturn occurs, and that as crisis recedes and growth returns approval and legitimacy will strengthen. This intuitive expectation also fits with what we know about the relationship of public opinion about politics to economic fortune in Russia and expectations about the political effect of different types of crisis. National economic affluence has been the most significant factor behind Putin and United Russia's (*Edinaya Rossiya*) political appeal. This finding is consistent with studies of the relationship between voting and economic affluence more generally: voters tend to vote according to their perception of how the national economy is doing rather than how they are faring personally (Kinder & Kiewiet 1981; Kiewiet & Lewis-Beck 2011).[10] In post-communist cases the relationship between national economic performance and public opinion is strengthened where there is clear executive authority over the economy; being able to take responsibility for economic success, or being unable to dodge blame for economic failure, strongly influences voting (Tucker 2006). The economic success that Russia enjoyed before the boom confirmed this. Close control over the economy built up support for Putin and United Russia. McAllister and White's examination of support for United Russia in the 2007 *Duma* elections found that the most significant factor behind the party's electoral success—it took 64% of the vote—was its association with Putin and his leading the country to greater economic prosperity; United Russia voters may not have believed that their own personal circumstances had improved but they did give the ruling party and Putin credit for the country's economic success and voted for it (McAllister & White 2008, pp. 949–50). Similarly Treisman (2011, p. 601) shows the strong influence of economic success—and high oil prices—on Putin's popularity; if Yel'tsin had had similar economic conditions to Putin he would have left office 'extremely popular', while if Putin had experienced the economic downturn of the Yel'tsin years his approval ratings would have been far lower.

From this we would expect regime support to dip as crisis hit, but then recover, especially as economic revival would be associated with the government's control over the economy. Further, as noted above, the fact that crisis was transmitted to Russia through a trade shock enabled Russia's leaders to point out that the source of their immediate problems lay overseas (Feklyunina & White 2011; Cooper 2011).

[10]There are cases where self-interest is more important than sociotropic voting, but in Russia the two seem to track one another closely and sociotropic voting has been a stronger predictor than narrow self-interest.

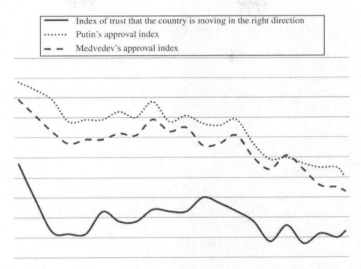

FIGURE 8. APPROVAL RATINGS FOR THE TANDEM AND TRUST IN RUSSIA'S FUTURE, SEPTEMBER 2008–JANUARY 2012.
Source: Based on Levada Centre monthly survey data, available at: http://www.levada.ru/indeksy, accessed 22 February 2012.

However, in practice the link between securing growth and political approval buckled not just during the crisis but also after it. Figure 8 shows the relationship between trust that the country is moving in the right direction and the popularity of Putin and Medvedev. As the crisis hit far more Russians were positive about the direction of the economy than felt that its direction was negative. Putin and Medvedev had high approval ratings, the former's rating being consistent with his long-term approval score, the latter hitting a high as he established himself in office and as a partner for Putin. As one would expect, trust and approval for both men fell as the crisis rolled over Russia in later 2008 and early 2009. Again, as one would expect, the drop in approval and fall in trust about the country's future bottomed out as the crisis peaked and the first tentative signs of recovery showed. Both trust in the country's future and approval for the Tandem began to increase during 2009 and into 2010 as the country came out of recession and growth returned. However, although economic recovery continued, trust in the future and approval ratings fell away again. Unlike the economy they never recovered to their pre-crisis levels and from the end of 2010 they fell. This is probably because Russians had not returned to believing that either their own household economy or the national economy had recovered, despite the actual economic recovery that was taking place in the country, and did not believe that the future would show any great improvement.

Figure 9 shows that the number of people who felt that their family was worse off than a year before has decreased since the crisis abated; however, people did not feel that they were better off. For many Russians, economic recovery seems to appear as a stabilisation of their losses rather than as growth. As Figure 10 shows, they did not expect this situation to improve over the course of the next year either, and were consistently sceptical about the prospects for improved economic circumstance over the course of the crisis and recovery

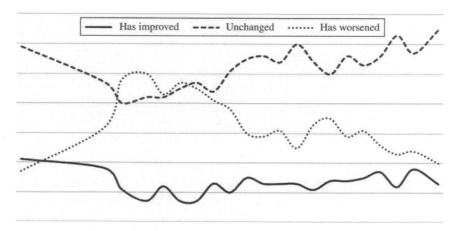

FIGURE 9. RUSSIANS' ASSESSMENTS OF THEIR FAMILIES' ECONOMIC FORTUNES: FAMILY ECONOMIC POSITION OVER THE LAST YEAR.

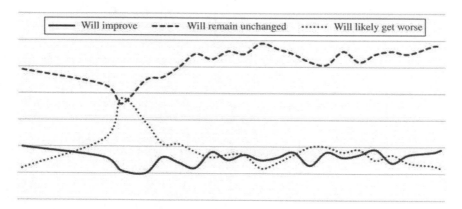

FIGURE 10. RUSSIANS' ASSESSMENTS OF THEIR FAMILIES' ECONOMIC FORTUNES: ASSESSMENT OF FAMILY ECONOMIC PROSPECTS OVER THE COMING YEAR.
Source: Calculated from Levada Centre (2012).

period. Figures 11 and 12 show that assessment of national economic fortunes mirrors assessments of family fortunes, at least at an aggregate level. Although the numbers thinking that national economic fortunes would improve over the next year (Figure 11) and five years (Figure 12) recovered after the peak of the crisis in 2009, the plurality remained pessimistic.

Not surprisingly, as Russians were either not experiencing economic recovery or did not believe that they were, or were ignorant of or dismissive of headline economic figures, trust in the country's future could not recover. Indeed, as Figure 8 shows, in 2011 it fell back to the level it had been at the depth of the crisis and correspondingly Putin and Medvedev's approval ratings fell below the levels they had been at during the crisis. This falling off of trust in the country's future and in approval for Putin and Medvedev showed through in the electoral cycle of 2011–2012. In the December 2011 *Duma* elections, United Russia's vote share dropped to 49.3% of the vote, from 64% in 2007; in the March 2012 presidential

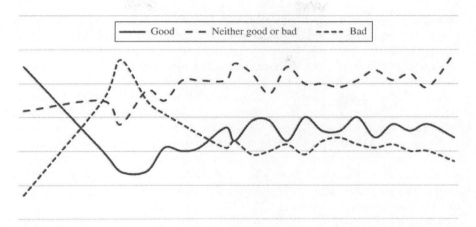

FIGURE 11. RUSSIANS' ASSESSMENTS OF NATIONAL ECONOMIC FORTUNES: NATIONAL ECONOMIC PROSPECTS OVER THE NEXT YEAR.

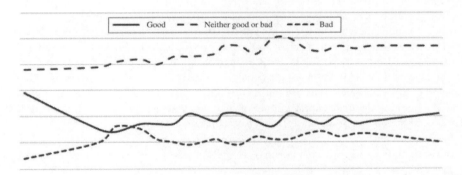

FIGURE 12. RUSSIANS' ASSESSMENTS OF NATIONAL ECONOMIC FORTUNES: NATIONAL ECONOMIC PROSPECTS OVER THE NEXT FIVE YEARS.
Source: Calculated from Levada (2012).

election, Putin secured 63.6% of the vote, which was less than Medvedev had secured in 2008 (70.3%) and less than he had secured in 2004 (71.3%). United Russia and Putin still won, of course, but the lower voter share shows that there was a significant negative political outcome from the crisis when one bears in mind that United Russia and Putin's vote were boosted by electoral fraud, severe constraints on participation by alternative candidates and parties, and tight control over the most effective means of campaigning in the media (Golos 2012, p. 8).

Why did economic recovery meet with such a lukewarm response? There are doubtless multiple reasons for this since individuals' experiences of crisis will differ. Part of the reason for the lukewarm response might also be that narratives about the handling of the crisis and its aftermath developed that portrayed government action as less than successful and warned of more crisis. No matter what any individual Russian's experience of crisis might have been, the discursive frame through which crisis has been explained by political elites was a negative one. These narratives seem to have been produced at all levels of

Russian politics and society, from within and without government, by experts, by politicians and by social actors, both organised and disorganised. Given that there will always be different beliefs about what these underlying causes of crisis are there will always be analysts who think that crisis has not been tackled correctly no matter that it is followed by growth in short order. There is an element of this in the contemporary Russian experience. In particular, there is a strong, and not incorrect, feeling that Russian post-depression growth is a case of its economy regressing to its mean: pre-crisis growth depended on global hydrocarbon prices and has followed their recovery.[11] However, this feeling has been amplified to create a broader perception of the inadequacy of Russia's response to crisis. We cannot hope to examine all of the narratives about the crisis that have emerged here or to trace in detail all of the ways that they have influenced each other and public opinion. Instead, what we will do is to look at how certain tropes have amplified the idea that Russia's response to crisis was not adequate.

The first source of this amplification is that, viewed in the light of Russia's recent economic history, crisis appears to be the norm rather than the exception: the 2008 crisis fits in with the pattern of Soviet economic collapse, transitional recession, rolling fiscal crisis in the 1990s, and the ruble crises of 1994 and 1998. Between the busts of the 1980s and 1990s and the boom of the 2000s there was no period of 'normal' economic development, of steady, moderate, incremental economic growth. This has made it easy to portray and see the crisis as a part of a longer set of problems that have not been dealt with in the past and which will not be dealt with through crisis management, no matter how necessary crisis management might be. In this reading of crisis the trade shock that Russia experienced in the autumn of 2008 becomes an excuse rather than the exogenous source of Russia's troubles, and ameliorating the trade shock will not resolve the fundamental structural problems that lay behind the boom−bust cycle. As one Russian economist put it:

> Russia's crisis is twenty years older than the global crisis .... The short period of fiscal and financial ecstasy is gone; when the leading countries of the world have solved the external signs of crisis Russia risks being left alone with its enduring crisis, which will be deeper than ever but which can no longer be attributable to international economic conditions. (Leskin 2009, p. 3)

This approach to crisis points to both institutional and ideational failure as the ultimate source of 'enduring crisis'. These failings are more destructive than the short-run crisis caused by exogenous factors; they predate and will outlast crisis, because they cannot be solved by third parties. The trade shock will abate when other economies' demand for raw materials picks up, but the 'enduring crisis' will, as its name suggests, endure. Institutional failure means that Russia, unlike other capitalist countries, neither has the public administration nor the political structures to undertake 'true' reform, meaning to respond fully to the problems that leave Russia vulnerable. Nor can this be done in a socially efficient way, leading society to see economic action as being taken in the interests of a common good. That cannot be visible in economic policy, because policy is not produced publicly through parliamentary institutions: the 'initial bailout was a top down ... process ... [not] subjected to independent scrutiny or legislative oversight or systematic winnowing of the turmoil victims' (Desai 2010, p. 144).

---

[11] See, for example, IEPP (2010), GU-VES (2009) and Akindova *et al.* (2011), for Russian literature on the subject. For Western analyses see Desai (2010), Hanson (2011) and Robinson (2011).

TRANSITION ECONOMIES AFTER 2008

Moreover, there is an impression that policy was not economically sound. Differences over economic philosophy are compounded in the Russian case by critiques of economic policy that ascribe it to private interests. The institutional environment in which policy making is hidden made this claim easier to make and harder to refute; hidden policy making can be portrayed as captured policy making. The closeness of political and economic elites reinforced this impression. This was the case both at national and regional levels. For example, regionally the Moscow city government announced that it would spend up to $2 billion bailing out developers, much of this being used to buy property from developers for cash (Maudlin 2008). On the one hand, this made sense since Moscow was at the heart of the construction boom and the hit that the construction sector was about to take when foreign loans came due was going to be extensive. On the other hand, however, it could be portrayed as serving private interests: the mayor of Moscow's wife, Elena Baturina, was then the largest developer in Moscow and was about to see her worth fall by about $3 billion (Serafin 2009).

Nationally the structure of the response to the crisis looked to be overwhelmingly in favour of economic elites since the government, both directly and indirectly, took over their debts by providing government credit guarantees, interest rate subsidies, stalling tax payments and setting preferential export and import tariffs. The chief beneficiaries of these policies were energy firms, metals producers and other rent-generating firms (GU–VES 2009, pp. 44–46). The cost fell both on households, as the falling value of the ruble eventually decreased real wages and purchasing power, and on those firms not able to access the government's largesse. Anti-crisis measures could thus be portrayed as supporting elite interests. This led to accusations that the response to crisis was perpetuating the very structures that had caused it. As Boris Nemtsov (2009) argued, the

> monstrous structure of the Russian economy, based as it is on monopolies and close ties between the authorities and oligarchic groups, is the main reason for the deep financial–economic crisis in Russia .... Putin's actions amount to supporting oligarchic groups and banks that are close to the government ... it is impossible to explain the social utility of saving the oligarchs.[12]

The difficulty of putting a line between private and common interests exposed the government to similar kinds of criticisms about 'socialism for the rich, capitalism for the poor' that have been levelled against governments elsewhere during the crisis. Some popular edge was given to this criticism by the protests against government policy (Teague 2011, pp. 423–24).

Political action might have eased these criticisms, but there seems to have been no consolidated or consistent attempt to explain the manner in which the crisis had been dealt with by the Russian leadership in late 2008.[13] None of the potentially politically positive benefits of the crisis strategy were defended, such as the fact that the state took back some more control over parts of Russian industry in the course of defending share prices. This may be because there was a tendency initially to blame the crisis on the West and to assert that it was a limited crisis (Feklyunina & White 2011). It may also have been the case that it was not believed that an economic argument needed to be put forward. This seems to be the impression of officials involved in economic policy interviewed in the spring of 2011. None were in the CBR but in other parts of the economic policy-making apparatus (including the

[12]See also Nemtsov and Milov (2009) and Robinson (2011).

[13]Of course, there were platitudes about defending the financial system and the currency.

Ministry of Economic Development, Ministry of Finance, the Prime Minister's Office). When asked about the policy response to the trade shock all thought that the policy reaction, although not without its problems, was essentially the default position and its rightness at the time and since was obvious; it was simply what happened when the oil price fell and the currency was threatened. The government, in other words, did not explain its policy, because it was doing what it had all along said it was going to do: spending reserves to deal with the erratic price cycle of commodities. When booming prices fell, the obvious thing happened: reserves were drawn on and applied where needed. As one Ministry of Finance official put it 'we do not really have models of economic policy to draw on in our work ... we have ideas about when we should and should not spend that are activated by the price of oil'.[14] This was the message that Medvedev (2008) put out in his 'state of the union' address to the Federal Assembly in November 2008. Apart from seeking to reassure Russians that the crisis that was then biting deep was going to be temporary and stating that it 'was not in vain that we built up our gold and currency and budget reserves', Medvedev had little to say about the crisis.

The change away from dealing with the crisis through defending the ruble that began around January 2009 should have neutralised this criticism. However, the idea that the response to crisis was wrong because of the institutional failure of Russian public administration never disappeared. Indeed, a part of the government reinforced the idea that policies to ease immediate crisis were not addressing the deeper-seated and more important symptoms of 'enduring' crisis. This happened because the 2008 crisis occurred as Russia's leaders became engaged in a prolonged critique of their own economy in the name of 'modernisation'. The call for modernisation recognised implicitly that economic growth during the boom had not enabled Russia to catch up with other states (Makarenko 2008, p. 35).

The association of modernisation with diversification away from energy highlighted the idea that the structure of the economy was the enduring problem that underpinned the crisis. This, albeit for different reasons, was the same point that opposition politicians like Nemtsov were making. In short, a part of the government legitimised opposition critiques of its own handling of the crisis. In 2009, modernisation was made pivotal to the definition of the anti-crisis response. This meant that the standard against which that response was judged was not the reversal of economic downturn, but the prevention of crisis in the future through modernisation. This was a very high standard and an impractical one. It confused short-term goals of dealing with crisis with long-term ones of structural reform, and tied recovery to something that might well have been difficult, if not impossible, to achieve even under favourable economic circumstances.

Judging anti-crisis measures against the goals of modernisation created an impression that they were a part of a long run of failure rather than a success since in this discursive frame economic growth, whether pre- or post-crisis, was a failure if it was not associated with diversification. We can see this logic at work right in the middle of 2009 in an interview given by Medvedev:

> I can tell you quite honestly that I am not happy with our economic structure. We were aware of this even before the crisis .... What we really should have done is diversified the structure of our economy to a greater extent .... We entered the crisis with the same raw materials structure that we had in the past .... Our economy's one-sided structure is reflected in the figures we are seeing today .... We will pull ourselves out of this crisis; however, the same situation could repeat itself several years down the road.

[14]Author interview with a mid-ranking Ministry of Finance official, Moscow, 7 April 2011.

> The patterns governing this crisis are not fully clear, and nobody knows when we might have another one like it. Thus, we must begin creating a new economic structure now. (Medvedev 2009a)

The stress on anti-crisis measures and modernisation being part and parcel of the same thing was a constant in Medvedev's speeches throughout his presidency and was especially prominent after early 2009. It was a theme in the revised 2009 budget and in the anti-crisis documents produced by the Russian government in 2009 (Russian Government 2009b, 2009c).[15] Medvedev and a section of the Russian government thus created a rhetorical position from which the efforts of the government as a whole could only be found wanting. Indeed, recovery itself could be regarded as a form of failure since it was associated with more rises in energy prices rather than with modernisation; such a way out of the crisis, Medvedev argued in December 2009—as the crisis was ending and growth returning to the economy—'leads nowhere. We need to get out of the crisis by reforming our own economy' (Medvedev 2009c). Over the course of 2009–2011, the development of thinking on modernisation from within Medvedev's circle and in his own speeches and writings increasingly implicated the political system as a barrier to tackling crisis in the right way. Documents and proposals from the Institute for Contemporary Development (seen as Medvedev's think-tank) such as 'Twenty-First Century Russia: Vision for the Future' and 'Finding the Future. Strategy 2012', or Medvedev's 'Go Russia!' or his 2010 blog on political reform, all linked crisis to political reform (INSOR 2010, 2011; Medvedev 2009b, 2010). The Institute for Contemporary Development documents in particular are vociferous in arguing that the crisis had proved that Russia's economic model of the 'years zero [the 2000s]' had failed and that it needed to be replaced; such a shift could not come through the anti-crisis programme since, although 'many crisis problems have been "extinguished" with money from federal budgets, their resolution had been set to one side. The result is a provisional stabilisation without modernisation; the crisis cannot break through institutional barriers' (INSOR 2011, pp. 79, 222). Breaking through institutional barriers required political change in its own right; it was not something that economic problems or policy would bring about on their own. Failure to produce deep political change, or to persuade people that the political changes announced were significant, all signified that economic crisis was not being dealt with and that it would not be dealt with.

The linking of political changes to crisis resolution could only create uncertainty about the future. Although the rhetoric of Medvedev and INSOR pushed change there were, as was widely recognised, 'limits to adaptation', as one columnist put it; there might be hints at change from 'high places' but the 'ship of state is on the same course as before . . . . Anxiety is growing about the future and hope that the current order of things will survive hard times is starting to melt away' (Ryabov 2009). The most obvious of these limits to adaptation was that no consensus emerged from within the executive on what substantive political changes were necessary to deal with crisis. There was a consensus on the need to tackle corruption, or on the need to reform aspects of public administration so as to ease the ingress of capital, but the relationship of these lower order changes to more fundamental issues about the conduct of national political life was not resolved.[16] Consequently it could only look as if

---

[15]There is an academic literature that does the same thing; see Babkin (2009) and Diskin (2009), for example.

[16]For some of the counterarguments to the Medvedev/INSOR line see Feklyunina and White (2011, pp. 398–401). Many of these counterarguments shared the initial assumption of Medvedev that there needed to be change in the political system to deal with both the immediate and the deeper crisis.

the executive was gridlocked on a key issue that a part of it deemed necessary to solve in order to resolve the crisis once and for all. This probably sent out political signals that supporting reform was a gamble that elite members might not want to take and, more broadly, that the factors that the President recognised as underlying crisis were not going to be dealt with.

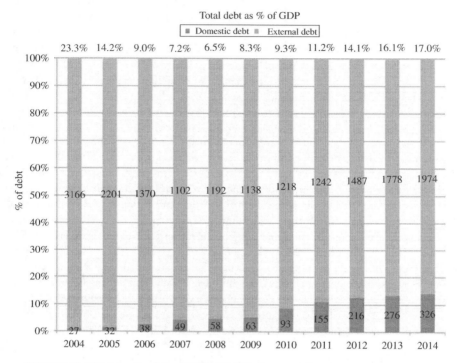

FIGURE 13. GOVERNMENT DEBT, 2004–2014 (BILLIONS OF DOLLARS AND % OF GDP).
Sources: Calculated using data from MinFin (2011, p. 7).

The 'modernisation–crisis–political reform' linkage and the impossible standard set by it for resolving crisis seems to have fed back into fear about the economic future. Over the latter half of 2011 and into 2012 there were a plethora of official and semi-official statements on the dangers of rising spending, inflation and vulnerability to another trade shock that fed fear of a new crisis.[17] The core of this fear is that the attrition of reserve funds during 2008–2009 gives less room for manoeuvre in any future manifestation of the 'enduring crisis'. The Reserve Fund has grown, but even though it has recovered from its low of R775.2 billion, in 2010 its projected figure of R1624.4 billion by 2014 was far less than the R4027.6 billion that the fund contained in 2008 (see Figure 7). This concern was exacerbated by worries that government spending plans and increased borrowing would both overheat the economy, stimulating inflation further, and leave Russia exposed to foreign debt. Figure 13 shows projections of borrowing to 2014. By 2014 borrowing was projected to be around

[17]See Aris (2011) for an example of media commentary about a coming new crisis. For official doubts about the future see, *inter alia*, the IMF's (2011) warnings about spending plans.

17% of GDP, closing on pre-crisis and pre-debt-payoff levels. The largest percentage growth in borrowing was to be domestic borrowing, following a trend established before the crisis. However, external government debt was also to grow and would be larger than the Reserve Fund. These borrowing figures, and the expenditure plans that underlay them, were predicated on high oil prices (about $120 a barrel). Future spending and borrowing plans thus provoke fear that structurally the economy was more or less in the same place as it was before the 2008 onset of crisis. How can it not be when there had not been a successful modernisation, as argued for by Medvedev and his supporters?

Conclusion

Russia was able to deal with the crisis that hit it in 2008 economically but handled it less well politically. Thanks to the oil boom the regime had the resources to deal with economic crisis, but the way that it responded to crisis looked to favour elite groups and this was not explained away. When policy did shift and seemed to offer greater hope to parts of society— like the citizens of 'monotowns'—it was hard to disentangle the effect of policy from that of changing external fortunes. As a result, and particularly in the light of arguments that were being made from within government about the need for modernisation, it appeared that Russia was recovering without getting better. The idea that the crisis was just one more manifestation of deeper problems, and that recovery without dealing with these problems lacked worth, made it hard to see that the crisis was over, although in economic terms it was when growth returned in late 2009. The fact that crisis was initiated by a trade shock did not work in favour of the government, therefore, and it was unable to take credit for economic success. Peplinsky's (2012, p. 136) argument that trade shocks have been less damaging than domestic financial crises because governments can 'portray themselves as innocent victims', and so avoid governmental change, is therefore not totally true of Russia.

The contexts in which a government tries to portray itself as a victim can be important too. When crisis is deepened by a preceding boom, when it looks to be part of a longer cycle of crisis, and when what needs to be done to escape crisis is defined broadly and independently of dealing with immediate economic problems, a government runs the risk of making itself and its response look inadequate, even if it was not fully to blame for crisis in the first place. This has been the case in Russia. Perceptions of an inadequate response to crisis did not lead to regime change, although there was government change of a sort. The change was the return of Putin, who had to deal with the notion, more widespread thanks to his predecessor, that economic change requires political change. How he deals with this and his success will determine how long the effects of the 2008 crisis will continue to reverberate through Russia.

University of Limerick

References

Aganbegyan, A. (2010) 'Uroki krizisa: Rossii nuzhna modernizatsiya i innovatsionnaya ekonomika', *EKO (Ekonomika i organizatsiya)—vserossiiskii ekonomicheskii zhurnal*, 1, pp. 34–61, available at: http://goo.gl/iWQvk, accessed 20 January 2012.
Ahrend, R. (2006) 'Russia's Post-Crisis Growth: Its Sources and Prospects for Continuation', *Europe-Asia Studies*, 58, 1, pp. 1–24.

TRANSITION ECONOMIES AFTER 2008

Akindova, N., Alekashenko, S. & Yasin, E. (2011) 'Scenarios and Challenges of Macroeconomic Policy', *Report at XII International Conference on Economic and Social Development, Moscow, April 5–7 2011* (Moscow, HSE Publishing House).

Aris, B. (2011) 'Crisis Watch: We are Getting Closer', *Moscow Times*, 4 October, available at: http://goo.gl/k434F, accessed 5 October 2011.

Babkin, K. (2009) *Razumnaya promyshlennaya politika. Ili kak nam vyiti iz krizisa* (Moscow, Mann, Ivanov i Ferber).

Bernhard, M., Reenock, C. & Nordstrom, T. (2003) 'Economic Performance and Survival in New Democracies', *Comparative Political Studies*, 36, 4, pp. 404–31.

Blanchard, O., Mitali, D. & Faruqee, H. (2010) 'The Initial Impact of the Crisis on Emerging Market Countries', *Brookings Papers on Economic Activity*, 1, pp. 263–307.

Chaisty, P. & Whitefield, S. (2012) 'The Effects of the Global Financial Crisis on Russian Political Attitudes', *Post-Soviet Affairs*, 28, 2, pp. 187–208.

Connolly, R. (2009) 'Financial Vulnerabilities in Russia', *Russian Analytical Digest*, 65, pp. 2–5, available at: http://www.css.ethz.ch/publications/pdfs/RAD-65.pdf, accessed 12 February 2010.

Connolly, R. (2012) 'The Determinants of the Economic Crisis in Post-Socialist Europe', *Europe-Asia Studies*, 64, 1, pp. 35–67.

Cooper, J. (2006a) 'Of BRICS and Brains: Comparing Russia, China, India and other Populous Emerging Economies', *Eurasian Geography and Economics*, 47, 3, pp. 255–84.

Cooper, J. (2006b) 'Can Russia Compete in the Global Economy?', *Eurasian Geography and Economics*, 47, 4, pp. 407–26.

Cooper, J. (2011) 'Russia and the Global Economic Crisis', in Wilhelmsen, J. & Wilson Rowe, E. (eds) (2011) *Russia's Encounter with Globalization. Actors, Processes and Critical Moments* (Basingstoke, Palgrave-Macmillan).

Desai, P. (2010) 'Russia's Financial Crisis: Economic Setbacks and Policy Responses', *Journal of International Affairs*, 63, 2, pp. 141–51.

Diskin, I. (2009) *Krizis … i vse zhe modernizatsiya* (Moscow, Evropa).

Dmitrieva, O. (2006) 'Formirovanie stabilizatsionnikh fondov: predposylki i sledstviya', *Voprosy ekonomiki*, 8, pp. 17–30.

EEG (2008) *Obzor ekonomicheskikh pokazatelei 13 fevralya 2008 goda*, 2 (Moscow, Expert Economic Group).

EEG (2010) *Obzor ekonomicheskikh pokazatelei 9 fevralya 2010 goda*, 2 (Moscow, Expert Economic Group).

EEG (2012) *Obzor ekonomicheskikh pokazatelei 13 fevralya 2012 goda*, 2 (Moscow, Expert Economic Group).

Feklyunina, V. & White, S. (2011) 'Discourses of "Krizis": Economic Crisis in Russia and Regime Legitimacy', *Journal of Communist Studies and Transition Politics*, 27, 3–4, pp. 385–406.

Gaddy, C. & Ickes, B. (2005) 'Resource Rents and the Russian Economy', *Eurasian Geography and Economics*, 45, 8, pp. 559–83.

Gaddy, C. & Ickes, B. (2010) 'Russia after the Global Financial Crisis', *Eurasian Geography and Economics*, 51, 3, pp. 281–311.

Garanina, O. (2009) 'What Beyond Oil and Gas? Russian Trade Specialisation in Manufactures', *Post-Communist Economies*, 21, 1, pp. 1–29.

Gasiorowski, M. (1995) 'Economic Crisis and Political Regime Change: An Event-History Analysis', *American Political Science Review*, 89, 4, pp. 882–97.

Golos (2012) 'Association GOLOS—Domestic Monitoring of Elections of the President of Russian Federation, 4 March 2012: Preliminary Report', *Russian Analytical Digest*, 110, pp. 8–16, available at: http://www.css.ethz.ch/publications/pdfs/RAD-110.pdf, accessed 4 May 2010.

Gurvich, E. (2006) 'Formirovanie i ispol'zovanie stabilizatsionnogo fonda', *Vorposy ekonomiki*, 4, pp. 31–55.

Gurvich, E., Lebedinskaya, E., Simachev, Y. & Yakovlev, A. (2010) *Russia Country Report* (Gutersloh, Bertelsmann Stiftung).

Gurvich, E., Vakulenko, E. & Krivenko, P. (2009) 'Tsiklicheskie svoistva budzhetnoi politiki v neftedobyvayushchikh stranakh', *Voprosy ekonomiki*, 2, pp. 51–70.

GU-VES (Gosudarstvenii universitet–Vyshaya shkola ekonomiki), Mezhvedomstvenii analiticheskii tsentr (MATs) (2009) 'Otsenka antikrizisnikh mer po podderzhke real'nogo sektora rossiiskoi ekonomiki', *Voprosy ekonomiki*, 5, pp. 21–46.

Haggard, S. & Kaufman, R. (1995) *The Political Economy of Democratic Transitions* (Princeton, NJ, Princeton University Press).

Hanson, P. (2007) 'The Russian Economic Puzzle: Going Forwards, Backwards or Sideways?', *International Affairs*, 83, 5, pp. 869–89.

TRANSITION ECONOMIES AFTER 2008

Hanson, P. (2011) 'Russia: Crisis, Exit and ... Reform?', *Journal of Communist Studies and Transition Politics*, 27, 3–4, pp. 456–75.

IEPP (2010) *Krizisnaya ekonomika sovremennoi Rossii* (Moscow, Institut ekonomiki perekhodnogo perioda).

IMF (2011) 'Russian Federation. 2011 Article IV Consultation', *IMF Country Report* 11/294 (Washington, DC, International Monetary Fund), available at: http://www.imf.org/external/pubs/ft/scr/2011/cr11294.pdf, accessed 15 January 2013.

INSOR (2010) *Rossiya XXI veka: obraz zhelaemogo zavtra* (Moscow, Institut sovremennogo razvitiya).

INSOR (2011) *Obretenie budushchego. Strategiya 2012* (Moscow, Institut sovremennogo razvitiya).

Kiewiet, D. R. & Lewis-Beck, M. S. (2011) 'No Man is an Island: Self-interest, the Public Interest, and Sociotropic Voting', *Critical Review*, 23, 3, pp. 303–19.

Kinder, D. R. & Kiewiet, D. R. (1981) 'Sociotropic Politics: The American Case', *British Journal of Political Science*, 11, 2, pp. 129–66.

Kudrin, A. (2006) 'Stabilizatsionnii fond: zarubezhnii i rossiiskii opyt', *Voprosy ekonomiki*, 2, pp. 8–45.

Kudrin, A. (2009) 'Mirovoi finansovii krizis i ego vliyanie na Rossiyu', *Voprosy ekonomiki*, 1, pp. 9–27.

Lane, D. (2011) 'The Impact of Economic Crisis: Russia, Belarus and Ukraine in Comparative Perspective', *Journal of Communist Studies and Transition Politics*, 27, 3–4, pp. 587–604.

Leskin, V. (2009) 'Rossiya do, vo vremya i posle global'nogo krizisa', *Rossiiskii ekonomicheskii zhurnal*, 3–8, pp. 3–34.

Levada Centre (2012) 'Rossiyane o svoem nastroenii i material'nom polozhenii, ekonomicheskoi i politicheskoi obstanovke v strane, krizise', available at: http://goo.gl/XbtV4, accessed 19 June 2012.

Makarenko, B. (2008) 'Vozmozhna li v Rossii modernizatsiya?', *Pro et Contra*, 12, 5–6, pp. 33–47.

Malle, S. (2009) *The Impact of the Financial Crisis on Russia* (Rome, NATO Defense College).

Maudlin, W. (2008) 'Russia Providing $200 Billion for Banks, Builders (Update 1)', *Bloomberg.com*, available at: http://goo.gl/0gm0B, accessed 17 December 2011.

McAllister, I. & White, S. (2008) '"It's the Economy, Comrade!" Parties and Voters in the 2007 Russian *Duma* Election', *Europe-Asia Studies*, 60, 6, pp. 931–57.

McAllister, I. & White, S. (2011) 'Democratization in Russia and the Global Financial Crisis', *Journal of Communist Studies and Transition Politics*, 27, 3–4, pp. 476–95.

Medvedev, D. (2008) 'Address to the Federal Assembly of the Russian Federation, November 5 2008', available at: http://goo.gl/6F9Bk, accessed 2 February 2012.

Medvedev, D. (2009a) '"Interview with *Kommersant*", 4 June 2009', available at: http://goo.gl/d4ziQ, accessed 13 December 2011.

Medvedev, D. (2009b) 'Rossiya, vpered!', available at: http://kremlin.ru/news/5413, accessed 13 December 2011.

Medvedev, D. (2009c) 'Speech at Council of Legislators. 28 December, 2009, Federation Council', available at: http://goo.gl/IeQbY, accessed 13 December 2011.

Medvedev, D. (2010) 'Nasha demokratiya nesovershenna, my eto prekrasno ponimaem. Zapis' v bloge Dmitriya Medvedeva posvyashchena razvitiyu Rossiiskoi politicheskoi sistemy', available at: http://kremlin.ru/news/9599, accessed 24 February 2011.

MinFin (2011) *Osnovnie napravelniya gosudarstvennoi dolgovoi politiki Rossiiskoi Federatsii na 2012–2014gg* (Moscow, Ministerstvo finansov Rossiiskoi Federatsii).

Myant, M. & Drahokoupil, J. (2012) 'International Integration, Varieties of Capitalism and Resilience to Crisis in Transition Economies', *Europe-Asia Studies*, 64, 1, pp. 1–33.

Nemtsov, B. (2009) 'Bankrotim oligarkhov—spasaem Rossiyu', *Yezhednevnii zhurnal*, 18 February, available at: http://www.ej.ru/?a=note&id=8825, accessed 12 December 2011.

Nemtsov, B. & Milov, V. (2009) 'Putin i krizis', available at: http://goo.gl/i5cQP, accessed 12 December 2011.

OECD (2009) *Russian Federation* (Paris, Organization for Economic Co-operation and Development).

OECD (2011a) 'Main Economic Indicators—Complete Database', available at: http://dx.doi.org/10.1787/data-00052-en, accessed 29 January 2012.

OECD (2011b) *Russian Federation* (Paris, Organization for Economic Co-operation and Development).

Peplinsky, T. (2012) 'The Global Economic Crisis and the Politics of Non-Transitions', *Government and Opposition*, 47, 2, pp. 135–47.

Robinson, N. (2007) 'So What Changed? The 1998 Economic Crisis in Russia and Russia's Economic and Political Development', *Demokratizatsiya*, 15, 2, pp. 245–59.

Robinson, N. (2009) 'August 1998 and the Development of Russia's Post-Communist Political Economy', *Review of International Political Economy*, 16, 3, pp. 433–55.

Robinson, N. (2011) 'Russian Patrimonial Capitalism and the International Financial Crisis', *Journal of Communist Studies and Transition Politics*, 27, 3–4, pp. 434–55.

Rose, R., Mishler, W. & Munro, N. (2011) *Popular Support for an Undemocratic Regime. The Changing Views of Russians* (Cambridge, Cambridge University Press).

Rosstat (2010) *Rossiya v tsifrakh* (Moscow, Federal'naya Sluzhba Gosudastvennoi Statistiki).

Rosstat (2011a) 'Economically Active Population', available at: http://goo.gl/ftkiR, accessed 26 February 2012.

Rosstat (2011b) 'Zanyatost' i bezrabotitsa', available at: http://goo.gl/FMvWF, accessed 26 February 2012.

Russian Government (2009a) 'Background Material for the March 19, 2009 Government Meeting', available at: http://government.ru/eng/docs/812/, accessed 24 March 2009.

Russian Government (2009b) 'Programma antikrizisnikh mer Pravitel'stva Rossiiskoi Federatsii na 2009 god', available at: http://premier.gov.ru/anticrisis/1.html, accessed 18 November 2010.

Russian Government (2009c) 'Pervoocherednie mery Pravitel'stva Rosii. Osnovniye napravelniya antikrisisnikh deistvii Pravitel'stva Rossiiskoi Federatsii na 2010 god', available at: http://premier.gov.ru/anticrisis/3html, accessed 18 November 2010.

Rutland, P. (2008) 'Putin's Economic Record: Is the Oil Boom Sustainable?', *Europe-Asia Studies*, 60, 6, pp. 1051–72.

Ryabov, A. (2009) 'Predely adaptsii', available at: http://www.gazeta.ru/column/ryabov/2955752.shtml, accessed 1 February 2012.

Serafin, T. (2009) 'Russia's Billionaire Drop-Offs', *Forbes.com*, available at: http://goo.gl/su8Me, accessed 17 December 2011.

Smith, B. (2004) 'Oil Wealth and Regime Survival in the Developing World, 1960–1999', *American Journal of Political Science*, 48, 2, pp. 232–46.

Teague, E. (2011) 'How did the Russian Population Respond to the Crisis?', *Journal of Communist Studies and Transition Politics*, 27, 3–4, pp. 420–33.

Treisman, D. (2011) 'Presidential Popularity in a Hybrid Regime: Russia under Yeltsin and Putin', *American Journal of Political Science*, 55, 3, pp. 590–609.

Tucker, J. (2006) *Regional Economic Voting: Russia, Poland, Hungary, Slovakia and the Czech Republic, 1990–1999* (Cambridge, Cambridge University Press).

Vavilov, A. (2010) *The Russian Public Debt and Financial Meltdowns* (Basingstoke, Palgrave).

Vlasov, S. (2011) 'Russian Fiscal Framework: Past, Present and Future. Do We Need a Change?', *BOFIT Online*, 5, available at: http://goo.gl/DomIA, accessed 5 January 2012.

World Bank (2010) *Russian Economic Report 22* (Moscow, World Bank).

Belarus' Anti-Crisis Management: Success Story of Delayed Recession?

DZMITRY KRUK

Abstract

The response of Belarus to the global economic crisis was shaped by a number of distinctive features of the Belarusian economy and of the economic policies implemented before the crisis. The specifics of anti-crisis management in Belarus resulted in a distribution of output losses for a number of subsequent periods and delayed recession. The scenario of stabilisation policies in Belarus can therefore be regarded as ineffective. The core reasons for this are an inappropriate choice of policy instruments and delayed exit from stabilisation policy. It is argued that this policy mix has long-term implications, including worsening economic growth prospects.

THE GLOBAL FINANCIAL CRISIS AFFECTED THE MAJORITY OF Central and East European countries rather similarly (Myant & Drahokoupil 2012). In the early stage—the second half of 2008 and 2009—the crisis was transmitted to this region through financial and trade linkages, resulting in severe GDP declines. In 2010–2011, the majority of Central and East European countries entered a recovery stage and restored output growth. The dynamics of output in Belarus were different. In 2009, real GDP grew by 0.2%, making Belarus the second country in the region, along with Poland, with positive output growth. In 2010 Belarus achieved GDP growth of 7.7%. Such dynamics appear puzzling given the reduction of export revenues and lower demand from major trading partners. However, given this unfavourable external environment, the Belarusian authorities resorted to a policy of stimulating domestic demand so as to maintain growth.

It has to be stressed that the government had a wider range of policy instruments at its disposal than other Central and East European countries. This is related to the unreformed nature of the Belarusian economy, characterised by substantial state ownership which makes direct intervention in the economy by the government the dominant mode of economic policy making. The authorities can guide the investment behaviour of economic agents, thus directly affecting domestic demand. Indeed, policy in the 2009–2010 period aimed to a

I would like to express my gratitude to M. Myant, J. Drahokoupil, K. Haiduk and the anonymous referees for their valuable comments and suggestions.

large extent at domestic demand stimulation in the specific context of state ownership of the majority of assets in the economy.

However, the policy of demand stimulation has its limits. It is considered reasonable in almost all theoretical approaches when actual output is lower than potential output. When this is not the case, stimulation of domestic demand can lead to accelerating inflation and through that, it is frequently argued, to a new economic downturn. Under such circumstances a policy of demand stimulation may cause deep and frequent macroeconomic fluctuations, rather than a smooth growth path around the potential level of output. Stabilisation policy should therefore be implemented with caution and a timely exit is required. However, in practice policy makers may face difficulties in identifying the type of output shock—whether it changes the shape of cyclical fluctuations, shifts the potential output level and/or its growth rate, or affects both—and correspondingly in choosing the appropriate policy.

Alongside the issue of the duration of stabilisation policy is the issue of selection of the policy type and of the precise instruments. Stabilisation policy may be based on monetary or fiscal measures but their outcomes generally differ. In the two decades before the crisis, there was a consensus towards expecting greater effectiveness from monetary policy as a countercyclical tool. In particular, it was widely argued that monetary policy aimed at stable inflation would also lead to equality between actual and potential output (Blanchard *et al.* 2010). This means that during a downturn or a slowdown, monetary policy can move output closer to its potential level, while having little effect on prices. In contrast, fiscal policy is subject to the so-called Ricardian equivalence, meaning that fiscal expansion is alternated with fiscal restriction maintaining a balanced budget in the long term, which might restrict its effectiveness as a countercyclical tool (Blanchard *et al.* 2010).

Moreover, the selection of policy tools within each policy type matters, as the nature of shocks affecting the economy may differ. In 2008, the majority of Central and East European countries faced shocks from external demand and several countries, including Belarus, operated exchange-rate pegs that limited scope for devaluation. However, domestic demand policies alone could not be adequate for combating external demand shocks. We can therefore argue that untimely exit from stabilisation policies or inappropriate choice of the type of policy or its instruments may delay the current recession or cause a new one. In the medium term, this effect may be treated as an inter-temporal redistribution of output losses. In the long term, there are a number of factors that can cause an adverse impact of stabilisation policy on economic growth (Kruk 2010a). The emergence of these factors is related to the accumulation of distortions in the course of stabilisation policy implementation. First, stabilisation policy may result in an increased level of public and external debt. If the latter reaches a certain critical level, debt can become a barrier to long-term growth (Reinhart & Rogoff 2010). Second, interventions by the government on the financial market may lower credit discipline and spread moral hazard.

The brief theoretical discussion above points to the hypothesis that anti-crisis macroeconomic management in Belarus from 2008 to the first half of 2011 could be considered as an inter-temporal redistribution of output losses. In particular, the cyclical expansion of 2010 was followed by downturn and then slowdown in 2011, as discussed below and shown in Figure 1. In contrast, economies of other Central and East European countries displayed a different dynamic: they recovered earlier in a more stable way, attaining positive growth in 2011.

In this essay we concentrate on the specific nature and characteristics of Belarusian anti-crisis macroeconomic management and its effectiveness in terms of its impact on the

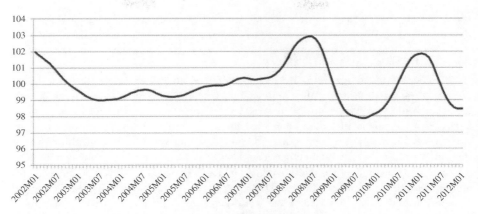

FIGURE 1. CYCLICAL COMPONENT OF GDP.

Note: These data are derived from monthly figures, following the method used by the OECD to smooth out irregularities and show trends more clearly. The data are derived from double usage of the Hodrick–Prescott filter for real GDP data with lambda 133108 (for the 10-year cycle) and 13.9 (for the one-year cycle). The double Hodrick–Prescott filter assumes that the cyclical component corresponding to a one-year cycle is used for smoothing the cyclical component corresponding to a 10-year cycle. The figure therefore shows the difference between a 10-year cyclical component and a one-year cyclical component. For an explanation of the advantages of the method, see http://www.oecd.org/std/ compositeleadingindicatorsclifrequentlyaskedquestionsfaqs.htm, accessed 15 August 2012.

Source: Author's own computations based on the data by Belarusian Statistical Committee (Belstat 2012).

business cycle. This effectiveness is measured by the degree and sustainability of smoothing of fluctuations and the impact on long-term growth. The next section covers the performance of the Belarusian economy during the crisis. The following section describes the anti-crisis macroeconomic policy agenda and its impact on further developments. A separate section focuses on the key economic policy tool, directed lending (using the term as in Stiglitz *et al.* (1993)), the use of which became more prominent during the crisis, and analyses its impact on long-term growth.

Peculiarities of the impact of the global crisis on the Belarusian economy

The Belarusian economy is often treated as a small open economy. Rapid growth of capital mobility and development of financial markets in recent decades left open economies exposed not only to trade flows, but also to movements of capital. Moreover, transition economies facilitated the inflow of foreign capital—in the form of foreign loans and Foreign Direct Investment (FDI)—through improvements in their domestic investment climates and provision of other 'sweeteners' for foreign investors. This increased their vulnerability to financial market shocks. During the 2003–2008 period the Belarusian growth model was based on domestic demand stimulation. The cornerstone of monetary policy was a currency peg, maintained despite a mounting current account deficit from 2006 onwards. As a result, the currency remained overvalued (Kruk *et al.* 2011). This peg was held thanks to substantial revenues from exports of oil products: the price of crude oil imports from Russia was much lower than the world market price, while Belarus processed this cheap oil into products sold at world market prices. Cheaper natural gas also contributed to the stability of the currency peg. When faced with a deterioration in external imbalances, the government took various emergency steps to maintain the currency peg, notably privatisations providing inflows on the financial account.

The mode of integration of the Belarusian economy into the world economy was rather different from that of the majority of post-socialist countries. In particular, FDI remained at a low level, while borrowing by the financial and non-financial sectors was rather modest. Both banks and non-financial institutions borrowed abroad only after 2006 and the volume of gross external debt in 2009 was rather modest, still not exceeding 30% of GDP, and almost half of this debt was in short-term commercial loans (NBB 2011). Sovereign borrowing in Belarus was mainly based on bilateral intergovernmental loans provided at negotiated interest rates and on special terms and conditions. Therefore, at the onset of the crisis, the Belarusian economy was weakly connected to the world economy, with foreign trade as the major channel for the transmission of the effects of the crisis onto the domestic economy.

The global financial crisis affected the state of foreign trade with a lag. Moreover, over the period from March to August 2008, soaring world prices of natural resources resulted in an increase of export revenues from oil products and potassium fertilisers. As a result, the government regarded the external shock as a short-term problem only and not as a serious threat to future growth. In the second half of 2008 the government therefore saw no need to make any changes in economic policy.

However, in the fourth quarter of 2008, foreign trade felt its first serious shock. First, demand in Russia—previously the major outlet for exports of capital goods—declined. Second, prices of natural resources began to fall. Third, several key trading partners, including Russia, Poland and Ukraine, saw currency depreciations in the third quarter of 2008, potentially improving their competitiveness levels, while Belarus still kept the exchange-rate peg to the US dollar. The Belarusian ruble also appreciated against the euro which, in turn, was depreciating against the US dollar. Price competitiveness in relation to the EU—the country's second most important trading partner—was therefore also deteriorating. The real effective exchange rate of the Belarusian ruble appreciated between July and December 2008 by roughly 23%.

Thus, in the second half of 2008, export revenues began falling as exporters had to grapple with dwindling demand for their products. However, the demand for imports did not adjust in line with this as importers had continued to increase output to meet economic growth targets communicated to them by the government. Disproportions between production costs, output volumes and finished product sales led to a massive growth in inventories, including both finished products and raw materials. Moreover, many enterprises maintained demand levels for foreign currency to buy imported inputs, although they were no longer exporting. The situation deteriorated further because of the difficulty of refinancing existing loans. As a result, in the second half of 2008, the net demand for foreign currency took a sharp upward turn, putting serious pressure on the exchange-rate peg.

Transmission of the crisis through trade channels was supplemented by transmission through informational ones, namely through propagating information asymmetry and uncertainty to other sectors of the economy (Kruk *et al.* 2009). Negative expectations caused an increase in the demand for foreign currency. Thus, both currency substitution—meaning the demand for hard currency (Feige & Dean 2002)—and financial dollarisation—meaning conversion into dollars of both deposits and loans (Ize & Parrado 2006)—increased. Traditionally, the high level of financial dollarisation in Belarus was mainly a consequence

TRANSITION ECONOMIES AFTER 2008

of a weak monetary policy that lacked credibility and generated fears that the currency would soon be floating (Kruk 2010b).[1]

The information effect—along with pessimistic expectations from economic agents—became a trigger both for the domestic currency market and for the credit and deposit markets, thereby transmitting negative impulses to financial intermediaries. Under these conditions of uncertainty and information asymmetry, banks could be expected to restrict credit and raise interest rates in order to offset newly detected risk factors. Furthermore, it could be expected that increasing financial dollarisation from the banks' liability side would at least partially turn into dollarisation on the asset side (Ize 2005; Ize & Yeyati 2003), as banks sought to reduce their currency risk by shifting the burden onto borrowers. However, this crisis transmission channel—through financial intermediation—also had significant peculiarities in Belarus, deriving from specific features of the banking system.

The banking system is the dominant segment of the financial system in Belarus, as the stock market is underdeveloped. One of the key features of this banking system—which makes it very distinct from other Central and East European countries—is the high share of state ownership. The state is the major shareholder in the two largest banks—Belarusbank and Belagroprombank—whose share in total assets and capital of the banking system is around 70%. This pattern of ownership creates scope for the use of additional policy instruments, supplementing the traditional tools of monetary policy, as government can directly shape the credit policy of commercial banks.

As shown in Table 1, instead of credit restrictions and credit rationing, the banking system as a whole increased its credit exposures. As shown in Table 2, instead of balancing the currency risks related to the rising share of foreign currency deposits, the majority of banks accumulated additional currency risks by granting new loans, largely in the national currency. Accumulation of credit and currency risks for the whole system was driven by state-owned banks, while private and foreign banks behaved in a more standard manner.

These specific features of the financial system delayed the onset of the crisis in Belarus. The government took no action in the face of changes in the external environment and postponed the introduction of anti-crisis policies until the beginning of 2009. It therefore took almost no steps against the growing external deficit, financial dollarisation and currency substitution. The rapidly growing demand for hard currency and the reduction of international reserves put severe pressure on the exchange-rate peg. The net demand for foreign currency was met by a reduction in the volume of international reserves, which meant automatic contraction of the money supply by the National Bank, as selling hard currency for national currency by a central bank results in a reduction in the volume of national currency in circulation. To absorb money supply contraction the authorities could have sterilised interventions by increasing money, for example, by the purchase of government bonds. However, this would have led to additional pressure on the exchange-rate peg. The implications of non-sterilisation would have been a liquidity shock for banks, which could have been transmitted to the real sector rather rapidly. In this situation, the National Bank chose a kind of compromise between the extremes, facing both problems, but trying to limit their scope.

[1]The problem of dollarisation has been deeply-rooted in Belarus from the mid-1990s. There was a declining trend for financial dollarisation in the 2002–2006 period. Later it stabilised and the fluctuations in 2007–2008 were limited, but during the financial crisis, and especially after the devaluation of the national currency at the beginning of 2009, it jumped and the deposit dollarisation ratio exceeded 50%.

TRANSITION ECONOMIES AFTER 2008

TABLE 1

CONTRIBUTION OF BANK GROUPS (BY TYPE OF OWNERSHIP AND SIZE) TO THE QUARTERLY %AGE GROWTH OF ASSETS EXPOSED TO CREDIT RISK

	Q3 2008	Q4 2008	Q1 2009	Q2 2009	Q3 2009	Q4 2009
Increase of assets exposed to credit risk	**15.5**	**8.5**	**10.5**	**7.9**	**5.9**	**8.5**
State-owned banks	10.6	8.5	8.4	6.8	6.7	0.9
Foreign banks	4.6	0.0	2.2	0.9	−0.8	43.8
Private banks	0.3	0.1	−0.1	0.2	−0.1	−13.7
Large banks	13.0	7.1	8.8	6.7	5.6	8.7
Mid-sized banks	1.7	1.0	1.5	0.7	−0.1	14.5
Small banks	0.8	0.4	0.2	0.5	0.3	−8.2

Note: Assets exposed to credit risk refers to the sum of assets that could lead to banks' losses because of non-fulfilment or under-fulfilment of obligations by the borrower.
Source: Author's own computations based on the data by the National Bank of the Republic of Belarus (NBB 2010).

Stabilisation policy agenda and its outcomes

Pressure on the exchange-rate peg pushed the government into seeking an IMF stand-by arrangement (SBA) which affected the economy in two ways. On the one hand, it was a stabilising factor, as the loans were used to increase international reserves and to reduce demand for foreign currency from households. The SBA also increased trust in the currency. On the other hand, the SBA required policy conditionality and limited the scope for macroeconomic policy autonomy. The commitments of the government under the SBA amounted to a stabilisation policy agenda for Belarus.

The main measures accepted by the government were: first, a single-step devaluation of the Belarusian ruble by 20.5% against the US dollar in January 2009, which resulted in the nominal effective exchange-rate devaluation of 12.5%; second, greater exchange-rate flexibility by changing the currency peg base from the US dollar to a basket of currencies (US dollar, euro, Russian ruble) with a wider band of fluctuation of up to 5%, later to be widened to 10%; third, improved fiscal stability through the commitment of the government to targeting a balanced central-government budget; fourth, freezing capital expenditures by the government, which was aimed at securing fiscal stability; fifth, increases in utility tariffs by roughly 15%; sixth, wage policy restrictions, which were aimed both at promoting fiscal stability and at enhancing more price competitiveness for exporters by holding down unit labour costs; and seventh, a ban on transfers of funds by central and local governments to their deposit accounts at state-owned banks, as these funds were the core source for the directed lending that had become an important tool of investment demand stimulation.

There were also a number of commitments to implement structural reforms. For instance, the government promised to privatise partially the two largest banks, to weaken direct price regulation, to spur privatisation—and for this purpose to establish a new Privatisation Agency—to restrict the scope for directed lending and to establish the Special Financial Agency for managing outstanding directed loans and for granting new ones. From the IMF's point of view, the SBA programme agenda was an attempt to solve short-term problems through managed macroeconomic adjustment to be followed by structural reforms (IMF 2009). As far as the Belarusian authorities were concerned, the policy measures under the SBA were probably perceived as an outside intervention tolerated under the threat to the

TABLE 2

ACCUMULATION OF CURRENCY RISKS BY BANKS

	Foreign currency component of outstanding loans, %		Borrowed funds in foreign currency, %		Net currency position, % of regulatory capital	
	1 October 2008	1 October 2009	1 October 2008	1 October 2009	1 October 2008	1 October 2009
State-owned banks	27.9	24.2	30.8	38.4	− 1.4	− 26.3
Foreign banks	68.2	68.3	49.5	68.1	2.7	17.4
Private banks	37.4	49.4	26.4	69.1	5.0	8.4
Large banks	31.1	27.2	31.8	40.0	− 1.3	− 21.6
Mid-sized banks	74.9	71.1	52.1	68.2	3.8	8.0
Small banks	47.9	50.8	44.7	71.4	2.4	9.2
Total	**36.0**	**31.7**	**33.9**	**43.8**	**− 0.2**	**− 15.3**

Notes: Foreign currency component—the share of loans/borrowed funds, where the sum of the contracted is nominated in foreign currency. Net currency position—the biggest value of a net long or short currency position. Currency position—the difference between assets and liabilities in a foreign currency. If the assets are greater/less than liabilities, the position is long/short. Net long (short) position—the sum of long (short) position in individual currencies for all currencies.
Source: National Bank of the Republic of Belarus (NBB 2010).

currency peg, which was seen as an essential element of the growth model. They remained unwilling to change from the model of the 2003–2008 period, while formally meeting the majority of commitments on short-term target indicators, and the government in some cases tried to find other instruments to compensate for the adverse impact on domestic demand.

The devaluation of early 2009 relieved the pressure on the currency market. Nevertheless, this devaluation was mainly compensatory, restoring competitiveness following depreciation of the currencies of the country's main trading partners during the second half of 2008. However, nominal devaluation of 20.5% against the US dollar, and by 12.5% in nominal effective exchange-rate terms, amounted to only a moderate real effective exchange-rate devaluation and the real effective exchange rate was still noticeably higher than in the first half of 2008. Its pre-crisis level was reached only in the second half of 2009, following increased flexibility under a modernised peg and a wider band of 10%. Thus, until 2011, the real effective exchange rate remained significantly overvalued against its equilibrium level (Kruk *et al.* 2011).

The authorities had no intention of encouraging a shift towards a higher level of exports. Domestic demand stimulation remained the core of their conception of GDP growth. The relatively modest devaluation during that period was associated with the need to establish a new and more credible peg, rather than with changing the incentives for economic agents. There were a number of policy commitments, implying the conservative fiscal and monetary policy favoured by the IMF. However, to avoid recession and maintain GDP growth rate, the government chose a strategy of formal compliance with the IMF's requirements, but a *de facto* continuation of the stimulation of domestic demand that actually contradicted the principles of the SBA.

During 2009, the government provided a number of fiscal and monetary incentives. However, commitment to the balanced budget pointed to monetary expansion as the primary policy tool. Thus, the SBA imposed restrictions on directed lending by limiting the government's deposits at commercial banks, the core source for directed loans before, and the government respected this restriction. At the same time, it substituted budget funds placed as deposits in banks by additional refinancing of banks by the National Bank of Belarus (NBB) which maintained the volume of directed loans in the economy. The share of the NBB's funds in banks' liabilities more than doubled during 2009, rising from 5.1% at the beginning of the year to 10.2% by the end of the year (NBB 2011). The banks then had to pass these funds on to the borrowers—typically at low interest rates—to promote capital investment.

Capital investment, as a rule, is the most sensitive to external shocks among the components of domestic demand and therefore tends to be volatile. In Belarus, capital investment dynamics were at first sight strange. Rather than adjusting downwards to the global recession, investment continued to grow in volume, an outcome that was mainly attributable to government intervention as bank loans became the driver of investment growth in 2009, as shown in Table 3.

This provided the government with an opportunity to boost a range of sectors, especially construction. Capital investment became the key source of economic growth in the crisis year. Besides new incentives, the government actively used administrative interventions. For example, large state-owned enterprises were required to fulfil investment targets set by the bureaucrats in the pre-crisis years and targets for output growth for state-owned enterprises remained an important policy measure in late 2008 and in the first half of 2009.

TRANSITION ECONOMIES AFTER 2008

TABLE 3
CONTRIBUTION TO CAPITAL INVESTMENTS GROWTH BY SOURCES OF FUNDING

	% of annual growth			Contribution of funding sources to growth, %		
	2008	2009	% change	2008	2009	Difference
Fixed capital investments	**23.5**	**4.7**	**− 18.8**	**23.5**	**4.7**	**− 18.8**
State budget	23.2	− 10.6	− 33.8	6.2	− 2.8	− 8.9
Enterprise equity	20.5	− 0.2	− 20.7	8.4	− 0.1	− 8.5
Third party borrowings	34.5	− 30.0	− 64.5	0.3	− 0.3	− 0.6
Foreign borrowings (excluding bank loans)	105.1	25.7	− 79.4	0.9	0.4	− 0.5
Bank loans	31.0	29.4	− 1.6	6.1	6.1	0.0
Loans from foreign banks	*− 43.7*	*2.8*	*46.5*	*− 0.6*	*0.0*	*0.6*
Loans from local banks	*38.1*	*30.5*	*− 7.6*	*6.3*	*5.7*	*− 0.7*
Personal savings	13.8	20.5	6.7	1.2	1.5	0.4
Extrabudgetary funds	− 22.6	− 9.0	13.6	− 0.1	0.0	0.1
Other sources	14.1	− 1.9	− 16.0	0.5	− 0.1	− 0.5

Source: Author's own computations based on data by Belarusian Statistical Committee (Belstat 2011).

For some enterprises, fulfilment of these targets implied significant losses, but the state compensated for this by linking administrative targets and monetary incentives. The need to fulfil these administrative targets was also an important cause of the build-up of inventories.

Given this emphasis on domestic demand stimulation, government policies towards household incomes were sending mixed signals. On the one hand, the government was obliged to implement fiscal restrictions and constrain wage growth in order to contain the demand for imports. These policies had been agreed with the IMF, stipulated in the signed memorandum of understanding with the Fund, and were expected to reduce pressure on the Belarusian currency market. On the other hand, Belarusian enterprises were forced by the government to respect pre-crisis targets for wage increases. Many enterprises did so, but at the cost of reduced competitiveness. At the macro-level, this led to increases in unit labour costs during the crisis years.

The reduction in real wages was very modest—0.4% annually—during the crisis years. However, real household incomes—including natural incomes, current transfers and property incomes—increased by 2.9% annually (Belstat 2011). This indicated rather weak adjustment in household consumption behaviour. The share of household consumer expenditure in GDP decreased only moderately, and this downward trend was not consistent throughout the recession period. For example, there was a spike in household propensity to consume in the third quarter of 2008, accompanied by a similar decline in the propensity to save. These dynamics were most likely linked to changes in consumer expectations and the accumulated imbalances in the finance sector. Household savings and consumption dynamics in 2009 show no clear adjustment trend. In turn, this produced a relatively favourable dynamic of household consumption relative to GDP.

Overall, in 2009, the major source of GDP growth was the increase in domestic demand. However, the policies of the domestic demand stimulation were weakened somewhat in the second half of 2009. Domestic demand was allowed to adjust to limit the growth of the external deficit. This explains a difference between the first and the second quarter of 2009 in the contributions of individual components to output growth, as shown in Table 4. However, this does not change the overall picture. In 2010, policies of domestic demand stimulation continued, leading to a similar composition of demand components as in the first half of 2009 (see Table 4).

On the one hand, the economic policy mix in Belarus in 2009 and the first half of 2010 was more or less successful, as it limited the depth of the recession and softened the impact of the crisis on households, as indicated in Figure 1. However, on the other hand, it should be emphasised that the economic policy aimed at preventing the recession in 2009 impeded adaptation of the economy that could have helped the country to deal with the accumulated structural imbalances. The foreign trade deficit remained the key problem, leading to increasing structural imbalances, including accumulation of external—mainly public—debt, increasing financial dollarisation, lowering capital productivity and a savings–investment imbalance. Moreover, the excessive efforts to stimulate domestic demand in 2009 and 2010 led to new disproportions, including inflationary pressure and the accumulation of additional risks in the banking system. Signs of overheating of the economy were evident in mid-2010, with pressures for price increases and growing unit labour costs. The government nevertheless remained wedded to its demand-stimulation policies.

The aftermath of the crisis resulted in a worsening position for Belarusian firms in foreign markets. Furthermore, the recession period coincided with a number of unfavourable shocks that were more political than economic in nature. Those included changes in the terms of trade in Russian crude oil and substantial increases in Russian natural gas prices. In sum, the depletion of old growth factors along with the accumulation of new structural imbalances reduced the potential of the Belarusian economy (Kruk 2010a).

These problems remained through 2011, after the policy of active domestic demand stimulation had been applied through the whole of 2010. In early 2011 the authorities failed to maintain the currency peg, as the external deficit grew with increased demand for imports and weak competitiveness of exports. The National Bank lost a substantial share of its international reserves and correspondingly could no longer support the national currency. The exchange rate began moving towards its long-term equilibrium level, pushing up inflation which, in turn, triggered an automatic macroeconomic adjustment by cutting the main macroeconomic indicators in real terms. Thus, short-term distortions, on top of long-term ones, precipitated a huge currency crisis leading to nominal devaluation of roughly 180% during the year, which led in turn to the recession in the real sector shown in Figure 1.

This demonstrates how economic policy, during the acute stages of the crisis, led to an inter-temporal redistribution of output losses, rather than being a case of successful anti-crisis management. However, that does not prove that application of a demand stimulus was necessarily inappropriate in total. It should be borne in mind that the stabilisation policy was carried out against the background of huge, accumulated structural distortions, above all of an overvalued pegged exchange rate which meant that demand stimulation led to external imbalance. It should also be recognised that a shorter period of demand stimulation could have brought positive results while avoiding the negative ones: the Belarusian authorities may have missed the time for exit from expansionary policy. Moreover, it remains difficult to compare the Belarusian experience with that of other countries because of the availability and accessibility of specific tools, notably directed lending, which is discussed in more detail in the next section.

TABLE 4

CONTRIBUTION OF THE DEMAND COMPONENTS TO GDP GROWTH, BY % INCREASE IN COMPONENTS, YEAR-ON-YEAR

| | 2007 | 2008 | 2009 | 2010 | 2011 | 2009 | | | | 2010 | | | |
						Q1	Q2	Q3	Q4	Q1	Q2	Q3	Q4
GDP	**8.6**	**10.2**	**0.2**	**7.6**	**5.3**	**1.1**	**− 0.4**	**− 0.8**	**1.0**	**4.0**	**8.9**	**6.7**	**10.3**
Final consumption expenditure	*7.0*	*9.1*	*0.0*	*6.1*	*2.1*	*2.9*	*− 0.7*	*− 1.7*	*0.0*	*2.8*	*8.0*	*5.0*	*8.1*
Households	7.1	9.1	0.1	5.9	1.9	2.9	− 0.6	− 1.6	0.1	2.6	7.9	4.8	8.2
General government	− 0.1	0.1	0.0	0.1	0.2	0.1	− 0.1	0.0	0.0	0.2	0.1	0.3	0.0
Non-profit institutions serving households	0.0	0.0	− 0.1	0.0	0.0	− 0.1	− 0.1	− 0.1	− 0.1	0.0	0.0	0.0	0.0
Gross capital formation	*5.6*	*10.3*	*− 1.2*	*6.5*	*1.2*	*3.4*	*2.6*	*− 2.7*	*− 6.7*	*− 1.8*	*4.4*	*8.9*	*12.7*
Gross fixed capital formation	5.2	8.1	1.9	6.0	4.3	6.1	6.1	2.7	− 5.9	− 1.1	4.7	6.4	12.5
Changes in inventories	0.4	2.3	− 3.1	0.5	− 3.1	− 2.7	− 3.5	− 5.4	− 0.8	− 0.8	− 0.4	2.5	0.2
Domestic demand	*12.6*	*19.5*	*− 1.2*	*12.6*	*3.3*	*6.3*	*1.9*	*− 4.4*	*− 6.7*	*0.9*	*12.4*	*13.9*	*20.8*
Net exports of goods and services	*− 1.5*	*− 9.4*	*2.1*	*− 4.0*	*3.8*	*− 6.4*	*− 2.8*	*4.6*	*10.4*	*3.6*	*− 2.7*	*− 7.5*	*− 7.4*
Statistical discrepancy	*− 2.5*	*0.2*	*− 0.7*	*− 1.1*	*− 1.8*	*1.1*	*0.5*	*− 1.1*	*− 2.7*	*− 0.5*	*− 0.8*	*0.3*	*− 3.1*

Note: Italics and bold—author's own emphasis.
Source: Author's own computations based on data by Belarusian Statistical Committee (Belstat 2012).

TRANSITION ECONOMIES AFTER 2008

Directed lending as a specific policy tool in Belarus

Directed lending was a distinctive feature of the Belarusian economy through the late 1990s and the 2000s. Before the crisis its role had been declining, giving way to more standard methods of credit allocation. During the crisis it became a core tool of stabilisation policy. It involved provision of a designated volume of loans to selected sectors—mainly agriculture and some branches of industry—and households—for housing construction—at interest rates below the market rate. The government's major objectives were stimulation of investment demand in the short run and intensification of capital accumulation in the long run. The implicit assumption was that market mechanisms could not provide the desired level of capital investments and capital accumulation for the economy. The expectation of underinvestment was related to the structural features of the Belarusian economy, which had not fundamentally changed since the times of the Soviet Union. A relatively small number of enterprises still produced a large proportion of output. They were mostly controlled by the government, which considered them to be of strategic importance. The implicit assumption was that long-term growth required capital investment into these core enterprises, and that this would not occur without government intervention.

In the early years, directed loans were mainly aimed at supporting industrial and agricultural enterprises, with the assumption that investment projects in large enterprises would ensure GDP growth. This, then, was a focus on the supply side of the economy and could be interpreted as softening budget constraints for these firms. Indeed, among the sector of state-owned enterprises, which were the key recipients of directed loans, some were profitable, while others needed financial support. The latter included firms from industry—especially light industry—and agriculture. Some enterprises were continuously generating losses or just covering their costs. It was therefore likely that at least some fraction of directed loans was wasted in low-productivity projects and there was some direct evidence for this (Korosteleva & Lawson 2010; Kolesnikova 2010).

The mode of directed loans provision changed in the 2000s. While supply side measures continued, demand side policies were also introduced. These policies include the provision of loans to potential users of capital goods. Two effects were expected. First, this policy could strengthen the demand for capital goods produced by large firms, thus increasing current output in the economy. Second, it was expected that over the medium to long term, users of capital goods would become more productive and thus contribute to output growth. This policy shift went with changes in the composition of borrowers. Initially it was producers of agricultural goods that received support to compete on international markets. Later, the purchase of capital goods from domestic producers of agricultural machinery was also subsidised. Firms thereby received support for selling on the domestic market instead of for competing on foreign markets. In other words, it led to a substitution of potential external demand by a guaranteed portion of domestic demand. A similar mechanism was used in the construction sector. Housing construction was supported through subsidised housing loans to households in need. Thus, in the first stages of the development of directed lending, large industrial companies were the borrowers, but later households and agricultural firms became the major recipients.

Directed loans were channelled through two banks in which the government was the main stockholder, with shares in their equity close to 100%. Economic authorities were thereby able to intervene directly in banks' credit policies by decisions from the president or the government. State-owned banks, in their turn, enjoyed some preferential treatment from the authorities, including implicit 100% guarantees on households' deposits and lax reserve requirements. By the mid-2000s this approach had been replaced by regular replenishment—usually at the end of the year—of the state-owned banks' equity capital from the state budget.

The government used directed loans as the major tool for stimulating domestic demand during the global crisis. As shown in Figure 2, there was a clear upward trend in their volume during 2009 both in absolute terms and as a proportion of total outstanding loans. By the end of 2009, the share of directed loans amounted to 46.2% by the IMF (2010) estimate.

In 2009–2010, the government and the NBB provided additional sources of liquidity for state-owned banks in order to maintain banks' solvency under the burden of directed loans. The NBB implemented this policy by relying on a standard set of liquidity injection instruments, but these were insufficient to compensate for a sharp increase in the volume of loans granted through 2009. The NBB therefore opened credit lines for five-year low-interest loans to these two banks of BYR4 trillion, about €1 billion as of that period. This was equivalent to about 7% of these banks' total assets, or about 45% of their regulatory capital. Moreover, the government continued to provide injections through replenishments of the equity capital of the state-owned banks, directly from the state budget. Thus, in December 2010, the shareholders' equity of three major state-owned banks was increased to raise their regulatory capital by 22%, a step that increased the regulatory capital of the entire banking system by 15%. The enormous volume of government's and NBB's liquidity injections revealed the lack of alternative sources of increasing capitalisation for state-owned banks, which had to reserve a large part of their portfolio for loans on government programmes.

The system of directed loans may have a limited growth-promoting effect, but it also has a significant potential to restrict growth. This is associated with lower efficiency of resource allocation, lower productivity of accumulated capital, reduced efficiency of financial intermediation and distortion of interest rate signals (Fry 1995). Some negative effects of directed lending can become visible in the short run. Thus, in conditions of stagnating or decreasing demand for money, an increase in the money supply to accommodate the

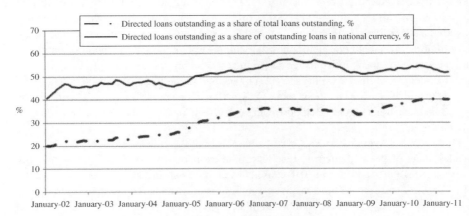

FIGURE 2. Directed Loans as a Share of Total Loans.

Note: We treat the sum of loans to agricultural firms in national currency and households in national currency as directed loans (for more details see Kruk (2011)).

Source: Author's own computations based on data from the National Bank of the Republic of Belarus (NBB 2011).

demand for directed loans creates inflationary pressure. In the longer term the use of directed lending to stimulate domestic demand may increase the magnitude of the business cycle, making fluctuations more frequent and volatile (Kruk 2011).

In Belarus, both long-term and short-term effects can be observed. As for the long-term effect, Belarus suffered from losses in efficiency of resource allocation and efficiency of financial intermediation (Korosteleva & Lawson 2010; Kruk 2011). However, over the 2000s, these growth restricting effects were offset by additional capital accumulation. The outcome has been estimated as an approximately neutral effect on the rate of long-term growth (Kruk 2011). Nevertheless, a more intense application of directed lending can have a decidedly negative long-term effect, as the consequences of poor allocation of resources, lower efficiency of financial intermediation and lower productivity of capital all become apparent.

In practice, negative short-term effects were felt quite quickly. Monetary policy over the 2009–2010 period resulted in inflation and an overvaluation of the national currency, which triggered a currency crisis and further recession in 2011 (Chubrik *et al.* 2012). Only after that did the government indicate the possibility of restricting directed loan provision to reduce inflationary pressure. Nevertheless, it was reluctant to abandon directed lending in 2012, still believing it to be a growth-enhancing mechanism.

Conclusions

In 2009, Belarus maintained economic growth, although at the very modest rate of 0.2%, despite the global recession and the huge drops in output in neighbouring countries. The economy then grew more rapidly in 2010 and 2011. This was achieved against the background of a substantial fall in external demand for Belarusian goods alongside a rather stable demand for imports. Growth was therefore achieved through the stimulation of domestic demand, led by higher investment and a growth in inventories. Companies piled up stocks because the government instructed them to maintain high output growth rates even in the face of the unfavourable business environment, while the growth in investment required a sharp increase in directed loans. The economic authorities also did their best to avoid falling household consumption, using administrative tools to maintain some growth in real wages. Changes to exchange-rate policy—meaning the level of the exchange rate and the degree of its flexibility—were rather modest and the current account deficit increased dramatically. The main tool to cover this deficit was foreign borrowing by the government, as other actors faced borrowing constraints on the global financial markets hit by the crisis.

However, the relatively successful macroeconomic dynamics actually meant a displacement of the challenges to the Belarusian economy to later periods. The intention to avoid recession at any cost in 2010 caused further problems in 2011. There were a number of reasons for this. First, there was not enough room for manoeuvre as stabilisation policy was carried out in the context of accumulated structural distortions. Second, although recession was delayed, that delay depended on the use of policy instruments that carried long-term dangers: Belarus responded to external shocks by stimulating domestic demand which led to a deterioration of the current account. Third, this expansionary policy appears to have been pursued for too long, overshooting its optimal term.

TRANSITION ECONOMIES AFTER 2008

The case of Belarus points to the importance of a timely exit from an expansionary policy. Instead, it was continued throughout the downturn and recovery stages, and then extended into the expansion stage. Moreover, the expansionary policy was the only stimulus to the economy and that made its continuation beyond the initial phase particularly dangerous. It can therefore be argued that future prospects would have been brighter had the stabilisation policy been used during the slowdown stage only. The peculiarities of the Belarusian economy and specific tools of stabilisation policy worsened prospects for long-term growth. The tool of directed lending, which was actively used for stabilisation policy, can be expected to have a growth-restricting effect for potential GDP. The crisis thus exacerbated a severe challenge for the Belarusian economy—the necessity to search for new sources of sustainable growth.

Belarusian Economic Research and Outreach Center

References

Belstat (2011) *Republic of Belarus: Statistical Yearbook* (Minsk, Belarusian Statistical Committee), available at: http://belstat.gov.by/homep/ru/publications/yearbook/2011/Yearbook_2011.rar, accessed 15 March 2012.

Belstat (2012) *National Accounts of the Republic of Belarus* (Minsk, Belarusian Statistical Committee), available at: http://belstat.gov.by/homep/ru/publications/sns/2012/national_accounts_2012.rar, accessed 15 March 2012.

Blanchard, O., Dell'Ariccia, G. & Mauro, P. (2010) 'Rethinking Macroeconomic Policy', *Journal of Money, Credit and Banking*, 42, s1, pp. 199–215.

Chubrik, A., Shymanovich, G. & Zaretsky, A. (2012) *Srednesrochnye Perspektivy Ekonomiki Belarusi Posle Krizisa Platezhnogo Balansa*, IPM Research Center Working Paper, WP/12/03 (Minsk, IPM Research Center).

Feige, E. & Dean, J. (2002) 'Dollarization and Euroization in Transition Countries: Currency Substitution, Asset Substitution, Network Externalities and Irreversibility', in Volbert, A., Melitz, J. & Furstenberg, G. M. (eds) *Monetary Unions and Hard Pegs: Effect on Trade, Financial Development and Stability* (Oxford, Oxford University Press), pp. 303–20.

Fry, M. J. (1995) *Money, Interest, and Banking in Economic Development* (Baltimore, MD, Johns Hopkins University Press).

IMF (2009) *Republic of Belarus: Financial System Stability Assessment*, IMF Country Report, 09/30 (Washington, DC, International Monetary Fund).

IMF (2010) *Republic of Belarus: Fourth Review under the Stand-By Arrangement*, IMF Country Report, 10/89 (Washington, DC, International Monetary Fund).

Ize, A. (2005) *Financial Dollarization Equilibria: A Framework for Policy Analysis*, IMF Working Paper, WP05/186 (Washington, DC, International Monetary Fund).

Ize, A. & Parrado, E. (2006) *Real Dollarization, Financial Dollarization, and Monetary Policy*, Central Bank of Chile Working Paper, 375 (Santiago de Chile, Central Bank of Chile).

Ize, A. & Yeyati, E. (2003) 'Financial Dollarization', *Journal of International Economics*, 59, 2, pp. 323–47.

Kolesnikova, I. (2010) *State Aid for Industrial Enterprises in Belarus: Remedy or Poison?*, Economics Education and Research Consortium Working Paper, 10/01E (Kiev, Economics Education and Research Consortium), available at: http://eerc.ru/default/download/creater/working_papers/file/f7787518ecb13f7fdd09e9c4f788c61a3eb92ef7.pdf, accessed 15 March 2012.

Korosteleva, J. & Lawson, C. (2010) 'The Belarusian Case of Transition: Whither Financial Repression?', *Post-Communist Economies*, 22, 1, pp. 33–53.

Kruk, D. (2010a) 'Vliyanie Krizisa na Perspektivy Dolgosrochnogo Ekonomicheskogo Rosta v Belarusi', in Pelipas, P. (ed.) (2010) *Natsionalnaya Konkurentosposobnost' Belarusi: Otvechaya na Sovremennye Vyzovy* (Minsk, Belprint), pp. 159–98.

Kruk, D. (2010b) *Dollarization in Belarus: Preconditions and Perspectives of Dedollarization Policies*, IPM Research Centre Policy Paper, PP/01/10 (Minsk, IPM Research Center).

Kruk, D. (2011) 'Vliyanie Direktivnogo Kreditovaniya na Dolgosrochnyi Ekonomicheskii Rost', *Bankauski Vesnik*, 4, 549, pp. 26–35, available at: http://nbrb/by/bv/narch/549/5.pdf, accessed 1 June 2012.

Kruk, D., Tochitskaya, I. & Shymanovich, G. (2009) *Vliyanie Globalnogo Ekonomicheskogo Krizisa na Ekonomiku Belarusi*, IPM Research Center Working Paper, WP/09/03 (Minsk, IPM Research Center).

Kruk, D., Zaretsky, A. & Kirchner, R. (2011) *Estimating the Equilibrium Exchange Rate in Belarus*, IPM Research Center Policy Paper, PP/01/2011 (Minsk, IPM Research Center).

Myant, M. & Drahokoupil, J. (2012) 'International Integration, Varieties of Capitalism and Resilience to Crisis in Transition Economies', *Europe-Asia Studies*, 64, 1, pp. 1–33.

NBB (2010) *Banking Sector of the Republic of Belarus as of 1 October, 2010* (Minsk, National Bank of the Republic of Belarus), available at: http://nbrb.by/system/banksector/2010/bs_20101001.pdf, accessed 1 March 2012.

NBB (2011) *Bulletin of Banking Statistics: Yearbook 2000–2010* (Minsk, National Bank of the Republic of Belarus), available at: http://nbrb.by/statistics/bulletin/2010/Bulletin_Yearbook2010.pdf, accessed 1 March 2012.

Reinhart, C. & Rogoff, K. (2010) 'Growth in a Time of Debt', *American Economic Review*, 100, 2, pp. 573–78.

Stiglitz, J. & Weiss, A. (1981) 'Credit Rationing in Markets with Imperfect Information', *American Economic Review*, 71, 3, pp. 393–410.

Stiglitz, J. E., Jaramillo-Vallejo, J. & Park, Y. C. (1993) 'The Role of the State in Financial Markets', in *World Bank Research Observer, Annual Conference on Development Economics Supplement* (Oxford, Oxford University Press), pp. 19–61.

Continuity and Change in the Enterprise Sector

Crisis and Upgrading: The Case of the Hungarian Automotive and Electronics Sectors

MAGDOLNA SASS & ANDREA SZALAVETZ

Abstract

By triggering a wave of organisational restructuring, reconfiguration of supply chains and consolidation of business processes at multinational companies, the crisis offered significant upgrading opportunities for peripheral actors in globalised production networks (the so-called global value chains). Drawing on Hungarian case studies of local subsidiaries in the automotive and electronics industries, this essay investigates the crisis-induced product, process and functional upgrading opportunities in low-cost locations. We show Hungary's high level of integration into global value chains and document the rapidly ongoing process of functional upgrading.

THE GLOBAL FINANCIAL AND ECONOMIC CRISIS AND THE ENSUING geographical and organisational consolidation triggered a restructuring of value-adding activities in sectors organised through globalised production networks (Cattaneo *et al.* 2010; Milberg & Winkler 2010; Sturgeon & Van Biesebroeck 2010). The latter can be conceptualised as 'global value chains' (GVCs), encompassing:

> the full range of activities that are required to bring a good or service from conception through the different phases of production—provision of raw materials; the input of various components, subassemblies, and producer services; the assembly of finished goods—to delivery to final consumers, as well as disposal after use. (Cattaneo *et al.* 2010, pp. 3–4)

The sharp contraction in demand in 2009 particularly affected the economies that had relied on integration into GVCs as a means of modernising their production capacity. However, the lead companies governing the GVCs reacted to the crisis by restructuring their value chains, which created upgrading opportunities for low-cost subsidiaries (Filippov & Kalotay 2011; Sturgeon & Kawakami 2011).

Using the example of selected new member states of the European Union, this essay investigates the crisis-induced opportunities for upgrading in the case of GVC actors at low-cost locations. Combining statistical analysis techniques with field interviews and case study

This research was undertaken in the framework of the OTKA project No. K83982.

investigations at a sample of 10 automotive and electronics subsidiaries in Hungary,[1] we point to a number of methodological problems that distort analyses of upgrading if they rely exclusively on commonly used indicators, such as the 'revealed comparative advantage' and the Lafay indices of trade specialisation (defined below). We document the rapidly ongoing process of functional upgrading, a process not captured by hard statistical indicators, but too important to be neglected.

As a first step we show Hungary's high level of integration into GVCs, using indicators that demonstrate changes in the country's position in the international division of labour, focusing on the crisis years. This is followed by case study investigations that document some practical and quality features of upgrading. Our analysis covers a period of four years between 2007 and 2012, with statistical data available for the period between 2007 and 2009 and case study information for the period to the end of 2010.[2] We focus on the impact of the crisis in the automotive and electronics sectors in Hungary, two industries with high involvement of GVCs.[3] On the basis of company interviews we examine the impact of the crisis and how the companies in question handled the problems it presented. We also investigate if the crisis environment impacted on local subsidiaries' upgrading by scrutinising process, product and functional upgrading.

We start with a short discussion of the theoretical and methodological background. In the following section, we present the results of our statistical analyses of the involvement of Hungary in GVCs. We then turn to the micro-level: based on case study analysis we briefly review the impact of the crisis on the companies in which we conducted qualitative investigations. We analyse the companies' product, process and functional upgrading efforts. The final section concludes and describes the limitations of our investigations.

Theoretical and methodological background

Advances in information and communication technologies, as well as multilateral, bilateral and unilateral liberalisation steps in international trade and capital flows, have accelerated

---

[1]Interviews with the senior management of respective companies were carried out by the authors in April–June 2010 and April–June 2011, with follow-up interviews conducted in 2012. For details, see the Appendix. Interviews were collected in the context of two projects financed by the Hungarian Scientific Research Fund (OTKA No. K83982 'Measuring the Upgrading Performance of TNCs' Hungarian Subsidiaries' and OTKA No. 68435 'International Relocations to Hungary—Theory, Facts, Statistical Analysis and International Comparison').

[2]The year 2007, and in some calculations 2008, serve as pre-crisis benchmark years. However, the use of 2010 is arbitrary and somewhat problematic, since it cannot be considered as the end year of the crisis. Our statistical analysis therefore uses 2007 and 2009 to quantify the impact of the crisis, while our case study investigations cover the longer period (2007–2010) to discern the surveyed companies' upgrading performance.

[3]The two industries feature important differences in terms of product variety, length of the technological cycle, extent of geographic dispersion of the value chain and the mobility of production activities and thus their geographical 'stickiness', meaning the extent to which they are bound to a current location. Accordingly, the automotive industry is more regionally organised while electronics is more rootless (Sturgeon & Van Biesebroeck 2010; Dicken 2011). In this essay we concentrate rather on their common features. Beyond the fact that the electronics industry is a key supplier of the automotive industry, the two industries have a lot in common. (Roland Berger Strategy Consultants estimate the share of electronics in cars was 23% in 2010 (see http://www.elektrobit.com/investors/financials/market_outlook/automotive_market_outlook, accessed 11 July 2012).) They are both intermediates-intensive. In both cases assembly and part production are geographically separated from headquarters-type services such as strategic planning and system integration, branding, design and science-based research. Peripheral actors in vertically integrated value chains also have quite limited opportunities for substantial position improvement in the value chain (Pavlínek & Ženka 2011; Sturgeon & Kawakami 2011).

the ongoing fragmentation and geographical dispersion of production. The accompanying organisational innovations in the business sphere produced important changes in the organisation and governance of the global economy. In an increasing number of industries, value-adding activities and international trade are structured around global value chains (Gereffi *et al.* 2005). In a holistic view of value creation, the concept of GVC (Gereffi 1999; Gereffi & Fernandez-Stark 2011) refers to all (tangible and intangible) activities—carried out by geographically dispersed, networked economic actors—that contribute to the creation and sale, and support the end use, of a product or service.

For low-income economy actors, integration into GVCs is a key opportunity for catching up in terms of accelerating growth and industrialisation and modernising production techniques (Pietrobelli 2008).[4] While insertion into the GVCs provides the firms with valuable opportunities for modernisation, peripheral GVC actors' competitiveness can be sustained only if they continuously upgrade their activities within a GVC, and move from low to relatively higher value-adding activities, thereby improving or at least sustaining their actual income (Buckley 2009; Ernst 2009; Winter 2010). Upgrading is manifested in a shift to increasingly sophisticated and higher unit-value products (product upgrading); in the improved efficiency and reliability of production processes as a result of improved production methods and technologies (process upgrading); and in the increased breadth and sophistication of activities, through assuming new, relatively more knowledge-intensive business functions and activities (functional upgrading). Finally, competitiveness can be sustained through inter-sectoral upgrading when firms move to new sectors with relatively higher gains, taking advantage of their accumulated knowledge and technological capabilities (Humphrey & Schmitz 2004).

Crisis-induced, steeply falling demand and increasing competitive pressures have two contradictory effects (Gereffi 2010; Milberg & Winkler 2010). The demand effect is the consequence of declining demand for the products of a given company, which induces lead firms to decrease their off-shoring activities and reduce in turn their purchases from suppliers. The counteracting 'substitution effect' leads to increasing purchases from suppliers as lead firms have incentives to off-shore or outsource more in order to increase competitiveness and efficiency and to lower prices. These two effects impact upon lead firms and suppliers differently (Fernandez-Stark & Bamber 2011). The impact on suppliers also differs according to their position in the value chain. Lead firms and 'tier-one suppliers'—that is, firms integrated with the lead firm to a great extent through common activities and cooperation—try to consolidate their activities and rationalise supply chains. Lower-tier suppliers that are integrated with the lead firm to a smaller extent usually aim at diversifying their activities in terms of producing more products or serving more buyers. They also try to diversify the products and services they provide through investment in technology and machinery and through such steps as obtaining certifications.

Various theories and empirical analyses try to capture the characteristics of the changes in the international division of labour and spread of GVCs. Among these, Yeats (1998) tried to assess the extent of global production sharing by analysing foreign trade in parts and components using the Standard International Trade Classification (SITC) Revision 2, concentrating on the SITC 7 product group (Machinery and transportation equipment), which represents around half of world trade in manufacturing products. Using Yeats' methodology,

---

[4]As Baldwin (2011) argues, industrialisation today occurs much faster than in the era of import-substitution industrialisation, as industrialising economies do not need to build the whole supply chain at home: their actors may simply join one.

TRANSITION ECONOMIES AFTER 2008

Kaminski and Ng (2001) carried out the same statistical analysis for the Central European economies. They showed that these economies became increasingly integrated into production networks of the European Union. They point to the advance especially in three sectors: furniture, which is characteristic of almost all analysed economies; automobiles, in the Czech Republic, Hungary, Poland, Slovakia and Slovenia; and information technology networks in Estonia and Hungary. Other more recent studies also underline that these countries are integrated to a relatively large and increasing extent into GVCs.[5]

The issue of upgrading in Central and Eastern European countries has been analysed mainly using the example of the automotive industry,[6] while Radošević (2005) and Szanyi and Sass (2012) give an overview of the evolution of the electronics industry. Our approach to upgrading differs from that of the previous papers. First, we concentrate on the short-term impact of, and firms' reactions to, the crisis, manifested in restructuring, consolidation and other organisational changes at the level of the multinational corporation (MNC), and relate these changes to subsidiaries' upgrading. Second, we analyse only foreign-owned companies, the upgrading and governance patterns of which differ from those of indigenous GVC participants. Besides that, our choice of concentrating on foreign-owned companies is also justified by the fact that in the automotive and electronics sectors these are the most important market players in Hungary. Moreover, upgrading issues can be viewed differently in the case of foreign affiliates, as there are power relations and intra-company factors at play. Finally, although we briefly review also the developments in the field of process and product upgrading, which is the main focus of the comparative analyses referred to above, we concentrate on the issue of functional upgrading (increasing the breadth and sophistication of activities through assuming new and more knowledge-intensive business functions and activities). This reflects the results of subsidiaries' improved capabilities as well as their intangible contributions to their MNC-owner-led GVCs.

When investigating functional upgrading in Central and Eastern Europe, most papers discuss only the presence and the evolution of the research and development (R&D) function in host-country subsidiaries. In contrast, we discuss functional upgrading in a broader sense, focusing on all possible intangible auxiliary functions, such as procurement, sales, ICT-related activities, human resources management and finance. In line with the methodological work developed by Sturgeon and Gereffi (2009), we investigate the increases in the breadth and the depth, meaning originality and knowledge content of business functions that pertain to local subsidiaries' mandates (Wang & Tunzelmann 2000).

Before proceeding to the statistical analysis and to the results of our case study investigations, a caveat ought to be made with respect to the surveyed subsidiaries' upgrading performance, a caveat that is particularly relevant at times of crisis: upgrading is not always up to the subsidiary. Theoretical investigations in international business literature, focusing on multinational companies' strategies and structures, have described how subsidiaries accumulate resources and specialised capabilities and try to extend and upgrade their activities and thereby improve their position within their multinational owner's network (Birkinshaw 1996, 2000; Birkinshaw & Hood 1998). The implicit, albeit unfounded, assumption of these papers is that upgrading depends mainly on subsidiaries' efforts. If they have a talented,

---

[5]See among others Cheung and Guichard (2009) or Stehrer *et al.* (2011).

[6]See for example, Pavlínek and Ženka (2011) for the Czech Republic, and Domanski and Gwosdz (2009) and Winter (2010) for Poland. Comparative analyses were provided, among others, by Pavlínek *et al.* (2009), Jürgens and Krzywdzinski (2009) and Szalavetz (2012).

entrepreneurial management, accumulate capabilities and intangible resources, they can upgrade and improve their position within the MNC.

Although some scholars have investigated explanations for cases when subsidiaries lose their positions within production networks, looking at host country comparative disadvantages and the lack of subsidiaries' local embeddedness,[7] few emphasise that the majority of the subsidiaries—especially peripheral ones and especially at times of crisis— have little power to influence headquarters' decisions (Bouquet & Birkinshaw 2008). Subsidiaries may pursue textbook-type strategies of accumulating capabilities, and have a proactive and entrepreneurial management: if their parent companies adopt a global centralisation strategy and believe in standardised management practices, they have little space for independent initiatives. If the parent company is acquired by an investor with such a strategy—takeovers were particularly frequent in the surveyed industries in the surveyed period—subsidiaries acting previously with relatively more independence in certain functions will have little voice following the takeover.

If the parent company decides to reconfigure resources and reallocate specific activities away from the peripheral subsidiary, the subsidiary has little power to counter this decision. If the parent company turns its attention to emerging economies, peripheral European subsidiaries will find it difficult to persuade their owners of the benefits of additional local investments. With this caveat in mind we now proceed to our analysis.

Hungary in GVCs

There are various approaches in the literature which try to measure the changes in the international division of labour and in the position of individual countries or groups of countries. In our essay we adapted the methodology of Yeats (1998). However, while Yeats used SITC Revision 2 classifications, we elaborated a similar, updated classification for SITC Revision 3, the product sub-categories of which are even more suitable for distinguishing between parts, components and readymade products for final use. We employ that new classification in order to show, using Eurostat trade data, how deeply Hungary is integrated into GVCs and how this changed during the crisis. We analysed data for the years before and during the crisis (2007 and 2009, respectively). Besides simple statistical indicators, we also deploy other composite indicators in order to show changes in revealed comparative advantages (RCA[8]) and levels of trade specialisation (Lafay indices[9]).

On the basis of the indicators presented in Table 1, we can state that SITC 7 parts and components play an important role in Hungarian foreign trade, which may be a good illustration for the high level of the country's participation in GVCs. They are

[7]See Dörrenbächer and Gammelgaard (2006) and references therein.

[8]The RCA index is calculated as RCA $= (X_{ij} - M_{ij})/(X_{ij} + M_{ij})$, where X is exports, M is imports, i refers to country and j to commodity. It can take a value between -1 (revealed comparative disadvantage of the given country in the production and export of the given product) and 1 (revealed comparative advantage).

[9]The Lafay index measures revealed comparative advantage or international specialisation. For country i good j $LFI_{ij} = 100[(X_{ij} - M_{ij})/(X_{ij} + M_{ij}) - \Sigma^N_{j=1}(X_{ij} - M_{ij})/ \Sigma^N_{j=1}(X_{ij} + M_{ij})]$ $(X_{ij} + M_{ij})/ \Sigma^N_{j=1}(X_{ij+}M_{ij})$, where X and M are exports and imports and N is the number of goods. Positive values again indicate a comparative advantage and specialisation in the production and export of a given product. The higher the value of the index, the higher is the advantage and level of specialisation. For more details see, e.g. Zaghini (2005), according to whom the Lafay index is a better choice for measuring trade specialisation in the era of GVCs.

TABLE 1
STATISTICAL INDICATORS OF TRADE IN PARTS AND COMPONENTS OF HUNGARY

	2007	2009
Parts and components exports (billion euros)	12.84	9.84
Parts and components imports (billion euros)	16.14	12.03
Parts and components trade balance (billion euros)	−3.30	−2.19
Share of parts and components in total exports (%)	18.45	16.53
Share of parts and components in total imports (%)	23.15	21.58
Parts and components RCA	−0.1139	−0.1003
Parts and components Lafay index	−0.0959	−0.7196

Source: Authors' own calculations based on Eurostat data, available at http://epp.eurostat.ec.europa.eu/newxtweb/, accessed 11 July 2012.

especially important in imports, representing more than one-fifth of the country's total imports. Their relatively high level, compared for example to that of parts and components exports, may give an indication of the country's participation in GVCs more on the assembly side, where local suppliers are relatively less able to provide these components.

On the basis of Figure 1, we can state that Hungary is similar to other countries of the region. In all four countries shown here parts and components play an important role both in exports and imports. However, there are differences in how the four analysed countries participate in GVCs. The Czech Republic appears to be the most integrated into production networks, with very high shares of parts and components in both imports and exports, even higher than in the case of Hungary. On the other hand, Slovakia has the highest share of imports in parts and components, higher than that of Hungary. However, in exports, Slovakia has the lowest shares, which indicates that its role is more as an assembly point for imported parts and components. Hungary, and especially the Czech Republic, sell a considerable volume of parts and components abroad relative to their total exports. Thus the

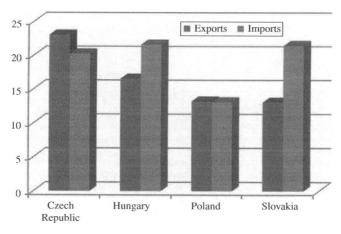

FIGURE 1. SHARE OF SITC 7 PARTS AND COMPONENTS EXPORTS AND IMPORTS IN TOTAL EXPORTS AND IMPORTS, 2009 (%).

Source: Authors' own calculations based on the data of Eurostat from COMEXT database, available at: http://epp.eurostat.ec.europa.eu/newxtweb/mainxtnet.do, accessed 11 July 2012.

very high share of trade in parts and components for the analysed countries indicates their participation in international production networks, especially given the dominance of foreign-owned enterprises in their production.

In Hungary, the impact of the crisis is more pronounced in imports, with a larger reduction both in absolute values and shares than in exports (as indicated in Table 1). However, the magnitude does not exceed two percentage points in terms of shares in totals. Our findings thus indicate only modest levels of changes overall (consistent with Stehrer *et al.* (2011)). The trade deficit for parts and components decreased between 2007 and 2009. However, the implications of the statistical indicators on the issue of upgrading are conflicting. RCA indices improved during the crisis, with the revealed disadvantage moving closer to zero, indicating probable upgrading, but Lafay indices showed declining comparative advantage and lower levels of specialisation. This conflicting result may be explained by the higher level of aggregation of the RCA index, which cannot take account of changes at the more disaggregated level.

While our statistical results may provide evidence for changes, or even for upgrading, during the crisis, we have to acknowledge that there are innumerable problems with the statistical approaches. There are no direct measures of GVC involvement and only proxies can be used, leading to difficulties of interpretation when the results conflict. Moreover, trade in parts and components does not necessarily equate with participation in global or regional production networks, or global or regional value chains. However, it is reasonable to assume that the overwhelming majority of cases of trade in parts and components in the countries considered here are connected to participation in GVCs. Furthermore, final products are omitted, which implies omitting assembly-type activities.

It is also problematic that only the SITC 7 product group is covered by the analysis. This does include the automotive and electronics sectors, but other GVC and non-GVC sectors are left out and it does not cover all parts and components, even for those two sectors. A significant share originates in other industries, such as in metallurgy, plastics, textile or glass production and even some service branches. As has been shown for the Czech Republic (Pavlínek *et al.* 2010) and Hungary (Rugraff & Sass 2012), many automotive suppliers in these countries come from outside the automotive sector. In the electronics sector, the extent of supplying from outside electronics is presumably lower than in the automotive industry, although plastics and rubber parts and components can be found there as well. Thus our method can only provide a partial picture. These two industries do not cover total foreign trade, and even GVCs of these two sectors are not covered fully. However, as we saw, these two sectors represent the bulk of foreign trade for the four analysed countries. Thus even results for these two sectors can give important insights into the level and characteristics of participation of Hungary in GVCs.

The conflicting results and their ambiguous interpretations justify supplementing our investigations on upgrading with firm-level case studies. We have concentrated on foreign-owned affiliates operating in Hungary, which are the most important players in the Hungarian automotive and electronics sectors.[10] Interviews were undertaken with 10 foreign-owned affiliates of multinational companies operating in Hungary; six automotive

---

[10]In the automotive industry, there were 141 companies on the list of automotive suppliers of the trade development agency, of which 110 were foreign-owned and 31 Hungarian-owned. In terms of employees, these 110 foreign-owned companies altogether employed more than 81,000 workers, while the 31 Hungarian-owned firms employed slightly less than 17,000 (Sass 2009).

and four electronics firms.[11] The automotive companies were, in all but one case, first-tier suppliers, meaning that they supplied the parts and components directly to the automotive assembly plants. However, some companies had a diversified product mix, and were also manufacturing parts and components to be supplied to first- and second-tier suppliers. Part of these first-tier suppliers' production was therefore classified as second or third tier.

Our sample was selected from the authors' database of case studies and journal articles on the activities of Hungarian subsidiaries in the chosen sectors. This sample selection method brings risks of selection bias: our sample consists of well-known 'blue chip' companies that may show above-average upgrading performance. Our six automotive companies represented more than 5% of total employment in the sector in 2010, while the electronics firms accounted for 14% of employment in their sector. In a period of 18 months, spanning 2010 and 2011, we contacted 18 firms, 10 of which were willing to contribute to the research. Interviews were conducted with 14 managers, mainly chief executive officers, and in some cases also with information technology, human resources or chief procurement officers.

The impact of the crisis and crisis-driven upgrading

The impact of the crisis

The demand effect of the crisis was deep and quite uniform in the companies surveyed. With two exceptions they all experienced a sharp drop in demand and the fall in orders was 30% on average. All the companies had a high export-to-sales ratio, averaging 85%. Thus they were mainly cross-border suppliers, of German or other Western European companies, the only exception being a supplier of the Hungarian branch of the Japanese manufacturer Suzuki. The immediate reaction to the crisis in almost all companies surveyed was a reduction in employment. At the same time, most companies tried to find means to minimise layoffs. Temporary agency workers would be terminated first. The highly skilled workers were typically retained, as companies tried to avoid harming their longer-term competitiveness.

In addition to the demand effects of the crisis our interviews also identified a substitution effect. Some of the companies took over orders from foreign and domestic competitors that were experiencing difficulties. Most spectacular was the case of a large automotive company that made huge investments to expand its Hungarian capacity precisely during the crisis period. Similarly, an electronics firm extended its capacities in Hungary. Another manifestation of the substitution effect was the case of an automotive company that took back previously outsourced tasks from suppliers in order to maintain its own level of employment. The companies also made some offensive adjustment steps, initiating production reorganisation in order to improve efficiency, looking for more efficient suppliers or for additional ones to increase competitive pressure on all of them, diversifying the product mix and finding new partners (Table 2).

We found evidence for both process and, to a lesser extent, product upgrading efforts during the crisis. Crisis-triggered process upgrading in terms of restructuring and production reorganisation was present in all of the companies. The crisis prompted a search for means to increase value added, enhancing the complexity of products and thereby strengthening

[11]As mentioned in footnote 3, given that the electronics industry is a key supplier of the automotive industry, the two parts of the sample overlap to some extent. Two companies classified as automotive in our sample manufacture automotive electronics products.

TRANSITION ECONOMIES AFTER 2008

TABLE 2
CRISIS-HANDLING AND UPGRADING AT THE COMPANIES SURVEYED

No.	Product upgrading	Process upgrading	Functional upgrading
1	Modification (improvement) of existing products	Reorganisation of production for increasing efficiency: redesign of the production line, introduction of IT-based troubleshooting by establishment of networked computers between manufacturing lines and technical staff, introduction of SAP (business management software)	Some development tasks allocated here: intra-function upgrading in R&D (though very limited); new tasks in procurement, but overall lower level of autonomy of the affiliate compared to the pre-crisis years
2	Modification (improvement) of existing products	Reorganisation of production for the more efficient use of capacities: rebuilding of the production line, introduction of digital manufacturing methods (shop-floor scheduling); attempt at the reorganisation of supplies (mainly in vain)	More intensive cooperation with R&D centres inside the company network, some development tasks
3	No new product, but modifications of existing ones	New investments, including in machinery	Upgrading in scope: provision of testing services for other subsidiaries as well, some development tasks; maintained R&D as the most important 'anti-crisis' measure, with new directions: hybrid and green topics
4	Directions of product development identified through a new strategy elaborated during the crisis (but no practical steps taken yet)	New machinery	More tasks allocated to the Hungarian affiliate (partly through relocation from the parent), especially R&D-related tasks (full development), in connection with that, development projects initiated (in cooperation with universities)
5	New products introduced	New process development projects in order to increase manufacturability, new investment (opening of a new plant, machinery)	More independence in selecting suppliers (responsibility for the whole Central and Eastern European region), consolidation of suppliers Upgrading in scope: R&D partly for other subsidiaries and for the parent, increased innovation activities partly in cooperation with universities
6	No upgrading	Revision of cost structures and modifying the organisation of production accordingly, taking back certain outsourced activities after cost revisions	Upgrading in scope: instrument development and machinery production for partner subsidiaries, deepening within the logistics function, loss of selected HR and communication tasks
7	Increasing the complexity of products (mounted products from components)	Reorganisation of production for the better use of capacities: redesign of the production line, changes in the system of shifts, multitasking (especially for white-collar workers—their partial insertion in blue-collar production tasks); process upgrading to reduce energy consumption; concentration on certain processes, outsourcing non-core ones	No functional upgrading: the Hungarian affiliate is independent, it undertakes almost all functions except for finance and credits, the parent (70% of shares owned) acts as a financial investor (though it is operating in the sector)

No.	Product upgrading	Process upgrading	Functional upgrading
8	Introduction of a new mounted product, production of new products transferred here continuously from the parent	Development and introduction of new technological solutions into production (partly related to the new product, partly to other products), process upgrading in order to decrease energy consumption	New functions: environmental management, intra-function deepening in general management corporate governance functions, and in technology and process development
9	Modified product	New machinery	New functions: strategy setting for the Hungarian subsidiary, procurement. Upgrading in scope: customer and after-sales service
10	Minimal (modified product for a new partner, sought for and found as part of crisis handling measures)	Minimal (modifications and technological solutions for the new partner to improve manufacturability)	Loss of procurement function, new function: marketing and sales and distribution, carried out at Eastern European level

Source: Interviews of the senior management of respective companies by the authors in April–June 2010 and April–June 2011, with follow-up interviews conducted in 2012. Interviews were collected in the context of two projects financed by the Hungarian Scientific Research Fund (OTKA No. K83982 'Measuring the Upgrading Performance of TNCs' Hungarian Subsidiaries' and OTKA No. 68435 'International Relocations to Hungary—Theory, Facts, Statistical Analysis and International Comparison').

companies' positions in the value chain. Various approaches and various methods were applied, as can be seen in detail in Table 2. While process upgrading was prevalent in the sample of companies, product upgrading was less common. Modifications of existing products or attempts at improving their quality were present in half of the sample. However, completely new products connected to new projects were introduced in only two companies. Some companies tried to increase the complexity of their products, for example by shifting into complex systems instead of simple panels, single parts or components.[12]

Following this brief review of the impact of product and process upgrading type reactions to the crisis, we now turn to an examination of the companies' functional upgrading.

Crisis-driven functional upgrading

Analyses of upgrading at firm level have typically been restricted to product and process upgrading. This section presents the results of our field investigations about the firms' post-crisis functional upgrading, meaning increases in the breadth and the depth of their mandates. Functional diversification can be considered quality upgrading, because it involves the uptake of relatively sophisticated, knowledge-intensive and higher-value-adding assignments that complement the production-related tasks. The expansion of locally assumed corporate functions supposes, and is usually accompanied by, learning and local capability accumulation. In line with analyses of business functions by GVC scholars (Brown 2008; Sturgeon 2008; Sturgeon & Gereffi 2009),[13] we asked the companies about the evolution in the number of business functions that have gradually been added to the subsidiaries'

[12]Our interviews showed product upgrading to be subject to major inter-subsidiary competition. Subsidiaries strove to gain the right to manufacture the newly introduced, and the technologically most complex, products. For this they had to present complex calculations—technical and business feasibility studies—and engage in intensive lobbying to influence parent companies' decisions.

[13]A number of recent national and international surveys have been launched to collect data on the geography and the sourcing of business functions; see http://epp.eurostat.ec.europa.eu/statistics_explained/index.php/International_sourcing_statistics, accessed 12 July 2012.

responsibility. However, subsidiary upgrading cannot be explained solely with data on the location of business functions within GVCs. Identical business functions, such as corporate finance, are performed by several subsidiaries in an MNC, with sizeable inter-subsidiary differences in the content and the knowledge-intensity of the tasks. It is therefore important to gain insights into the quality of business functions performed at specific locations.

A theoretical approach to the quality of business functions performed at individual locations is presented in Sato and Fujita's (2009) paper. The authors tried to assess the depth of capabilities for every function along the value chain, devising four capability levels to express the originality of the firm's contribution: operational; assimilative; adaptive; and innovative. Operational-level capabilities are self-explanatory: the firm is able to operate the existing technology. At the assimilative level, the firm has mastered the technology and is able to maintain stable and continuous operation over time. The adaptive level means the firm is able to make minor, incremental, yet original, improvements to the existing technology. The innovative level refers to a substantial original contribution by the recipient firm, either as an improvement to the received technology or as the creation of something new, 'with significant elements of originality and novelty compared to the existing technology' (Sato & Fujita 2009, p. 16).

Departing from Sato and Fujita's taxonomy of business function complexity we asked the managers to describe the quality level, and the evolution, of selected business functions and to compare it with the knowledge content and originality of similar business functions performed at the corporate or regional headquarters. We have also tried to reveal whether crisis triggered any kind of business function consolidation at the MNC level and whether the Hungarian subsidiaries could benefit from the consolidation moves. We therefore tracked the quantitative evolution of the local subsidiaries' assignments, asking whether they managed in the second half of the 2000s to complement their core function with production-related support activities or advanced functions that enhance the intangible value of products, such as R&D or marketing. In addition, we inquired about the evolution of the complexity and skill-intensity of the business functions and tried to identify inter-subsidiary differences in the quality of specific business functions. We asked the interviewed officials to describe, with as much detail as possible, the content of their tasks, the mandate of the local subsidiary related to the given function and to compare their own responsibility—the knowledge-intensity and the creativity requirement of their tasks, as well as their decision-making autonomy—with those of their partners at the corporate or regional headquarters.

Finally, we asked the interviewed managers about the perceived impact of the crisis on the evolution of the locally assumed business functions. Our interview questions were open ended, which allowed us to adapt to emerging themes and get into more details on issues relevant for the company. Our findings are summarised in subsections as follows.

Three dimensions of functional upgrading

Our interviews revealed that, by the end of the 2000s, Hungarian participants in electronics and automotive GVCs had moved far beyond the status of single-function manufacturing establishments, with mandates restricted to production. Beyond their core activities, local manufacturing facilities performed a wide range of support functions in-house. These included administrative, accounting and clerical functions, maintenance, HR, IT, quality control, transportation, warehousing, management of environmental affairs, process engineering and corporate governance. However, most of the locally performed support functions were restricted to subsidiaries' own operation-related necessities. Moreover, marketing, brand building and sales were in most cases missing from the firms' function portfolios: these were carried out in the majority of the cases by the corporate or regional headquarters. Product development and design were among the least frequently devolved functions.

As the local manufacturing subsidiaries expanded their output, new support functions were added to their portfolios so as to ensure smooth operation. Changes in the scale of production, meaning tangible investment in new capacity, were strongly correlated with intangible investment into the local subsidiaries' organisational capital. Moreover, in a self-reinforcing manner, expansion in various support functions required additional investment into the firms' organisational and management functions: they also became increasingly complex.

Our interviews revealed a similar pattern of functional diversification throughout the whole sample. The inception and the expansion of manufacturing activity were followed by a rapid—meaning within a period of between two and four years—expansion of locally performed functions: this was the initial functional diversification. This period saw the establishment of the support functions necessary for the local operation. With the expansion of production, support functions became increasingly diversified. Beyond a threshold production size, peripheral firms' support function portfolios became increasingly diversified. This included the addition both of size-related new functions, such as corporate social responsibility and communication, and of functions related to core operation functions, such as IT, process engineering, logistics and quality control. After an initial period, the pace of functional diversification abated: only a few further support functions were added to the subsidiaries' portfolios, with the in-sourcing of previously outsourced functions,[14] or as a consequence of global strategy changes, such as takeovers, changes in the product or production expansion due to additional relocation moves.

Functions added in later stages included vocational training and research and development. Along with the expansion of production, several local subsidiaries faced increasingly pressing shortages of skilled technicians and of blue-collar workers and had to invest in on-the-job training. R&D was limited in most cases to process development, testing, instrument development and product upgrading. The processes of assuming the new functions often followed a textbook upgrading path: accumulation of credibility, location of initial, low value-adding process development and testing tasks, followed by increasingly sophisticated assignments, expansion of the local R&D staff and finally location of an R&D department.

This process, referred to as upgrading in depth, occurs in most business functions. For example, in the case of procurement, efforts from a subsidiary to increase its responsibilities coincided with parent companies' intentions to cut costs by localising purchases. The tasks of monitoring local and regional supply, identifying potential subcontractors and auditing them—by rigorously applying the parent companies' standard supplier auditing practices—were delegated to subsidiaries. By gaining new responsibilities, some of the firms became specialised in particular functions in addition to their core activities.

In contrast to this gradual functional diversification, the crisis-induced transformation of the intra-MNC distribution of functional responsibilities meant that, in some cases, the upgrading process took another dimension. An automotive subsidiary reported managing

[14]This was reflected in our interview with the CEO of Company no. 8 (see Appendix for details): 'With the expansion of production it was no longer sufficient to pay an environmental consultancy firm's employee to spend half a day a week at the company and manage the accumulated environmental affairs. We had to hire a full time environmental engineer'.

the procurement of selected components not only for its own operational needs but for some partner subsidiaries as well: it negotiated over MNC-wide quantities and organised for the intra-MNC distribution of these components. An electronics subsidiary was entrusted with selected after-sales customer support services also on behalf of its partner subsidiaries in its MNC owner's network. Another electronics subsidiary gradually developed into an Eastern European regional sales and marketing centre, covering 13 countries in the region. At the same time, there were also cases of downgrading. Three subsidiaries experienced the loss of previous functions as a result of crisis-induced MNC-level organisational consolidation.

All-in-all, the firms experienced crisis-induced reconfiguration of GVCs that was complex and multidirectional. MNCs' organisational structures undergo constant changes: the decentralisation of previously centrally managed business functions may go hand-in-hand with the outsourcing of others or with the consolidation of previously distributed functions. In summary, we identified three dimensions of functional upgrading. Upgrading across functions—functional diversification—occurred almost automatically and in an organic and self-reinforcing manner parallel to the expansion of production. The second dimension of functional upgrading (to be detailed below) is intra-function upgrading or upgrading in depth: this was manifested in the increased originality of subsidiaries' contributions. The third dimension can be referred to as upgrading in scope, which refers to the acquisition of MNC-wide, or at least regional, responsibilities. In contrast to the first two dimensions of upgrading, related to local subsidiaries' own operational necessities, upgrading in scope occurs if the subsidiary performs certain tasks on behalf of other subsidiaries, so that one subsidiary's capabilities and competencies are used by the parent company or by other corporate entities, usually as a result of the consolidation of the given business function to the subsidiary in question.

Upgrading in depth—business functions are complex and decomposable

In order to get some insights into the quality of business function-related activities, we asked the interviewed officials to describe the content of their tasks and compare them with those performed by their counterparts at partner subsidiaries or at the corporate or regional headquarters. Answers to our open-ended questions revealed that business functions are complex and decomposable, consisting of many sub-functions. Headquarters usually do not delegate the responsibility for a complete business function to subsidiaries: they delegate responsibility only for selected sub-functions. There are therefore sizeable inter-subsidiary differences in the quality and value-adding capability of individual business functions.

This can be illustrated with the case of corporate finance. The mandates of most chief financial officers of MNCs' peripheral subsidiaries are limited to 'core financials', meaning that they produce detailed financial information and present it in the course of internal reporting. Activities include cost accounting and analysis, banking, and reporting to local tax authorities. The local chief financial officer's task is to adopt and introduce all changes in MNC-wide financial policy and valuation methods, such as changes in the financial structure or in the methods of process analysis, or if new bank tender schemes are introduced.

The next quality level is operational planning, forecasting—such as working capital requirements or potential provision requirements—and carrying out risk management and insurance activities, in strict conformity with the MNC owner's principles and methods. Local chief financial officers may be entrusted with various analytical tasks, such as analysis of local banks' new products or various risk analyses. These are prepared in accordance with detailed templates sent from headquarters. Chief financial officers transmit and put into practice the headquarters' cost containment and cost reduction requests but, even in this latter instance, there is little room for individual initiatives. Thus it is usually not the local chief financial officer who designs and carries out local business process reengineering. As noted by the CEO of company no. 5: 'Creativity is required mainly to explain the numbers'.

The next quality level includes tasks such as subsidiary-level risk management and/or treasury management. However, assuming the responsibility of managing subsidiary level resources, designing and developing financing alternatives or taking financing decisions, are all excluded for local subsidiaries. The top quality level, that of 'value-added finance', is hardly attainable for peripheral, local subsidiaries. Although the shifting content of chief financial officers' roles away from core financial activities to value-added finance is commonplace in both international business (Hope 2006) and sociological literature (Zorn 2004), local chief financial officers in the companies we analysed were rarely entrusted with decision support tasks, such as modelling the impact of alternative financing decisions, participating in strategic decisions or inventing new ways to leverage capital.

The above list of activities, tasks and responsibilities related to one specific business function serves as an illustration to our finding that business functions are decomposable, consisting of several sub-functions. Some sub-functions consist of routine tasks and are easy to codify. Other sub-functions necessitate non-routine, cognitive and analytical competencies (Autor *et al.* 2003). The partial off-shoring of functions may result in sizeable inter-subsidiary differences in the content and the knowledge-intensity of apparently identical functions.

There were similar differences in quality for several other functions, such as human resource management, logistics, procurement, IT and R&D. Our sample contains cases ranging from minimal to considerable local autonomy, creativity and responsibility. Over time the knowledge content of subsidiaries' function-specific contributions increased to some extent at each of the surveyed companies. While intra-function upgrading, similar to upgrading across functions, was going on gradually and quasi-automatically over time—in line with the evolution of local subsidiaries and with their efforts to build trust and gain recognition of their evolving capabilities from the parent companies—crisis significantly accelerated this process. Upgrading in depth intensified as a consequence of the overall efforts to reorganise and streamline production, increase process efficiency and cut costs.[15] Moreover, cases of upgrading in scope, meaning when local subsidiaries acquired regional or MNC-wide responsibilities as a result of crisis-driven organisational consolidation, also triggered substantial upgrading in depth.

---

[15] As one of the CEOs of company no. 9 put it: 'We are involved in new projects earlier. Now, we are also involved in preparatory activities before the launch of the manufacturing operations of new products: instead of waiting for the parent company to organise for the transportation of the required machinery, we are entrusted to select, often together with the representative of the customer, and purchase the production equipment'.

TRANSITION ECONOMIES AFTER 2008

Functional upgrading performance is hard to measure

Upgrading in depth did not necessarily increase local value added in a quantifiable manner. New responsibilities, new tasks and new sub-functions were added to local functional officers' existing ones. However, officers' salaries did not increase as a consequence of the new and increasingly sophisticated tasks. Neither could they employ additional assistants. In some cases specific functions-related employment did increase, not necessarily as a result of upgrading in depth, but sometimes rather because the expansion of production multiplied the tasks of functional officers. Upgrading that resulted in the increase of specific functions-related employment had a direct and immediate impact on subsidiaries' value added. It should be noted that this impact could be countered by changes in the profitability of the local operations, the other factor that influences the extent of the local value added.

In summary, upgrading, and particularly upgrading in depth, is hard to quantify, as it does not necessarily leave a trace in the subsidiary's accounts. Indicators that refer to upgrading include employment in specific functions—this directly influences local value added, although the indicator is not strongly correlated with the quality level of certain functions—and the value of intangible assets, although valuations are usually distorted and weakly comparable across subsidiaries. Although indicators such as investment in training, and in IT systems, or the costs of technical and management consultancy are also related to upgrading, causal relations, as well as the direction of causality, are ambiguous. Furthermore, the value of these indicators may be distorted by a number of other factors. Thus, for example, investment in training increases if the local company wins government support for training people. Technical and management consultancy fees—if paid to related companies within the MNC—may be part of creative accounting, as the valuation of such headquarters services is not market-based. Overall, the impact of upgrading is practically impossible to measure: it is associated with the intangible value of the subsidiary itself, the headquarters' recognition of subsidiary-specific capabilities and their willingness to take advantage of these capabilities. This type of gradually and meticulously accumulated intangible capital can quickly become obsolete as a result of external factors, such as takeovers, shifts to centralised management practices or deteriorating political and institutional conditions in the host country.

Conclusion

The point of departure of our essay was that by triggering a wave of organisational restructuring at multinational companies, involving the reconfiguration of supply chains and the consolidation of business processes, crisis offered significant upgrading opportunities for peripheral GVC actors. We analysed the case of Hungary which, similarly to other new member states, is deeply integrated into GVCs, especially in the automotive and electronics sectors. We have taken a snapshot of crisis-related product and process upgrading, concentrating on foreign-owned affiliates in Hungary,[16] and investigated their functional upgrading experience. We found that crisis-triggered upgrading was manifested first—as a

---

[16]Our focus on foreign-owned subsidiaries can be considered an important limitation of the essay. The differences between the upgrading patterns of domestic-owned companies and foreign subsidiaries, the scope for indigenous technological and non-technological capability building and the differences in the evolution perspectives of the Southeast Asian (see for example, Hobday & Rush 2007; Chin 2010) and the Central European electronics and automotive sectors are issues for further research.

short-term reaction to falling demand—in MNCs' organisational restructuring. The consolidation of the product and function portfolio and organisational restructuring had beneficial side-effects for some subsidiaries: they could diversify their product portfolios and carry out product upgrading. MNC-level restructuring moves had process-upgrading effects as well, a feature present in all the interviewed companies.

Our investigations produced two major findings in relation to functional upgrading. On the one hand, we revealed that functional upgrading—more specifically, intra-function upgrading and upgrading across functions—was an organic process going on in line with subsidiaries' continuous capability accumulation. This process was markedly accelerated by MNCs' crisis-triggered organisational consolidation moves, inducing upgrading in scope at some subsidiaries which, in turn, gave a new impetus to their upgrading in depth. On the other hand, a key objective of subsidiaries' functional upgrading efforts was to demonstrate their capabilities, increase the knowledge-intensity of their activities, and thereby win recognition from the parent company. The managers' perception was that functional upgrading would strengthen the subsidiary's position in inter-subsidiary competition for increasingly complex and technology-intensive products. In short, functional upgrading facilitates subsidiaries' search for product upgrading by influencing headquarters–subsidiary power relations.

Two open questions remain; whether these moves in upgrading were of a temporary nature and, on the other hand, whether the crisis was used as an excuse to push through long-awaited measures at the level of the multinational companies which had been postponed because of a fear of resistance from workers and local managers.

Research Centre for Economic and Regional Studies, Hungarian Academy of Sciences

References

Autor, D. H., Levy, F. & Murmane, R. J. (2003) 'The Skill Content of Recent Technological Change: An Empirical Exploration', *Quarterly Journal of Economics*, 118, 4, pp. 1279–333.

Baldwin, R. (2011) *Trade and Industrialisation after Globalisation's 2nd Unbundling: How Building and Joining a Supply Chain are Different and Why it Matters*, NBER Working Paper, 17716 (Cambridge, MA, National Bureau of Economic Research).

Birkinshaw, J. (1996) 'How Multinational Subsidiary Mandates are Gained and Lost', *Journal of International Business Studies*, 27, 3, pp. 467–95.

Birkinshaw, J. (2000) *Entrepreneurship in the Global Firm* (London, Sage Publications).

Birkinshaw, J. & Hood, N. (1998) 'Multinational Subsidiary Evolution: Capability and Charter Change in Foreign-Owned Subsidiary Companies', *Academy of Management Review*, 23, 4, pp. 773–95.

Bouquet, C. & Birkinshaw, J. (2008) 'Weight versus Voice: How Foreign Subsidiaries Gain Attention from Corporate Headquarter', *Academy of Management Journal*, 51, 3, pp. 825–45.

Brown, S. (2008) 'Business Processes and Business Functions: A New Way of Looking at Employment', *Monthly Labor Review*, 131, 12, pp. 51–70.

Buckley, P. (2009) 'The Impact of the Global Factory on Economic Development', *Journal of World Business*, 44, 2, pp. 131–43.

Cattaneo, O., Gereffi, G. & Staritz, C. (eds) (2010) *Global Value Chains in a Postcrisis World. A Development Perspective* (Washington, DC, The World Bank).

Cheung, C. & Guichard, S. (2009) *Understanding the World Trade Collapse*, OECD Economics Department Working Papers, 729 (Paris, Organisation for Economic Co-operation and Development).

Chin, G. T. (2010) *China's Automotive Modernization: The Party-State and Multinational Corporations* (New York, Palgrave Macmillan).

Dicken, P. (2011) *Global Shift. Mapping the Changing Contours of the World Economy* (6th edn). (Thousand Oaks, CA & London, SAGE Publication).

TRANSITION ECONOMIES AFTER 2008

Domanski, B. & Gwosdz, K. (2009) 'Toward a More Embedded Production System? Automotive Supply Networks and Localized Capabilities in Poland', *Growth and Change*, 40, 3, pp. 452–82.

Dörrenbächer, C. & Gammelgaard, J. (2006) 'Subsidiary Role Development: The Effect of Micro-Political Headquarters–Subsidiary Negotiations on the Product, Market and Value-Added Scope of Foreign-Owned Subsidiaries', *Journal of International Management*, 12, 3, pp. 266–83.

Ernst, D. (2009) 'A New Geography of Knowledge in the Electronics Industry? Asia's Role in Global Innovation Networks', *Policy Studies*, 54 (Honolulu, East West Center).

Fernandez-Stark, K. & Bamber, P. (2011) 'The Offshore Services Value Chain: Upgrading Trajectories in Developing Countries', *International Journal of Technological Learning Innovation and Development*, 4, 1–3, pp. 206–34.

Filippov, S. & Kalotay, K. (2011) 'Global Crisis and Activities of Multinational Enterprises in New EU Member States', *International Journal of Emerging Markets*, 6, 4, pp. 304–28.

Gereffi, G. (1999) 'International Trade and Industrial Upgrading in the Apparel Commodity Chain', *Journal of International Economics*, 48, 1, pp. 37–70.

Gereffi, G. (2010) *The Economic Crisis: A Global Value Chain Perspective. Presentation at Globalisation and Employment: Global Shocks, Structural Change and Policy Response*, 21 June (Geneva, International Labour Office), available at: http://www.ilo.org/wcmsp5/groups/public/@ed_emp/documents/presentation/wcms_142223.pdf, accessed 11 July 2012.

Gereffi, G. & Fernandez-Stark, K. (2011) *Global Value Chain Analysis: A Primer* (Durham, NC, Center on Globalization, Governance and Competitiveness, Duke University), available at: http://www.cggc.duke.edu/pdfs/2011-05-31_GVC_analysis_a_primer.pdf, accessed 11 July 2012.

Gereffi, G., Humphrey, J. & Sturgeon, T. (2005) 'The Governance of Global Value Chains', *Review of International Political Economy*, 12, 1, pp. 78–104.

Hobday, M. & Rush, H. (2007) 'Upgrading the Technological Capabilities of Foreign Transnational Subsidiaries in Developing Countries: The Case of Electronics in Thailand', *Research Policy*, 36, 9, pp. 1335–56.

Hope, J. (2006) *Reinventing the CFO: How Financial Managers Can Transform Their Roles and Add Greater Value* (Boston, MA, Harvard Business Press).

Humphrey, J. & Schmitz, H. (2004) 'Governance in Global Value Chains', in Schmitz, H. (ed.) *Local Enterprises in the Global Economy* (Cheltenham, Edward Elgar), pp. 95–109.

Jürgens, U. & Krzywdzinski, M. (2009) 'Changing East–West Division of Labour in the European Automotive Industry', *European Urban and Regional Studies*, 16, 1, pp. 27–42.

Kaminski, B. & Ng, F. (2001) *Trade and Production Fragmentation. Central European Economies in European Union Networks of Production and Marketing*, World Bank Policy Research Working Paper, 2611 (Washington, DC, The World Bank).

Milberg, W. & Winkler, D. (2010) *Trade Crisis and Recovery. Restructuring of Global Value Chains*, World Bank Policy Research Working Paper, 5294 (Washington, DC, The World Bank).

Ng, F. & Yeats, A. (1999) *Production Sharing in East Asia. Who Does What for Whom and Why?*, World Bank Policy Research Working Paper, 2197 (Washington, DC, The World Bank).

Pavlínek, P., Domański, B. & Guzik, R. (2009) 'Industrial Upgrading Through Foreign Direct Investment in Central European Automotive Manufacturing', *European Urban and Regional Studies*, 16, 1, pp. 43–63.

Pavlínek, P. & Ženka, J. (2011) 'Upgrading in the Automotive Industry: Firm-Level Evidence from Central Europe', *Journal of Economic Geography*, 11, 3, pp. 559–86.

Pavlínek, P., Ženka, J. & Žížalová, P. (2010) 'Functional Upgrading through Research and Development in the Czech Automotive Industry', *Proceedings of the XXII Conference of the Czech Geographic Society*, Ostrava, 31 August–3 September (Ostrava, Czech Geographical Society and the University of Ostrava), pp. 483–488), available at: http://konference.osu.cz/cgsostrava2010/dok/Sbornik_CGS/Socioekonomicka_geografie/Functional_upgrading_through_research.pdf, accessed 11 July 2012.

Pietrobelli, C. (2008) 'Global Value Chains in the Least Developed Countries of the World: Threats and Opportunities for Local Producers', *International Journal of Technological Learning, Innovation and Development*, 1, 4, pp. 459–81.

Radošević, S. (2005) 'The Electronics Industry in Central and Eastern Europe: A New Global Production Location', *Papeles del Este: Transiciones poscomunistas*, 5, 10, pp. 1–15.

Rugraff, E. & Sass, M. (2012) 'Válság és relokációs fenyegetés a feltörekvő országokban: a magyar autóipar esete', *Külgazdaság*, 56, 9–10, pp. 4–29.

Sass, M. (2009) 'Eltérő örökség és eltérő politikák—hasonló eredmények. Autóipari beszállítók Csehországban és Magyarországon', presentation at the 17th annual conference of the *Hungarian Association of Logistics, Purchasing and Inventory Management*, 11–13 November, Balatonalmádi.

Sato, Y. & Fujita, M. (2009) *Capability Matrix: A Framework for Analyzing Capabilities in Value Chains*, IDE Discussion Papers, 219 (Tokyo, Institute of Developing Economies).

Stehrer, R., Ali-Yrkkö, J., Hanzl-Weiss, D., Foster, N., Rouvinen, P., Seppälä, T., Stöllinger, R. & Ylä-Anttila, P. (2011) *Trade in Intermediate Products and EU Manufacturing Supply Chains*, WIIW Research Reports, 369 (Vienna, The Vienna Institute for International Economic Studies).

Sturgeon, T. J. (2008) 'Mapping Integrative Trade: Conceptualising and Measuring Global Value Chains', *International Journal of Technological Learning, Innovation and Development*, 1, 3, pp. 237–57.

Sturgeon, T. J. & Gereffi, G. (2009) 'Measuring Success in the Global Economy: International Trade, Industrial Upgrading, and Business Function Outsourcing in Global Value Chains', *Transnational Corporations*, 18, 2, pp. 1–35.

Sturgeon, T. J. & Kawakami, M. (2011) 'Global Value Chains in the Electronics Industry: Characteristics, Crisis, and Upgrading Opportunities for Firms from Developing Countries', *International Journal of Technological Learning, Innovation and Development*, 4, 1–3, pp. 120–47.

Sturgeon, T. J. & Van Biesebroeck, J. (2010) *Effects of the Crisis on the Automotive Industry in Developing Countries. A Global Value Chain Perspective*, World Bank Policy Research Paper, 5330 (Washington, DC, The World Bank).

Szalavetz, A. (2012) 'The Hungarian Automotive Sector: A Comparative CEE Perspective with Special Emphasis on Structural Change', in Welfens, P. J. (ed.) *Clusters in Automotive and Information and Communication Technology. Innovation, Multinationalization and Networking Dynamics* (Berlin & Heidelberg, Springer), pp. 241–70.

Szanyi, M. & Sass, M. (2012) 'Relocations in the Electronics Sector: The Case of Hungary', *Two Essays on Hungarian Relocations*, CERS-HAS Discussion Papers, 23 (Budapest, Institute of Economics, Research Centre for Economic and Regional Studies, Hungarian Academy of Sciences), pp. 25–55.

Wang, Q. & von Tunzelmann, N. (2000) 'Complexity and the Functions of the Firm: Breadth and Depth', *Research Policy*, 29, 7–8, pp. 805–18.

Winter, J. (2010) 'Upgrading of TNC Subsidiaries: The Case of the Polish Automotive Industry', *International Journal of Automotive Technology and Management*, 10, 2–3, pp. 145–60.

Yeats, A. (1998) *Just How Big is Global Production Sharing?* World Bank Policy Research Paper, 1871 (Washington, DC, The World Bank).

Zaghini, A. (2005) 'Evolution of Trade Patterns in the New EU Member States', *Economics of Transition*, 13, 4, pp. 629–58.

Zorn, D. M. (2004) 'Here a Chief, There a Chief: The Rise of the CFO in the American Firm', *American Sociological Review*, 69, 3, pp. 345–64.

Appendix

TABLE A1
COMPANIES IN THE SAMPLE

Company no.	Sector	Number of employees (end 2010, rounded)	Interviewed manager	Location	Dates of interview
1	Automotive	600	CEO, HR officer	Western Transdanubia	25 March 2011, 1 March 2012
2	Automotive	300	CFO	Northern Hungary	6 April 2011
3	Automotive (electronics)	400	CEO	Northern Hungary	20 May 2011
4	Electronics	6,800	CEO, procurement officer	Southern Transdanubia	20 September 2010, 31 May 2012
5	Electronics	2,500	CEO, financial officer	Northern Hungary	7 April 2010, 28 June 2012
6	Electronics	1,600	CEO	Western Transdanubia	17 March 2011
7	Automotive (electronics)	1,100	CEO	Central Hungary	16 June 2011
8	Electronics	900	CEO	Northern Great Plain	6 April 2011
9	Automotive	700	CEO, IT manager	Southern Great Plain	27 May 2010, 20 April 2012
10	Automotive	1,100	CEO	Northern Hungary	5 May 2011

Source: Authors' compilation.

Actions and Reactions of Russian Manufacturing Companies to the Crisis Shocks from 2008–2009: Evidence from the Empirical Survey

KSENIA GONCHAR

Abstract

This essay explores the nature of the 2008 crisis and the channels through which it affected the performance of firms in Russia. Based on the findings of a manufacturing industry survey, the evidence suggests that all manufacturing firms were affected by the crisis and that there is no single and dominant transmission channel. Crisis reactions were significantly related to participation in international markets, although participation in trade, in external borrowing or FDI cannot explain recession by themselves. The reversal of growth was mainly caused by demand shock and, following that, by financial constraints. Thus the hypothesis that blames overheating of internal demand in the years prior to the crisis seems to receive statistical backing. Globalised companies, though hit by external shocks, were better prepared to pay the cost and balance the consequences of the crisis.

MANY OBSERVERS EXPECTED THE RUSSIAN ECONOMY TO BE adequately protected from the effects of the global financial crisis of 2008–2009. In contrast to the crisis of 1998, when Russia defaulted on its debts, the country had accumulated reserve assets, benefiting from several years of current account and fiscal surpluses. Firms had also accumulated internal cash reserves and had developed experience from coping with the previous crisis. However, as indicated in the introduction to this issue, the Russian economy experienced severe decline in GDP in 2009, raising questions as to how the external financial crisis could lead to so dramatic a downturn in real output. Dooley and Hutchison (2009), studying the transmission of the crisis to emerging markets, suggested that these countries were adequately prepared for less violent financial shocks from the rest of the world, but the policy measures taken were

The author has benefited from valuable comments, feedback and suggestions by Martin Myant and other participants at the COST Action ISO 902 Systemic Risk and Financial Crisis network workshops and from anonymous referees. I would also like to thank the Basic Research Programme at the National Research University Higher School of Economics (HSE) for financial support and the Ministry for Economic Development of the Russian Federation for making the manufacturing industry survey feasible.

TRANSITION ECONOMIES AFTER 2008

TABLE 1
GDP Growth by Main Sectors (Value Added) in Russia, 2007–2011

	2007	2008	2009	2010	First quarter 2011	Second quarter 2011
GDP growth	8.5	5.2	−7.8	4.0	4.1	3.4
Tradable sectors	3.6	−0.2	−8.0	6.3	8.3	4.7
Agriculture, forestry	1.3	6.4	1.3	−10.7	1.1	0.5
Extraction industries	−2.2	1.0	0.5	4.7	2.4	2.2
Manufacturing	7.5	−2.1	−14.9	12.3	12.9	6.9
Non-tradable sectors	12.4	9.2	−7.2	2.9	2.4	2.4
Electricity, gas, water	−3.4	0.7	−5.0	5.5	−0.3	2.0
Construction	13.0	11.1	−14.6	−0.7	0.8	0.1
Trade	11.7	9.9	−6.2	5.0	1.3	2.3
Transport, communication	4.8	5.2	−8.5	7.7	5.1	3.7
Financial services	29.1	13.5	2.2	−2.4	2.0	2.5

Source: Russian statistical agency and World Bank, 2011, available at: http://documents.worldbank.org/curated/en/2011/09/15115904/growing-risks, accessed 12 April 2012.

insufficient protection as the situation in US financial markets deteriorated through 2008. Other authors point to structural imperfections leading to a specific vulnerability of their economies. Mitra *et al.* (2010) name high trade integration of transition economies and overheating in the boom years as an explanation for the deep contraction. Connolly (2012), on the other hand, found that trade vulnerabilities were of little explanatory value and identified the core explanation of the effects of the crisis in the degree to which foreign savings were used to fuel domestic credit booms. Myant and Drahokoupil (2011, 2012) write that the differences in the severity of the effects of the crisis on transition economies depended on differences in the extent and forms of international integration, meaning the extent of dependence on inflows of external finance, the degree of dependence on exports of goods and the importance to the economies of remittances from citizens working abroad. These in turn reflected 'post-communist' heritages, as well as policies pursued during and after transition. Table 1 shows a further feature of the effects of the crisis on the Russian economy: there was substantial heterogeneity in both the downturn and the recovery across sectors. Manufacturing industries showed matching decline in 2009 and recovery in 2010 and 2011. Extraction industries, heavily dependent on exports, grew gradually and did not decline seriously in 2008–2009.

What follows from these insights, however, is not straightforward. Aggregate data conceal considerable variations across firms. This essay attempts to demonstrate and understand those variations in the case of manufacturing industry by looking at how managers acted in response to the shocks. The goal is to identify the nature of the shocks and details of the channels through which they affected firm performance, thereby also showing which types of firms were hit hardest by the crisis. These questions are addressed empirically using microeconomic data. In the rest of the essay we first discuss the literature that guided the empirical research; then we describe the overall setting of the Russian manufacturing sector from the perspective of possible causes of its downturn in Russia. The following section describes the data and research hypothesis; and finally we present the models and estimation results.

Related literature and context

Research into the causes and consequences of a crisis has long been associated with the business cycle literature and has matured into a body of study that focuses particularly on issues related to finance. Burns and Mitchel (1946) created a theoretical framework for conceptualising responses to shocks. Haberier (1958), in his literature survey, listed many possible causes of crisis, as discussed in business cycle literature, including credit changes, over-investment, costs of production, under-consumption and mass psychology. More recent neoclassical models of economic fluctuations (Kydland & Prescott 1980, 1982) have focused on external sources of economic crisis, such as increases in productivity due to technological innovations. Since then many works have been devoted to identifying the driving forces behind business cycles and have thereby extended theory in a number of directions.

However, the very fact of such variety raises the question of which explanations are likely to be applicable to the current crisis. Ohanian (2010), in his essay on neoclassical business cycle theories, argues that the 2008 economic crisis cannot be satisfactorily understood within current classes of economic models and discusses how business cycle literature could be adapted to capture the key elements of the real crisis events. The analysis that follows builds from works on crises that can be grouped under five headings.

First, there are theories and empirical literature that explain recession in the non-financial business sector by the failure of financial institutions and the declining value of assets. These failures lead to reductions in output, consumption and employment (Carlstrom & Fuerst 1997; Gertler & Kiyotaki 2010).

Second, there is the literature that explains international business cycles by focusing on heterogeneous firm productivity (Ghironi & Melitz 2005). Such authors developed a model of international trade and macroeconomic dynamics, and show a positive cross-country correlation between foreign and domestic GDPs. Close to this work is the study by Rotemberg (2009) which showed how interconnectedness, meaning the number of other firms to which one firm is linked by lending or borrowing, can increase difficulties of firms in times of reduced access to cash.

Third are works that blame economic policies for the recession when those policies distort incentives and increase uncertainties about the economic environment (Taylor 2010).

Fourth, there are works that deal with the specific causes and consequences of crisis in emerging economies (Claessens 2010; Mitra 2010; Yakovlev *et al.* 2010; Connolly 2012; Myant & Drahokoupil 2011, 2012).

The fifth grouping includes managerial literature that views crisis as one of the pressures associated with globalisation and technological advance in the new, dynamic and changeable world of destabilised economies, dominated by uncertainties of all kinds. This literature suggests that ineffective management practices, inflexible organisational forms and inefficient technology systems can be responsible for crisis events (Turner 1976). The main casualties could be expected to be the fragile bureaucratic organisations that are incapable of coping efficiently with the challenges of the crisis (Castells 1996).

At the time of writing, the evidence on how the crisis affected individual firm performance is relatively scarce and offers different results. An example is the work of Claessens *et al.* (2011), who used firm-level statistics from Worldscope data on balance sheets, cash flow and income statements for listed manufacturing companies covering 42 advanced and emerging countries, including 105 Russian firms. The authors studied three possible channels for

TRANSITION ECONOMIES AFTER 2008

transmission of the crisis—financial, trade and demand—following the effects on profitability, sales and capital expenditure. The main finding was that the crisis had a bigger negative impact on the firms that were the most sensitive to demand and trade changes while the impact of financial openness was more limited.

Bricogne *et al.* (2009) explain the heterogeneous performance of French exporters during the crisis trade shocks of 2008. They found that impact of the crisis was not affected by firm size, but that firms in sectors structurally more dependent on external finance were the most seriously affected. Kolasa *et al.* (2010), on the basis of Polish firm-level data, found that foreign ownership provided a higher degree of resilience to the crisis and explained this effect by intra-group lending mechanisms supporting affiliates facing external credit constraints. Levchenko *et al.* (2010) showed that US firms producing intermediate inputs experienced significantly higher percentage reductions in both imports and exports.

Some papers analyse the reaction of firms to crisis rather than transmission channels. For example, Babecký *et al.* (2011) used a large panel of Czech manufacturing firms with 50 or more employees to study employment decisions of firms in pre-crisis and crisis times. They reported increased sales and wage elasticities of firms in crisis. The survey evidence showed that cost reductions by Czech firms were achieved mainly through adjustment of employment levels, of the duration of the working day and of non-labour costs.

Firm-level data on Latin American countries, collected by the World Bank Enterprise Survey in 2006 and 2010, showed how firms adjusted their funding strategies to crisis conditions: firms whose access to financing deteriorated relied more on bank and supply-chain financing; foreign firms or firms that were part of a group made greater use of internal funds, while firms that both exported and imported relied more on bank credits to fund their investment projects (Leitner & Stehrer 2012).

Finally, we may learn from recent publications that study the response of firms to the financial crises of the 1990s. Thus, Kim *et al.* (2012) demonstrated that, in contrast to the French exporters in 2008, firm size mattered for the fate of Korean manufacturing firms in 1998. They used the Korean data on more than 4,000 publicly-listed and privately-owned firms to show that during the 1997–1998 Korean financial crisis small firms with more short-term foreign debt were more likely to suffer larger sales declines and to experience bankruptcy. Large firms with greater exposure to foreign debt performed better during that crisis. Moreover, exporting firms were more likely to survive the crisis than the average for Korean firms.

Statistical evidence suggests that many of the abovementioned sources could cause a downturn in manufacturing industries in Russia, although the results reported in Table 1 are mixed. Thus, if global financial markets are mostly responsible for the crisis transmission, then sectors producing tradable goods should have been hit harder than those producing non-tradable goods. This was not the case. In both parts of the economy we see sectors hit hard, manufacturing among tradable goods and construction among the non-tradable. Agriculture, forestry and financial services actually reported growth in the crisis year of 2009, although agriculture collapsed later because of a drought that cannot be blamed on the economic crisis.

Apart from branch of activity, firm size might also be expected to affect reactions to crisis. The largest firms might have been expected to perform better than the average, being protected by economies of larger scale, by accumulated reserves and by political capital. On the other hand, bigger companies were involved in international trade and

TRANSITION ECONOMIES AFTER 2008

TABLE 2
PERFORMANCE OF THE 400 LEADING RUSSIAN COMPANIES ACROSS SELECTED SECTORS

Sector	Number of 'leading' companies, 2010	Sales growth rate, 2009 − 2008, %	Profit/loss rate
Industry total, including	168	− 9.2	11.4
Oil and natural gas	13	− 6.6	19.0
Electricity	25	14	1.8
Steel	13	− 30.3	− 2.6
Machine building	37	− 18.3	− 4.8
Food processing	27	8.8	6.5
Chemical and petrochemical	19	− 20.9	9.7
Non-ferrous metallurgy	9	− 17.4	17.2
Timber	5	4.8	7.1
Construction materials	3	− 21.7	5.7
Banks	30	34.3	1.4
Transport	26	1.2	7.9
Retail trade	43	6.3	2.2
Wholesale trade	37	6.6	3.6
Telecommunications	9	5	12.5
Construction	14	− 1.5	− 10.9

Note: A leading company is defined as one for which sales exceeded $500 million in 2009. *Source*: Based on the data of the rating agency Expert, 2010, No. 39, available at: http://expert.ru/ratings/table_611687/, accessed 12 April 2012.

borrowed internationally to a much greater extent than middle-sized firms and could therefore have declined more steeply. Table 2 shows mixed results. Some of the biggest firms outperformed the market—banks and construction are the clearest examples—while others—notably the biggest steel companies—effectively defined the downward trend in their sectors.

Questions of the importance of trade effects also inevitably arise in view of the level of internationalisation of the Russian economy which is substantially below that of other transition countries. Thus, between 2005 and 2009 the combined volume of Russian exports and imports relative to GDP declined from 57% to 48%, both relatively low figures, while FDI followed the cyclical trend, also remaining at a low level in terms of

TABLE 3
INDICATORS OF RUSSIA'S INTEGRATION INTO THE WORLD ECONOMY, 2005−2010

	2005	2006	2007	2008	2009	2010
Export, percentage change	6.3	7.9	7.2	− 5.6	− 8.8	
Export share in GDP, %	35	34	30	31	28	29
Import share in GDP, %	22	21	22	22	21	20
FDI, current (billions of dollars)	12.9	29.7	55.1	75.0	36.8	42.9
Manufactures exports (% of merchandise exports)	18.8	16.5	17.0	16.7	17.2	

Note: Foreign direct investment shows the net new investment inflows from foreign sources less disinvestment, summing equity capital, reinvestment of earnings, other long-term capital and short-term capital as shown in the balance of payments.
Source: The World Bank statistical database, available at: http://data.worldbank.org/indicator, accessed 20 October 2011.

TRANSITION ECONOMIES AFTER 2008

TABLE 4
Inventories to Sales Ratios by Sector, 2007–2009

	2007	2008	2009	2009 as % from 2007
Extractive industries	8.8	9.7	10.0	113.0
Manufacturing	15.5	16.0	18.5	119.2
of which;				
Food	13.6	12.1	11.5	84.9
Textiles	18.9	19.3	19.2	102.0
Timber	13.9	15.1	14.5	104.4
Chemicals	11.9	8.6	12.8	107.7
Steel	13.1	10.6	17.3	131.7
Machine building	22.6	29.8	26.1	115.6
Electrical, electronic and optical equipment	18.9	22.0	24.3	128.9
Transport equipment	37.9	45.7	62.4	164.9

Source: Our estimates on the basis of Russian statistical agency data, Promyshlennost' Rossii (2010, pp. 296–98).

international comparisons, as shown in Table 3. Manufacturing industry continued to reduce its export share and increase its import share. For example, the share of machines and equipment in total exports declined from 8.8% in 2000 to 5.7% in 2010, while the share of these goods in imports grew from 31.4% to 44.5% (Torgovlya Rossii 2011, pp. 203–4).

Another possible explanation for declining output is that firms reduced production because they had accumulated a large volume of inventories prior to the crisis. This could then have caused a larger reduction in output than the fall in demand. Table 4 shows that the inventories to sales ratio in 2009 was highest in the transportation equipment sector, followed by machinery, electrical equipment, electronics and optical equipment. In total this ratio in 2008–2009 increased by one-fifth, and could therefore have added to the severity of the crisis. One explanation for the suboptimal stock levels might relate to firms supplying manufactured products for export or to the depressed construction sector. When demand for these products fell, production was already under way for those products with longer gestation periods and final products therefore ended up in inventories. Cost inflation after exchange rate depreciation could also be blamed: company managers tried to accumulate as large a level of input stocks as possible prior to expected price increases. The abilities of Russian companies in inventory management may also be important. Just-in-time production is rare. Companies still typically keep large stocks of materials and components so as to meet the risks of supply insecurity.

A further possibility is that the downturn in Russia was caused primarily by transmission of the financial crisis through international financial markets. The fact of high corporate debt levels would seem to support this argument. A rapid growth of domestic demand, higher than the increase in domestic production, was supported by external borrowing and high levels of imports in the lead-up to crisis. Companies could borrow in foreign currency, enjoying lower interest rates and better conditions of borrowing than available on the domestic financial market. Aleksashenko *et al.* (2011) estimated that at the end of 2009 Russian corporate debt in total was equivalent to 65% of GDP, while external debt was 36% of the total corporate debt. As shown in Figure 1, financing through international capital markets doubled between 2005 and 2008 and reached a level equivalent to 10.7% of GDP. It dropped significantly in the crisis period and continued to decline as the economy recovered.

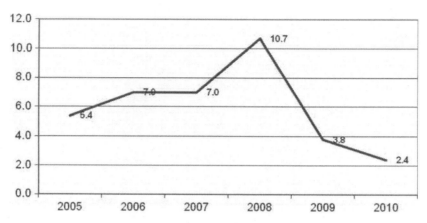

FIGURE 1. Financing via International Capital Markets, Gross Inflows, % of GDP.
Source: World Bank database, available at: http://databank.worldbank.org/Data/Views/Reports/TableView.aspx? IsShared=trueandIsPopular=country, and Trading Economics database, available at: http://www. tradingeconomics.com/russia/financing-via-international-capital-markets-gross-inflows-percent-of-gdp-wb-data.html, accessed 22 January 2013.

However, there are reasons for doubting the importance of this as an explanation for the downturn in Russia. First, the share of Russian firms integrated into the international financial system is not large enough for financial transmission channels to appear as a credible source for the general downturn. We do not have aggregated data for the share of firms borrowing internationally, but survey results show only 8% of surveyed firms that reported on this theme financing their investment through foreign banks, as shown in Figure 2. The majority used internal cash or applied to the Russian commercial banks. However, firms that used external finance both from domestic and foreign banks produced two-thirds of the sample's output in 2007, immediately prior to the crisis. Moreover, Russian commercial banks

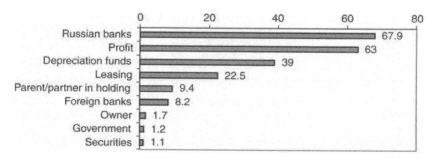

FIGURE 2. Financing Sources of Investments, % of Responding Firms among Investing Firms.
Note: The indicators are constructed from the answers to the question: 'Which sources did your enterprise use to finance investments between 2005 and 2008?' The respondent could give any number of answers from the list of possible options shown in Appendix A.
Source: HSE survey of manufacturing industry, 2009.

borrowed extensively in the West. This transmission mechanism therefore appears potentially important.

A further possibility is that the recession was the result of economic policies leading to a poor investment climate. The Russian economy entered the crisis in a strong fiscal and foreign exchange position. It had established substantial reserve assets, avoided public debt and implemented a gradual and controlled currency depreciation. Together these smoothed the crisis shocks and helped to avoid the worst case scenario. However, this policy hit the positions of import-dependent firms and thereby contributed to recession. Yakovlev *et al.* (2010) found that aggressive borrowing by large companies and their outward investment, combined with their growing inefficiency, can be explained by the distortions created by the specific policy measures introduced prior to crisis. These include expansion of the public sector and public demand, restrictions on foreign investors and shareholders, and growing arbitrary informal relations between the government and big businesses. The anti-crisis policy added to these distortions, while aid was made available mostly for the largest inefficient companies.

Finally, we cannot ignore the argument from management literature that recession is fuelled by such factors as bad management and technological backwardness. The crisis could have exposed a large number of fragile and inefficient firms, previously kept afloat for various reasons and by various means, sometimes protected by enormous distances, sometimes by the low level of competition, and sometimes to satisfy social goals of keeping people employed in small towns where no alternative jobs were available. Internal demand was inflated prior to the crisis enabling many enterprises with very low levels of productivity to survive in the market. Gonchar and Kuznetsov (2008) reported an enormous intersectoral dispersion of value-added productivity between the best 20% and the worst 20% of Russian manufacturing firms, with some of the former up to 25 times as productive as some of the latter. At least one-third of active companies exhibit extremely low levels of productivity. It is plausible to suggest that for this inefficient third the crisis shock was unmanageable.

Although there were different possible channels for crisis transmission, firms were frequently hit by more than one of them. Moreover, different types of firms could react differently to the same form of external shock. The following sections aim to provide empirical evidence for possible determinants of output changes and the reactions of firms.

Data and summary statistics

Data for the study come from the manufacturing firms' survey conducted by the Higher School of Economics, Moscow, in spring 2009. The methodology used was face-to-face interviews with top company managers. The sample included 957 firms in eight manufacturing industries in Russia, randomly structured across sectors and size-groups of enterprises. The sample covered medium-sized and large enterprises that employ 100–10,000 people. This therefore excluded both very large and small firms. In total the sample represented 8% of the total population of manufacturing industry output and 5% of employment. The surveyed firms were located in 48 Russian regions and 357 cities. The composition of the sample is presented in Table 5.

The questionnaire included more than 100 questions about company goals, performance and behaviour with some additional questions related to the evaluation of the causes and consequences of the crisis and preferences for government anti-crisis policies. Firm

TRANSITION ECONOMIES AFTER 2008

TABLE 5
SAMPLE STRUCTURE BY SECTOR AND BY FIRM SIZE, % OF THE TOTAL

Sector	%
Food	24.6
Textiles and garments	9.3
Timber	8.5
Chemicals	9.2
Steel	10.2
Electrical, electronic and optical equipment	12.2
Transport equipment	9.0
Machine building	17.0
TOTAL	100
Firm size	
Under 250 employees	45.0
251–500	24.1
501–1,000	16.5
Over 1,000 employees	14.4
TOTAL	100
Number of observations	957

Source: Author's calculation.

characteristics include two-digit industry codes, number of employees, age of the firm, ownership structure and participation in integrated business groups. Sales, inventory and employment company data from 2009 were extracted from the register and linked to the survey information in the year 2011.

Hypothesis and methodology

We test two competing hypotheses:

(1) Crisis in the manufacturing industry was the product of various dependencies from the outside world, particularly dependence on external finance, international markets or foreign owners.
(2) Crisis is explained by the endogenous structural weaknesses of firms, which experienced suboptimal credit-led growth prior to the crisis and contracted dramatically as soon as the partly artificial domestic demand collapsed. Various inefficiencies and poor inventory management also fit among these structural weaknesses.

In the real world, external and internal factors often operate together, their influences overlapping, and the boundaries between the two are not always distinct. Nevertheless it is useful to study their relative importance as crisis determinants, especially given the unique opportunity to use direct answers from company managers received in the middle of crisis, rather than relying on proxies.

There are several methodological difficulties. First, there is definitional uncertainty between crisis and normality in the perceptions of company managers, especially given the socially constructed nature of both (Drennan & McConnell 2007). The companies grew

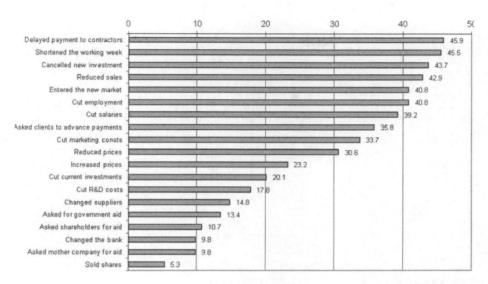

FIGURE 3. ANTI CRISIS ACTIONS AS A MEASUREMENT OF CRISIS EFFECTS: SHARE OF FIRMS REPORTING FOLLOWING MEASURES, %.
Source: HSE survey of manufacturing industry, 2009.

rapidly several years prior to the crisis and a normal cyclical slowdown could be identified by managers with crisis. Second, there is the problem of measuring the impact of the crisis. This could be measured by a number of indicators, notably falling sales, reduced profit, cuts in employment, exit from some markets or rising debts. Subjective perceptions of the crisis may focus on lack of cash or lack of control over a general business situation and rising levels of uncertainty. We therefore estimate three different indicators associated with crisis. The first is the percentage fall in sales from 2008 to 2009. However, about 28% of the sample continued growing through 2008 and 2009, and simultaneously reported problems associated with crisis. Therefore we constructed an additional index summing different reactions of management to the crisis, since the questionnaire included the corresponding question with 19 possible options and the respondent could choose any number of answers.[1] The idea behind this index is that if companies practised active layoffs, cut costs, applied for assistance from the state or from the other sources, then probably they were hit more than firms that did not react. We assume that the action is taken when the constraint is serious. On average firms reported between four and five actions, with the highest figure being 18. Figure 3 shows that the actions of managers are dominated by various cost-saving measures, starting from delayed payments to reduction of sales, salaries and costs.

However, this measurement also has its drawbacks, because companies that did not invest would not report an investment decline. Therefore the cumulative index is biased towards more sophisticated firms. To cope with this possible bias, we added an estimate of the probability of measures that were the most difficult in the Russian context, personnel layoffs and/or cuts in pay. Table 6 uses indicators for dependent variables across two groupings,

[1] The question was as follows: 'If your firm encountered problems associated with the crisis, which actions have you undertaken to solve the problems?'.

TABLE 6

STATISTICS OF DEPENDENT VARIABLES ACROSS SECTORS

	Mean sales growth/decline rate, %		Mean number of reported anti-crisis actions		Share of firms which reported layoffs and/or pay cuts, %	
	Among declining firms, %	Among growing firms, %	Among declining firms	Among growing firms	Among declining firms, %	Among growing firms, %
Food	−24.0	25.8	4.1	3.2	40.2	30.0
Textiles and garments	−25.8	21.0	5.4	4.3	54.6	45.8
Timber	−34.6	20.9	6.0	6.5	78.6	75.0
Chemicals	−27.0	36.2	5.3	3.6	66.1	25.0
Steel	−37.9	27.6	5.6	4.8	67.1	61.5
Electrical, electronic and optical equipment	−30.2	29.0	5.7	3.7	64.3	36.4
Transport equipment	−40.2	97.8	5.4	3.5	60.7	17.6
Machine building	−34.6	25.7	6.1	4.5	77.9	51.5
Total	−31.6	32.0	5.4	3.7	63.1	36.4
Number of observations	585	241				

Source: Author's calculation from the HSE (Higher School of Economics, Moscow) survey of manufacturing industry data from spring 2009, as referred to in the text.

firms that declined and firms that continued with robust growth between 2008 and 2009. It shows significant variety in output dynamics across and within sectors. However, it is noteworthy that growing firms reacted to the crisis with about half as many measures and they practised layoffs and/or cuts in pay significantly less often.

Table 7 sets out basic differences in the descriptive statistics for the independent and dependent variables. The story that these figures tell is very inconclusive. Exceptionally low figures for sales dynamics (a decline of 28.1%) in the group of firms that reported a poor financial position is understandable: these firms also responded with the highest number of actions, and more than 80% of them laid people off. Comparable output contraction (by 25.3%) was recorded only in the group of firms which reported a collapse in demand. Thus we may expect that recession followed demand collapse and debt crisis. It remains to be seen how both are related to trade integration and other dependencies from the outside world. A binary correlation setting firms with cash and demand problems against their levels of external dependency proved insignificant.

Our data allow for testing of several indicators of external dependency. More than two-thirds of the sample are integrated into the outside world through trade, international borrowing or foreign ownership and, on average, this globalised group performed better in the crisis than purely national firms. To test the relative importance of the form of international participation, we divided trade integrated companies into four groupings, those with 'no international trade' as a reference category, two-way international traders, only exporters and only importers. It was

TRANSITION ECONOMIES AFTER 2008

TABLE 7
LIST OF INDICATORS, DEFINITIONS AND HYPOTHESIS

Indicator and coding	Definition and hypothesis	Descriptive statistics of dependent variables		
		Sales growth rate 2008– 2009, %	Number of anti-crisis actions	Layoffs and/ or pay cuts, % of firms
Two-way international traders	Firms engaged both in export and import. We expect that the variable captures the highest level of trade integration, and if the globalisation logic of crisis transmission holds, then this group will be hit most			
Yes = 1		−6.3	5.6	58.1
No = 0		−17.0	4.4	54.2
Exporters	Exporters that do not import. Their level of trade integration is lower than in the group of two-way traders, but they avoided the effects of higher import costs after devaluation			
Yes = 1		−23.7	4.9	65.4
No = 0		−10.4	4.8	53.1
Importers	Importers that do not export. These firms were hit by Ruble devaluation, but avoided the external demand shock			
Yes = 1		−10.5	4.8	48.4
No = 0		−13.5	4.8	57.0
Firms under foreign ownership	Measured as a dummy, if the firm has any FDI. This factor may work both as a sign of vulnerability (foreign owners adjust output and employment decisively) or as a stabiliser, because foreign-owned firms as a rule are more efficient and cash rich			
Yes = 1		−8.3	4.6	47.4
No = 0		−14.4	4.9	56.8
Borrowed from foreign banks	External borrowers will be hurt by the world financial crisis directly. On the other hand these firms were strong enough prior to the crisis and could bear the crisis costs without dramatic cost saving measures			
Yes = 1		10.2	5.4	54.5
No = 0		−14.5	4.8	55.5
Leader/laggard	Dummy built from self-assessments of competitive position of the firm against the best performing national leader in the market. We expect that weak firms are more likely to be hit, because of their fragile finances, organisation and technical capabilities			
2 = Leader		−14.6	5.0	54.9
1 = Laggard		−11.9	4.7	55.9
Inventories growth rate 2009/2008	We expect that sales and stock dynamics are interconnected so that higher stock accumulation leads to lower output	In the sample average sales declined by 13%, while stock levels increased by 7%		
Inventories/ sales ratio in 2007	High stock levels prior to the crisis led to output decline and anti-crisis actions. This may reflect the poor inventory management	24% on average, ranging from 16% in the food sector to more than 30% in electronics and transport equipment		
Demand collapse	Variable built from respondent's assessment of problems, emerging from the 2008 crisis, which takes values from 1 to 3. The higher value indicates greater relative importance of the demand shock			

151

TRANSITION ECONOMIES AFTER 2008

TABLE 7
(CONTINUED)

Indicator and coding	Definition and hypothesis	Descriptive statistics of dependent variables		
		Sales growth rate 2008–2009, %	Number of anti-crisis actions	Layoffs and/or pay cuts, % of firms
Problem does not exist = 1		11.6	2.9	28.0
Problem not too acute = 2		− 6.0	3.9	40.7
Very acute problem = 3		− 25.3	6.0	73.5
Public procurement collapse	Values analogous to those for the previous variable. We expect that public procurement decline affected downturn and anti-crisis reactions			
Problem does not exist = 1		− 13.0	4.6	53.8
Problem not too acute = 2		− 10.9	4.6	51.8
Very acute problem = 3		− 16.7	6.0	67.6
Credit cost increased	Values analogous to those for the previous variable. We expect that firms hit by high credit costs fell victim to the failure of local financial institutions, which in turn were affected by international borrowing			
Problem does not exist = 1		− 14.6	3.5	48.6
Problem not too acute = 2		− 6.1	4.6	48.9
Very acute problem = 3		− 16.3	5.9	64.5
Cash position of the firm	Variable built from self-assessment of the financial position of the firm at the end of 2008. A good financial position implies that a firm avoided severe crisis effects			
Poor = 1		− 28.1	6.6	80.9
Satisfactory = 2		− 11.8	4.6	53.4
Good = 3		− 7.0	4.1	42.5
Firm in a holding company	Needed to control for the vulnerability of the firm to the decisions of the mother company and limited freedom of the dependent firm within a holding structure to take anti-crisis decisions			
Yes = 1		− 14.56	4.6	26.0
No = 0		− 12.5	5.4	30.3
Size groups, number of employees	Control variable			
<250 = 1		− 15.9	4.5	53.4
251–500 = 2		− 14.1	4.8	57.6
501–1,000 = 3		− 10.8	4.8	52.2
>1,000 = 4		− 6.3	5.8	62.3

intended to capture the difference in performance of globalised firms depending on the nature of their problems. Thus, if exporters faced mainly demand problems, many importers, especially importers of machinery and equipment, launched the new investment cycle for equipment and technologies' upgrade prior to the crisis and could experience the double shock, from increased credit costs and from national currency devaluation. A counterargument is that in Russia, as elsewhere, the most efficient and larger firms self-select into international markets. Their resistance to shocks could therefore be higher than within the group of less efficient companies that target only the domestic market for sales and supplies.

The hypothesis about the determinants of the recession not directly related to the outside world is tested with the help of several indicators: size of the firm, its competitive position relative to the national market leader, participation in a holding-company structure and sectoral dummies that capture unobserved sectoral trends, like price dynamics and performance prior to the crisis. In addition, we construct two variables to assess the role of inventory accumulation. Thus we test the hypothesis that weak and inefficient firms, smaller companies and firms in particularly depressed sectors are more likely to be hit, because of their fragile finances, organisation and technical capabilities. Many inefficient firms grew extensively prior to the crisis thanks to the inflated domestic demand, generated mainly by construction and private consumption, as well as by the credit boom. They proved particularly vulnerable to the sudden reversal of domestic demand and the resulting reversal in growth could be exceptionally severe. With respect to the role of size, two options are possible. Larger firms should have better access to finance, and smaller firms would therefore be expected to reduce output more sharply. Alternatively, larger firms may be less flexible and more bureaucratic. Their reaction to the crisis might therefore be inadequate to the challenges.

Model and findings

We estimate three models and use an identical set of explanatory variables.

$$\log Y_{1i} = \beta_0 + X_i'\beta + \sum_{j=1}^{7} \gamma_j D_{ji} + \varepsilon_i \tag{1}$$

$$Y_{2i} = \beta_0 + X_i'\beta + \sum_{j=1}^{7} \gamma_j D_{ji} + \varepsilon_i \tag{2}$$

$$\text{Prob}\,(Y_{3i} = 1) = \text{probit}\left(\beta_0 + X_i'\beta + \sum_{j=1}^{7} \gamma_j D_{ji} + \varepsilon_i\right) \tag{3}$$

where i is the enterprise, X_i' are the tested determinants of crisis and D_i are sectoral dummies. The first model is a standard OLS (ordinary least squares) regression on sales growth/decline ratio $Y_1 = \log\,(1 + (\text{sales2009} - \text{sales2008})/(\text{sales2008}))$. The second model is the MLE (maximum-likelihood estimation) Poisson regression on the number of reported anti-crisis actions (Y_2). Finally, the third model is the probit regression on the likelihood of layoffs and/ or pay cuts (Y_3). Results are presented in Table 8.

The findings provide evidence that practically all firms were affected by the crisis. Even firms that did not reverse growth reported hardships and undertook active measures to smooth out the consequences of financial and market distress. The crisis affected enterprises

TRANSITION ECONOMIES AFTER 2008

TABLE 8
REGRESSION RESULTS

	OLS on logged sales growth rate 2009/2008	Poisson MLE on the number of reported anti crisis measures	Probit on probability of layoffs and/or pay cuts
Two-way international traders	0.1312**	0.2069***	−0.0358
Exporters	0.007	0.0688	0.0263
Importers	0.045	0.1569**	−0.1654
Firms with foreign owner	−0.0624	−0.1307*	−0.1502
Borrowers from the foreign banks	0.1135	0.0588	0.1862
Leader/laggard	−0.0663*	0.0979**	0.076
Inventories growth rate 2009/2008	0.1402***	−0.0303	−0.1237
Inventories/sales ratio in 2007	−0.0096	0.0391*	0.0328
Demand collapse	−0.1441***	0.2891***	0.5449***
Increased credit cost	−0.0159	0.2143***	0.1969**
Public procurement collapse	0.009	0.0509*	−0.0155
Cash position of the firm	0.0815**	−0.1611***	−0.4668***
Firm in holding	−0.036	0.2151***	0.2835*
Size group of the firm	0.0424**	0.0127	0.0212
Textiles	−0.0003	0.0636	0.1938
Timber	−0.2996***	0.2445***	0.8299***
Chemicals	−0.0815	0.0501	0.3494
Steel	−0.2792***	0.1842**	0.6077**
Electrical, electronic and optical equipment	−0.13*	0.1017	0.3648
Transport equipment	−0.3036***	0.0822	0.2931
Machinery	−0.1913***	0.2117***	0.7496***
_cons	0.076	0.064	−1.25***
N	745	743	751
Rsq	0.23	0.14	0.18

Notes: * $p < 0.05$; ** $p < 0.01$; *** $p < 0.001$; food industry is a reference category among sectoral dummies. Non-trading firms is a reference category among groups of international traders.

by much more than one mechanism, usually with several that probably complemented each other. Our initial question, over whether outside dependencies or internal inefficiencies made firms particularly vulnerable, therefore found no conclusive answer.

It is not legitimate to assume that trade integration did not matter, despite the finding that international trade does not explain recession and instead is positively associated with the higher growth rate for the two-way traders. This group also shows a significantly larger number of reactions than non-traders, with a negative, albeit not significant, probability of layoffs. A wide variety of anti-crisis reactions in the group of two-way international traders may also be explained by the higher degree of sophistication of these firms: they not only practised cost-economising measures, but could also rely on cash reserves and market power to enter new markets, manipulate prices, change suppliers and/or delay payments, measures beyond the financial reach of less favourably placed firms.

Contrary to our expectation, there is no evidence that the group of only importers contracted more severely than non-trading companies, though this group undertook significantly more anti-crisis measures. Thus we may conclude that trade integration of manufacturing firms, especially two-way trade, was rather a factor stabilising sales, although it increased the likelihood and variety of reported constraints. This can be explained by self-selection of efficient companies into international markets, following from their underlying productivity advantage. Internationalised firms were severely hit by the turbulences on markets, but had sufficient resources and market power to cope with the shocks.

The effect of other measures of globalisation—foreign ownership and borrowing from foreign banks—is less precisely estimated. The coefficient by FDI firms in the specification of the second model is negative and significant only at the 10% level: the number of reactions was lower than within the group of firms with national owners. The coefficient for layoffs was negative and insignificant. Thus we may conclude that FDI and foreign borrowing did not influence the impact of the crisis on firms or their reactions. Neither of these internationalised groups were associated with layoffs or pay cuts.

The differences across industries are more important in explaining the severity of recession and reactions of firms than are other structural factors. Firms in the steel[2] and timber industries declined dramatically, irrespective of the markets they served. They reported a significantly higher number of reactions and actively practised layoffs. This reflects the particular vulnerability of steel and timber companies to the combination of demand and price dynamics on the external and domestic markets during the 2008–2009 period.

Prior accumulation of inventories does not explain output decline. We can only confirm that the dynamics of inventory accumulation interacts with the dynamics of output and the stock growth rate is significantly and positively associated with the sales growth rate. No evidence was found that firms used inventories to smooth production when demand dropped. On the contrary, firms that invested in inventories, measured by the stock growth rate in 2008–2009, were more likely to maintain robust sales growth. This applies at the 1% significance level. Poor inventory management, measured by the 2007 inventory/sales ratio, is only modestly associated with the reported anti-crisis actions and has a negative, albeit not significant, coefficient when the probability of layoffs is regressed. Firms that were part of holding companies did not suffer steeper declines than independent entities, although they reported significantly more reactions and layoffs. We did not find evidence for the proposition that smaller firms were hit harder than larger, or that leaders did better in the crisis than laggards.

Concluding remarks

The evidence presented in this essay suggests that all manufacturing firms were affected by the 2008–2009 crisis, and there is no single and decisive explanation for the dominant transmission channel. Our analysis showed that it is not sufficient to measure the crisis with the conventional indicators of output downturn, because firms with more favourable starting positions could sustain sales and yet be hit in other directions, leading to cuts in investment and R&D projects, reduced geographical expansion or employment cuts. The indicator of anti-crisis actions as a measure of crisis impact provided interesting results, especially in combination with the more conventional sales dynamics indicator.

Overall, the cross-sectional differences between international traders and non-traders in the intensity of actions that can reduce costs and stabilise performance suggests that crisis

[2]There is a possible problem with these findings from the sample selection: the largest holding companies in steel production, which employ more than 10,000 people, were not surveyed. The high vulnerability of steel companies should therefore be interpreted with caution. The sample here is made up from second-rank producers which target mostly local markets and sell to the depressed domestic construction sector.

reactions were significantly related to participation in international markets. However, trade channels do not explain recession, nor do external borrowing or FDI. Reversed growth was mainly caused by the demand shock and following that by financial constraints. For both, unobserved sectoral characteristics rather than the direction of trade mattered. Thus the hypothesis blaming overheating of internal demand in the years prior to the crisis seems to receive statistical backing. In the case of the Russian medium-sized manufacturing companies we did not find empirical evidence for an explanation of the crisis from the failure of financial institutions and the declining value of securities.

We are not able to give a conclusive answer on whether external dependencies or internal structural weaknesses mattered most. The two effects cannot be separated. Abnormal domestic demand growth prior to the crisis was fuelled by high primary materials prices on the international markets and by external borrowing by Russian banks. This allowed inefficient firms to borrow and customers to pay far above reasonable limits. The globalised companies, though hit by external shocks, were better prepared to pay the cost and balance the consequences of the crisis.

This finding carries implications for policy making. While the government introduces import duties to protect the domestic market and devalues the exchange rate to protect exporters, the latter are rather punished than protected. In the real world, firms' imports complement their exports, through the diversified sources of supply of materials and components from the international market. Therefore expanded export and import opportunities in manufacturing industries can have a positive effect on firm performance, in spite of emerging dependencies.

National Research University—Higher School of Economics

References

Aleksashenko, S., Mironov, V. & Miroshnichenko, L. (2011) 'Rossiiski krisis i antikrisisnii paket: tseli, masshtabi, effectivnost', *Voprosy Ekonomiki*, 2, pp. 23–49.

Babecký, J., Galuščák, K. & Lízal, L. (2011) *Firm-Level Labour Demand: Adjustment in Good Times and During the Crisis*, Czech National Bank Working Paper Series, No. 15, December (Prague, Czech National Bank).

Bricogne, J. C., Lionel Fontagné, L., Gaulier, G., Taglioni, D. & Vicard, V. (2009) *Firms and the Global Crisis: French Exports in the Turmoil*, Banque de France Working Paper, No. 265 (Paris, Banque de France).

Burns, A. F. & Mitchel, W. C. (1946) *Measuring Business Cycles* (New York, National Bureau of Economic Research).

Carlstrom, C. T. & Fuerst, T. S. (1997) 'Agency Costs, Net Worth, and Business Fluctuations: A Computable General Equilibrium Analysis', *American Economic Review*, 87, 5, pp. 893–910.

Castells, M. (1996) *The Rise of the Network Society* (Malden, MA, Blackwell).

Chari, V. V. & Kehoe, P. J. (2009) 'Confronting Models of Financial Frictions with the Data', available at: http://research.stlouisfed.org/conferences/policyconfpapers2009/Chari_Kehoe.pdf, accessed 6 August 2012.

Claessens, S. (2010) 'The Financial Crisis Policy Challenges for Emerging Markets and Developing', *The Journal of Applied Economic Research*, 4, 2, pp. 177–96.

Claessens, S., Tong, H. & Wei, S. J. (2011) *From the Financial Crisis to the Real Economy: Using Firm-level Data to Identify Transmission Channels*, NBER Working Paper, 17360, August (Cambridge, MA, National Bureau of Economic Research).

Connolly, R. (2012) 'The Determinants of the Economic Crisis in Post-Socialist Europe', *Europe-Asia Studies*, 64, 1, pp. 35–67.

Cravino, J. & Llosa, L. G. (2010) 'The Behavior of the Firm Size Distribution during Recessions', unpublished manuscript.

TRANSITION ECONOMIES AFTER 2008

Didier, T., Hevia, C. & Schmukler, S. L. (2011) *How Resilient Were Emerging Economies to the Global Economic Crisis*, World Bank Policy Research Working Paper, 5637 (Cambridge, MA, National Bureau of Economic Research).

Dooley, M. P. & Hutchison, M. M. (2009) *Transmission of the US Subprime Crisis to Emerging Markets: Evidence on the Decoupling–Recoupling Hypothesis*, NBER Working Paper, 15120, available at: http://www.nber.org/papers/w15120, accessed 6 August 2012.

Drennan, L. T. & McConnell, A. (2007) *Risk and Crisis Management in the Public Sector* (London, Routledge).

Gertler, M. & Kiyotaki, N. (2010) *Financial Intermediation and Credit Policy in Business Cycle Analysis*, Working Paper, available at: http://www.princeton.edu/~kiyotaki/papers/gertlerkiyotakiapril6d.pdf, accessed 10 October 2011.

Ghironi, F. & Melitz, M. J. (2005) 'International Trade and Macroeconomic Dynamics with Heterogeneous Firms', *Quarterly Journal of Economics*, 120, 3, pp. 865–915.

Gonchar, K. & Kuznetsov, B. (eds) (2008) *Rossiiskaya promyshlennost' na etape rosta. Faktori konkurentosposobnosti firm* (Moscow, Higher School of Economics).

Haberier, G. (1958) *Prosperity and Depression: A Theoretical Analysis of Cyclical Movements* (3rd edn) (London, Allen and Unwin).

Kim, Y. J., Tesar, L. & Zhang, J. (2012) *The Impact of Foreign Liabilities on Small Firms: Firm-Level Evidence from the Korean Crisis*, NBER Working Paper, 17756, January (Cambridge, MA, National Bureau of Economic Research).

Kolasa, M., Rubaszek, M. & Taglioni, D. (2010) 'Firms in the Great Global Recession: The Role of Foreign Ownership and Financial Dependence', *Emerging Markets Review*, 11, 4, December, pp. 341–57.

Kydland, F. E. & Prescott, E. C. (1980) 'A Competitive Theory of Fluctuations and the Feasibility and Desirability of Stabilization Policy', in Fischer, S. (ed.) *Rational Expectations and Economic Policy* (Chicago, IL, University of Chicago Press), pp. 169–98.

Kydland, F. E. & Prescott, E. C. (1982) 'Time to Build and Aggregate Fluctuations', *Econometrica*, 50, 6, pp. 1345–70.

Leitner, S. M. & Stehrer, R. (2012) *Access to Finance and Composition of Funding during the Crisis: A Firm-level Analysis for Latin American Countries*, The Vienna Institute for International Economic Studies Working Papers, 78 (Vienna, Vienna Institute for International Economic Studies).

Levchenko, A. A., Logan, T. L. & Tesar, L. (2010) 'The Collapse of International Trade during the 2008–09 Crisis: In Search of the Smoking Gun', *IMF Economic Review*, 58, 2, pp. 214–53.

Mitra, P. K. (2010) 'The Impact of Global Financial Crisis and Policy Responses: The Caucasus, Central Asia and Mongolia', *Global Journal of Emerging Market Economies*, 2, 189, available at: http://eme.sagepub.com/content/2/2/189, accessed 6 August 2012.

Mitra, P., Selowsky, M. & Zalduendo, J. (2010). *Turmoil at Twenty: Recession, Recovery, and Reform in Central and Eastern Europe and the Former Soviet Union*, World Bank, available at: https://openknowledge.worldbank.org/handle/10986/2682, accessed 5 May 2011.

Myant, M. & Drahokoupil, J. (2011) *Transition Economies: Political Economy in Russia, Eastern Europe, and Central Asia* (Hoboken, NJ, Wiley-Blackwell).

Myant, M. & Drahokoupil, J. (2012) 'International Integration, Varieties of Capitalism, and Resilience to Crisis in Transition Economies', *Europe-Asia Studies*, 64, 1, pp. 1–33.

Ohanian, L. (2010) 'The Economic Crisis from a Neoclassical Perspective', *Journal of Economic Perspectives*, 24, 4, pp. 45–66.

Promyshlennost' Rossii (2010) *Statisticheskii sbornik* (Moscow, Rosstat).

Rotemberg, J. (2009) *Liquidity Needs in Economies with Financial Obligations*, CQER Working Paper 09-01 (Atlanta, GA, Federal Reserve Bank of Atlanta).

Taylor, J. B. (2010) 'Getting Back on Track: Macroeconomic Policy Lessons from the Financial Crisis', *Federal Reserve Bank of St. Louis Review*, 93, 3, pp. 165–76.

Torgovlya Rossii (2011) *Statisticheskii sbornik* (Moscow, Rosstat) available at: http://www.gks.ru/wps/wcm/connect/rosstat/rosstatsite/main/publishing/catalog/statisticCollections/doc_1139916653609, accessed 30 April 2012.

Turner, B. (1976) 'The organizational and interorganizational development of disasters', *Administrative Science Quarterly*, 21, 3, pp. 378–97.

Yakovlev, A., Simachev, Y. & Danilov, Y. (2010) 'The Russian Corporation: Patterns of Behaviour during the Crisis', *Post-Communist Economies*, 22, 2, pp. 129–40.

TRANSITION ECONOMIES AFTER 2008

Appendix A Selected questions asked during the interview and used in this study

1. Type of economic activity.
2. Number of workers included in staff list in 2007 and 2008.
3. Total value of sales in 2007 and 2008.
4. Is your establishment an independent (autonomous) firm or a part of holding company group?
5. What share of common stock belongs to the following groups of owners: (1) Russian private owners; (2) foreign private owners; (3) federal authorities; (4) regional/local authorities?
6. Did your establishment sell goods to the following customers in 2008: government, foreign companies working in Russia, exports?
7. Did you import material inputs and parts? If yes, what is the share of imports in the total input costs in 2008?
8. Did you invest in machinery and equipment? If yes, what is the share of imported machines and equipment in total investment?
9. Please evaluate how the competitiveness of your firm has changed relative to the leaders in the sector in 2005–2008.
10. Evaluate the financial position of your enterprise by the end of 2008 (one answer—good, satisfactory, bad).

	We are not behind (leaders)	We are behind, but the gap closes	We are behind, the gap is constant	We are behind, and the gap becomes wider	Hard to answer
Russian leaders					
Foreign leaders					

11. Which sources did your enterprise use to finance investments between 2005 and 2008? Any number of answers: Russian commercial banks; international commercial banks; financial leasing; trade credit (supplier or customer); non-financial firms-partners; financial market; depreciation; profit.
12. What management methods are used in your establishment? A list of 13 technologies is offered, including 'Just-in-time' production.

		This problem does not apply	The problem exists, but is not too acute	Very acute problem
a.	Demand contraction	1	2	3
b.	State procurement contraction	1	2	3
c.	Non-payment for products sold	1	2	3
d.	Use of barter or promissory notes	1	2	3
e.	Credit cost increase	1	2	3
f.	Credit term decrease	1	2	3
g.	New requirements for collateral	1	2	3
h.	Advanced payments—requirement from subcontractors	1	2	3
i.	Dramatic worsening of the financial position, bankruptcy threat	1	2	3
j.	Others (specify)		2	3

TRANSITION ECONOMIES AFTER 2008

13. How serious for your enterprise are problems stemming from the current crisis?
14. If your enterprise was hit by the crisis, which of the following actions did you take to solve the problem (any number of answers):

> Reduced sales
> Cut employment
> Shortened the working week
> Cut salaries
> Asked clients to pay in advance
> Cut planned investment
> Cut current investment
> Entered a new market
> Increased prices
> Reduced prices
> Asked shareholders (owners) for aid
> Asked mother company for aid
> Asked for government aid
> Changed bank
> Changed suppliers
> Sold shares
> Cut marketing expenditure
> Cut R&D expenditure

Banks—the Role of Ownership and Regulation

Central and East European Bank Responses to the Financial 'Crisis': Do Domestic Banks Perform Better in a Crisis than their Foreign-Owned Counterparts?

RACHEL A. EPSTEIN

Abstract

In the context of transition, nine out of the 10 post-communist countries that ultimately joined the European Union reluctantly privatised the bulk of their banking sectors with foreign capital. The financial crisis of 2008–2009 therefore sparked fears that foreign banks would remove their operations from their Central and East European markets because of a 'home bias' in lending. Such fears were predicated on the widely held beliefs that banks' loyalties lie with their home markets and that it is therefore desirable to protect domestic bank ownership to help combat an economic downturn. This essay casts doubt on the value of banking sector protectionism by comparing foreign and domestic bank behaviour in Central and Eastern Europe during the crisis. The essay finds no consistent relationship between domestic control and either limited economic vulnerability or countercyclical lending.

NINE OUT OF THE 10 POST-COMMUNIST COUNTRIES THAT joined the EU since 2004 sold the bulk of their banking sectors to foreign owners, mostly to West European banking groups. It is now normal in Central and Eastern Europe for banking sectors to be at least 70% foreign owned. By 2009, foreign bank ownership exceeded 80% in seven Central and East European countries. Although Central and East European politicians had been reluctant to privatise formerly state-owned banks primarily with foreign capital, a series of banking crises, in connection with pressure from international financial institutions, ultimately pushed them to do so (Bonin *et al.* 1998; Epstein 2008a; Bonin & Schnabel 2011). After enjoying several years of explosive credit growth, in part because of foreign lenders, the question of whether foreign bank ownership increased the region's vulnerability emerged again in the wake of

I would like to thank Jan Drahokoupil, Martin Myant and two anonymous reviewers for their comments on earlier drafts of this paper. I am also grateful to Stephen Bloom for his input on the Latvian section of the article. Erica Fein, Balazs Martonffy, and Gosia Pawlak all provided invaluable research assistance. The Faculty Research Fund and the Professional Research Opportunities Fund at the University of Denver, as well as the Colorado European Union Center of Excellence at the University of Colorado at Boulder, provided field research support.

Lehman Brothers' collapse in 2008 when the threat of capital outflows from the region became acute.

One way to assess the consequences of foreign bank ownership in a financial crisis is to compare foreign banks' behaviour to that of domestically controlled banks. If domestic banks give states more control over credit allocation and a channel through which to promote countercyclical lending in a crisis, it may be the case that high levels of foreign ownership are particularly dangerous to a country in a financial crisis; but if the problem for crisis-ridden economies is an overall lack of confidence, then it may be that domestically controlled banks offer no additional value. And to the extent that they are less well capitalised than their foreign counterparts, domestic banks may actually pose a threat to an economy in a financial crisis or economic downturn.

The central argument here is that foreign compared to domestic ownership is not decisive in explaining the compounding or countercyclical role of financial institutions in an economic downturn. I examine the behaviour of foreign banks in Central and Eastern Europe and then use comparative evidence from domestically controlled banks in Poland, Hungary, Latvia and Slovenia to assess the argument. The relevant measures are whether domestically controlled banks contribute more or less than their foreign counterparts to an economy's vulnerability in the run-up to a crisis and whether either foreign or domestic banks reduce credit in a crisis or engage in countercyclical lending instead.

In broad outline, foreign banks did contribute to selected countries' vulnerabilities in the run-up to the crisis, both through cross-border and foreign currency lending. But a number of domestically controlled banks in Central and Eastern Europe did this as well—regardless of whether those domestic Central and East European banks were state owned or privately owned. Second, foreign banks did not 'cut and run' in the 2008–2009 crisis. Although there is a debate about why Western banks maintained their exposures (EBRD 2009; IMF 2010; Pistor 2011; De Haas *et al.* 2012; Kudrna & Gabor, in this collection) the relevant conclusion here is that although there was a slow-down in the growth of credit from foreign-owned banks to the region, it did not cause devastating capital outflows that characterised the Asian financial crisis of 1997–1998.

The central contribution of this essay is to provide detail on domestic bank behaviour in the crisis in order to assess whether states gain advantage and limit vulnerability by preserving domestic bank ownership. The general answer to this question is that sometimes states and economies benefit from their domestic banks and at other times they do not. Poland's majority state-owned bank, PKO Bank Polski (PKO BP), was conservative in the pre-crisis phase. Then, PKO BP played a countercyclical role in the post-Lehman crisis, partly in conscious response to its own managers' perceptions that foreign-owned banks in the country were pulling back on credit provision. By contrast, Latvia's domestically but privately controlled Parex Bank engaged in risky behaviour in the run-up to the crisis, borrowing from abroad and contributing to the country's foreign exchange exposure. Parex Bank's failure required a costly nationalisation and was the proximate cause for Latvian officials to call on the IMF for assistance. Hungary's OTP Bank is a separate kind of case. It is majority foreign owned, though through dispersed shareholdings. Thus OTP's Hungarian managers both contributed to Hungary's difficulties by following foreign banks into foreign exchange lending, and also had a countercyclical role when the crisis hit by serving as a channel for the government's stimulus plan. Slovenia by contrast is the only post-communist country that is in the EU that followed a West European model of financial

TRANSITION ECONOMIES AFTER 2008

sector protectionism, resulting in less than 30% foreign ownership of the country's banks. Because Slovenia's domestically controlled (and state controlled) banks engaged in large-scale cross-border borrowing in the run-up to the crisis, however, they also contributed to Slovenia's vulnerability.

Given the success of PKO BP in both limiting Poland's vulnerability in the run-up to the crisis and in increasing its own balance sheet through the crisis, one might conclude that of the possible domestic ownership models that yield better outcomes for an economy during a crisis, it is state ownership that matters.[1] Taking into account the Slovenian case, however, where state-owned banks took on risk before the crisis and failed to boost lending during the crisis, the state ownership variable alone was not decisive. What set the Polish case apart was the fact that it had a more conservative regulatory framework than some other post-communist countries, its macroeconomic situation did not deteriorate to the same extent as in the Baltic republics, Hungary, Slovenia or elsewhere in South-Eastern Europe, and its biggest bank, PKO BP, while owned by the state, had also been very attuned to risk and market principles because of the ongoing presumption that ultimately the bank would be fully privatised. Thus maintaining the bank's value was the first priority for management. An optimal mix of state influence alongside market discipline was also a key to the economic success of the most effective high performing Asian economies, at least according to the World Bank's analysis (World Bank 1993).

The study of domestic bank behaviour compared to that of foreign banks has implications for how both transition and advanced economies alike treat their banking sectors. With few exceptions, the older EU members have protected domestic bank ownership, despite the European Commission's efforts over decades to create a single European market in financial services (Barth *et al.* 2006). Moreover, the eurozone debt crisis has highlighted how the fragmented banking market fails to support the single currency (Véron 2011).[2] Yet despite the tension between retaining national banking champions and economic integration, Western states have used the financial crisis and national bank bail-out schemes to consolidate national control rather than dispense with it (Donnelly 2011; Epstein 2012). But if domestic ownership *per se* is not necessarily a source of prudence in the run-up to a crisis and is also not a source of countercyclical lending during a crisis, then the findings here would suggest reasons for the older EU member states to follow their post-communist counterparts and cede control over bank ownership. Alternatively, to the extent that certain patterns of cooperation between domestically controlled and state-owned banks and political authorities exist, and those patterns of cooperation can limit vulnerability and also support economic activity in a downturn, then states pursuing domestic ownership may want to secure channels of influence to ensure that domestic bank ownership serves its desired purpose.

Domestic bank ownership in comparative perspective

In comparative political economy, financial systems are the starting point for understanding firms' time horizons, states' labour market structures and also their adjustment strategies

---

[1]Also see De Haas *et al.* (2012, p. 13) for the relatively stronger countercyclical role of state-owned banks when examining the larger 'emerging Europe' region, which includes 30 countries.

[2]Also see the work by Epstein (2012).

(Katzenstein 1978; Zysman 1983; World Bank 1993; Deeg 1999; Hall & Soskice 2001; Wade 2004; Hancké *et al.* 2007). To the extent that bank behaviour was coordinated by institutional complementarities, state intervention and social norms, rather than by markets alone, domestic bank ownership was perceived to be critical to the functioning of the economic model. But even in liberal market economies, states have used banks for political ends, not least by assigning lending targets during crises to stimulate economic activity. This essay specifies the conditions under which domestic banks can or cannot contribute to states' economic adjustment in an age of unprecedented financial liberalisation and from a position of dependent market capitalism (Nölke & Vliegenthart 2009). In contrast to earlier work on the role of finance in facilitating adjustment, the evidence here is that domestic banks have only a limited role to play.

Many states have used domestically controlled banks to pursue certain kinds of economic development and competitiveness. Strategies have included using subsidised interest rates to target particular industries or exporters and to boost public goods such as mass housing. States have also imposed portfolio requirements on banks in order to prevent the development of asset bubbles, particularly in real estate. Moreover, by setting prudential limits on, for example, real estate lending, states have tried to ensure that sufficient capital has flowed to manufacturing or other sectors with perceived social returns, and not primarily to consumption or other less productive asset classes. Historically, some states have been more successful than others at directing credit in ways that produce stability, prosperity and competitiveness. Although all of the high performing Asian economies used some elements of a directed credit strategy, those with the best outcomes included Japan, Korea and Taiwan (World Bank 1993). These countries' success was in part marked by their retreat from directed credit once firms achieved competitiveness.

More recently, China has achieved growth with relative stability, in large measure through state control of most of the country's financial intermediation. Banks in China are not only domestically controlled, but also state controlled. Savers in China, and most particularly individuals, pay a high price for China's economic model as it is currently configured. With inflation outpacing returns on savings deposits by several percentage points, there is nevertheless intense pressure on citizens to save because of the absence of a social safety net and because of the private imperative to acquire housing. In light of capital controls, however, there are few investment alternatives to deposits in state-owned banks. State control over savings, reminiscent of the 'Asian Tiger' model of earlier decades, has allowed China to not only try to 'pick winners' in industry (in green technology, among others), but also to invest overseas and intervene in currency markets as a means by which to maintain relative export competitiveness. Thus state-controlled banks in China are the central linchpin of the entire economic model.[3]

In addition to developmental goals, states have also sought domestic control over banks to prevent vulnerability and promote adjustment in the international system. As Robert Wade (2007, p. 84) has written:

> No country should let its banking system be taken over by foreign banks—even though in developing countries Western banks are likely to be more 'efficient' than domestic ones—for at

[3]On China's banks, see Barboza (2011, p. A1). On China's support for green energy technology, see Bradsher (2010, p. A1).

TRANSITION ECONOMIES AFTER 2008

times of crisis banks rely heavily on their home state and are likely to sacrifice operations in developing countries in order to protect their home base.

The suspicion that states would use their banks to combat the 2008–2009 financial crisis for national ends was borne out by lending targets, stimulus programmes and monitoring efforts. In China, banks were the central channel through which stimulus was administered. In some West European countries, regulators urged their own banks to deleverage from foreign markets (Bakker & Gulde 2010, p. 21) or to pull out of foreign markets entirely.[4] In Austria, a country with three major multinational banking groups in addition to smaller ones, the government required supported banks to try to make 200% of state participation capital available to Austrian businesses. Greek banks operating internationally faced similar conditions. The Greek banks were also warned by their central bank governor George Provopoulos not to send rescue funds to foreign markets. ING of the Netherlands also received government assistance and agreed in return to extend $32 billion in credit to domestic businesses and consumers. Similarly, German banks boosted lending to the small and medium-sized enterprise (SME) segment of the German economy. French banks committed to increasing domestic lending by 3–4% in the context of the bail-outs there, while UK banks receiving assistance also agreed to lending targets (the so-called Merlin Agreements). The US government stipulated no formal requirements for American banks, but those receiving assistance were asked to report back regularly on growth in domestic lending.[5] Though the domestic lending conditionalities were generally couched as targets, banks were under pressure to comply given their dependence on the domestic political system and its regulators for their continued existence—much as Robert Wade anticipated they would be.

The ability of states to use domestically controlled banks for countercyclical purposes during the crisis was no accident. While the social returns on banking sector protectionism are controversial, there is little doubt that states actively retain domestic control over banks, both to protect their economic models and to provide tools in a crisis. In conscious response to the introduction of the common market in the 1980s and financial liberalisation in the EU more generally, Spanish and Italian banks undertook domestic consolidation and foreign expansion in the 1990s and 2000s with state support as a strategy for avoiding foreign takeovers (Guillén & Tschoegl 2008). German and French banks have relied on their country-specific corporate governance rules to achieve the same ends (Culpepper 2011). Even the UK, one of the world's most orthodox liberal economies, had cordoned off its SME segment for British banks (Macartney 2012). In Asia, only Korea has seen its foreign bank ownership levels rise, but that is because of IMF and US Treasury pressure in the context of the country's bail-out in the 1997–1998 financial crisis (Kirshner 2006, pp. 13–14; Martinez-Diaz 2009).

All of the efforts to resist high levels of foreign bank ownership among most of the world's major industrialised and emerging economies would suggest that domestically controlled banks effectively serve a range of economic and political functions. But do they? And do they perform better in a crisis? The evidence from Central and East European

---

[4]For example, 'Athens ... ordered Greek banks to pull out of the Balkans' (as given in Engdahl (2009)).

[5]The information on government requirements attached to bank bail-outs (except for Germany) comes from IIF (2009) and 'Homeward Bound', *The Economist*, 5 February 2009. The information on Germany is from the author's interview with three Commerzbank bankers (Frankfurt, 15 June 2011).

domestically controlled banks suggests that concern about foreign ownership, at least with respect to vulnerability in a financial crisis and the capacity of states to adjust to a downturn, may be misplaced. Central and Eastern Europe, as a region, has the highest penetration of foreign bank ownership in the world. At the same time, it has some major domestically controlled (if not always majority domestically owned) players. As the following sections will show, foreign banks in Central and Eastern Europe did contribute to some countries' vulnerabilities, but did not cut and run from the region as had been anticipated. In addition, domestic Central and East European banks played a stabilising role in some cases but some also contributed to economic vulnerability. Based on a brief review of foreign bank behaviour as well as four, more detailed case studies from Poland, Latvia, Hungary and Slovenia, I conclude that foreign or domestic ownership is not a meaningful predictor of bank behaviour.

Bank behaviour in the 2008–2009 crisis: foreign and domestic banks

Foreign bank behaviour in the crisis

Foreign banks contributed to unsustainable credit booms prior to the crisis in a number of countries (Duenwald *et al.* 2005; De Haas *et al.* 2012, p. 13). The problem was especially pronounced in Central and East European states with currency boards, where currency pegs reassured foreign lenders and insulated them from the eroding effects of inflation (Bakker & Gulde 2010). Foreign banks also heightened vulnerability in Central and Eastern Europe by lending in foreign currencies. Loans in Swiss francs, euros and yen were attractive to consumers and businesses because they carried lower interest rates than the equivalent products in local currencies. Foreign exchange exposure varied significantly across countries, however. In 2008, 14% of Czech loans and 22% of Slovak loans were in foreign currency, while in both Romania and Bulgaria foreign exchange loans were close to 58% of all loans (Raiffeisen Research 2009).

Given the very high levels of foreign bank ownership and the foreign exchange exposure of particular countries, there was widespread fear in 2008 and early 2009 that Central and Eastern Europe would suffer economic collapse. Observers concluded that as the Western banks that had invested in Central and Eastern Europe came under funding pressure after the Lehman Brothers' collapse in September 2008, they would move out of the region. On his blog, Paul Krugman equated Central and Eastern Europe in 2008 with East Asia in 1997, suggesting that foreign-owned banks were poised to 'cut and run'. *The Times* argued that Eastern Europe threatened to drag the rest of the continent down into 'the goulash', implying that a crisis in Eastern Europe threatened to cause major economic problems for the rest of the continent. The negative sentiment was shared by a number of major publications, in addition to industry reports.[6]

Fears about how foreign banks would behave reflected long-held beliefs about the political nature of banks and where their loyalties ultimately lie—with their home

[6]See King (2009). For similar conclusions, see Engdahl (2009), Champion *et al.*, (2009) and Cox and Garnham (2009). Industry reports were also negative: see Citigroup, 'Western Europe's Banks: Eastern Europe's Problem?', 13 October 2008; Deutsche Bank, 'CEE Banking Systems—Risks of a Systemic Banking Crisis?', 15 October 2008; and Merrill Lynch, 'A Review of Exposures to CEE', 27 October 2008. Only the *Economist* was more sanguine, arguing that it was unlikely that a Western bank would 'pull the plug' on a Central and East European subsidiary: 'The Whiff of Contagion: Ex-Communist Economies', *The Economist*, 28 February 2009, p. 29.

TRANSITION ECONOMIES AFTER 2008

markets. In the event, however, foreign banks did not cut and run from the region in the aftermath of the Lehman failure. Output declines in Central and Eastern Europe were very severe but this was due more to faltering trade than contagion as a result of funding flows (EBRD 2009). There were no bank failures or closures in the region that were the responsibility of foreign-owned entities. Some Western banks did ultimately dispose of their Central and East European holdings,[7] but those Central and East European banks were ultimately purchased by eager new entrants who did nothing to depress Central and East European bank prices (including Santander of Spain and Sberbank of Russia). While the reasons for Western banks' continuing exposures are debated (EBRD 2009; IMF 2010; Pistor 2011; De Haas *et al.* 2012; Kudrna & Gabor, in this collection), the focus here is on whether domestic banks served a more constructive role for their home economies than their foreign-owned counterparts.

PKO Bank Polski in Poland: countercyclical stabiliser

PKO Bank Polski was one of two major savings banks stemming from the state-socialist era and considered for privatisation during the 1990s. Different governing coalitions had varying approaches to its ownership, with some arguing for full privatisation and others urging continued state control and even market expansion through the takeover of other Polish banks (Epstein 2008a). By 2011, PKO BP had the largest market share in Poland, measured both in terms of loans and deposits (Raiffeisen Research 2011), and remained state owned (at just over 51%), albeit with a relatively independent board of directors. PKO BP's dominant market position actually resulted from the crisis. Pekao SA, owned by Unicredit of Italy, had formerly been the largest by all measures, but was overtaken by PKO BP as the latter undertook more lending and management and had a rights issue while other banks were pulling back their activities. PKO BP did not contribute to the country's economic vulnerability before the crisis and also undertook significant countercyclical lending beginning in early 2009 when economic conditions in Central and Eastern Europe (and also in Western Europe) deteriorated. By these measures, PKO BP provides justification for domestic control over banks and casts doubt on whether high levels of foreign ownership are desirable.

Although approximately 34% of all loans were denominated in foreign currency in 2011 in Poland (just over half of the levels in Hungary and Romania) risks were limited, despite złoty depreciation, by pre-crisis lending standards (Raiffeisen Research 2011, p. 38). PKO BP neither borrowed heavily from abroad to finance lending in Poland prior to the crisis nor became a major player in foreign exchange lending. Its conservative strategy in the decade before the crisis can be explained in part by ongoing debates in Poland about whether and when the bank should be fully privatised.[8] Having built a reputation for safety prior to Lehman Brothers' collapse in September 2008, PKO BP was in a strong position to play a countercyclical role in the ensuing crisis.

In January 2009, members of the PKO management board became aware that CitiBank of the United States and ING of the Netherlands had ordered their subsidiaries in Poland first to stop offering any new loans, and second, to invigorate efforts to collect deposits. UniCredit

---

[7] Allied Irish Bank and Volksbank of Austria are two examples.

[8] Author's interview with a former Polish Deputy Minister for Foreign Affairs, Warsaw, 22 June 2011.

169

of Italy followed a similar, though less severe, strategy. In the meantime, all other banks operating in Central and Eastern Europe were facing conditions on lending from home governments that were bailing them out. This included Commerzbank, owner of BRE Bank in Poland, which was required to provide €5 billion in additional lending to Germany's SMEs in exchange for a large government capital injection, ultimately totalling €18 billion, which also resulted in 25% German state ownership.

In response to the decreasing commitment of foreign banks to the Polish economy, one PKO BP management board member noted in January 2009 that the Polish economy needed funding, and that PKO BP had always been very close to its clients, and therefore knew and understood its clients well, and that PKO BP never faced restrictions on lending from a foreign parent bank. Taking advantage not only of PKO BP's conservative brand but also capitalising on the perceived safety of the bank, given its majority state ownership which was still a reputational boon in post-communist Poland, PKO launched one of only two successful rights issues in Europe in the summer of 2009 (the other being the state-owned Nordea Bank of Sweden). Funds obtained from the PKO BP issue were 5.125 billion złoty, about $1.7 billion, and were used primarily to support new lending, allowing the bank to 'continue [its] mission' in the crisis.[9]

In addition to shoring up the bank's capital position with a major rights issue, PKO BP also successfully expanded its deposit base during the crisis. PKO BP had always had the largest branch network in the country. Its strong physical and marketing presence encouraged Polish depositors, who were increasingly uncertain about how foreign-owned banks would behave in the crisis, to move their money over to PKO.[10] In 2009, when safety rather than returns was paramount in the minds of savers, PKO did not overpay for this additional liquidity.

At the same time, given the worsening global economic conditions and spreading uncertainty, including in the Polish economy, PKO implemented stringent risk management that monitored the economic situations of clients. The bank expanded the definition of what constituted a 'bad loan' to include those loans that were not only in default, but also that were at risk of moving into default because of the deteriorating economic circumstances of clients. Extensive monitoring in connection with early-warning systems gave bank managers the confidence to continue to do business. Meanwhile, foreign banks were often trying to offload clients and shrink their balance sheets, further contributing to PKO's client base. Thus in 2009, PKO was only one of two banks in Poland—the other was the small and privately owned Polish Getin Bank—to increase its balance sheet, both in terms of the deposit base and in terms of assets.[11]

Also helpful to the Polish economy, and indicative of the pressure that foreign banks were under in 2009, was PKO's loan to the state-owned social insurance entity, Zakład Ubezpieczeń Społecznych (Social Insurance Institution, ZUS). Because of Poland's early retirement age, the partial privatisation of the pension system, and constitutional debt limits, funding the 'pay-as-you-go' pillar of Poland's pension scheme had, at times, required ZUS to seek out private creditors. Without sufficient funds from the state, ZUS turned to private markets in the summer of 2009, but virtually no bank was willing to lend, despite the very

---

[9]Author's interview with a PKO BP management board member, Warsaw, 22 June 2011.

[10]Author's interview with a former chief economist at a foreign-owned bank in Poland, Warsaw, 22 June 2011.

[11]Author's interview with the PKO BP management board member. For 2009, PKO BP's assets increased by 17%, while its deposit base grew by 22% (PKO BP 2010a, p. 4).

TRANSITION ECONOMIES AFTER 2008

high margins being offered, 6.42%, and its very short term of six months to one year. Ultimately PKO stepped into the breach, although management denied there was political pressure to do so. Rather, PKO managers claim to have reasoned that ZUS's state-backed status meant that the loan was guaranteed. This was further proof that if foreign banks were not willing to lend to a state-backed entity such as ZUS under such auspicious conditions— those being high margins, a state guarantee and short duration—then they had certainly been instructed not to lend at all (Kostrzewa & Mięczński 2009).

As noted previously, the crisis afforded PKO BP opportunities to expand its operations. By 2011, the bank had regained its dominant position on all measures: capitalisation, assets and deposit market share. It had overtaken Commerzbank in terms of overall market capitalisation, and in 2011 was enjoying year-on-year profit growth of 39.5%, with a cost-to-income ratio of less than 39%. It was also the biggest lender to 'institutional clients' in 2011, including to SMEs, larger corporations and also local governments and municipalities (PKO BP 2010b, p. 10). Poland was the only EU member to escape recession in 2009. There are many reasons for this: one understudied reason might be the performance of PKO BP.

Although PKO PB was majority state owned through the crisis period, state policy did not guide the bank. Rather, its independent board of directors did. Thus politicians have asked questions of the bank and solicited the bank's assessment of the economic situation, but there was no political pressure to expand credit through the crisis, and no 'blatant requests' for particular segments of the economy or for particular borrowers. Although PKO BP's perception that it had a 'mission' to continue to provide credit to the Polish economy through the crisis has social overtones, there was also a commercial logic to PKO BP's use of its local knowledge, network and reputation for safety to expand its operations during the crisis. According to one sceptic, however, PKO's success during the crisis can be attributed to 'luck' as much as to anything else, in the sense that regulation had protected the Polish banking sector from excessive risk while the economy was insulated from the downturn because of its comparatively large domestic market.[12] Such scepticism aside, however, without a large domestic bank in Poland during the crisis it is not clear where borrowers whose loans were not being renewed would have gone. In view of PKO's apparent success then, it is surprising that the subject of PKO's further privatisation has not gone away (Kruk 2011).

If all domestically controlled, or even state-owned, banks performed as well as PKO BP did on behalf of the Polish economy through the crisis, there would be strong justification for protecting domestic bank ownership. As the cases from Latvia, Hungary and Slovenia show, however, domestic bank ownership is no guarantee of bank support for an economy. The uneven performance of domestically controlled, state-owned and domestically managed banks from the remaining three cases casts doubt on the relationship between domestic control over financial institutions and countercyclical behaviour.

Parex Bank in Latvia: pro-cyclical risk-taker

The economic and financial crisis in Latvia both started earlier than elsewhere in Eastern Europe and resulted in one of the most severe output declines of any country in the world.

---

[12]Author's interview with the former chief economist at a foreign-owned bank in Poland, Warsaw, 22 June 2011.

TRANSITION ECONOMIES AFTER 2008

Output declined by 25%, unemployment reached 21%, and between 2007 and 2011, the country lost 10% of its population to emigration (Buckley 2011).[13] The biggest domestically controlled bank, Parex, acted in parallel with its foreign competitors, intensifying the credit boom before the crisis, but because it was domestically controlled, it then fell to the Latvian state to either wind down the bank in 2008 or bail it out. Latvia chose the latter, with IMF and EU assistance, which by 2011 had cost the state 5% of Latvia's 2008 GDP.

Before Parex Bank's nationalisation in 2008, it had been owned by Viktors Krasovickis and Valerijs Kargins, who had extensive experience in international banking and finance. They had been the first to win a hard currency trading license from the Soviet Union in 1990 and went on to run a 'highly entrepreneurial' bank, 'complete with all the baggage', implying a high volume of bad loans (Åslund & Dombrovskis 2011, pp. 39–40). In its pro-cyclical risk-taking, however, Parex Bank, Latvia's second largest before the crisis, did not distinguish itself from its foreign counterparts of similar size. With just over 60% foreign bank ownership in Latvia in 2007—low for a post-communist member of the EU—Parex Bank's main foreign competitors were all from Sweden: Swedbank, SEB and Nordea. Together with Parex, these financial institutions had three-quarters of Latvia's banking assets. The balance was held by 30 smaller banks (Åslund & Dombrovskis 2011, p. 19; EBRD 2008, p. 146).

Macroeconomic conditions, regulatory permissiveness and bank behaviour (both foreign and domestic) contributed to the crisis. The EBRD reported that in 2007, Latvia had among the highest ratios of domestic credit to GDP in the Central and Eastern Europe region at 78% (EBRD 2008, p. 144). Loose monetary policy set by the US Federal Reserve and the European Central Bank, high Latvian inflation, especially of wages, and the country's peg to the euro boosted credit demand. Demand was strongest in consumption and housing, while relatively little credit went to productivity enhancement, such as research and development (EBRD 2009, p. 184). Given negative real interest rates and the perceived certainty, ultimately proven correct, that lenders would not suffer from a depreciation of the lat, the incentive for consumers was to borrow while the incentive for lenders was to bring cheap liquidity from abroad and enjoy large margins in Latvia.[14]

None of the major banks had a robust local deposit base in Latvia. Swedbank, SEB and Nordea mostly financed lending in Latvia through borrowing from their parent banks in Sweden. Similarly, although Parex Bank had no foreign parent from which to borrow, it did rely on European wholesale markets. To the extent Parex attracted depositors, they were often from abroad. This helps explain why, by the autumn of 2008 and particularly following the Lehman Brothers' collapse in September 2008, depositor flight brought Parex Bank to the brink (EBRD 2009, p. 184), as did the freezing up of interbank markets more generally.

It was Parex Bank's failure that was the proximate cause of Latvia's resort to the IMF in the autumn of 2008. By that time, new credit was scarce, asset prices were in decline, and output was already in freefall. Foreign banks had stopped lending and foreign depositors were leaving. Negative economic trends were linked in part to a widespread recognition by 2007 that boom dynamics were unsustainable. In response, the Latvian authorities put new

---

[13]Buckley (2011) and 'Latvia Weighs Human Cost of its Austerity Programme', *Financial Times*, 6 November 2011.

[14]See Bakker and Gulde (2010) on this dynamic in all the countries with currency boards.

TRANSITION ECONOMIES AFTER 2008

restrictions on lending, including higher reserve requirements for banks and stricter mortgage regulation. Meanwhile, Sweden's SEB and Swedbank slowed credit growth by early 2007, although Nordea increased their market share. But it was the global economic downturn that caused the dramatic reversal in credit flows and output in countries like Latvia. By October 2008, Parex Bank was facing a deposit run and a credit lock-out just as syndicated loans were due. With a fifth of the country's banking assets at stake, the Latvian government opted to nationalise Parex, with the state initially buying a 51% stake from Krasovickis and Kargins for two lats (Åslund & Dombrovskis 2011, p. 35).

Given that Parex's loans were due in late 2008 and were worth close to 5% of Latvia's GDP, and given the crisis of confidence in the banking sector, reflected in deposit flight, the government began negotiating an assistance package with the IMF in November 2008. The package would ultimately be worth €7.5 billion, or approximately 37% of the country's GDP. It was conditioned on the state raising its stake in Parex to 85%, and was financed not only by the IMF but also by the EU, the Nordic countries, and several Central and East European states. Much of the planned assistance was in anticipation of a final bank bail-out bill equal to 15–20% of GDP, which ultimately was more than proved necessary.

Not only did Parex Bank contribute to Latvia's vulnerability in the run-up to the crisis, but the principal owners, Krasovickis and Kargins, continued to impose costs on the bank even after the government takeover. Those additional costs suggest that, depending on the sophistication of policy makers, domestically controlled banks, under certain circumstances, may do more harm to an economy than their foreign counterparts. For example, apparently without the government's knowledge, both men liquidated their own deposits in the bank between the government takeover on 8 November 2008 and the 20 November. This was after significant government infusions of liquidity—thus Krasovickis and Kargins were benefiting directly from the nationalisation (Baltic News Service 2009; Sloga 2009a; Sloga 2009b). It is also not clear that government control ensured the best outcome from the Latvian public's point of view. An independent audit of Parex Bank's nationalisation questioned whether the bank was truly systemic, pointing out that approximately 60% of its clients were not residents, including individuals on money laundering lists. At the same time, state and local government deposits amounted to only 160 million lats. Casting further doubt on the soundness of government deliberation was the fact that efforts to declassify the minutes from the meetings in which increasing government ownership was agreed failed because the Finance Ministry and the Financial and Capital Market Commission both wanted to maintain confidentiality (Sloga 2009b).

Two other developments bear on Parex Bank's ownership structure. In April 2009, the EBRD took a 25% stake in the bank to help fund its recovery and to instil greater confidence in the bank and Latvia's economy more generally. Given the EBRD's involvement and its track record in helping to privatise Central and East European enterprises with foreign capital, this was certainly an indication that the bank would ultimately be re-privatised via an international bidding process, which would probably increase foreign bank ownership levels in Latvia. In addition, Parex Bank was, after the original bail-out, broken into two parts. 'Citadele', the well performing entity, existed alongside a 'bad bank' that was tasked with recouping anything it could from still non-performing or doubtful loans. To the extent that such loans are eventually repaid in part or in full, then the overall cost of Parex Bank's failure could turn out to be substantially less than the 5% of Latvia's 2008 GDP recorded thus far.

The contrast between PKO BP in Poland and Parex Bank in Latvia is striking. In addition to their different ownership structures, they also functioned in distinct regulatory environments and macroeconomic policy contexts. The comparison clearly shows that states cannot rely on domestic bank owners to secure better economic outcomes in a crisis, but there could nevertheless be advantages in having domestic banks that are susceptible to political influence. Even if PKO BP had an independent board of directors and managers, the fact that the state was asking particular questions might have created a sense of shared purpose between PKO BP and government officials, both in the run-up to the crisis and during the crisis itself. However, there clearly was no sensibility around protecting a collective enterprise in Latvia, even after Parex Bank's nationalisation, even though the eventual marginalisation of its former owners did help the bank recover.

One might conclude from Parex Bank that the international financial institutions in the 1990s were correct to argue in favour of foreign bank ownership. In addition to capital, the international financial institutions argued, foreign owners would bring know-how and technology. The international financial institutions also hoped they would disrupt communist-era networks that would otherwise lead to risky lending in the transition (Epstein 2008a, 2008b). Indeed, Åslund and Dombrovskis (2011) concluded that Parex Bank was mismanaged by its domestic owners. However, given the very similar behaviour of Parex to the three major foreign-owned banks, it is not clear that foreign ownership produces better outcomes either. The central difference between Parex and the other three was that the Swedish banks had well funded parents to fall back on and came from a set of countries that demonstrated a long-term political commitment to Latvia and the other Baltic states. Such commitments are rare in the world of bank rollover agreements and support packages (Roubini & Setser 2004). Thus, if the Polish–Latvian comparison demonstrates anything, it is that foreign or domestic bank ownership *per se* does not determine whether bank behaviour will be compounding or countercyclical in a crisis.

To further assess domestically controlled banks, we now turn to two other countries that were hit particularly hard by the economic crisis: Hungary and Slovenia.

OTP in Hungary: contributor to the crisis and conduit of state stimulus

OTP in Hungary contributed to the economic crisis there by borrowing from abroad and then issuing foreign exchange loans, much like foreign banks operating in the country. Indeed on this score, 'Foreign exchange loans were extended by all major banks in Hungary irrespective of whether they [were] foreign owned' (Molnár 2010, p. 11). When the Hungarian forint lost value, the debt burdens of borrowers suddenly grew, and OTP's non-performing loans increased. The bank then required a loan of €1.4 billion from the Hungarian government in March 2009 when OTP lost access to liquidity on international markets. Those funds were used to finance Hungarian enterprises. Government assistance was in turn tied to lending to Hungarian corporations and the SME segment, which amounted to Ft248 billion in 2009 (OTP 2009, p. 5). Given the bank's relatively strong performance through the crisis, OTP paid those funds back to the government a year ahead of schedule.

OTP is privately owned, with the majority of shareholders coming from abroad, but it is a Hungarian-run multinational banking group that has operations in Hungary, Bulgaria, Croatia, Slovakia, Romania, Ukraine, Serbia, Russia and Montenegro. In 2009, 97% of its

TRANSITION ECONOMIES AFTER 2008

shares were owned by domestic and foreign private institutional investors while 2% were owned by employees and 1% by the Hungarian Treasury, down from 7% in 2008. Although by March 2011 OTP was over 70% foreign owned, through the dispersed holdings of foreign institutional investors, the bank had a Hungarian identity and its Chairman and CEO, Sándor Csányi, had strong connections across Hungary's political spectrum.[15]

In the run-up to the financial crisis, OTP pursued strategies that, had they been successful, might have mitigated the worst effects of the crisis. However, OTP also contributed to Hungary's vulnerability. One aspect of this was the introduction in 2000 of a housing subsidy programme. Intended to bolster the housing market and also to create incentives for buyers and builders to expand the existing stock of homes, the programme both provided a subsidy on the interest homebuyers paid and gave them a generous tax deduction on the expense of the loan, so generous in fact that estimates suggest the cost of the programme might have reached 1.5–2% of GDP by the end of 2002 (Rózsavölgyi & Kovács 2005, p. 3). Because the subsidy benefit was only legally allowed to be administered by Hungary's mortgage banks, few commercial actors stood to gain: the main beneficiaries were OTP, UniCredit of Italy and FHB, another Hungarian lender specialising in mortgages. Within a short time, OTP had two-thirds of the rapidly growing mortgage market (Molnár 2010, p. 14).

To the extent that the OTP management helped negotiate the home mortgage interest subsidy and loan tax deduction, the bank used its political influence to boost Hungary's housing market while also reaping significant competitive advantages. In addition, since there was no modelling of the programme's costs into the future and therefore no specific budgeting, the programme exacerbated an already deteriorating fiscal situation. The programme's expense, in connection with ongoing tensions between the government and the central bank that had resulted in restrictive monetary policy, led to a significant scaling back of mortgage subsidies by the end of 2003.

The fallout from housing subsidies points to OTP's continuing efforts to protect its market position. Although the government programme was scaled back, there was nevertheless strong demand for housing loans. Given Hungary's high interest rate environment, it became economically plausible, beginning in 2004, to issue foreign exchange loans on a large scale, in yen, euros and Swiss francs. Although OTP's CEO Csányi argued in September of 2011 that he had tried to stop foreign exchange loans because they were risky, it is also the case that OTP would have benefited from restricted competition in mortgage lending, and especially by keeping foreign exchange loans out of the market as they were cheaper than OTP could offer with what remained of the government subsidy programme. OTP failed in this lobbying effort, however, and as CIB Bank, owned by Intesa SanPaolo of Italy, and K&H Bank, owned by Belgium's KBC, embarked on foreign exchange lending, OTP quickly followed suit (Ferenc 2011). Because of the inability to forecast the coming crisis from the United States and the presumption that Hungary would ultimately join the eurozone, foreign exchange loans were generally not perceived as risky. By 2008, loans in a foreign currency as a percentage of all loans in Hungary were 61.4% (Raiffeisen Research 2011, p. 41).

In the crisis itself, which for Hungary struck most strongly following Lehman's collapse in September 2008, OTP's Hungarian identity and domestic management proved helpful to

---

[15]Author's interviews with Hungarian bankers, Budapest, 20 June 2011.

TRANSITION ECONOMIES AFTER 2008

the economy and to its political leaders. First, although Hungary's loan-to-deposit ratio was among the highest in Central and Eastern Europe at 140%, OTP's own loan-to-deposit ratio was significantly lower, meaning that while the bank had borrowed from abroad in the run-up to the crisis, its deposit base was stronger than those of its foreign competitors (Várhegyi 2010). OTP's strength in this regard is similar to PKO's in Poland: because OTP had had a Hungarian brand for nearly 60 years, a certain segment of the population was always inclined to patronise it, particularly pensioners.[16] OTP also had the most extensive branch network in the country, which contributed to its deposit gathering. Its loan-to-deposit ratio shows that OTP took fewer risks than its foreign counterparts.

In view of foreign banks' sudden reluctance to extend new credit because of the crisis, the Hungarian government tried to use its assistance to domestic banks to effect a modest stimulus. However, this effort was not as successful as Polish PKO's independent—meaning without government funding—initiative to expand lending in the crisis. In Hungary, three banks qualified for government assistance: OTP, FHB (the mortgage lender) and the Hungarian development bank, MFB. While FHB was the only bank to receive a capital injection in March 2009, of Ft30 billion that raised the state's ownership stake to 43%, all three Hungarian banks received unsubsidised loans from the government, of Ft120 billion, 400 billion and 170 billion, respectively. These measures were conditional upon the supported banks financing or refinancing corporate loans, extending credit to non-financial enterprises and increasing loan portfolios, or in the case of FHB, at least not decreasing its total portfolio (Molnár 2010, p. 12). Similar domestic lending targets were a central feature of bank assistance packages across the EU in the crisis. Despite government assistance, OTP's loans to clients fell by a percentage point between 2007 and 2009, in contrast to PKO BP (Várhegyi 2010, p. 843).

In the spring of 2010, Victor Orbán's *Fidesz* won a supermajority in parliament and passed legislation of critical importance to the Hungarian banking sector. The most significant was the annual bank levy of 0.5% of assets over Ft50 billion. It is not clear whether OTP had a hand in the bank levy's design, although Csányi is on record as saying that while the bank tax would be difficult for OTP, 'it is necessary for the country, and Prime Minister Orbán, to match the deficit margin for 2010'.[17] OTP was one of the few banks of the largest 10 that was able to maintain profitability, in spite of the levy. It was also the last bank, according to financial analysts, that passed the cost of the levy onto consumers (Várhegyi 2010, pp. 834–35 and 839–40).

The *Fidesz* government also introduced two foreign exchange mortgage relief schemes and, like the banking levy, all banks, whether domestic or foreign, faced the same conditions. While the lump-sum repayment plan was costly for the banks, because it fixed the exchange rate at Ft180 to the Swiss franc, with banks covering two-thirds of the cost and the government one-third, the small number of eligible participants minimised those costs. The alternative, which fixed premiums in the medium term but extended the life of the loan, was more likely to affect banks' balance sheets. However, foreign banks in particular were

[16]Author's interviews with Hungarian bankers, Budapest, 20 June 2011.

[17]'Orbán és Csányi a bankadóról', *Népszabadság Online*, 8 July 2010, available at: http://nol.hu/gazdasag/egy_asztalnal_orban_viktor_es_csanyi_sandor, accessed 20 February 2013. Hungarian bankers employed by foreign-owned banks speculate that Csányi was consulted on the bank levy bill before it was passed. Author's interviews with Hungarian bankers, Budapest, 20 June 2011.

concerned about both measures and took their complaints to the IMF and European and Hungarian authorities, with OTP noticeably absent from these efforts.

There is some evidence that OTP enjoyed a favourable market position in Hungary because of the bank's Hungarian identity and management. Having its roots in the pre-communist era, OTP garnered clients' loyalty by virtue of its domestic brand and its perceived association with the Hungarian state. In addition, there is indirect evidence that OTP had special access to the public policy apparatus, and benefited from it. Its mortgage lending business grew enormously from the housing subsidy programme of the early 2000s. Subsequently, the bank levy seems to have been structured in ways that did not put OTP at the same competitive disadvantage as the bank's foreign competitors, which explains why OTP was one of the few top banks that reported profits in the years after the financial crisis began. Despite this favourable treatment, however, OTP contributed to Hungary's vulnerability in the run-up to the financial crisis by building up foreign exchange exposure in ways that proved unsustainable (Jenkins & Sovago 2011).

The advantage for both Poland and Hungary of having had one major domestically controlled bank through the crisis was that Hungarian and Polish clients stayed with their domestic bank, or even gravitated towards it. Keeping or attracting clients was a function of both banks' long histories and associations with their respective states. In Parex Bank's case, however, foreign depositors were prone to withdraw. Thus one conclusion about domestic bank ownership and its possible salutary effects in a crisis is that it is not just the behaviour of the bank that matters, but also the behaviour of populations around the concept of domestic bank ownership. In addition, because OTP lost access to international credit markets and required government assistance, Hungarian authorities were then in a position to impose conditions on the bank related to increased lending. Thus countercyclical lending was possible although, in contrast to Poland's PKO BP, increased lending was not the result. OTP's portfolio actually shrank slightly, because, at least according to the bank, demand for credit diminished (OTP 2009, p. 5). In sum then, it may have been better for the Hungarian economy to have had about 20% of the banking market subject to some political influence during the worst of the financial crisis. However, those advantages must be weighed against the apparently damaging effect OTP had on Hungary's vulnerability given the bank's embrace of the government's housing subsidy programme and also foreign banks' foreign exchange lending model.

Slovenia: the risks of cross-border borrowing

Slovenia is different from Poland, Hungary and Latvia in one critical way that is useful for the assessment of domestic bank responses to the financial crisis. Rather than selling the bulk of its banking sector to foreigners, the country elected instead to limit foreign bank ownership to 30% or less for most of the post-communist period. While arguments in favour of domestic control over finance suggest this should have improved the country's fortunes through the financial crisis, that turned out not to be the case. After the Baltic republics, Slovenia was among the hardest hit by the economic downturn with a contraction in output of 8% in 2009, the most severe in the eurozone (EBRD 2010, p. 144; Raiffeisen Research 2011, p. 46). Not only did Slovenia's economy suffer as a result of the crisis, but so too did its model of low party polarisation and strong social dialogue (Guardiancich 2012). One reason for Slovenia's difficulties was that although its major banks were domestically controlled and state controlled, they nevertheless engaged in extensive cross-border borrowing in the run-up to the crisis, thus increasing the country's vulnerability, much like in Hungary and Latvia.

The two biggest banks, Nova Ljubljanska Banka (NLB) and Nova Kreditna Banka Maribor (NKBM) were both state controlled. Together they accounted for close to half of Slovenia's banking market before the crisis began, but by 2011 served only 40% of the market (EBRD 2010, p. 144; 2011, p. 157). Although both banks passed the European Banking Authority's stress test in the summer of 2011, NLB, the country's largest bank, did so by a slim margin and was required to raise additional capital by the spring of 2012. Non-performing loans for these banks were estimated at 15% by the middle of 2011 with Slovenia suffering from a slow recovery, hampered by exceptionally weak domestic demand. While Slovenia had long been encouraged by the IMF, World Bank and EBRD to expand foreign investment in its banking sector, the country repeatedly refused to do so, reneging on a commitment to Belgium's KBC, for example, to sell it a controlling stake in NLB (Lindstrom & Piroska 2007; Epstein 2008b, p. 895). KBC's limited access in Slovenia, in addition to other difficulties, led the bank to try to exit the Slovenian market altogether by 2012, possibly by selling its minority stake in NLB to Santander of Spain.

Since a growing source of finance in Slovenia between 2005 and 2008 was cross-border borrowing, it is not clear that domestic bank ownership in Slovenia was necessarily a source of stability. Over the course of those four years, the percentage of loans funded by customer deposits fell from 99% to 62%, while foreign borrowing grew to €12 billion. Foreign finance was offered on short maturities, which meant that when the crisis peaked in late 2008 and 2009, it was no longer possible for Slovenian banks to roll over loans using the same foreign sources. Net capital outflows amounted to over €3 billion in 2009, and continued in 2010. Consequently, the Slovenian state stepped in with a capital injection for NLB, guarantees for all the local banks and additional liquidity through the state's own issue of bonds. Government borrowing to assist the banks contributed to the growth in Slovenia's deficit in 2009 to 5.5% of GDP, which, as also happened in many eurozone countries, violated the Stability and Growth Pact and prompted the EU's 'excessive deficit procedure'. Slovenian banks, unlike others profiled here, also benefited from European Central Bank financing because of Slovenia's membership in the eurozone since 2007. Perhaps surprisingly, the combination of domestic ownership and eurozone membership also failed to save the country from foreign exchange exposure. Lending spreads, especially to the corporate sector, were among the highest in the eurozone. Thus Swiss franc borrowing also took place in Slovenia in the run-up to the crisis, especially in the housing loan market, although the level subsequently fell over time.[18]

Critics of Slovenian state ownership of finance argue that while the crisis illustrated the hazards of the Slovenian model, the government used the crisis to enhance its power over the banking sector rather than to divest from it. Chief among the critiques is that the state-controlled banks, 'in a time of intense lending activity … paid little attention to the risks and not only financed projects based on their economic viability but also on other reasons'. Critics also claim that in highly profitable times, managers distributed gains to

[18]'Economic Issues: The Economic Crisis Interrupted Slovenia's Efforts in Achieving the Strategic Objectives and Revealed Structural Maladjustment of its Economy', *UMAR Economic Issues*, 13 August 2010; 'Impact of the Crisis on the Credit Market in Slovenia', *Economic Issues 2011*, pp. 89–116; and Bank of Slovenia (2009) 'Stability of the Slovenian Banking System' (Ljubljana, Bank of Slovenia).

shareholders rather than boosting capital adequacy. Moreover, despite high levels of state and domestic ownership, lending was slower to recover in Slovenia than in the rest of the eurozone.[19]

In July 2010, Slovenia joined the OECD, which brought renewed pressure on the country to reduce the state's role in banking. International organisations generally judged Slovenia's corporate governance as weak, with poor payment discipline among firms. Thus, in the run-up to Slovenia's OECD membership, the country established the Capital Assets Management Agency that in turn developed a plan, delivered to the Slovenian government in June 2011, to reduce the state's stake in a range of companies, including NLB and NKBM. While the plan would not eliminate state ownership or even state control, it would, for example, reduce the state's ownership stake in NLB from 55% to 25%. However, sceptics doubted whether political support could be mobilised even for this limited change.[20]

Conclusion: does foreign bank ownership matter, and what kind of domestic bank performs better in a crisis?

The former governor of the Bank of Mexico and former minister of finance in Mexico, Guillermo Ortiz, argued that, in the post-Lehman financial crisis, foreign banks in emerging markets were 'reducing their exposure ... prompting damaging credit crunches, and using profits obtained from subsidiaries to recapitalise parent banks'. He claimed further that emerging markets 'should implement a new model of international banking that limits global banks' expansion' (Ortiz 2012). Whether this is a sound prescription, however, depends on whether domestic banks serve their economies better than their foreign counterparts. So far, the evidence on this question is mixed.

In Poland, PKO BP pursued its commercial interests in the crisis in ways that allowed the bank to expand its market share along several dimensions. Although state owned, it was not directed by the state to engage in countercyclical lending. Its domestic status appears to have been part of the explanation for its behaviour during the crisis in so far as its local, and autonomous, management perceived opportunities in the Polish economy at precisely the moment when foreign owners became risk-averse. In addition, Polish clients moved their business there, both for safety and for opportunity, the latter when foreign banks would not renew credit lines. But PKO BP 'got lucky', as one former chief economist at a major foreign-owned bank put it, because the macroeconomic environment was better in Poland than elsewhere in post-communist Europe. In addition, the regulatory environment had not been as permissive, which limited risky behaviour, especially in foreign exchange lending. Thus to the extent that domestic bank ownership yields advantages to states, it is by virtue of an optimal combination between state influence and market exposure. In PKO's case, the ongoing presumption of eventual privatisation resulted in a conservative strategy among bank managers. This finding is reminiscent of earlier conclusions about why Japan, South

---

[19]The quotation is from *Economic Issues 2011*, p. 89. Also see p. 92 of the same report on low credit activity in Slovenia, in addition to Cerni (2012).

[20]Slovenian Press Agency, 'Slovenia to Slash Majority Stake in NLB to 25%', 29 February 2012. Also see ''Economic Issues: The Economic Crisis Interrupted Slovenia's Efforts in Achieving the Strategic Objectives and Revealed Structural Maladjustment of its Economy', *UMAR Economic Issues*, 13 August 2010, p. 4.

Korea and Taiwan reaped bigger rewards from state control over finance than some other Asian economies.

However, in none of the other three cases did the domestically controlled (Parex in Latvia), domestically run (OTP in Hungary) or state-owned (in Slovenia) banks perform as well as PKO BP in Poland, or even necessarily out-perform their foreign counterparts. In all cases they borrowed from abroad in the run-up to the crisis, contributing to their countries' vulnerability. In all cases they required assistance from the state, which in some instances was costly (particularly in Latvia and Slovenia). While OTP was useful as a conduit for Hungary's state-directed stimulus that targeted SMEs, neither Parex Bank in Latvia nor the two major Slovenian banks were capable of boosting their local economies in the crisis. This raises the question of whether domestic bank ownership is really better for countries in a crisis, as some very eminent scholars and practitioners have argued.

While this essay concludes that in transition states domestic bank ownership *per se* did not produce more desirable outcomes in the crisis, it is also clear that, given the presence of other conditions, domestic control over finance could, in theory, limit vulnerability. China limited its own vulnerability, at least to external shocks, precisely by controlling intermediation and capital flows. However, whether the kinds of controls China exercises, which make the difference between vulnerability and security, are compatible with the democratic governance and economic integration that Central and East European states seek, is doubtful. It is also unclear whether China has guaranteed its financial security in the long term, or whether state-led finance implies its own vulnerabilities, namely the inability to 'pick winners', resulting in excessive credit to real estate and unpromising technology sectors.

For states that seek to retain some domestic control over finance, or even to increase that control, several other conditions must be in place for such control to serve a national purpose linked to limiting vulnerability and promoting recovery and adjustment in a crisis. Most important would be restricting cross-border borrowing, expansion of local deposit bases as the foundation for domestic lending, and developing knowledge of the local market that could be used in connection with the state's resources to combat an economic downturn. Such strategies, of course, have a serious downside. One of the international financial institutions' central arguments in favour of opening post-communist banking markets to foreign investors was that banks could then be the conduit through which capital from Western Europe could fund development in the East, as it did before the crisis to an impressive extent (EBRD 2009). Whether there is a way to reap the benefits of European integration and globalisation more generally without also suffering undue risk will undoubtedly be the central debate for transition states in the recovery phase. However, when it comes to bank ownership, foreign or domestic, the findings of this essay suggest that the political debate is currently misconstrued. Foreign or domestic ownership is not a decisive factor that can be considered independently of other variables. The history of a bank, the perceived attractiveness of its particular brand, its sources of funding and specific relationship to the state all bear on potential performance.

University of Denver

TRANSITION ECONOMIES AFTER 2008

References

Åslund, A. & Dombrovskis, V. (2011) *How Latvia Came through the Financial Crisis* (Washington, DC, Peterson Institute for International Economics).

Bakker, B. B. & Gulde, A. (2010) *The Credit Boom in the EU New Member States: Bad Luck or Bad Policies?*, IMF Working Paper 130 (Washington, DC, International Monetary Fund).

Baltic News Service (2009) 'Godmanis: pirms "Parex bankas" pārnemšanas lielākie akcionāri no bankas nēmuši laukā naudu', 23 July, available at: http://www.diena.lv/sabiedriba/politika/godmanis-pirms-parex-bankas-parnemsanas-lielakie-akcionari-no-bankas-nemusi-lauka-naudu-679528, accessed 20 February 2013.

Barboza, D. (2011) 'As its Economy Sprints Ahead, China's People are Left Behind', *New York Times*, 10 October.

Barth, J. R., Caprio, G. Jr & Levine, R. (2006) *Rethinking Bank Regulation: Till Angels Govern* (New York, Cambridge University Press).

Bonin, J. P., Mizsei, K., Székely, I. & Wachtel, P. (1998) *Banking in Transition Economies: Developing Market Oriented Banking Sectors in Eastern Europe* (Cheltenham, Edward Elgar Publishing Limited).

Bonin, J. P. & Schnabel, I. (2011) 'The Great Transformation: From Government-owned to Foreign-controlled Banking Sectors', *Economics of Transition*, 19, 3, pp. 397–405.

Bradsher, K. (2010) 'On Clean Energy, China Skirts Rules', *New York Times*, 9 September, p. A1.

Buckley, N. (2011) 'Economy: New Hope', *Financial Times*, 13 December.

Cerni, B. (2012) 'Slovenian Banks Unwilling to Lend Despite ECB Financing', *Bloomberg*, 3 February.

Champion, M., Slater, J. & Mollenkamp, C. (2009) 'Banks Reel on Eastern Europe's Bad News', *Wall Street Journal*, 18 February.

Cox, A. & Garnham, P. (2009) 'Moody's Warns of Eastern Europe Risk', *Financial Times*, 17 February.

Culpepper, P. D. (2011) *Quiet Politics and Business Power: Corporate Control in Europe and Japan* (New York, Cambridge University Press).

De Haas, R., Korniyenko, Y., Loukoianova, E. & Pivovarsky, A. (2012) *Foreign Banks and the Vienna Initiative: Turning Sinners into Saints*, EBRD Working Paper 143 (London, European Bank for Reconstruction and Development).

Deeg, R. (1999) *Finance Capitalism Unveiled: Banks and the German Political Economy* (Ann Arbor, MI, University of Michigan Press).

Donnelly, S. (2011) 'The Public Interest and the Economy in Europe in the Wake of the Financial Crisis', *European Political Science*, 10, 3, pp. 384–92.

Duenwald, C., Gueorguiev, N. & Schaechter, A. (2005) *Too Much of a Good Thing? Credit Booms in Transition Economies: The Cases of Bulgaria, Romania and Ukraine*, IMF Working Paper 128 (Washington, DC, International Monetary Fund).

EBRD (2008) *Transition Report 2008: Growth in Transition* (London, European Bank for Reconstruction and Development).

EBRD (2009) *Transition Report 2009: Transition in Crisis?* (London, European Bank for Reconstruction and Development).

EBRD (2010) *Transition Report 2010: Recovery and Reform* (London, European Bank for Reconstruction and Development).

EBRD (2011) *Transition Report 2011: Crisis and Transition: The People's Perspective* (London, European Bank for Reconstruction and Development).

Engdahl, W. F. (2009) 'Next Wave of Banking Crisis to come from Eastern Europe', *Global Research Online*, 18 February.

Epstein, R. A. (2008a) *In Pursuit of Liberalism: International Institutions in Post-communist Europe* (Baltimore, MD, Johns Hopkins University Press).

Epstein, R. A. (2008b) 'The Social Context in Conditionality: Internationalizing Finance in Post-communist Europe', *Journal of European Public Policy*, 15, 6, pp. 880–98.

Epstein, R. A. (2012) 'A European Banking Union Could Save the Euro', *US News and World Report*, available at: http://www.usnews.com/opinion/articles/2012/06/29/a-european-banking-union-could-save-the-euro, accessed 23 January 2013.

Ferenc, M. L. (2011) 'Az OTP elleni bankháború vezetett a devizahitel-robbanáshoz', *HVG Online*, 9 November, available at: http://hvg.hu.gazdasag/20111105_OTP_bankok_devizahitelezes_okai, accessed 30 August 2012.

Guardiancich, I. (2012) 'The Uncertain Future of Slovenian Exceptionalism', *East European Politics and Societies*, 26, 2, pp. 380–99.

Guillén, M. F. & Tschoegl, A. (2008) *Building a Global Bank: The Transformation of Banco Santander* (Princeton, NJ, Princeton University Press).

Hall, P. A. & Soskice, D. (eds) (2001) *Varieties of Capitalism: The Institutional Foundations of Comparative Advantage* (New York, Oxford University Press).

Hancké, B., Rhodes, M. & Thatcher, M. (eds) (2007) *Beyond Varieties of Capitalism: Conflict, Contradictions, and Complementarities in the European Economy* (New York, Oxford University Press).

IIF (2009) *Fragmentation of the International Financial System: Analysis and Recommendations*, IIF Staff Paper (Washington, DC, Institute of International Finance).

IMF (2010) *Regional Economic Outlook: Europe: Building Confidence* (Washington, DC, International Monetary Fund).

Jenkins, P. & Sovago, M. (2011) 'Foreign Currency Mortgages Now Threaten Hungary', *Financial Times*, 13 December.

Katzenstein, P. (ed.) (1978) *Between Power and Plenty: Foreign Economic Politics of Advanced Industrialized States* (Madison, WI, University of Wisconsin Press).

King, I. (2009) 'Eastern European Crisis May Put Us All in the Goulash', *The Times*, 19 February.

Kirshner, J. (2006) 'Globalization and National Security', in Kirshner, J. (ed.) (2006) *Globalization and National Security* (New York, Routledge), pp. 1–33.

Kostrzewa, L. & Mięczński, P. (2009) 'Emerytury na kredyt. ZUS nie ma, więc pożycza w bankach', *Gazeta Wyborcza*, 10 June.

Kruk, M. (2011) 'Poland Scraps PKO Bank Polski Share Offer for Now', *Dow Jones News*, 16 December.

Lindstrom, N. & Piroska, D. (2007) 'The Politics of Privatization and Europeanization in Europe's Periphery: Slovenian Banks and Breweries for Sale?', *Competition and Change*, 11, 2, pp. 115–33.

Macartney, H. (2012) *From Merlin to Oz: Limited Lending to the UK's Small- and Medium-Sized Enterprises*, unpublished manuscript.

Martinez-Diaz, L. (2009) *Globalizing in Hard Times: The Politics of Banking-Sector Opening in the Emerging World* (Ithaca, NY, Cornell University Press).

Molnár, M. (2010) *Enhancing Financial Stability Through Better Regulation in Hungary*, OECD Economics Department Working Papers 786, 17 June, available at: http://dx.doi.org/10.1787/5kmd41chjg34-en, accessed 4 April 2012.

Nölke, A. & Vliegenthart, A. (2009) 'Enlarging the Varieties of Capitalism: The Emergence of Dependent Market Economies in East Central Europe', *World Politics*, 61, 4, pp. 670–702.

Ortiz, G. (2012) 'It is Time for Emerging Markets to Lead Reform of Banking', *Financial Times*, 5 March.

OTP (2009) *OTP Bank Annual Report* (Budapest, OTP Bank).

Pistor, K. (2011) 'Governing Interdependent Financial Systems: Lessons from the Vienna Initiative', *Journal of Globalization and Development*, 2, 2.

PKO Bank Polski (2010a) *Directors' Report for the Year 2009* (Warsaw, PKO BP).

PKO Bank Polski (2010b) *2010 Annual Report* (Warsaw, PKO BP).

Raiffeisen Research (2009) *CEE Banking Sector Report: Rough Playing Field ... Committed Players* (Vienna, Raiffeisen Research).

Raiffeisen Research (2011) *CEE Banking Sector Report: Banking Sector Convergence 2.0* (Vienna, Raiffeisen Research).

Roubini, N. & Setser, B. (2004) *Bailouts or Bail-Ins? Responding to Financial Crises in Emerging Economies* (Washington, DC, Institute for International Economics).

Rózsavölgyi, R. & Kovács, V. (2005) 'Housing Subsidies in Hungary: Curse or Blessing?', *ECFIN Country Focus*, 2, 18, pp. 1–6.

Sloga, G. (2009a) 'Zatlers: jānodrošina maksimāla atklātība par Parex pārnemšanu', *Diena*, 28 September.

Sloga, G. (2009b) 'Vairās uznemties atbildību', *Diena*, 29 September.

Várhegyi, É. (2010) 'A válság hatása a magyarországi bankversenyre', *Közgazdasági Szemle*, 8, October, pp. 825–46.

Véron, N. (2011) 'Testimony on the European Debt and Financial Crisis', *Breugel Policy Contribution*, 2011, 11.

Wade, R. (2004) *Governing the Market: Economic Theory and the Role of Government in East Asian Industrialization* (Princeton, NJ, Princeton University Press).

Wade, R. (2007) 'The Aftermath of the Asian Financial Crisis: From "Liberalize the Market" to "Standardize the Market" and Create a "Level Playing Field', in Muchhala, B (ed.) (2007) *Ten Years After: Revisiting the Asian Financial Crisis* (Washington, DC, Woodrow Wilson International Center for Scholars), pp. 73–94.

World Bank (1993) *The East Asian Miracle: Economic Growth and Public Policy* (New York, Oxford University Press).

Zysman, J. (1983) *Governments, Markets, and Growth: Financial Systems and the Politics of Industrial Change* (Ithaca, NY, Cornell University Press).

The Return of Political Risk: Foreign-Owned Banks in Emerging Europe

ZDENEK KUDRNA & DANIELA GABOR

Abstract

Political risk—risk that investments are damaged by policy action of authorities—increased during the financial crisis due to controversies about the distribution of accumulated losses among stakeholders. Authorities interconnected by cross-border banks considered unilateral policies that minimised losses for domestic stakeholders at the expense of their foreign counterparts. This is at odds both with the assumption behind financial integration which presumes multilateral responses to cross-border shocks and with the typical definition of political risks that ignores the fact that not only host-country, but also home-country authorities can create such risks. This paper recasts the definition of political risk and reviews instances when political risk materialised within the EU banking market between 2007 and 2011. The analysis reveals that the EU regulatory framework needs to be enhanced to contain resurgent political risks systematically rather than through *ad hoc* interventions of the EU and international bodies.

THE INTERTWINING OF EMERGING ECONOMIES WITH THE capital markets of advanced countries through financial globalisation has been perceived as a mutually advantageous process. Banks from advanced countries gained access to more profitable banking opportunities in emerging markets, while the host countries received capital and banking know-how and shortened the time necessary to build up governance and regulatory frameworks for banks (EBRD 2007; Mishkin 2006; Berglöf & Bolton 2002). Consequently, the mutual benefits for home and host countries were such that they were prepared to cooperate and remove obstacles to the operation of transnational banks.

However, the long-term interest in cooperation may be challenged by short-term shocks, such as financial crises. Crises tend to create economic losses that need to be distributed across stakeholders, including foreign banks and local populations. Distribution of losses is bound to be more controversial than the distribution of benefits of financial cooperation. It may create short-term incentives for non-cooperation as home and host countries try to minimise their own losses and ignore the cross-border effects of their policies. Such unilateralism may then undermine the long-term consensus in favour of financial globalisation in emerging and advanced economies alike.

The new EU member states made transnational banking central to their development models by selling all large banks to foreign investors (EBRD 2007). They thereby provided the most important test case of commitment to cross-border cooperation in banking. The foreign-dominated model appeared to work well before the crisis, although it also contributed to excessive credit booms and foreign currency indebtedness that made economies more vulnerable to external shocks (Allen *et al.* 2011; EBRD 2010b; Kudrna 2010). When the crisis translated vulnerabilities into losses, authorities had to deal with their distribution between banks and their borrowers, which could be affected by various policies. For example, banks can be forced to restructure and prolong mortgages without any compensation, while borrowers might be forced to pay their debts, despite questionable banking practices during their origination. Similarly, taxpayers might be forced to pay extra taxes to stabilise banks or banks might be taxed more to ease additional fiscal burdens imposed on households. In short, when banks are foreign-owned, various policies may shift crisis-related burdens between foreigners and locals.

Using banks to protect the real economy or relying on the states' fiscal resources to stabilise banks is not unusual. However, in countries with largely domestic bank ownership there is no stark division between foreign and domestic stakeholders. In new member states, any extra burden shifted onto banks relieves primarily the domestic borrowers, while amplifying losses borne by banks' foreign shareholders. During hard times this inevitably creates short-term political incentives for imposing disproportionate burdens on foreigners. Furthermore, similar distributional conflicts may arise from the policy decisions in the home countries of cross-border banks affected by crisis. Where governments are reluctant to absorb fully the costs of bank rescue, or attribute the crisis to vulnerabilities particular to cross-border banking, regulatory responses may seek to shift resources from foreign subsidiaries. Governments may believe that the resources of subsidiaries abroad, rather than state support, should be used to repair the balance sheets of parent banks. Whether authorities act on these incentives is an important question for the debate about the political and economic sustainability of financial globalisation. It is one of the pertinent aspects of the regulators' dilemma of how to secure advantages of financial integration while containing its risks (Kapstein 1989).

We argue here that the distributional conflict can be understood in terms of political risk. In the next section, we review and recast the definition of political risk in order to capture its symmetrical nature, which means that not only investors from advanced home countries face political risks, as the existing literature assumes, but also that emerging market host countries are exposed to risks arising from political and regulatory developments in home countries. The third section reviews cases where such political risks materialised within the EU banking market during the 2007–2011 period. These cases have demonstrated that, even though the legal framework of the single market in financial services does substantially constrain the most extreme forms of political risk, it still allows for more subtle types. Although these risks were contained by successful *ad hoc* improvisations, we conclude that further institution building within the EU is necessary to cover political risks arising from the mismatch between the national regulatory frameworks on the one hand and the global integration of financial markets on the other.

Transmission of political risks within integrated transnational banks

The Financial Times Lexicon (2012) defines political risk as the risk associated with operating or investing in a country where political changes may have an adverse impact on earnings or returns. This risk exists in any economy, but is generally higher in politically unstable countries.[1] Political risk is relevant for both domestic and foreign investors, but higher for the latter as they have more limited access to political, legal and regulatory recourse in the host country. Especially during times of economic hardship or political instability, foreign investors tend to face higher political risks stemming from policies that depart from the pre-crisis consensus.

Political risk is part of the bundle of country risks, which includes various overlapping types of risks related to the exchange-rate regime, capital flows, macroeconomic policies or sovereign solvency (Bremmer & Keat 2010, p. 65). Most of these risks are generated by rare events, the occurrence and timing of which are difficult or impossible to predict.[2] The operational definitions in the literature therefore tend to list typical instances of political risk, rather than attempting to provide some overarching definition that would clearly separate political risk from other country risks (MIGA 2011; Bremmer & Keat 2010; Moran 2001; Moran *et al.* 2008). Table 1 provides one such definition which is used by the Multilateral Investment Guarantee Agency (MIGA) of the World Bank.

TABLE 1

MULTILATERAL INVESTMENT GUARANTEE AGENCY (MIGA) DEFINITION OF POLITICAL RISK

Specific source of political risk	Explanation
Transfer and convertibility restrictions	Risk of losses arising from an investor's inability to convert local currency into foreign exchange for transfer outside the host country.
Expropriation	The loss of investment as a result of discriminatory acts by any branch of the government that may reduce or eliminate ownership, control, or rights to the investment, either as a result of a single action or through an accumulation of acts by the government.
Breach of contract	Risk of losses arising from the host government's breach or repudiation of a contractual agreement with the investor, including non-honouring of arbitral awards.
Non-honouring of sovereign financial obligations	Risk of losses due to non-compliance of government guarantees securing full and timely repayment of a debt that is being used to finance the development of a new project or the enhancement of an existing project.
War, terrorism or civil disturbances	Risk of losses due to: the destruction, disappearance or physical damage as a result of organised internal or external conflicts, politically motivated acts of violence by non-state groups or social unrest.
Other adverse regulatory changes	Risk of losses for foreign investors stemming from arbitrary changes to regulations.

Source: Based on MIGA (2010, p. 21).

The MIGA definition includes the two types of biases characteristic of most of the literature on political risk. First, it is almost entirely focused on the catastrophic forms of political risk. Second, it presumes that political risk is asymmetric—a one-way street—where investment can be damaged only by political changes in the host country, but not in the home country. These are important omissions that may lead to underestimation of risks related to financial integration within the single banking market.

[1] See Bremmer (2006) for discussion of the relationship between political risk and stability.

[2] Some aspects of political risk are related to Knightian uncertainty rather than risk with known probabilistic distribution, which also hampers attempts to quantify these risks for risk management purposes.

TRANSITION ECONOMIES AFTER 2008

Subtle forms of political risks within the EU

The advantage of the focus on the catastrophic forms of political risk is that the events that translate a risk into a loss are relatively easy to verify. This is crucial for the insurance contracts offered by private or public insurance organisations such as MIGA.[3] However, there are more subtle forms of political risk, not related to any single dramatic event, but stemming from incremental sequences of relatively minor or deeply technical policy decisions. Such risks are part and parcel of everyday economic processes and most firms manage them through participation in the policy-making process. However, the foreign control of any important sector of the economy opens specific possibilities for more or less tacit discrimination and hence contributes to more subtle forms of political risk.

International investment treaties provide some protection against discrimination of foreign-owned firms. Typically, they entitle foreign investors to the same treatment as domestic firms in the same sector. However, if there are no important domestic firms in that sector, then such clauses provide only limited protection from unexpected policy changes. Especially during recession, when distributional conflicts intensify, it is politically tempting to impose extra burdens on sectors controlled by foreign investors, whose voice in a jittery politics tends to be more limited compared to that of domestic actors. It is therefore important for the debate about the sustainability of financial integration to understand the factors that shape political risk in cross-border banking.

The subtle forms of political risk are more relevant in the EU context characterised by relative political stability and robust legal constraints. EU treaties guard against capital controls, expropriations or explicit discrimination of foreign investors and other catastrophic forms of political risk listed in Table 1. At the same time, EU legislation still leaves space for the more subtle forms, especially with regard to regulatory and taxation policies. Member states guard their rights to set taxes, enabling them to impose sector-specific taxes (Genschel 2011). Similarly, EU regulatory policies are usually defined only as minimum common standards, leaving member states free to impose additional sectoral rules as long as they do not contradict some higher-level rules.[4] Member states can therefore change regulations so that they deliver the desired distributional outcome without necessarily breaching the letter of EU rules. Whether they implemented such policies is again important for the debate about sustainability of financial integration throughout the difficult times of crisis.

Symmetry of political risk

The second limiting assumption of the existing literature is that the political risk originates only in the host country. This is largely an empirical artefact stemming from its traditional focus on the catastrophic risks faced by foreign firms—especially those in extractive industries—in developing countries. However, there is no *a priori* theoretical justification for this asymmetry; once countries are interconnected by cross-border investments, adverse policy change that affects the investor in any of these countries is likely to impact investments of the given investor in all the other countries. At the same time, the salience of such spillovers is likely to differ across industries.

[3]See Lu *et al.*, (2009) for a review of the political risk insurance industry.
[4]See Kudrna (2012) for a related example.

186

In manufacturing, non-financial services or utility industries the political risk spillovers from home to host countries are less relevant than in banking. If the home-country government of an energy firm decides to ban nuclear technology, it does not have a direct impact on nuclear power plants owned by the same firm abroad. Similarly, if home-country authorities change product regulations, foreign plants of the same firm can either adapt or simply source the input no longer available from the home country on international markets. However, if the home country limits the financial flows between the parent bank and its host-country subsidiary, the impact on the financial stability of the subsidiary may be dramatic. Although power plants, car factories or supermarkets owned by a transnational firm tend to be connected by common management, brands and logistics, their internal operations are less integrated and thus less dependent on each other than is the case for transnational banks.

Cross-border banks gain considerable efficiencies from integrating their internal functions across national boundaries. They tend to concentrate strategic decision-making, capital management, risk management and auditing at the headquarters, while other activities such as back-office, information technologies, liquidity management or asset and liabilities management also tend to be concentrated on the group level, but not necessarily in the home country (BIS 2010; Van den Spiegel 2008). However, the most important channel for transmission of political risks between home and host countries is the internal capital market. Parent banks distribute capital through internal markets to the best-performing subsidiaries, enabling those to overcome the constraints of underdeveloped capital markets in the countries where they operate. Subsidiaries of multinational banks then take into account a broader series of considerations when deciding the pace of credit expansion, including macroeconomic conditions in home countries and alternative profit opportunities in other subsidiaries of the same banking group (De Haas & van Lelyveld 2010). This makes internal liquidity flows sensitive to economic and political developments in home and host countries alike.

The reliance on internal capital markets allows transnational banks to 'price-in' changes in political risks in both home and host countries. For domestic banks, lending rates typically reflect the costs of liquidity on domestic money markets and some mark-up. In contrast, transnational banks deploy 'internal prime rates' that price overall market conditions for the banking group and country risk premiums for subsidiaries (Bruno & Shin 2011; Van Groeningen 2010). In this sense, the reallocation of liquidity through internal capital markets reflects the move away from traditional relationship-based loan pricing to market-based instruments for pricing credit and other risks, including political ones (Norden & Wagner 2007). This level of internal integration of transnational banks makes it certain that shocks originating in any country of operations would be transmitted through internal capital markets to all other countries with a strong presence of a given bank. In principle, this could make transnational banking more resilient as it can pool risks and shocks more broadly and stable subsidiaries may enhance the stability of an ailing parent bank as much as a stable parent may support vulnerable subsidiaries. However, the increased resilience is contingent on how home- and/or host-country authorities respond to the crisis.

Policy responses and changes in political risk

Home- and host-country authorities may perceive the role of internal capital markets very differently. Host-country authorities may view it as a way to reduce banks' funding costs that increases the availability of credit in underdeveloped financial systems. However, they can also consider the internal prime rates as a non-transparent transfer pricing mechanism potentially enabling the abuse of market power or tax evasion as well as undermining the transmission of monetary policy signals. Policy autonomy is further undermined where internal capital markets act as an important conduit for the transmission of global shocks (Gabor 2012; Cetorelli & Goldberg 2012). A tightening of funding conditions for the parent bank may force subsidiaries with large funding gaps, meaning large loan-to-deposit ratios, to turn to domestic money markets. The increased demand for domestic liquidity may push up interest rates and thus worsen funding conditions for the entire banking system in the host country. Furthermore, subsidiaries of banking groups reliant on wholesale funding curtail credit much faster than domestic banks funded from local deposits (De Haas & van Lelyveld 2011). Hence, host-country authorities may welcome opportunities to regain more control over the domestic subsidiaries of transnational banks. Similarly, home-country authorities may welcome increased profit opportunities and diversification, but remain concerned about credit and liquidity risks involved in transnational banking and may prefer to reduce exposure of parent banks under their supervision. In short, cross-border integration of banks is a contested development and what was generally accepted during the boom times may be questioned during the crisis. This increases the uncertainty of unexpected regulatory responses, inevitably heightening political risks associated with transnational banking.

Uncertainty is only heightened during financial crises that put supervisory authorities into a much more powerful position *vis-à-vis* supervised banks. Crisis makes asset prices much more volatile, and supervisors may therefore not accept banks' prudential calculations without question. At the same time, crisis puts banking capital under pressure, and bankers are therefore keen to avoid disputes with supervisors that might force them to raise more capital. When banks actually receive some form of public support or state aid, national authorities may even acquire some formal co-decision powers. Hence, the treatment of units of transnational banks in other countries would reflect not only commercial considerations of bankers, but to a large extent also those of their national supervisors. However, the mandate of supervisors in the EU member states—even home supervisors of large transnational banks—is concerned, almost exclusively, with national financial stability. This makes national supervisors somewhat reluctant to accept any pooling of risks that leaves 'their' parts of transnational banks more exposed to problems from other countries. In short, a more powerful position of national supervisors heightens the political risk that the banking investment might be damaged by regulatory changes in any host or home country.

National authorities may opt for two principal responses to the shocks affecting transnational banking, multilateral or unilateral. The former considers cross-border externalities of the domestic policy response and engages the counter-party in finding a cooperative response that minimises the joint negative impact on all sides. In contrast, the unilateral strategy aims to minimise the impact on the single economy and, in its extreme form, completely disregards all spillovers to other economies. An example of the multilateral strategy is a situation when home and host actors jointly agree not to limit exposure of banks to their economies in order to prevent a credit crunch. Such an agreement is not automatic, because in times of crisis countries may prefer a unilateral policy response that limits the exposure of important banks by their withdrawal from other countries. Whereas the coordinated multilateral response requires commitment from host and home authorities, unilateral non-cooperative strategies disregard the impact of domestic policies on other economies and require no commitment to cooperation.

Financial globalisation is predicated on the assumption that political risks are negligible, because bankers and supervisors would respond to crises in a multilateral coordinated fashion. However, their commitment to multilateral cooperation is only voluntary, as there is no legally binding arrangement preventing unilateral responses, not even within the EU (Kudrna 2012). Unilateral responses therefore not only remain plausible, but also quite likely given the national mandates of national banking supervisors. Whether bankers and supervisors choose to cooperate across borders or not remains an empirical question with important policy implications for long-term sustainability of transnational banking.

Policy responses to crisis

In the boom years preceding the crisis, foreign-owned banks financed rapid credit expansion in many new EU member states (De Haas *et al.* 2012; EBRD 2010b; Aydin 2008). Low interest rates and exchange-rate stability, predicated on expected progress towards eurozone entry, encouraged particularly rapid growth of foreign currency lending that exposed households to exchange-rate risk, but seemingly eliminated currency mismatches for transnational banks (Rosenberg & Tirpak 2008). Several attempts by host regulators to curb lending in foreign currencies were largely frustrated by regulatory arbitrage. For instance, parent banks provided direct cross-border credit to companies based in host countries (Pistor 2010). Banks from the old EU countries therefore built up $1.3 trillion exposure to economies on the Eastern periphery of the EU, with Austrian banks accounting for almost 20%, followed by German and Italian banks (15% and 17%). Once the post-Lehman freezing of international financial markets increased funding stress for parent banks, banks and supervisory authorities in home and host countries had to respond to the new circumstances that threatened a systemic crisis in all new and some old member states (Gabor 2010; Kudrna 2010).

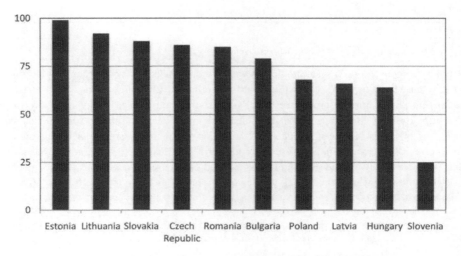

FIGURE 1. FOREIGN BANKS' ASSETS IN TOTAL BANKING ASSETS (2009).
Source: Bankscope database, available at: https://bankscope2.bvdep.com/version-2012713/ home.serv? product=scope2006, accessed 24 July 2012.

TRANSITION ECONOMIES AFTER 2008

This section reviews the policy responses of host countries as well as home countries that are connected through the major transnational banks (see Figure 1 and Table 2). It identifies instances when unilateral policy proposals heightened political risks and traces multilateral responses aimed at containing them before they could escalate into some form of 'regulatory war'. The evidence presented suggests that, although political risks increased due to unilateral policy proposals both in host and home countries, they were successfully contained by *ad hoc* policy improvisation.

TABLE 2
MATERIALISATION OF POLITICAL RISKS DURING THE FINANCIAL CRISIS (2007–2011)

Date	Policy initiative creating political risk	Final outcome of the initiative
March 2009	EU-level proposal for support of some banks in new member states.	Failed attempt to implement a formal EU-level multilateral programme.
January 2009	Vienna Initiative 1.0	Informal, but successful multilateral cooperation of transnational banks.
June 2010	Unilateral transposition of the Consumer Credit Directive in Romania.	Contested aspects withdrawn after the intervention of the European Commission and IMF.
June 2010	Introduction of special banking taxes in Hungary.	Unilateral imposition of taxes on foreign-owned sectors, including banks.
December 2011	Forced mortgage replacement scheme in Hungary.	Multilateral compromise achieved after pressure from international organisations
June 2010	Personal bankruptcy law in Latvia.	Multilateral compromise satisfied Nordic parent banks.
November 2011	Unilateral ceilings on internal lending to new member states suggested by Austria.	Reclassified as mere recommendation after Commission intervention.
January 2012	Vienna Initiative 2.0	Ongoing search for multilateral framework conditioned on EU reforms.

Source: Authors.

Failed proposal for EU-level multilateral scheme

A policy response to such systemic threats was obviously needed. It could come either on a case-by-case basis or more systematically as a coordinated EU policy (Gros 2009). Austria led an effort to design a systematic response and tested its political feasibility at the informal ECOFIN Council in March 2009. The idea did not receive sufficient support, as the problems of banks in new member states were not of equal concern to all EU members (Haeberle 2009). The Council refused to consider a systematic EU solution and declared that the affected EU countries would be supported on a case-by-case basis. Although the Austrian initiative was unsuccessful, its preparatory meetings led to the less formal 'Vienna Initiative'.

Successful multilateral improvisation: Vienna Initiative 1

The Vienna Initiative (VI—formally known as the European Bank Coordination Initiative) was launched as a forum for coordination and information sharing among international financial organisations, the European Commission, home and host authorities of cross-border banking

TRANSITION ECONOMIES AFTER 2008

groups and the largest financial groups involved in the new member states.[5] It was based on mutual *'quid pro quo'*. International and national authorities provided banks with detailed information on the course of macroeconomic stabilisation and international reserves that were crucial for their risk assessment (IMF 2010a, p. 63).[6] In exchange, banks committed to sustaining certain levels of external financing for their subsidiaries that supported the overall objectives of macroeconomic stabilisation. To this end, specific agreements on liquidity support and recapitalisation of local subsidiaries were signed for Hungary, Romania and Latvia (EBRD 2010a, p. 1).

The initiative was also important for the integrity of the single banking market. Almost all important Austrian, Belgian, French and Greek banks active in the new member economies received some form of financial support from their home-country governments (Unicredit 2009, p. 13). The Commission and other parties to the VI not only had to ensure compliance with EU state aid rules, but also to prevent the introduction of protectionist rules into public aid packages that could restrict liquidity and capital support of the banks' host-country subsidiaries.

The VI successfully maintained commitment of parent banks to their subsidiaries in the new member states most affected by the crisis. At the same time, it revealed the limits of an improvised multilateral solution beyond the most immediate crisis. As banks became concerned that subdued loan demand would result in idle liquidity trapped at some subsidiaries, they watered down their commitments (Nietsche 2010). Whereas the first VI agreement for Romania included detailed commitments to specific capital adequacy ratios and recapitalisation parameters depending on pre-agreed stress-test indicators, in the later cases of Hungary and Latvia conditions were far less specific and practically superseded by commitments under respective IMF stand-by agreements for these countries.

The absence of a credible framework for the coordinated resolution of distributional conflicts in cross-border banking saw the emergence of various unilateral initiatives to which we now turn.

Unilateral policy responses proposed by host countries

The VI initiative helped to contain the initial impact of the crisis on new EU economies and banks. However, as the political and economic pressures created by continued recession increased, so did the incentives of host-country authorities to shift some of the burden onto foreign banks. Three countries—Romania, Hungary and Latvia—formulated specific legislative proposals that clearly threatened unilateral policy responses.

[5]The VI was concerned with the following 21 countries, which does not necessarily imply that all host authorities participate in every activity: Albania, Belarus, Bosnia & Hercegovina, Bulgaria, Croatia, Czech Republic, Estonia, Hungary, Latvia, Lithuania, Former Yugoslav Republic of Macedonia, Moldova, Montenegro, Poland, Romania, Russia, Serbia, Slovak Republic, Slovenia, Turkey and Ukraine. The most active host countries are Austria, Italy and Sweden. The participating international financial institutions are the European Bank for Reconstruction and Development (EBRD), the International Monetary Fund (IMF), the World Bank and the European Investment Bank. The EU stakeholders are the European Commission (DG ECFIN), the European Banking Authority and also the European Central Bank (ECB) which participates as an observer. The following banks participated in various activities of the Vienna Initiative: Bayerische Landesbank, Eurobank EFG, Erste Bank, Intesa Sanpaolo, KBC, National Bank of Greece, OTB Bank, Piraeus Bank, Raiffeisen Bank International, Societe Generale, Swedbank and Unicredit. The European Banking Federation also took part.

[6]International financial institutions also committed €33 billion to emerging Europe, some of which was channelled through transnational banks. However, these were general funds for mitigating the crisis and were not a direct consequence of the VI (EBRD 2012).

Hungarian policy response: from multilateral to unilateral and back

The Hungarian government approach to banking sector regulation offers the prime case of a unilateral policy response. Financial and social stability was threatened by rapid currency depreciation in the aftermath of Lehman's collapse, due to the high share of foreign currency loans—particularly Swiss francs—in household credit. Hungary was the first EU country to request IMF assistance in November 2008 and, with IMF blessing, it adopted a moratorium over house repossessions related to non-performing foreign currency mortgages (Gabor 2010).

The new Hungarian government elected in May 2010 promised to reverse the social costs of austerity by asking 'the strongest participants of the economy [to] help those who are in distress' (Bryant 2010). It introduced a series of changes in tax and regulatory rules that shifted the costs of the crisis onto foreign investors. In June 2010 it announced a levy based on the size of banks' balance sheets that was much higher than similar taxes in other countries (Kudrna 2010). The IMF decried the bank levy as 'distortive ... harmful to the economy', warned about adverse reactions from foreign banks that would negatively impact credit growth, and immediately suspended its programme in Hungary (Than & Dunai 2010). Even though the Hungarian government remained committed to the fiscal tightening programme originally agreed with the IMF, the disagreement that ended the relationship arose from the government's rejection of the IMF's view that 'sustainable consolidation will require durable, non-distortive measures', such as spending cuts (IMF 2010b). Indeed, the Hungarian government announced further taxes in November 2010, designed to impact exclusively on foreign-dominated, highly profitable sectors such as retail, energy and telecommunications.

Further regulatory measures aimed at reducing households' burden of foreign currency debt were introduced in May 2011. Foreign banks were consulted over the initial proposals, which were multilateral in their character as they appeared to reconcile the conflicting priorities of home and host actors. Distressed borrowers were allowed to switch their foreign currency mortgages to a fixed exchange rate, higher than the pre-Lehman level, but around 25% less than the market rate at the time. In return, the government agreed to suspend the moratorium on repossessions, which would allow banks to recover the collateral of non-performing loans and proceed, at a gradual pace, to resell the houses. To ease the social costs of repossessions, a state fund would purchase the homes of some distressed borrowers or provide interest rate subsidies to those willing to move to smaller homes.

The Hungarian government, however, departed from its erstwhile multilateral approach by announcing an early repayment scheme for foreign currency mortgages in September 2011. Although the law stopped short of imposing mandatory forint refinancing at the preferential rate that banks feared the most, it forced banks to assume losses between the preferential and the market-level exchange rate, if affected households decided to convert their mortgages to the local currency. The scheme would primarily benefit wealthier households with forint savings or ready access to forint loans for the lump-sum repayment, hence only a 10–15% take-up rate was expected (Kester 2011a).

Initially the Hungarian government resisted the widespread contestations of the mortgage scheme, including harsh assessments of the impact for banking sector stability from home-country authorities, Austria in particular, the European Commission and the ECB (2011). Instead, the Hungarian Competition Authority raised the stakes by announcing an investigation into cartel activity in the household mortgage market, citing significant rises in interest rates immediately after the introduction of the FX-currency mortgage repayment

TRANSITION ECONOMIES AFTER 2008

scheme. The government also threatened to hike up the special bank tax to cover any bank compensation payments ruled by European institutions (Dunai 2011).

Eventually, however, market pressures forced Hungarian actors to reconsider the unilateral imposition of mortgage relief plans. Hungary faced increasing difficulties in servicing its large funding requirements and reluctantly returned to the negotiation table with both foreign banks and the IMF as it strove to prevent a sovereign downgrade to non-investment grade. An agreement between government and banks to share the costs for easing Hungarian households' debt burden was eventually reached in December 2011. The new deal envisaged partial debt cancellation for overdue loans, new conditions for Swiss franc mortgages for non-delinquent borrowers where the government assumed some of the currency risk and, crucially, allowed banks to deduct around 30% of the early repayment scheme losses from the 2012 bank tax (Kester 2011b). The government also promised to phase out the special bank tax by 2014. The return to a multilateral policy response, together with expectations of IMF support, contributed to the stabilisation of the forint in early 2012.

Romania: reinterpreting the EU consumer credit directive

In Romania the threat of a unilateral policy response took the form of an overly strict interpretation of an EU directive. In June 2010, the Romanian Authority for Consumer Protection (RACP) presented the law transposing the EU Directive 48/2008, harmonising the regulation of consumer credit across Europe and improving consumer protection by stronger competition in the banking sector. This came at a particularly tense moment, when indebted households voiced increasingly stronger complaints over changes in interest rates on foreign currency loans, and especially mortgages. In the aftermath of Lehman's collapse, banks had unilaterally increased rates, citing 'liquidity conditions on the money market' that increased the internal reference rates typically used by transnational banks as benchmarks for calculating rates applicable in different countries of operation.

The RACP draft proposed to reorganise the regulatory terrain around household credit and impose restrictions on potential abuses of banks' dominant positions. It drew on the directive's provisions intended to curb 'hidden taxes' attached to consumer credit, such as cash-handling fees or risk commissions or early repayment charges that prevent consumers from choosing the most competitive loan conditions. These provisions also reduce banks' scope for varying interest rate spreads, reflecting internal prime rates (Silaghi 2010). However, the RACP modified the original directive in three distinct ways. First, it extended the new set of rules beyond consumer credit to mortgages, which breached explicit limits on the scope of application specified in the directive. Second, it proposed the retroactive imposition of new rules on existing loans, not only on new ones as recommended by the directive. Third, the later proposal also introduced mandatory refinancing rules requiring banks to enable existing borrowers with a good credit record to benefit from a relaxation of banks' lending conditions and the new interest rate provisions by allowing them to refinance without any additional costs arising from a re-evaluation of creditworthiness.

The new legislation exposed conflicting positions among host-country actors, as well as the difficulties involved in imposing tighter regulation on foreign-owned banks (Singer 2007). The central bank questioned the RACP's interventions in what it viewed as its exclusive regulatory purview and expressed concerns about the profitability and stability of the banking system under the new legislation. Indeed, from the central bank viewpoint, the regulatory initiative threatened to derail the VI and raised the uncomfortable prospect of capital flight, should cross-border banks decided to relocate capital (Chiru 2010).

The Romanian parliament initially approved some of the proposed measures in November 2010, despite intense bank lobbying. However, as the international and home-country actors rallied behind the central bank position, the decision was reversed in December 2010. Parliament voted to exclude some of the most controversial aspects, including the retroactive extension to existing loans and the mandatory refinancing requirement. The European Commission threatened pre-infringement procedures and the IMF threatened the suspension of the January 2011 stand-by tranche. The IMF explained its intervention in domestic politics as a consequence of its involvement with the VI, where it used its leverage on behalf of the Romanian state to persuade parent banks of the importance of continued exposure to new member states' banking systems (Deacu 2010). The unilateral initiative was therefore dropped in favour of a multilateral compromise.

Latvia: unilateral mortgage relief prevented

The Latvian parliament passed a new personal bankruptcy law at the same time as Hungary introduced the special bank tax. The law significantly strengthened the position of debtors relative to creditors and required Latvian banks to absorb a higher proportion of losses stemming from the collapsed real-estate bubble that they had helped to fuel. The law allowed borrowers who had been declared bankrupt to write off their debt after one year if they repaid 50% of what they owed, after two years if they repaid 35% and after three years if they repaid only 20%. In practical terms, debtors are only liable to pay back the market value of their collateral rather than the actual amount of the loan (Danske Bank 2010, p. 1). The law also required banks to cover the administrative costs of the personal bankruptcy procedure (Mullett 2010).

Unlike the Hungarian case, the changes in mortgage law were prepared in consultation with parent banks as well as with the IMF and EU representatives overseeing the Latvian stabilisation programme. An earlier version was passed by parliament in June 2010, but was vetoed by the Latvian president who considered some of the banks' objections. The initial proposal would have allowed debt to be forgiven, by paying 30% of a debtor's income for two years (Eglitis 2010), and made no distinction between people who had taken loans for their own property and those who had speculated on the real-estate market (Mullett 2010).

The version eventually signed into law was seen by Nordic parent banks as a viable multilateral compromise (Braslina 2010). Although the law pushed a higher proportion of mortgage resolution costs onto banks, it was not expected to have any immediate effect on Latvian banks or their Nordic parents. Swedbank, SEB, Nordea and DnB NORD, which dominated the Latvian market, wrote off over €900 million in bad loans, including many of those covered by the new legislation (Eglitis 2010). However, the limits placed on the recovery process would make loans more risky for banks, requiring borrowers to put up more of their own funds in the future, thus making repetition of the pre-crisis credit boom less likely.

All three cases of unilateral policy responses in Hungary, Romania and Latvia commanded considerable political support during their reading in the respective parliaments, with both government and opposition parties voting for them. This points to the popular appeal of unilateral policy responses in domestic politics. At the same time, the

TRANSITION ECONOMIES AFTER 2008

involvement of international and host-country actors persuaded host-country authorities to reconsider their proposals and opt for multilateral compromises.

Unilateral policies proposed by a home country

We have argued that political risk related to cross-border banking is symmetric in the sense that while home-country actors are exposed to policy risks stemming from the actions of host-country actors, so the reverse also applies. The VI successfully prevented unilateral policies in early 2009, but the deepening eurozone crisis reinforced incentives for home countries to consider such policies. A new rule imposed by Austria on subsidiaries' lending provides the case in point, also confirming the symmetric nature of political risk.

Austria: limits on host-country lending

Austria was instrumental in the success of the multilateral VI. However, throughout the second half of 2011, the eurozone crisis triggered an increasing scrutiny of European banks' vulnerabilities and widespread speculation that the exposure of Austrian banks to new member state countries threatened the country's AAA rating (McGovern & Sidliarevich 2011).[7] Despite protests that Austrian banking models in new member countries engendered little vulnerability, the Austrian central bank eventually announced new regulatory measures in November 2011. It imposed a 110% cap on subsidiaries' loan-to-deposit ratios, thus curbing Austrian banks' use of cross-border funding and inducing them to rely on local deposits instead. The new provision would only apply to new lending, so that subsidiaries with existing funding gaps would not have to immediately adjust their lending activity.

The reactions of the various host-country regulators to the Austrian decision illustrate the difficulties of *ad hoc* multilateral improvisation during crisis. On the one hand, the Austrian regulators presented the move as the outcome of collective regulatory efforts, 'discussed in principle with regulators in most neighbouring countries' (McGovern & Sidliarevich 2011). In a sense, the measures did reflect the VI's recommendations, which explicitly acknowledged the possibility that macro-prudential tools, such as loan-to-deposit ratio caps, may be necessary to curb rapid asset side growth financed through cross-border lending. From this perspective, the Austrian regulators argued, the new measures only sought to speed up the agreed changes for strengthening the ability of large, cross-border banking groups to withstand shocks in particular funding markets. Indeed, for the Austrian regulators, the new measures contravened in timing rather than in spirit the VI resolutions, working 'in the interests of both the Austrian banks and of the host countries, because basically it is about strengthening the sustainability of the business model in these countries' (Wagstyl & Buckley 2011).

However, host-country regulators interpreted the new Austrian rule as a unilateral action. The new member state authorities denied that any multilateral consultation had taken place (Wagstyl & Frey 2012). They pointed to the lack of measures that would contain the cross-border spillovers of the Austrian interference with banks' internal capital markets and regarded the decision as being prompted by political concerns over Austria's sovereign rating rather than as an effort designed to accelerate multilateral resolutions. The Hungarian

[7]The combined assets of the three largest Austrian banks in the region surpassed Austria's annual GDP.

and Romanian actors, who had previously backed away from unilateral policy responses, were particularly vocal about the 'beggar thy neighbour' aspects of the Austrian policy. They argued that the measures to strengthen the parent-banks' balance sheets would prompt these to repatriate capital, thereby harming financing and growth prospects for host countries.

Extended negotiations to settle the controversy eventually resulted in a dilution of the initial provisions. Once the European Commission formally set to examine host-countries' claim that unilateral measures were infringing freedom of capital movement, the Austrian regulator took a more flexible position, clarifying that the loan-to-deposit caps were issued as a guideline rather than a rule since failure to comply involved no formal sanctions (Wagstyl & Frey 2012). This dilution, effectively amounting to a 'humbling' example of the dangers associated with *ad hoc*, unilateral initiatives, motivated home countries to strive for coordinated responses and set the scene for a second round of the Vienna Initiative that took place in March 2012.

Return to multilateralism: Vienna Initiative 2

During the second half of 2011 funding pressures again reached a point when uncoordinated withdrawal of transnational banks from Central and Eastern Europe became a distinct possibility. In response, the VI was re-launched in January 2012 to meet this threat. As in 2009, its goal was to prevent uncoordinated unilateral policies, but the focus of its work moved from forging short-term financing agreements to advocacy of long-term regulatory reforms that would render the cross-border banking model sustainable in turbulent times.

Eurozone uncertainty as well as Greek debt restructuring weighed heavily on parent banks, as they scrambled to increase capital–asset ratios above 9% to meet new global and EU rules by the mid-2012 deadline. At the same time, banks faced increasing losses in many host countries and struggled to contain them due to political and procedural obstacles to the resolution of non-performing assets. Although the biggest cross-border banks seemed committed to the region, some of their smaller competitors were selling Central and Eastern European subsidiaries to buyers from Russia, which was not necessarily welcomed by host-country authorities. As the economic and political risks kept rising, so did the need for cooperation.

The Vienna Initiative 2 provided a quick fix for the international coordination problem. It was less *ad hoc* than in 2009 as it formalised its operations by appointing a steering committee and a chair—the governor of the central bank of Poland—to coordinate and disseminate the outputs of its deliberations. The Initiative operates by setting up working groups including all interested stakeholders. These explicitly recognise potential conflicts between home and host actors and try to formulate policy recommendations that reconcile them. The VI also launched a regular publication—the *Deleveraging Monitor*[8]—compiled by the participating international financial institutions in order to report financial flows to and out of host countries.

The policy recommendations of both rounds of the VI are based on the premise that the cross-border banking model is fundamentally sound, albeit in need of more intensive policy

[8]Available at: http://www.eib.org/attachments/vienna-2-0-sc_-warsaw-12-july-2012-deleveraging-monitor_letterhead.pdf, accessed 4 August 2012.

cooperation of home- and host-country authorities in order to contain financial contagion and political risks during economic downturns. Thus, the VIs have effectively provided a platform for transnational banks to intervene in multilateral regulatory deliberations and to contain unilateral initiatives where they were less likely to have political leverage. Indeed, the four policy papers published so far point to the VIs as a mechanism for internalising the preferences of transnational banks, as often occurs in collective transnational regulatory initiatives (Tsingou 2010). The first paper suggested market-based approaches, rather than regulatory measures to restrict foreign currency lending, emphasising the importance of developing local currency and capital markets that would reduce dependence on foreign funding (EBCI 2011a). The second focused more narrowly on increasing the capacity of host countries to absorb EU funds that would prop up demand for co-financing bank loans (EBCI 2011b). The third set of recommendations focused on reforms that would enable smoother resolution of non-performing loans (EBCI 2012a). These three reports primarily reiterated the usual list of institutional reforms provided by the international financial institutions and EU authorities for any candidate or transition country, although they acknowledge potential conflicts between home and host authorities more openly than was customary before the crisis. Finally, the fourth report recommended ways of implementing Basel III capital requirements without triggering a credit crunch in host economies and was dominated by the banks' desire to pool capital and liquidity freely across their subsidiaries, without restrictions imposed by the related party transactions (EBCI 2012b).

The key challenge remained regulatory fragmentation along national lines. The absence of jurisdiction and authority matching the geographic scope of cross-border banks creates strong incentives for unilateral policy responses and thus increases political risks. The proposals of the VI rely heavily on the supervisory colleges and the cross-border stability group that are supposed to develop *ex ante* agreements on the resolution of cross-border EU banks in crisis. However, the EU failed to agree on any binding rules and postponed any legislative decisions beyond 2015 (EC 2010). There is therefore no credible commitment to multilateral cooperation that could contain political risks stemming from unilateral policy responses and the VI was unlikely to progress until the EU reached some agreement. This remained a serious limitation for its long-term regulatory reform ambitions.

However, it is also possible that the eurozone crisis might induce a breakthrough agreement on banking union, which would shift regulation, supervision and resolution of the largest European banks to the EU level. That would allow for major progress in the VI agenda as well. At the same time, the escalation of the crisis may also destroy the cross-border banking model as the conflicts between home and host actors force banks to disintegrate into highly autonomous, separately capitalised national subsidiaries reliant on the rules and markets of the host country (Helleiner & Pagliari 2011). Such circumstances may also coincide with political risks beyond the subtle tax and regulatory measures, potentially all the way to the imposition of capital controls or even asset nationalisations.

Conclusion

The financial crisis brought to the fore many types of risk that had been practically disregarded by the globalised financial markets during the preceding boom years. Political risk that investment would be damaged by policy changes is one of these resurgent risks that question the sustainability of globalised finance in crisis circumstances. We reviewed instances of political risks in the new EU member states that host the most globalised banking sectors worldwide. The evidence so far suggests that the need to distribute crisis-related losses between banks and their borrowers or other policy concerns increased political risks by inducing authorities in Hungary, Austria, Romania and Latvia to propose unilateral policies that seemed unacceptable before the crisis. However, *ad hoc* improvisation facilitated by international bodies such as the EBRD, IMF and European Commission prevented their implementation in starkly unilateral forms. In all cases, authorities renegotiated their proposals with transnational banks and supervisors from other countries concerned. The final policy responses were therefore largely multilateral as they considered policy spillovers to other home and host countries that were made interdependent by the presence of integrated transnational banks.

The political risks involved in the EU banking system have some specific characteristics that were not previously explored in the related scholarly and policy literature. First, the EU legal framework constrains catastrophic forms of political risks stemming from nationalisations or currency controls: it therefore takes more subtle forms arising from changes in tax and regulatory policies. Second, foreign investments in banking create a two-way channel for transmission of political risks between the host and home countries. Hence, foreign investment into a bank in the new EU member states can be adversely affected not only by policy changes in these countries, but also by policy changes in their country of origin. Therefore, political risks in transnational banking are not asymmetric, originating only from the host country, as is traditionally assumed in the existing literature, but symmetric, originating in both home and host countries. The evidence from the Austrian case supports our conjecture.

Overall, the policy responses pertinent to the distribution of crisis-related losses between domestic borrowers and foreign-owned banks seem to proceed in a cycle starting with multilateral approaches, continuing with unilateral ones and then returning to multilateral policies. The initial response to crisis took the form of multilateral cooperation on the platform of the VI. Subsequently, Hungary, Romania, Latvia and Austria formulated unilateral policies that disregarded the adverse impacts in other countries. However, before they could be implemented, all four countries succumbed to external pressures and renegotiated their policies towards more balanced multilateral actions. The funding pressures in Western European markets triggered a further round of multilateral coordination under the Vienna Initiative 2. This aimed specifically at long-term regulatory reforms to render the internal capital markets model of cross-border banking sustainable in times of instability through *ex ante* coordination that would resolve the conflicting national incentives engendered by such a model. However, we argued, the long-term regulatory reform ambitions underpinning the new VI are unlikely to materialise without significant progress in the supervision, regulation and resolution of the banking crisis at the European level.

Experience so far shows that the existing EU and international arrangements do have a capacity to manage conflicting interests of home and host actors. However, the *ad hoc* nature of these arrangements and strong involvement of non-EU actors such as the IMF and EBRD in problems of the single banking market, suggest that further institution building is necessary in order to secure credible commitment to multilateral policy responses. The mismatch between the transnational banks and essentially national regulation and supervision continues to generate unconstrained political risks that may eventually

TRANSITION ECONOMIES AFTER 2008

undermine support for financial globalisation in the EU and worldwide. The financial crisis revealed that, despite the three decades of common EU banking policies, the answer to Kapstein's (1989) dilemma of how to secure advantages of financial integration, while containing its risks, remains elusive.

University of Vienna

Bristol Business School, University of the West of England

References

Allen, F., Beck, T., Carletti, E., Lane, P., Schoenmaker, D., & Wagner, W. (2011) '*Cross-Border Banking in Europe: Implications for Financial Stability and Macroeconomic Policies*', CEPR Report, London, available at: www.cepr.org/pubs/books/CEPR/cross-border_banking.pdf, accessed 2 April 2013.

Aydin, B. (2008) *Banking Structure and Credit Growth in Central and Eastern European Countries*, IMF Working Paper, 08/215 (Washington, DC, International Monetary Fund).

Berglöf, E. & Bolton, P. (2002) 'The Great Divide and Beyond: Financial Architecture in Transition', *Journal of Economic Perspectives*, 16, 1, pp. 77–100.

BIS (2010) *Funding Patterns and Liquidity Management of Internationally Active Banks*, CGFS Paper, 39 (Basel, Bank for International Settlements).

Braslina, A. (2010) 'Latvia's New Insolvency Law Shifts Responsibility to Banks', *Reuters*, 26 July, available at: http://www.finanznachrichten.de/nachrichten-2010-07/17513038-latvia-s-new-insolvency-law-shifts-responsibility-to-banks-020.html, accessed 14 November 2011.

Bremmer, I. (2006) *The J Curve: A New Way to Understand Why Nations Rise and Fall* (New York, Simon and Schuster).

Bremmer, I. & Keat, P. (2010) *The Fat Tail: The Power of Political Knowledge in an Uncertain World* (Oxford & New York, Oxford University Press).

Bruno, V. & Shin, H. S. (2011) *Capital Flows, Cross-Border Banking and Global Liquidity*, Princeton University Working Paper (Princeton, NJ, Princeton University).

Bryant, C. (2010) 'Hungary Tax Move Alarms Investors', *Financial Times*, 10 November, available at: http://www.ft.com/cms/s/0/9b744750-ece9-11df-9912-00144feab49a.html#axzz2Io3rSH3L, accessed 15 November 2011.

Cetorelli, N. & Goldberg, L. (2012) 'Follow the Money: Quantifying Domestic Effects of Foreign Bank Shocks in the Great Recession', *American Economic Review*, 102, 3, pp. 213–8.

Chiru, L. (2010) 'Cinteză, BNR: Băncile ar putea pierde 600 mil. euro din aplicarea Ordonanței 50, unele vor cere despăgubiri statului', *Ziarul Financiar*, 20 September, available at: http://www.zf.ro/banci-si-asigurari/cinteza-bnr-bancile-ar-putea-pierde-600-mil-euro-din-aplicarea-ordonantei-50-unele-vor-cere-despagubiri-statului-7335075, accessed 15 November 2011.

Danske Bank (2010) 'EMEA Daily', *Danske Research*, 27 July.

De Haas, R., Korniyenko, Y., Loukoianova, E. & Pivovarsky, A. (2012) *Foreign Banks and the Vienna Initiative: Turning Sinners into Saints*, EBRD Working Paper, 143 (London, European Bank for Reconstruction and Development).

De Haas, R. & van Lelyveld, I. (2010) 'Internal Capital Markets and Lending by Multinational Bank Subsidiaries', *Journal of Financial Intermediation*, 19, 2, pp. 1–25.

De Haas, R. & van Lelyveld, I. (2011) *Multinational Banks and the Global Financial Crisis: Weathering the Perfect Storm?* EBRD Working Paper, 135 (London, European Bank for Reconstruction and Development).

Deacu, C. (2010) 'FMI nu da transa fara modificarea OUG 50', *Bursa*, 29 October, available at: http://www.bursa.ro/presiunea-bancilor-da-roade-fmi-nu-ne-da-transa-fara-modificarea-oug-50-99870&s=banci_asigurari&articol=99870.html, accessed 15 November 2011.

Dunai, M. (2011) 'Hungary May Raise Bank Tax if Courts Strike FX Scheme', *Reuters*, 22 November, available at: http://www.reuters.com/article/2011/11/22/hungary-banks-idUSL5E7MM3WK20111122, accessed 10 January 2012.

EBCI (2011a) *Report by the Public–Private Sector Working Group on Local Currency and Capital Markets Development* (Brussels, European Bank Coordination Initiative).

EBCI (2011b) *Report by the Public–Private Sector Working Group on Role of Commercial Banks in the Absorption of EU Funds* (Brussels, European Bank Coordination Initiative).

EBCI (2012a) *Report by Working Group on NPLs in Central, Eastern and Southeastern Europe* (Brussels, European Bank Coordination Initiative).

EBCI (2012b) *Working Group on Basel III Implementation in Emerging Europe* (Brussels, European Bank Coordination Initiative).

EBRD (2007) *Transition Report: Finance in Transition* (London, European Bank for Reconstruction and Development).

EBRD (2009) *Transition Report: Transition in Crisis?* (London, European Bank for Reconstruction and Development).

EBRD (2010a) *Vienna Initiative* (London, European Bank for Reconstruction and Development).

EBRD (2010b) *Transition Report 2010: Recovery and Reform* (London, European Bank for Reconstruction and Development).

EBRD (2012) *Vienna Initiative – Moving to a New Phase* (London, European Bank for Reconstruction and Development).

EC (2010) *Communication on an EU Framework for Crisis Management in the Financial Sector* (Brussels, European Commission).

EC (2012) *Full Forum Meeting of the European Bank Coordination 'Vienna 2.0' Initiative* (Brussels, European Commission).

ECB (2008) *EU Banking Structures* (Frankfurt, European Central Bank).

ECB (2011) *Opinion of the European Central Bank on Foreign Currency Mortgages and Residential Property Loan Agreements* (Frankfurt, European Central Bank).

Gabor, D. (2010) '(De)Financialization and Crisis in Eastern Europe', *Competition and Change*, 14, 3–4, pp. 248–70.

Gabor, D. (2012) 'Managing Capital Accounts in Emerging Markets: Lessons from the Global Financial Crisis', *Journal of Development Studies*, 48, 6, pp. 714–31.

Genschel, P. (2011) 'One Trap, Many Exits, but No Free Lunch: How the Joint-Decision Trap Shapes EU Tax Policy', in Falkner, G. (ed.) (2011) *The EU's Decision Traps: Comparing Policies* (Oxford, Oxford University Press).

Gros, D. (2009) 'Collapse in Eastern Europe? The rationale for a European Financial Stability', Voxeu.org, 25 February, available at: http://www.voxeu.org/article/saving-eastern-europe-contagion-starts, accesed 2 April 2013.

Haeberle, A. (2009) 'Not Exactly Stimulating', *Corporate Finance in Emerging Europe*, 1, 2, p. 11.

Helleiner, E. & Pagliari, S. (2011) 'The End of an Era in International Financial Regulation?: A Postcrisis Research Agenda', *International Organization*, 65, 1, pp. 169–200.

IMF (2010a) *Regional Economic Outlook: Europe—Building Confidence* (Washington, DC, International Monetary Fund).

IMF (2010b) *Statement by the IMF Mission to Hungary*, IMF Press Release, 10/295 (Washington, DC, International Monetary Fund).

Kapstein, E. B. (1989) 'Resolving the Regulator's Dilemma: International Coordination of Banking Regulations', *International Organization*, 43, 2, pp. 323–47.

Kester, E. (2011a) 'Vienna Furious at Hungary Plan for Mortgage Reprieve', *Financial Times*, 12 September, available at: http://www.ft.com/cms/s/0/9cbcdbac-dd5e-11e0-9dac-00144feabdc0.html#axzz1nUvRqTZC, accessed 15 November 2011.

Kester, E. (2011b) 'Hungary and its Banks Shake Hands', *Financial Times*, 15 December, available at: http://blogs.ft.com/beyond-brics/2011/12/15/hungary-and-its-banks-shake-hands/#axzz1o8frlwSW, accessed 10 January 2012.

Kudrna, Z. (2010) 'Financial Crisis: Testing the Relationship between Foreign Banks and the New EU Members', *Emecon: Employment and Economy in Central and Eastern Europe*, 1, 1, pp. 1–19.

Kudrna, Z. (2012) 'Cross-Border Resolution of Failed Banks in the EU after the Crisis: Business as Usual', *Journal of Common Market Studies*, 50, 2, pp. 283–99.

Lu, K. W., Verheyen, G. & Perera, S. M. (eds) (2009) *Investing with Confidence: Understanding Political Risk Management in the 21st Century* (Washington, DC, World Bank).

McGovern, R. & Sidliarevich, A. (2011) 'Austrian Bank Regulators Set "Public Precedent" for Supervision', *Financial Times*, 24 November, available at: http://www.ft.com/cms/s/2/1b5f6a48-1684-11e1-be1d-00144feabdc0.html#axzz1mjLnSkqf, accessed 10 January 2012.

MIGA (2011) *World Investment and Political Risk* (Washington, DC, Multilateral Investment Guarantee Agency of the World Bank Group).

Mishkin, F. S. (2006) *The Next Great Globalization: How Disadvantaged Nations Can Harness Their Financial Systems to Get Rich* (Princeton, NJ, Princeton University Press).

Moran, T. H. (2001) *International Political Risk Management: Exploring New Frontiers* (Washington, DC, World Bank).

Moran, T. H., Weste, G. T. & Martin, K. (2008) *International Political Risk Management: Needs of the Present Challenges for the Future* (Washington, DC, World Bank).

Mullett, A. (2010) 'Insolvency Law Approval has Banks Seething', *Baltic Reports*, 27 July, available at: http://balticreports.com/?p=22115, accessed 15 November 2011.

Nietsche, W. (2010) *The Vienna Initiative/European Bank Coordination Initiative—Assessment and Outlook* Working Paper, 4/2010 (Vienna, Federal Ministry of Finance of Austria).

Norden, L. & Wagner, W. (2007) 'Credit Derivatives and Loan Pricing', *Journal of Banking and Finance*, 32, 12, pp. 2560–9.

Pistor, K. (2010) *Into the Void: Governing Finance in Central and Eastern Europe*, WIDER Working Paper, 65 (Helsinki, World Institute for Development Economics Research).

Rosenberg, C. & Tirpak, M. (2008) *Determinants of Foreign Currency Borrowing*, IMF Working Paper, 173 (Washington, DC, International Monetary Fund).

Silaghi, C. (2010) *Jocul de-a soarecele si pisica. OU50 si Directiva Europeana*, Centrul Roman de Politici Europene Policy Brief, 4 (Bucharest, Centrul Roman de Politici Europene).

Singer, D.A. (2007) *Regulating Capital: Setting Standards for the International Financial System* (Ithaca, Cornell University Press).

Than, K. & Dunai, M. (2010) 'IMF and EU Suspend Talks with Hungary', *Reuters*, 17 July, available at: http://www.reuters.com/article/2010/07/17/us-hungary-imf-idUSTRE66G0RT20100717, accessed 15 November 2011.

Tsingou, E. (2010) 'Regulatory Reactions to the Global Credit Crisis: Analysing a Policy Community Under Stress', in Helleiner, E., Pagliari, S. & Zimmermann, H. (eds) (2010) *Global Finance in Crisis: The Politics of International Regulatory Change* (London, Routledge).

Unicredit (2009) *CEE Banking Outlook: Risk Appetite Crucial to Win the Upside* (Vienna, Unicredit Group).

Van den Spiegel, F. (2008) 'Roundtable on the Review of the Financial Conglomerates Directive', *Brussels*, Center for European Policy Studies, Presentation, 8 September, available at: http://ec.europa.eu/internal_market/financial-conglomerates/docs/efcc_newsletter_sep2008.pdf, accessed 15 January 2012.

Van Groeningen, S. (2010) 'High Fixed Interest Margins in Romania', available at: http://stevenvangroningen.eu/high-fixed-interest-margins-in-romania, accessed 2 August 2012.

Wagstyl, S. & Buckley, N. (2011) 'Crisis Hits Central and Eastern Europe', *Financial Times*, 22 November, available at: http://www.ft.com/cms/s/0/6a22d214-1530-11e1-855a-00144feabdc0.html#axzz2Io3rSH3L, accessed 10 January 2012.

Wagstyl, S. & Frey, E. (2012) 'Austria Clarifies Plan to Curb Eastward Lending', *Financial Times*, 17 January, available at: http://www.ft.com/cms/s/0/764cf35c-4137-11e1-936b-00144feab49a.html#axzz1mjLnSkqf, accessed 18 January 2012.

Index

Note:
Page numbers in **bold** type refer to figures
Page numbers in *italic* type refer to tables

accumulated capital 114–16, 135
aid: state 30–2, 188, 191
Aleksashenko, S.: *et al* 145
anti-crisis policy 17–19, 22–6, 29–34, 89–90,
  95–7, *150–2*, 153–5; Belarus 103–18;
  macroeconomic 104–5; response 96, 154
anti-cyclical policy 14, 22
anti-politics 42–4
anti-unemployment 25
Asia 167–8, 180; financial crisis (1997–8) 164
Asian Tiger model 166
Åslund, A. 57; and Dombrovskis, V. 174
asset bubble 166
assets 107, 170–1, 197; state ownership 104
austerity 19, 37, 41–2, 48–50, 53–7, 63–8,
  192; full-scale 52; pragmatic 74; public 8;
  reactions 71–2; reforms 48; short-term 76
Austria 9, 167, 189–92, 195–8
authoritarianism 9, 44
automotive sector: Hungary 121–39
autonomy 108, 131, 134, 188
avoidance: crisis 41–55
AvtoVaz 89–90

Babecký, J.: *et al* 143
bail-outs 68, 165–7, 173
balanced budget 13, 22, 26, 35, 38, 49, 84
Balcerowicz, L. 43, 51–2
Baltic Republics 1–4, 7–10, 14, 47–8, 56–79,
  165, 177
Bank Deposit Protection Act (Slovakia 2008)
  30
bank levy 176–7, 192–3
bank loans 3, 110, *111*
Bank of Mexico 179
Bank Stabilisation Assistance Act (Slovakia
  2009) 30
banking 27, 32–3, 47, 59, 86–9, 106–7, 144;
  behaviour 168–80; Central and East
  European 163–82; commercial 146; cross-
  border 183–91, 194–8; domestic 14, 67,
  163–84; failures 169; foreign 58, 66, *109*,
  146, 163–82, 183–201, 193; investment 188;

markets 180, 183–5, 198; private *108–9*,
  163–4; responses 10, 163–82; stability 17,
  28; transnational 183–90, 196–8
bankruptcy 21, 143; personal 190, 194; state
  20–1, 26
banks: parent 170, 179, 184, 187–8, 191, 194–
  6; state-owned 107–8, *109*, 114–15, 163–6,
  178–80
Baturina, E. 95
Belagroprombank (Belarus) 107
Belarus 2–4, 9; anti-crisis management 103–
  18
Belarusbank 107
Belgium 175, 178, 191
benefits 45; child 53; cuts 22, 26, 34–8;
  sickness 64; social *21*, 22, 26, 34, 45–6, 64;
  state 14, 21, 25–6; unemployment 20, 25–6,
  37, 64, 68
Berlin, I. 44
Bielecki, J. 43–5, 51
bilateral liberalisation 122–3
Blair, A. (Tony) 44
Boni, M. 45, 51
boom 74–5, 87–8, 94–6, 172, 188, 197; credit
  141, 153, 168, 172, 184, 194
borrowing 20; cross-border 33, 165, 177–80;
  domestic 99, 184; external 85, 140, 145,
  151, 156; foreign 86–9, *111*, 116, 145, 155,
  178; increased 89, 98; international 144–6,
  150, *152*; private 85
BRE Bank (Poland) 170
Bricogne, J.C.: *et al* 143
Buckley, N.: and Wagstyl, S. 195
budget *63*, 85; balanced 13, 22, 26, 35, 38, 49,
  84; capital 63–4; consolidation 74;
  constraints 19, 114; federal 97; private 85;
  public 13; revision 89; state 23, 26–7, 31,
  37–8, 50–1, 84, 115
budget deficit 5, 17–20, 25–7, 31, 46, **49**;
  decrease 21–3, 49; increase 28, 38, 48; state
  26–7
Bulgaria 1, 7, 168, 174
Burns, A.F.: and Mitchel, W.C. 142

INDEX

capital 30, 44, 105–7, 135, 179–80, 194;
  accumulation 114–16, 135; budgets 63–4;
  equity 115; expenditure 22, 29, 108, 143;
  flight 62, 88, 194; flows 122–3, 180, 185;
  foreign 45, 163, 173; increase 196; injection
  170, 176–8; international 47; investment
  110–11, 114; markets 183, 187–8, 195–7;
  outflows 164, 178; political 68, 143;
  productivity 112; raising 178; regulatory
  115; social 45; working 133–4
Capital Assets Management Agency 179
capitalism 72, 75, 80, 94–5; market 45, 166
caretaker government 22, 25
Cattaneo, O.: *et al* 121
Central Bank of Russia (CBR) 84, 88–9, 95–6
Central and Eastern Europe (CEE) 41–2, 47,
  62, 103–4, 107, 124, 196; banking 163–82;
  political economy 13–40
centre-right politics 46
child benefits 53
China 2–5, 166–7
CIB Bank (Hungary) 175
CitiBank (US) 169
Civic/Citizens' Platform (*Platforma
  Obywatelska*) 27–9, 41–8, 51–4
Civil Development Forum (*Forum
  Obywatelskiego Rozwoju*, FOR) 51–2
Claessens, S.: *et al* 142
commercial banking 146
commercial loans 106
Commerzbank (Poland) 170–1
Commonwealth of Independent States (CIS)
  1–4, 8–10
communism 51, 80, 174; post- 41–4, 90, 141,
  163–5, 170–2, 177–80, 183
consolidation 61; budget 74; fiscal 31–3, 36,
  61–5, 68–9
Consumer Credit Directive (CCD) *190*, 193–4
Convergence Programme (2010) 19, 25, 69
cooperation 183–4
corporate debt 145
corporate loans 176
corporate tax 34, 65
cost reduction 134, 149, *151*, 155–6
countercyclical lending 163–9, 177–9
countercyclical stabilisation 169–71
credit 58, 95, 153; allocation 114, 164; boom
  141, 153, 168, 172, 184, 194; bubble 47;
  demand 172; domestic 172; growth 148,
  163–4, 173, 187–9; halt 5, 15; household 3,
  192; private 3, 47; provision 19, 164; supply
  59
crisis: Asian financial (1997–8) 164; avoidance
  41–55; enduring 90–9; Eurozone 52–3,
  195–7; fiscal 86, 94; impact 15–17, 85–7,
  128–35; shocks 140–59

crisis management 57, 65, 70, 74, 89; Central
  and Eastern Europe 13–40
crisis responses 59–61; Russia 80–102
cross-border banking 183–91, 194–8
cross-border borrowing 33, 165, 177–80
cross-border investment 186
cross-border shocks 183
Csányi, S. 175–6
currency: foreign 88, 106–8, 168–9, 192;
  substitution 106–7
currency peg 110–12, 168; stability 106
cuts 13; benefits 22, 26, 34–8; employment
  149; expenditure 15, 19–23, 35, 42, 50–4,
  63, 192–3; government 50; investment 47–
  8, 155; lending 27, 87; pay 14, 26, 34–6, 64,
  149–50, *151–2*, 153–5; public-sector pay 14,
  26, 34–6; tax 7, 34
cyclical policy: anti- 14, 22
Czech Republic 5, *16–18*, 19–27, 38, 124–7

debt 48–50, 58, 65, 68, 140, 193, 197;
  corporate 145; external 19, 83, **98**, 106,
  112; foreign 86, 98, 143, 184, 192;
  government 10, 14, *18*, 20, **49**, **98**, 99;
  public 36, 41, 46–52, 83–5, 112, 147;
  reducing 53–4, 193; rising 10, 26–7, 149;
  state 8, 13, 17, 28
deficit 48–50, 65, 68, 85; external 111; fiscal
  17, 29, 74; government 33–4, *66*; reduction
  37, 53–4; rising 48; trade 112, 127
delayed recession 103–18
Deleveraging Monitor 196
demand: decreasing 145, 150, 153, *154*;
  domestic 59, 110, 145, 148, 153, 156;
  external 114–16; shocks 140, *151*
demand stimulation 38, 108; domestic 104,
  110–12, 115–16
democracy 2–3, 13, 41–3, 63, 81
deposits 169, 176; government 173
depression 3–5, 9, 19–20, 80
Desai, P. 94
devaluation 8, 47, 62, 106, 143, 147, 192;
  exchange rate 108–10, 156; external 62–3,
  70, 75; internal 8, 57, 62–3, 71, 74–7
developed countries 56
developing countries 166–7, 186
directed lending 108–16
disability pension 36
DnB NORD 194
dollarisation: financial 106–7
Dombrovskis, V.: and Aslund, Å. 174
domestic banks 14, 67; ownership 165–8, 184;
  performance 163–82
domestic borrowing 99, 184
domestic credit 172

INDEX

domestic demand 75, **76**, 110, *113*; artificial 148; decreasing 59; increasing 145, 153, 156; stimulation 104, 110–12, 115–16
domestic investment 175, 185
domestic lending 167
domestic liquidity 188
domestic markets 73, 114, 153–5
domestic stakeholders 184
Dooley, M.P.: and Hutchison, M.M. 140
double-digit inflation 58
downgrading 133
Drahokoupil, J.: Lesay, I. and Myant, M. 7–8, 13–40; and Myant, M. 141
Duma elections (Russia) 90–3

East-Central Europe 13–40
Eastern Europe 50, 72, 75, 133, 168
economic growth 26–9, 41, 45–6, 53, 56, 96, 116; declining 54; incremental 94
economic integration 2–3, 165
economic liberalism 43–4
economic policy 53, 73, 95, 112; divisions 41–55
economic recovery 4, 17, 56, 80–2, 91–3
economic reform 41–2, 46, 52–6, 70, 74
economic vulnerability 141, 163–4, 169
economy 1, 13; decline 20, 65; political 13–40
education 14, 64, 70; reforms 70
Elcoteq 75
election cycles 80–2, 92
elections 32–3, 37, 54; defeat 19; *Duma* 90–3; general 67; legislative 81; parliamentary 25–31, 41, 52, 67–8; presidential 67
electronics sector: Hungary 121–39
employment 87–8, 147–8; cuts 149; opportunities 7, 15; protection 7–8, 17, 20, 24, 35; raising 45, 74; reduction 33, 36, 128, 142
Epstein, R. 9, 163–82
equity capital 115
Estonia 3, 7, 47, 58–75, **76**, 124
Estonian Telecom 65
Europe 5, 48–9, 54–7, 71–2, 75, 84; banking 163–82; Central and Eastern (CEE) 50, 72, 75, 133, 168; East-Central 13–40; Eastern 50, 72, 75, 133, 168; emerging 183–201; political economy 13–40; South-Eastern 1–3, 165; Western 2–4, 7–10, 14, 42, 167, 180, 298
European Bank for Reconstruction and Development (EBRD) 172–3, 178, 198
European Banking Authority (EBA) 178
European Central Bank (ECB) 172, 178, 192
European Commission (EC) 25, 28, 31, 49, 52–3, 165, 190–8
European Crisis Committee (2009) 29

European Union (EU) 23–5, 41–3, 57–9, 73–7, 163–7, 176–8, 196–9; assistance 37, 67, 172; funding 28, 31, 63–4, 68; Structural Funding 47, 68–70, 75
Euroscepticism 24, 197
Eurozone 26–8, 47, 62, 76, 80, 87, 175–9; crisis 52–3, 195–7; entry 68–70, 74
exchange rate 62–3, 75, **76**, **85**, 112, 176; devaluation 108–10, 156; pegs 104–8; stability 189
excise duties 82, 85
Eximbanka (Slovakia) 30
expenditure: capital 108, 143; cuts 15, 19–23, 35, 42, 50–4, 63, 192–3; government 7, 17, 28, 47, 50, 54, 98; increased 22, 33, 47, 82, 98; planned 31; public 21–2, 28–9, 33, 46–9, 52, 59, 67; reduced 28, 33–4, 66; social 29, 48, 75, 90; state 4–5, 13–14, 15, 17, 22–3, 29, 35
export revenue 103, 106
exports 26, 47, 66–8, 126–7, 141, 150, 156; reduction 4, 9, 15, 59, 143
external borrowing 85, 140, 145, *151*, 156
external debt 19, 83, **98**, 106, 112
external deficit 111
external demand 114–16
external devaluation 62–3, 70, 75
external finance 141–3, 146–8, 191
external markets 155
external shocks 14, 106, 110, 180, 184

Fedak, J. 51
FHB Mortgage Bank (Hungary) 175–6
Fico, R. 29–32
Fidesz party (Hungary) 35–7, 176
finance: external 141–3, 146–8, 191
Financial and Capital Market Commission (Latvia) 173
financial crisis: Asia (1997–8) 164
financial dollarisation 106–7
financial flows 187, 196
financial globalisation 183–4, 189, 199
financial integration 183–6, 199
financial intermediation 107, 115–16
financial liberalisation 166–7
financial stability 187, 192
first-tier suppliers 128
fiscal consolidation 31–3, 36, 61–5, 68–9
Fiscal Council (Hungary) 33, 36
fiscal deficit 17, 29, 74
Fiscal Discipline Law (Latvia) 70
fiscal policy 19, 56–7, 66, 70, 77, 89, 110
fiscal retrenchment 22, 26, 74, 77
fiscal stabilisation 33, 108
fiscal stimulus 24–5, 28, 31
fiscal surplus 83, 140
flat tax 23, 27, 35, 43, 48

INDEX

flexicurity package 64
foreign banking 58, 66, *109*, 146, 183–201, 193; performance 163–82
foreign borrowing 86–9, *111*, 116, 145, 155, 178
foreign capital 45, 163, 173
foreign currency 88, 106–8, 168–9, 192
foreign debt 86, 98, 143, 184, 192
foreign direct investment (FDI) 73, 105–6, 140, *144*, 155–6
foreign exchange 86, 147; exposure 164, 168, 178
foreign investment 46, 63, 84, 175, 183–6, 192, 198
foreign lending 163, 169, 174, 179, 189, 192–3, 197
foreign markets 114, 167
foreign ownership 9, 143, 150, *151*, 155
foreign trade 106, 112, 125–7
Forum Obywatelskiego Rozwoju (Civil Development Forum, FOR) 51–2
France 167, 191
free market 7, 10, 21, 29, 43, 54
Freedom Union (*Unia Wolności*, UW) 43, 46, 51
Fujita, M.: and Sato, Y. 131
functional upgrading 121–4, *129*, 130–5
funding 35, 47, 169–70, 180, 188, 193, 198; government 176; structural 47, 68–70, 75

Gabor, D.: and Kudrna, Z. 9, 17, 183–201
Gazeta Wyborcza 44
Gereffi, G.: and Sturgeon, T. 124
Germany 5, 10, 59, **60**, 167, 170, 189
Getin Bank (Poland) 170
global shocks 188
global value chains (GVCs) 121–31, 135
globalisation 142, 153–6, 180, 197–8; financial 183–4, 189, 199
Go Russia! (Medvedev) 97
Gonchar, K. 9, 140–59; and Kuznetsov, B. 147
Gonser, M. 73
government: borrowing 178; caretaker 22, 25; debt 10, 14, *18*, 20, **49**, **98**, 99; deficit 33–4, *66*; deposits 173; funding 176; intervention 9, 46–8, 114; investment 54; policy 14, 95; revenue *6*, *23*, *66*, 85
government expenditure 28, 47, 98; cuts 50; increased 7, 17, 54
Gowin, J. 54
Gray, J. 44
Greece 2, 5–7, 68, 71, 167, 191, 197
gross domestic product (GDP) 13–14, 22–6, 32–6, 47–53, 66–8, 172–5, 178; declining 1–4, 15, 28, 37, 48, 103, 140; growth 23, 59, *61*, 90, 110–11, 114, *141*

growth 2–4, 94; credit 148, 163–4, 173, 187–9; economic 26–9, 41, 45–6, 53–6, 94–6, 116; gross domestic product (GDP) 23, 59, *61*, 90, 110–11, 114, *141*
Gyurcsány, F. 33

Haberier, G. 142
hegemonic ideology 54
home-country 183, 187–8, 191, 195–7
host-country 183, 187–8, 191–7
household credit 3, 192
housing subsidy programme 175–7
Hungary 13–22, 32–7, 164–5, 168, 171, 174, 191–8; automotive sector 121–39; Chamber of Commerce and Industry 33; Competition Authority 192; electronics sector 121–39; in global value chains (GVCs) 125–8
Hutchison, M.M.: and Dooley, M.P. 140

ideological liberalism 45, 52
ideology 41, 44; hegemonic 54; political 17–23
imports 116, 126–7, 150, *151*, 153, *154*, 156; reduced 143
income tax 30–4, 43, 48, 65, 72–3; cuts 34
indexation 34; pensions 26–8
inflation 59, *61*, 68, 84, 166; double-digit 58; rising 104, 112
ING Group 169
Institute for Contemporary Development (INSOR) 97
institutional reform 197
integration 45, *144*; economic 2–3, 165; financial 183–6, 199; internal 187; international 141; trade 150, 154
intermediation: financial 107, 115–16
internal capital markets 187–8, 195
internal devaluation 8, 57, 62–3, 71, 74–7
internal integration 187
international borrowing 144–6, 150, *152*
international division of labour 122–5
international integration 141
international markets 140, 148, 153–5, 174, 187
International Monetary Fund (IMF) 70, 110–11, 115, 167, 177–8, 193–4, 198; assistance 19–22, 37, 164, 172–3, 192; stand-by arrangement (SBA) 33–4, 108–10, 191
international trade 122–3, 142–4, 150, 154–5
intervention: government 9, 46–8, 114; state 45, 166
Intesa SanPaolo (Italy) 175
inventory accumulation 153–5
inventory management 145; poor 148, *151*, 155

206

INDEX

investment 103, 153, 185; banking 188; capital 110–11, 114; cross-border 186; cuts 47–8, 155; demand 114; domestic 175, 185; foreign 46, 63, 84, 175, 183–6, 192, 198; government 54; intangible 132; private 47–8; public 29, 47–8, 53; revenue 85; tangible 132

Italy 68, 167–70, 175, 189

Japan 166, 179–80
junk contracts 41
just-in-time production 145

K&H Bank (Hungary) 175
Kaczyński, L. 44, 49, 52
Kaminski, B.: and Ng, F. 124
Kapstein, E.B. 199
Kargins, V.: and Krasovickis, V. 172–3
Kattel, R.: and Raudla, R. 8, 56–79
KBC Bank (Belgium) 175, 178
Keynesian economics 7–8, 19–24, 28–30, 59
Kim, Y.J.: et al 143
Kolasa, M.: et al 143
Komorowski, B. 52
Korea (Republic of) 166–7, 179–80
Krasovickis, V.: and Kargins, V. 172–3
Krugman, P. 56, 62, 168
Kruk, D. 9, 103–18
Kudrna, Z.: and Gabor, D. 9, 17, 183–201
Kuokstis, V.: and Vilpisauskas, R. 62, 74
Kurzarbeit scheme 25, 30, 35
Kuznetsov, B.: and Gonchar, K. 147

labour market 20, 29–32, 36–7, 165–6; flexibility 68, 73–5
Lagarde, C. 56
Latin America 50, 143
Latvia 56–75, 168, 171–4, 177–80, 191, 194–5, 198
Law and Justice Party (*Prawo i Sprawiedliwość*, PiS) 27, 43–4, 48
layoffs 149–50, *150–2*, 153–5
left-right politics 13–14, 17, 20–35, 38, 44–6
left-wing politics 22, 25, 44
Lehman Brothers: collapse (2008) 59, 164, 168–9, 172, 175–6, 179, 192–3
lending *see* loans
Lesay, I.: Myant, M. and Drahokoupil, J. 7–8, 13–40
Leskin, V. 94
Levchenko, A.A.: et al 143
levy 176–7, 192–3
Lewandowski, J. 43
Liberal Democratic Congress party (*Kongres Liberalno-Demokratyczny*, KLD) 43
liberal reform 41, 45–6, 52

liberalisation 57; bilateral 122–3; financial 166–7; multilateral 122–3; trade 57; unilateral 122–3
liberalism 41; economic 43–4; ideological 45, 52; political 43; pragmatic 41–55; social 43
liquidity 30, 88, 115, 170–4, 178, 191–3, 197; domestic 188
Lithuania 3, 58–75, **76**
loan-to-deposit ratio 176, 188, 195–6
loans 14–15, 86, 168–73, 193; bank 3, 110, *111*; commercial 106; corporate 176; countercyclical 163–9, 177–9; cuts 27, 87; directed 108–16; domestic 167; foreign 163, 169, 174, 179, 189, 192–3, 197; non-performing (NPLs) 174, 178, 192, 197; refinancing 106; repayment 88; uncollateralised 88; unsubsidised 176
lobbying 19, 175, 194
lower-tier suppliers 123
loyalty 163, 177

Maastricht criteria 19, 25, 28, 65, 68, 74
McAllister, I.: and White, S. 81, 90
macroeconomic policy 29, 30, 108, 174, 185, 191; anti-crisis 104–5
management: crisis 13–40, 57, 65, 70, 74, 89, 90–9
manufacturing companies: Russian 140–59
market capitalism 45, 166
market power 154–5, 188
markets: banking 180, 183–5, 198; capital 183, 187–8, 195–7; domestic 73, 114, 153–5; external 155; foreign 114, 167; free 7, 10, 21, 29, 43, 54; international 140, 148, 153–5, 174, 187; labour 20, 29–32, 36–7, 68, 73–5, 165–6
Medvedev, D. 80–2, 89–93, 96–9
Mexico, Bank of 179
MFB Bank (Hungary) 176
Michnik, A. 44
Mikloš, I. 32
minimum wage 37, 68
Mitchel, W.C.: and Burns, A.F. 142
Mitra, P.: et al 141
modernisation 80, 96–9, 123
Molnár, M. 174
monetary policy 104, 110
monoprofil'nie gorody (monotowns) 89–90, 99
mortgage relief 193–5
Motor Industry Association (MIA) 30
Multilateral Investment Guarantee Agency (MIGA) 185–6
multilateral liberalisation 122–3
multilateralism 183, 188–91, 194–8
multinational corporations (MNCs) 124–5, 131–6

INDEX

Myant, M.: and Drahokoupil, J. 141; Drahokoupil, J. and Lesay, I. 7–8, 13–40

National Anti-Crisis Plan (*Národní protikrizový plán vlády*) 24
National Bank of Belarus (NBB) 107, 110–12, 115
National Economic Council of the Government (*Národní ekonomická rada vlády*, NERV) 24
National Economic and Social Council (*Nemzeti Gazdasági és Társadalmi Tanács*, NGTT) 35–6
National Interest Reconciliation Council (*Országos Érdekegyeztető Tanács*, OÉT) 35–6
National Reserve Fund (Russia) 88
National Wealth Fund (Russia) 83–4, **88**
nationalisation 164, 172–4, 198
nationalism 8, 20–2, 27, 35, 43–4, 72–4
Nemtsov, B. 95–6
neo-liberal reform 29, 32, 74
neo-liberalism 7–10, 13–14, 20–6, 27, 35–7, 43–4, 56–7; nationalist 72–4; pragmatic 72–4
Netherlands 167–9
nominal wages 58–9, 62
non-performing loans (NPLs) 174, 178, 192, 197
Nordea Bank (Sweden) 172–3, 194
North Atlantic Treaty Organisation (NATO) 73
Nova Kreditna Banka Maribor (NKBM, Slovenia) 178–9
Nova Ljubljanska Banka (NLB, Slovenia) 178–9

Občanská demokratická strana (Civic Democratic Party, ODS) 24–5
Ohanian, L. 142
oligarchy 8, 74, 95
Orbán, V. 176
Organisation for Economic Co-operation and Development (OECD) 50, 84, 179
Ortiz, G. 179
OTP Bank (Hungary) 164, 174–7
output: declining 142, 145, 150, 155, 169–72; dynamics 150; growth 103, 114; shock 104
overheating 58–9, 74, 98, 112
ownership: domestic banks 165–8, 184; foreign 9, 143, 150, *151*, 155; state 103–4, 107, 170, 179

parent banks 170, 179, 184, 187–8, 191, 194–6
Parex Bank (Latvia) 66–8, 164, 171–4, 177, 180

pay cuts 64, 149–50, *151–2*, 153–5; public-sector 14, 26, 34–6
pegs: currency 106, 110–12, 168; exchange rate 104–8
Pekao SA 169
pension reforms 50–2
pensions 14, 64, 89; cuts 34; disability 36; increase 26–8; indexation 26–8; privatisation 29, 38, 50–2, 170
Peplinsky, T. 99
peripheral subsidiaries 125, 133–4
personal bankruptcy 190, 194
Petru, R. 52
PKN Orlen 45
PKO Bank Polski 45, 164–5, 169–71, 174–80
Platforma Obywatelska (Civic/Citizens' Platform, PO) 27–9, 41–8, 51–4
Poland 13–19, 27–9, 124, 164–5, 168–70, 179–80, 196; economic policy 41–55
Polanyi, K. 72
policy: anti-cyclical 14, 22; economic 41–55, 73, 95, 112; elites 73, 77; fiscal 19, 56–7, 66, 70, 77, 89, 110; government 14, 95; improvisation 190; making 9, 14–15, 37, 95; monetary 104, 110; pro-cyclical 22, 33, 66, 84, 171–4; reforms 65; regulatory 186, 198; responses 13–17, 20, 57, 61, 88, 96, 189–97; socioeconomic 43, 46, 53; stabilisation 103–4, 108–17, 194
Polish Peasants' Party (*Polskie Stronnictwo Ludowe*, PSL) 44, 51–2
political capital 68, 143
political economy 13–40
political ideology 17–23
political liberalism 43
political reform 97–8
political risk 183–201
politics: anti- 42–4; centre-right 46; left-right 13–14, 17, 20–35, 38, 44–6; left-wing 22, 25, 44; pre-crisis 80; right-wing 22, 25–35, 44
Pollitt, C. 57
populism 20–4, 35–7, 43–6
post-communism 41–4, 90, 141, 163–5, 170–2, 177–80, 183
Powszechny Zakład Ubezpiecze⊠ (PZU) 45
pragmatic liberalism 41–55
Prawo i Sprawiedliwość (PiS, Law and Justice) 27, 43–4, 48
private banking *108–9*, 163–4
private borrowing 85
private credit 3, 47
private investment 47–8
privatisation 45, 49, 57, 108, 163–5, 169–71, 179; pensions 29, 38, 50–2, 170
pro-cyclical policy 22, 33, 66, 84, 171–4
process upgrading 123–4, *129–30*, 135–6

208

INDEX

product upgrading 124, *129–30*, 132, 135
production 123, 128; costs 142; improved 123; just-in-time 145; networks 121, 125–7; reduced 145
productivity: capital 112; decreased 114–16, 147; increased 58–9, 142, 172
progressive taxation 20–1, 30, 49, 65
protectionism 163–7, 191
protests 71–2, 95
Provopoulos, G. 167
public budget 13
public debt 36, 46, 83, 112, 147; decline 50–1, 84–5; increase 41, 48–9, 51–2
public expenditure 21, 29, 48; cuts 28, 46, 52, 59; increase 22, 33, 67
public investment 29, 47–8, 53
public opinion 14, 81, 90, 94
public-sector pay: cuts 14, 26, 34–6; increase 22, 28–9, 33
Purfield, C.: and Rosenberg, C. 59, 72
Putin, V. 80–2, 89–95, 99

quality upgrading 130

Radičová, I. 31–2
Radošević, S. 124
Rae, G. 8, 41–55
rainy-day fund 59, 66
Raudla, R.: and Kattel, R. 8, 56–79
recession: delayed 103–18
recovery: economic 4, 17, 56, 80–2, 91–3
reform 33, 44–6, 49, 82, 98, 197; austerity 48; economic 41–2, 46, 52–6, 70, 74; education 70; government 46; institutional 197; liberal 41, 45–6, 52; neo-liberal 29, 32, 74; pension 50–2; political 97–8; regulatory 196–8; structural 96, 108; tax 34–5, 54
Reform Alliance 33–4
regulatory capital 115
regulatory policy 186, 198
regulatory reform 196–8
Reserve Fund (Russia) 83–4, 88, 98–9
responses: banking 10, 163–82; crisis 59–61, 80–102; multilateral 183, 190–1, 194–8; neo-liberal 13–14, 20, 26; policy 13–17, 20, 57, 61, 88, 96, 189–97
retirement 45, 49–54; early 33, 36, 170
retrenchment 22, 26, 74, 77; fiscal 56, 59, 63, 70
revealed comparative advantages (RCA) 125–7
revenue: export 103, 106; government 6, *23, 66,* 85; increase 35; investment 85; loss 85; tax 5, 15, 67
right-wing politics 22, 25–35, 44
Robinson, N. 8, 80–102
Rogoff, K. 62

Romania 9, 168, 174, *190*, 191–8
Romanian Authority for Consumer Protection (RACP) 193
Rose, R.: *et al* 81
Rosenberg, C.: and Purfield, C. 59, 72
Rostowski, J. 46, 51
Rotemberg, J. 142
Roubini, N. 62
Russia 2–9, 19, 57, 105–6, 174, 196; crisis response 80–102; *Duma* elections 90–3; National Reserve Fund 88; National Wealth Fund 83–4, **88**; Reserve Fund 83–4, 88, 98–9, *see also* Soviet Union
Ryabov, A. 97

sales 132; decline 149, *150*, 153; growth *144, 150–2*, 153–5
Santander 178
Sass, M.: and Szalavetz, A. 9, 121–39; and Szanyi, M. 124
Sato, Y.: and Fujita, M. 131
SEB (*Skandinaviska Enskilda Banken*) 172–3, 194
second-tier suppliers 128
security: social 20, 36
shocks 42; crisis 140–59; cross-border 183; demand 140, *151*; external 14, 106, 110, 180, 184; global 188; output 104; trade 81, 88–90, 94–9
sickness benefits 64
simple polities 8–10, 72–5
Slovak Banking Association (SBA) 30
Slovak Guarantee and Development Bank (SZRB) 30
Slovakia *16*, 17–19, *21–3*, 29–32, 47, 124–6, 174; Bank Deposit Protection Act (2008) 30; Bank Stabilisation Assistance Act (2009) 30
Slovenia 47, 124, 164–5, 168, 171, 174, 177–9
small and medium enterprises (SMEs) 35, 167, 170–1, 174, 180
Smer-sociálna demokracia party (Direction-Social Democracy) 29–32
social benefits *21*, 45–6, 64; cuts 22, 26, 34
social capital 45
Social Democrats 7–8, 14, 20–6, 29–32, 37
social expenditure 29, 48, 75, 90
social liberalism 43
social security 20, 36
socialism 33, 43, 95
Socialist Party (*Magyar Szocialista Párt*) 32–3
socioeconomic policy 43, 46, 53
Solidarity Electoral Action (*Akcja Wyborcza Solidarność*, AWS) 43, 46, 51
solidarity movement 42–4
South Korea 166–7, 179–80

209

INDEX

South-Eastern Europe 1–3, 165
Soviet Union 72, 114, 172, *see also* Russia
Spain 68, 167, 178
spending *see* expenditure
stabilisation 97, 155–6; countercyclical 169–71; fiscal 33, 108; policy 103–4, 108–17, 194
Stabilisation Fund 59, 84, **88**
stability: banking 17, 28; exchange rate 189; financial 187, 192
Stability and Development Plan (*Plan stabilności i rozwoju*) 27
stand-by arrangement (SBA) 33–4, 108–10, 191
Standard International Trade Classification (SITC) 123–7
state: aid 30–2, 188, 191; bankruptcy 20–1, 26; benefits 14, 21, 25–6; debt 8, 13, 17, 28; intervention 45, 166; ownership 103–4, 107, 170, 179
State Audit Office (SAO) 36
state budget 23, 31, 37–8, 50–1, 84, 115; deficit 26–7
state expenditure 4–5, 13–14, 17; cuts 15, 22–3, 35; rising 29
state-owned banks 107–8, *109*, 114–15, 163–6, 178–80
stimulation: demand 38, 104, 108
stimulus: fiscal 24–5, 28, 31
stimulus package 24, 31–2, 59, 89–90
stock market 50, 82, 86
Structural Funding (EU) 47, 68–70, 75
structural reform 96, 108
Sturgeon, T.: and Gereffi, G. 124
subsidiaries 124–5, 128–31, 135–6, 187–8, 191; cap 195; peripheral 125, 133–4
subsidiary upgrading 131
substitution: currency 106–7; effect 123, 128
supply chains 123, 143; reconfiguration 121, 135
surplus: fiscal 83, 140
Swedbank 172–3, 194
Sweden 67, 172–4
Szacki, J. 44
Szalavetz, A.: and Sass, M. 9, 121–39
Szanyi, M.: and Sass, M. 124
Széll Kálmán Plan (Hungary 2011) 36

Taiwan 166, 180
tax 13–14, 82, 184; changes 192, 198; corporate 34, 65; cuts 7, 34; deduction 175; direct *23*, 27, 38, 64; evasion 188; flat 23, 27, 35, 43, 48; hidden 193; income 30–4, 43, 48, 65, 72–3; increase 20–2, 25, 49, 63; indirect *23*, 27, 38, 64; progressive 20–1, 30, 49, 65; reduction 21, 24–6; reforms 34–5,

54; regressive 46; revenue 5, 15, 67; value added (VAT) 27–8, 32–6, 46, 49, 64–5
Thatcherism 46, 54
tier-one suppliers 123
Times 168
Topolánek, M. 24–6
trade *126*, 140; deficit 127; effects 144; faltering 169; foreign 106, 112, 125–7; integration 150, 154; international 122–3, 142–4, 150, 154–5; liberalisation 57; shocks 81, 88–90, 94–9; specialisation 122, 125
trade unions 23–30, 34, 71–4
training voucher scheme 68–9
transnational banking 183, 187–90, 196–7; integrated 184–9, 198
Treisman, D. 90
tripartite structure 7, 19, 25, 28–9, 34–5
Tusk, D. 43–6, 52–4
two-way traders 150, *151*, 154

Ukraine 1–5, 19, 106, 174
unemployment *61*, 65, 172; anti- 25; reducing 36–7, 52; rising 15, 24–6, 41, 59, 74–5, 87, 89
unemployment benefits 20, 25, 68; cuts 26, 37; increase 64
Unicredit 169–70, 175
unilateral liberalisation 122–3
unilateralism 9, 183, 188–91, 194–8
unions: trade 23–30, 34, 71–4
United Kingdom (UK) 1, 5, 167
United Russia (*Edinaya Rossiya*) 81, 90–3
United States of America (USA) 5, 84, 141, 167–9, 172, 175
upgrading 121–39; functional 121–4, *129*, 130–5; process 124, *129–30*, 135–6; product 124, *129–30*, 132, 135; quality 130; subsidiary 131

value added tax (VAT) 46, 64–5; increase 27–8, 32–6, 49
value chains: global (GVCs) 121–31, 135
value-adding activities 121–3, 132–3
Vienna Initiative (EDCI) 190–1, 196–8
Vilpisauskas, R.: and Kuokstis, V. 62, 74
Vneshekonombank (Russia) 88
vulnerability 98, *152*, 166, 173–80, 195, 268; economic 141, 163–4, 169

Wade, R. 166–7
Wagstyl, S.: and Buckley, N. 195
Wałęsa, L. 43
Walicki, A. 44
Washington consensus 57
welfare state 72, 77
Western Europe 2–4, 7–10, 14, 42, 167, 180, 198

INDEX

White, S.: and McAllister, I. 81, 90
workfare society 45
working capital 133–4
World Bank 165, 178, 185; Enterprise Survey
  (2006 & 2010) 143

Yakovlev, A.: *et al* 147
Yeats, A. 123–5
Yel'tsin, B. 90

Zakład Ubezpieczeń Społecznych (Social
Insurance Institution, ZUS) 51, 170–1

www.routledge.com/9780415639125

Related titles from Routledge

Development Policies of Central and Eastern European States
From Aid Recipients to Aid Donors
Edited by Ondřej Horký-Hlucháň

The states from Central and Eastern Europe that joined the EU in 2004 and 2007 provide a fascinating series of case studies for scholars interested in politics, IR and development studies. The journey from recipients of aid to aid donors is interesting because their policy to become aid donors gives us an insight into governmental structures in CEE states, foreign policy priorities, public opinion, the role of NGOs/civil society and how well CEE states have taken on board the EU acquis (the EU's rule book). The book also explores whether the development cooperation programmes of the majority of CEESs reflect the so-called "transition experience" of moving from authoritarianism and socialism to democracy and modern liberalism.

This book was published as a special issue of *Perspectives on European Politics and Society*.

Ondřej Horký-Hlucháň is a Research Fellow in the Institute of International Relations, Prague.

Simon Lightfoot is Senior Lecturer in European Politics, University of Leeds.

December 2012: 246 x 174: 144pp
Hb: 978-0-415-63912-5
£85 / $145

For more information and to order a copy visit
www.routledge.com/9780415639125

Available from all good bookshops

www.routledge.com/9780415500227

Related titles from Routledge

Elites and Identities in Post-Soviet Space

Edited by David Lane

The dissolution of the communist system led to the creation of new states and the formation of new concepts of citizenship in the post-Soviet states of Central and Eastern Europe.

This book addresses how domestic elites (regional, political and economic) influenced the formation of national identities and the ways in which citizenship has been defined. A second component considers the external dimensions: the ways in which foreign elites influenced either directly or indirectly the concept of identity and the interaction with internal elites. The essays consider the role of the European Union in attempting to form a European identity. Moreover, the growing internationalisation of economies (privatisation, monetary harmonisation, dependence on trade) also had effects on the kind of 'national identity' sought by the new nation states as well as the defining by them of 'the other'.

This book was originally published as a special issue of *Europe-Asia Studies*.

April 2012: 246 x 174: 214pp
Hb: 978-0-415-50022-7
£85 / $145

For more information and to order a copy visit
www.routledge.com/9780415500227

Available from all good bookshops